The American West on Film

The American West on Film

Johnny D. Boggs

Hollywood History

An Imprint of ABC-CLIO, LLC
Santa Barbara, California • Denver, Colorado

Library of Congress Cataloging-in-Publication Data

Names: Boggs, Johnny D., author.
Title: The American West on film / Johnny D Boggs.
Description: Santa Barbara, California : ABC-CLIO, an imprint of ABC-CLIO, LLC, [2020] | Series: Hollywood history | Includes bibliographical references and index.
Identifiers: LCCN 2019026693 (print) | LCCN 2019026694 (ebook) | ISBN 9781440866760 (hardcover) | ISBN 9781440866777 (ebook)
Subjects: LCSH: Western films—History and criticism. | West (U.S.)—In motion pictures.
Classification: LCC PN1995.9.W4 B64 2020 (print) | LCC PN1995.9.W4 (ebook) | DDC 791.43/6278—dc23
LC record available at https://lccn.loc.gov/2019026693
LC ebook record available at https://lccn.loc.gov/2019026694

ISBN: 978-1-4408-6676-0 (print)
      978-1-4408-6677-7 (ebook)

24 23 22 21 20   1 2 3 4 5

This book is also available as an eBook.

ABC-CLIO
An Imprint of ABC-CLIO, LLC

ABC-CLIO, LLC
147 Castilian Drive
Santa Barbara, California 93117
www.abc-clio.com

This book is printed on acid-free paper ∞

Manufactured in the United States of America

Contents

Series Foreword

Just exactly how accurate are Hollywood's film and television portrayals of American history? What do these portrayals of history tell us, not only about the events they depict but also the time in which they were made?

Each volume in this unique reference series is devoted to a single topic or key theme in American history, examining 10–12 major motion pictures or television productions. Substantial essays summarize each film, provide historical background of the event or period it depicts, and explain how accurate the film's depiction is, while also analyzing the cultural context in which the film was made. A final resources section provides a comprehensive annotated bibliography of print and electronic sources to aid students and teachers in further research.

The subjects of these Hollywood History volumes were chosen based on both curriculum relevance and inherent interest. Readers will find a wide array of subject choices, including American Slavery on Film, the Civil War on Film, the American West on Film, Vietnam on Film, and the 1960s on Film. Ideal for school assignments and student research, the length, format, and subject areas are designed to meet educators' needs and students' interests.

Preface

In 1903, *The Great Train Robbery*, a 12-minute short film written, directed, and produced by Edwin S. Porter (1870–1941), depicted a Western outlaw gang's train robbery and the aftermath. Historian Richard Slotkin wrote, "The film was a commercial success on a scale that no single movie had previously achieved" (Slotkin 1993, 231) and established the Western as one of moviemaking's most popular genres.

Gilbert M. Anderson (ca. 1882–1971), who played various characters in *The Great Train Robbery*, soon became famous portraying "Broncho Billy" in 148 short films. With moviemaking headquarters relocating from the East Coast to Hollywood, California, by 1915, Shakespearean-trained actor William S. Hart (1864–1946) replaced Anderson as the next Western star in features such as *Hell's Hinges* (1916) and *Tumbleweeds* (1925), while director John Ford (1894–1973) became known for his Westerns, including *Straight Shooting* (1917) and *3 Bad Men* (1926). The advent of sound allowed moviegoers to hear gunshots and hoofbeats, but the box-office failures of *The Big Trail* and *Billy the Kid* (both 1930) and *Cimarron* (1931) reduced most Westerns made in the 1930s to low-budget programmers.

That changed in 1939. The financial success of *Stagecoach* and other A-list Westerns re-established the genre as one of the most popular—a trend that continued well into the 1960s. By the mid-1970s, the Westerns' run had ended. Although a few movies—including *Dances with Wolves* (1990) and *Unforgiven* (1992), both Best Picture Academy Award winners—revived some interest, the Western never regained its hold in Hollywood.

Westerns often reflect the time in which they are produced more than they reflect the time in which they are set. Those released during World War II often depicted a reluctant hero forced to stand up against tyranny (1942's

The Spoilers) or sent a hero against menacing gangs (1942's *Tombstone: The Town Too Tough to Die*). Westerns during the 1950s highlighted Cold War paranoia (1959's *No Name on the Bullet*); the blacklist (1954's *Silver Lode*); the need to come together as a country (1953's *Escape from Fort Bravo*); or even parodied the TV Western craze (1951's *Callaway Went Thataway*). By the 1960s, Hollywood illustrated the end of the old West (*Ride the High Country* and *The Man Who Shot Liberty Valance*, both 1962) and the struggles (1962's *Lonely Are the Brave*) and humor (1965's *The Rounders*) of the new West. The 1970s of Watergate and Vietnam brought about "revisionist" Westerns, which painted the frontier's settlement as far from glamorous (1972's *The Culpepper Cattle Co.*) and lawmen far from noble (1975's *Posse*).

So what exactly is a Western?

Westerns can include the colonial frontier (1939's *Allegheny Uprising*); the 1820s–1840s mountain-men era (2015's *The Revenant*); the Native American West (1981's *Windwalker*); the 1836 battle of the Alamo (1960's *The Alamo*); the 1840–1850s overland trails journeys (1951's *Westward the Women*); the Civil War West (1999's *Ride with the Devil*); the rodeo West (1943's *A Lady Takes a Chance*); and the post–World War II West (1971's *The Last Picture Show*). But for the purpose of this book, the West is confined to that traditional period beginning at the end of the Civil War and to the early 1900s.

Movies rarely got the facts right in most genres, but movies aren't about history; ideally, they're about entertainment. *The American West on Film* examines 11 movies, arranged chronologically by year of first release, beginning in 1939 when Westerns returned to A-list status. Each film represents a subcategory of post–Civil War Western history or a specific Western event or figure, and each chapter compares the movie's version of the truth to what most historians believe happened. Also, each chapter shows how the films represent the times during which they were released. For 1939, *Union Pacific* is used as that year's relaunch of big-budget Westerns and for its historical depiction of the building of the Transcontinental Railroad.

Two movies are used for each of the following three decades, the golden years of Hollywood Westerns. From the 1940s, *The Ox-Bow Incident* (1943) is one of the rare adult-themed Westerns made during World War II, and it represents frontier and vigilante justice; while *Red River* (1948) established John Wayne as an actor and depicts cowboys, cattle drives, and cattle towns—all Western staples. In the 1950s, *High Noon* (1952) embodies the Cold War scare of the midtwentieth century as well as towns and lawmen of the nineteenth century; and *The Searchers* (1956) represents Anglo–Native American relations and a drastic change in how Hollywood began depicting its heroes. For the 1960s, *The Magnificent Seven* (1960) illustrates the Old West's gunfighter culture as well as the shift in Hollywood toward movies with multiple heroes, and *Butch Cassidy and the Sundance Kid* closes out the Western's golden era as 1969's box-office champion that renewed inter-est in one of the historical West's notorious outlaw gangs.

With the popularity of Western films fading by the 1970s, *Little Big Man* (1970) represents George Custer and the 1876 Battle of the Little Big Horn, and it serves as an allegory for Vietnam and the My Lai massacre. *Young Guns* (1988) helped revive movie Westerns in the late 1980s and led to renewed interest in outlaw Billy the Kid. *Tombstone* (1993), which has risen to cult status, illustrates the 1881 Gunfight at the O.K. Corral. And *The Assassination of Jesse James by the Coward Robert Ford* (2007) depicts the Western as an art film and offers a fairly accurate examination of an often-filmed Old West legend.

FURTHER READING

King, Susan. 2011. "Classic Hollywood: Western Film Pioneers Have Silent-Era Roots." *Los Angeles Times*, July 25, 2011. https://www.latimes.com/entertain ment/la-xpm-2011-jul-25-la-et-classic-hollywood-20110725-story.html

Nelson, Andrew Patrick. 2015. *Still in the Saddle: The Hollywood Western, 1969–1980*. Norman: University of Oklahoma Press.

Slotkin, Richard. 1993. *Gunfighter Nation: The Myth of the Frontier in Twentieth-Century America*. New York: Harper Perennial.

Wright, Will. 1975. *Six Guns & Society: A Structural Study of the Western*. Berkeley: University of California Press.

Acknowledgments

Every time I tackle a book about Western history and/or Western films, I think, *This ought to be fun*—and every time I find myself buried in contradictory information, staying up late trying to solve one mystery or track down some elusive fact, often wondering what I've gotten myself into again. The more I do this, the more I realize it's a miracle any movie ever makes it to the big screen, or that any book about any movie or movies ever gets finished. For *The American West on Film*, I am indebted to historian Richard W. Etulain for recommending me for this job; Michael Millman, at ABC-CLIO, for thinking that I could handle this project; for the solid yet unheralded copy editors, who catch my myriad mistakes; and for my editor, Patrick Hall, who, like the grizzled trail boss/lawman/cavalry sergeant in many a B Western, guided, corrected, and ramrodded this green dude and shaped this book into something far, far better than I could have completed on my own. I also tip my cowboy hat to friends and colleagues at Western Writers of America and other Western historians, writers, filmmakers, and archivists I've met over the years for their insight, assistance, and knowledge.

Finally, I thank my wife, Lisa, and my son, Jack, for allowing me to watch old movies—sometimes even sitting through them with me—in the name of research and letting me disappear for hours into my office, which, once again, I have left trashed with books, newspaper printouts, magazines, and notes.

Introduction

"Go West, young man, and grow up with the country," is often attributed to journalist Horace Greeley (1811–1872). That's not exactly what Greeley said, but in the August 25, 1838, issue of the *New-Yorker*, Greeley did write: "If any young man is about to commence the world, with little in his circumstances to possess him in favor of one section more than another, we say to him, publicly and privately, Go to the West; there your capacities are sure to be appreciated, and your industry and energy rewarded. . . . The West is the land of promise and of hope; let all who are else hopeless, turn their eyes and, when able their steps toward it" (Greeley 1838, 361).

Westward exploration and expansion began shortly after the first Europeans arrived on the Atlantic Seaboard. The travels of Daniel Boone (1734–1820) led to frontier settlements in the trans-Appalachian Mountains, and Boone kept pushing west, eventually dying in St. Charles, County Missouri. The Louisiana Purchase of 1803 more than doubled the size of the United States by including all or parts of the present-day states of Arkansas, Colorado, Iowa, Kansas, Louisiana, Minnesota, Missouri, Montana, Nebraska, New Mexico, North Dakota, Oklahoma, South Dakota, Texas, and Wyoming. On May 14, 1804, Meriwether Lewis (1774–1809) and William Clark (1770–1838) led the 42-member Corps of Discovery on an exploratory trip along the Missouri River, returning to St. Louis, Missouri, on September 23, 1806, after having traveled more than 8,000 miles. Texas won its independence from Mexico in 1836 and spent nine years as an independent republic, but its admission into the Union in December 1845 led to a boundary dispute and triggered the Mexican-American War (1846–1848). The peace treaty signed at Guadalupe Hidalgo (now part of Mexico City) gave the United States all or parts of present-day Arizona, California, Colorado,

Nevada, New Mexico, Utah, and Wyoming. The Oregon Treaty of 1846 established the Canadian-U.S. border at the 49th parallel and officially gave the United States the present-day states of Idaho, Montana, Oregon, and Washington. In 1853, the United States, seeking a possible southern railroad line across the continent, and Mexico negotiated the Gadsden Purchase, named after American diplomat James Gadsden (1788–1858), which added another 29,670 square miles in present-day Arizona and New Mexico and established the Mexico-U.S. border.

The demand for beaver pelts and other furs led to the establishment of trading posts on the frontier and sent fur trappers, or mountain men, into the Rocky Mountains in search of beaver. The 1806–1807 expedition of Zebulon Pike (1779–1813) in the American Southwest helped open the fur trade on the upper Arkansas River. However, a change in European fashion to silk hats, along with a rapidly declining beaver population, ended the fur-trapping period around 1840. But the opening of the rich farmlands in Oregon and the discovery of gold in California in the late 1840s sent hundreds of thousands of Americans to the western United States along the California and Oregon trails.

Though much westward expansion had occurred during the first half of the nineteenth century, the years after the Civil War (1861–1865) saw rapid expansion and Anglo settlement of the West.

The Homestead Act of 1862 increased the settlement of the western lands. The law allowed any head of a family, or an individual over the age of 21, or an individual fulfilling a military service requirement to pay $14 to file on 160 acres of federal public land. After living on the land and making improvements, such as a home and/or agriculture, the applicant gained title to that land. Additional provisions were later added to the act, and after the Civil War, more than 270 million acres in the West had been claimed and developed.

African Americans, many of whom had been freed from slavery after the Civil War, came west. Some enlisted in Army units such as the 9th and 10th Cavalry and the 24th and 25th Infantry—all regiments that were first sent to the American West. Twelve African American settlements had been established in Kansas by 1881. Other African Americans founded towns in Nebraska, Colorado, and New Mexico; and between 1865 and 1920, more than 50 such settlements were established in present-day Oklahoma, including freedmen towns founded by the former slaves of Cherokee, Creek, Seminole, Chickasaw, and Choctaw Indians.

The Dawes Severalty Act of 1887 distributed land in what had been Indian Territory to the heads of tribal families or individual tribal males, and it eventually opened the rest of what is now Oklahoma to non-Native Americans. In 1889, President Benjamin Harrison (1833–1901) opened unoccupied lands in Oklahoma for settlement by non-American Indians. An estimated 50,000 to 60,000 migrants took part on the first day of the first land run, or land rush. Other runs followed with the opening of other parts of Oklahoma, including the 6-million-acre Cherokee Outlet in 1893 when some 100,000 people raced for homesteads.

The completion of the first Transcontinental Railroad in 1869, from Omaha, Nebraska, to Sacramento, California, made westward travel easier. Other railroads followed. Discoveries of gold, silver, or other precious metals sent swarms of people to California, Nevada, Colorado, New Mexico, Arizona, the Black Hills of present-day South Dakota, and elsewhere.

But there was a cost for this rapid growth.

European settlers introduced diseases to Native American populations that had no immunity to smallpox and other contagious diseases. The results were often devastating to the Native peoples. "By the early 1870s, the ancestral tribes of the middle and upper Missouri—the Omahas, Poncas, Pawnees, Arikaras, Mandans, Hidatsas, Assiniboines, and Blackfeet—had been subdued," historian R. G. Robertson wrote. "Weakened by smallpox and harassed by their enemies, these previous rulers of the Great Plains no longer held sway in their own land" (Robertson 2001, 293–294). The introduction of alcohol to Native Americans, who had little tolerance for liquor, also proved deadly—a trend that has not diminished. "Deaths related to alcoholism are four times higher for Indians than for the general population; 70 percent of all treatments provided by physicians at Indian Health Service clinics are for alcohol-related disease or trauma" (Mancall 1997, 6). Railroads altered the migratory paths of animals on which Native peoples depended for their survival. Once many tribes were confined to reservations, the government tried to convert hunter-gatherers into farmers.

The encroachment of white settlers into what had been, or still were, the homelands of Native American tribes led to violent confrontations. A group of peace commissioners in its report to President Andrew Johnson (1808–1875) in 1868 said:

> If the lands of the white man are taken, civilization justifies him in resisting the invader. Civilization does more than this; it brands him as a coward and a slave if he submits to the wrong. Here civilization made its contract and guaranteed the rights of the weaker party. It did not stand by the guarantee. The treaty was broken, but not by the savage. If the savage resists, civilization, with the ten commandments in one hand and the sword in the other, demands his immediate extermination. (Rives, Rives, and Bailey 1870, 449)

Conflicts between Indian tribes and the U.S. military or white settlers erupted throughout the West—no different east of the Mississippi River between the late 1600s and into the mid-1800s. By the 1830s, several Southeastern Native American tribes, including many Cherokees and Seminoles, had been relocated to reservations west of the Mississippi River.

In the West, relations between the U.S. military and Apaches deteriorated in 1861 when a young army officer, searching for a kidnapped boy and some stolen cattle, tried to hold Apache leader Cochise and his family hostage.

Prisoners on both sides were executed, and the war between the United States and various Apache tribes continued until 1886. Dakota Indians of Minnesota retaliated after the U.S. government ignored treaty provisions that included delivering food and other goods, launching the Dakota War of 1862. More than 600 white settlers were killed. Dakota deaths have been estimated at slightly more than 100, but after the war, a military commission sentenced 303 Dakotas to death and 16 others to prison sentences. After President Abraham Lincoln and lawyers reviewed the transcripts, Lincoln sent a list of 39 names to General Henry H. Sibley (1811–1891) to be executed. One man was spared at the last minute, but on December 26, 1862, 38 Dakotas were hanged before an estimated 4,000 spectators on a specially built gallows in Mankato, Minnesota—the largest mass execution in U.S. history.

In 1864, Colorado volunteers under John M. Chivington (1821–1894) massacred more than 200 Cheyenne Indians at Sand Creek, Colorado, touching off years of violence on the Great Plains, while the rush of white settlers to the gold fields in Montana and the government's establishment of three forts for protection, a clear violation of a previous treaty, led to Red Cloud's War, named after the Lakota leader, in 1866–1868. In the Pacific Northwest, the Modocs went to war in 1872–1874 in one of the United States' costliest wars of the nineteenth century, during which 159 Modoc men, women, and children fought against roughly 1,000 U.S. soldiers before surrendering. Comanches, Kiowas, and Cheyennes fought against men slaughtering the buffalo herds in the 1860s and the 1870s from Texas to Kansas before Quanah Parker surrendered his Comanche band in 1875. The discovery of gold in the Black Hills, land belonging to the Lakotas, touched off a war that led to the deaths of George Armstrong Custer (1839–1876) and his immediate command at the Little Big Horn River in southern Montana in 1876 and, eventually, the Lakotas' surrender and placement on reservations. In 1877, the Nez Perce under Chief Joseph resisted a forced removal from their homelands in the Pacific Northwest and began a desperate flight to freedom in Canada before being stopped in Montana's Bear Paw Mountains, just 40 miles from the international border.

By the mid-1880s, most of the Native American tribes had been relocated to reservations, sometimes in their ancestral homelands, other times not. The Dawes Act of 1887 sliced up reservations in Indian Territory (present-day Oklahoma) further by having tribal members pick or be assigned 160-acre or 80-acre lots. American Indian historian Kent Blansett, a Cherokee, Creek, Choctaw, Shawnee, and Potawatomi descendant, said:

> The Dawes Act was one of the most devastating and destructive polices to tribal sovereignty in history. It carried out earlier policies of assimilation by forcing native peoples to assume a capitalist and proprietary relationship with property. . . . Many of the reformers' ideas backfired and caused irrevocable damage to

tribal governments and culture. The act liquidated tribal lands, while individual ownership further aided in the checker-boarding effect on many reservations. (Crutchfield 2011a, 162)

Between 1860 and 1890, Dee Brown wrote in his seminal *Bury My Heart at Wounded Knee* that "the culture and the civilization of the American Indian was destroyed, and out of that time came virtually all the great myths of the American West—tales of fur traders, mountain men, steamboat pilots, goldseekers, gamblers, gunmen, cavalrymen, cowboys, harlots, missionaries, schoolmarms, and homesteaders. Only occasionally was the voice of an Indian heard, and then more often that not it was recorded by the pen of a white man" (Brown 1981, xi).

Wars were not limited to the military or white settlers against Native Americans. After the Civil War, feuds broke out between white settlers, leading to wars over cattle ranges and/or free enterprise in Colfax County and Lincoln County, New Mexico; Johnson County, Wyoming; Mason County, Texas; Pleasant Valley, Arizona. Range wars were fought over cattle and sheep. "Cattlemen did not like sheep because they believed the smaller animals with their sharply pointed hoofs cut the range grasses and made the ground stink so that cattle wouldn't use it," Candy Moulton wrote. "Quite simply, they did not want to share the range. But certainly some ranchers saw sheep as an opportunity, another way to turn grass into a commodity in the form of meat or wool" (Moulton 2011). Between 1866 and 1878, an estimated 20 to 30 men were killed in El Paso County, Texas, over the rights to salt fields.

The West also became known for bands of outlaws. Brothers Frank James (1843–1915) and Jesse James (1847–1882) of Missouri, both former Confederate-leaning guerrilla soldiers during the Civil War, led a notorious group of bank, train, stagecoach, paymaster, and even fairground robbers whose crimes are alleged to have reached from Northfield, Minnesota, to Muscle Shoals, Alabama, and from Huntington, West Virginia, to Muncie, Kansas. Their crime spree, which likely started in 1866 and no later than 1869, ended when gang member Robert Ford (1862–1892) murdered Jesse for the reward, and Frank surrendered shortly thereafter and was acquitted in two trials. In the 1890s, the Dalton brothers (Grat, 1861–1892; Bob, 1869–1892; and Emmett, 1871–1937) were accused of robbing banks and trains from California to Oklahoma. Their career ended when they tried to rob two banks simultaneously in their hometown of Coffeyville, Kansas. Grat, Bob, and two other gang members were killed, and Emmett was wounded and spent 14 years in prison. Four town citizens, including the town marshal, were also killed. In the late 1880s, a group of outlaws known as the Wild Bunch, Kid Curry's Gang, and the Hole in the Wall Gang, operating out of Wyoming and across much of the West, became known as highly efficient bank and train robbers. Members included Robert Leroy

Parker (1866–1908), alias Butch Cassidy; Harry Alonzo Longabaugh (ca. 1867–1908), alias the Sundance Kid; and Harvey Logan (1865–1904), alias Kid Curry. Curry killed himself after being surrounded by a posse near Parachute, Colorado. Cassidy and Sundance are believed to have fled the United States to Argentina and Bolivia, where both most likely were killed in the mining village of San Vicente after a gunfight with Bolivian officials and citizens.

To combat lawlessness, towns often hired professional gunmen as marshals. James Butler "Wild Bill" Hickok (1837–1876), who shot and killed Davis Tutt (1836–1865) in a rare walk-down, face-down gunfight, served as a constable in Monticello Township, Kansas; as marshal of Hays, Kansas; as a deputy U.S. marshal in Kansas; and as marshal of Abilene, Kansas, where he shot and killed gambler Phil Coe (1839–1871) and then accidentally killed one of his own deputies who was running to assist. Pat Garrett (1850–1908) was elected sheriff of Lincoln County, New Mexico, in 1880, and began hunting outlaw Henry McCarty (ca. 1859–1881), alias Billy the Kid, even before taking office. Garrett killed the Kid on July 14, 1881. Wyatt Earp (1848–1929) served in law enforcement in Lamar, Missouri, and Wichita and Dodge City, Kansas, before he arrived in the silver-mining boomtown of Tombstone, Arizona. There, on October 26, 1881, Earp, who had been deputized as an assistant marshal, joined his brothers, city marshal Virgil Earp (1843–1905) and deputy marshal Morgan Earp (1851–1882), and gambler and good friend John "Doc" Holliday (1851–1887) to allegedly disarm several cowboys. The resulting gunfight, which lasted no longer than 30 seconds, left three cowboys dead and Virgil, Morgan, and Holliday wounded, and it became known as the "Gunfight at the O.K. Corral," even though it did not take place at that location.

Lawlessness also led to the establishment of the Texas Rangers, a partisan militia since the early 1820s, as special state police force in 1874. Other states and territories, such as Colorado and Arizona, had similar Ranger organizations. In settlements far from courthouses, peace officers, and judges—and sometimes even when the law was close—vigilantes carried out their own brand of justice, running some undesirables out of town and lynching others.

During the years after the Civil War, the West also gave birth to one of its most iconic images: the cowboy. Cowboys, usually young men, worked for wages of around a dollar a day to take care of cattle on ranches or on cattle drives. The drives came about shortly after the Civil War, when longhorns were abundant in Texas and beef was in demand across the country, especially in the East. Railroads had reached Kansas by that time, so cattlemen or ranchers would hire cowboys to push herds of cattle from southern Texas to Kansas cattle towns such as Baxter Springs, Abilene, Ellsworth, Newton, Wichita, Caldwell, and Dodge City. Cowboys also drove cattle to help stock northern ranges in Wyoming, Montana, and the Dakotas. The era of the long cattle drives was brief, roughly 1866–1885, but it left a lasting impression across the world.

In fact, the dynamic period of western expansion was short, starting at the end of the Civil War and lasting until the end of the nineteenth century. On December 29, 1890, the 7th Cavalry—George Custer's former regiment—clashed with Lakota Indians at Wounded Knee, South Dakota. At least 150 Lakotas—most of them women and children—were killed in what is considered the last fight of the Indian Wars. Not quite three years later, Frederick Jackson Turner's "The Significance of the Frontier in American History," read at the World Columbian Exposition in Chicago, cited the 1890 Census report that the American frontier had vanished.

The frontier had closed, and Old West had become part of history.

FURTHER READING

Bell, Bob Boze. 2000. *The Illustrated Life & Times of Wyatt Earp*. Phoenix, AZ: Tri Star—Boze Publications, Inc.

Boardman, Mark. 2015. "Go West, Young Man? Did Anybody Actually Say That Famous Phrase?" *True West*, June 5, 2015. https://truewestmagazine.com/go -west-young-man

Boggs, Johnny D. 2003. *Great Murder Trials of the Old West*. Plano: Republic of Texas Press.

Brown, Dee. 1981. *Bury My Heart at Wounded Knee: An Indian History of the West*. New York: Pocket Books.

Cox, Mike. 1991. *The Texas Rangers: Men of Action & Valor*. Austin, TX: Eakin Press.

Cozzens, Peter. 2016. *The Earth Is Weeping: The Epic Story of the Indian Wars for the American West*. New York: Alfred A. Knopf.

Crutchfield, James A., ed. 2011a. *The Settlement of America: Encyclopedia of Westward Expansion from Jamestown to the Closing of the Frontier: Volume I*. Armonk, NY: Sharpe Reference.

Crutchfield, James A., ed. 2011b. *The Settlement of America: Encyclopedia of Westward Expansion from Jamestown to the Closing of the Frontier: Volume II*. Armonk, NY: Sharpe Reference.

Dary, David. 1982. *Cowboy Culture: A Saga of Five Centuries*. New York: Avon Books.

Dykstra, Robert R. 1983. *The Cattle Towns*. Lincoln: University of Nebraska Press.

Fehrenbach, T. R. 1983. *Lone Star: A History of Texas and the Texans*. New York: American Legacy Press.

Gard, Wayne. 1954. *The Chisholm Trail*. Norman: University of Oklahoma Press.

Gardner, Mark Lee. 2010. *To Hell on a Fast Horse: Billy the Kid, Pat Garrett, and the Epic Chase to Justice in the Old West*. New York: William Morrow.

Greeley, Horace. 1838. "The Pre-emption System." *New-Yorker* 5 (August 25): 361.

Guinn, Jeff. 2011. *The Last Gunfight: The Real Story of the Shootout at the O.K. Corral—And How It Changed the American West*. New York: Simon & Schuster.

Gwynne, S. C. 2010. *Empire of the Summer Moon: Quanah Parker and the Rise and Fall of the Comanches, the Most Powerful Indian Tribe in American History*. New York: Scribner.

Hatch, Thom. 2014. *The Last Outlaws: The Lives and Legends of Butch Cassidy and the Sundance Kid*. New York: New American Library.

Hutton, Paul Andrew. 2016. *The Apache Wars: The Hunt for Geronimo, the Apache Kid, and the Captive Boy Who Started the Longest War in American History*. New York: Crown.

Lamar, Howard R., ed. 1998. *The New Encyclopedia of the American West*. New Haven, CT: Yale University Press.

Mancall, Peter C. 1997. *Deadly Medicine: Indians and Alcohol in Early America*. Ithaca, NY: Cornell University Press.

Metz, Leon Claire. 2003. *The Encyclopedia of Lawmen, Outlaws, and Gunfighters*. New York: Facts on File, Inc.

Michno, Gregory F. 2009. *Encyclopedia of Indian Wars: Western Battles and Skirmishes, 1850–1890*. Flagstaff, AZ: Mountain Press Publishing Company.

Moulton, Candy. 2005. *Chief Joseph: Guardian of the People*. New York: Forge.

Moulton, Candy. 2011. "Conflict on the Range: On the trail of the Colorado and Wyoming Sheep and Cattle Wars." *True West*, August 29, 2011. https://truewest magazine.com/conflict-on-the-range

O'Dell, Larry. 2011. "ALL-BLACK TOWNS." *Encyclopedia of the Great Plains*. plainshumanities.unl.edu/encyclopedia/doc/egp.afam.006

Rives, F., J. Rives, and George A. Bailey. 1870. *Congressional Globe and Appendix: Second Session Forty-First Congress: In Seven Parts: Part VII, Appendix to Congressional Globe*. Washington, DC: Office of the Congressional Globe.

Robertson, R. G. 2001. *Rotting Face: Smallpox and the American Indian*. Caldwell, ID: Caxton Press.

Rosa, Joseph G. 1974. *They Called Him Wild Bill: The Life and Adventures of James Butler Hickok*. Norman: University of Oklahoma Press.

Stiles, T. J. 2003. *Jesse James: Last Rebel of the Civil War*. New York: Vintage Books.

Utley, Robert M. 1984. *The Indian Frontier of the American West, 1845–1890*. Albuquerque: University of New Mexico Press.

Utley, Robert M. 1987. *High Noon in Lincoln: Violence on the Western Frontier*. Albuquerque: University of New Mexico Press.Wallis, Michael. 2007. *Billy the Kid: The Endless Ride*. New York: W. W. Norton & Company.

Utley, Robert M., and Wilcomb E. Washburn. 1977. *The American Heritage History of the Indian Wars*. New York: American Heritage Publishing Company.

Chronology

April 3, 1860	The first riders leave St. Joseph, Missouri, and San Francisco, California, to launch the Pony Express, which can deliver mail over a 1,800-mile route in 10 days.
February 4, 1861	Apache leader Cochise meets with Lt. George Bascom, commanding a detail ordered to retrieve a six-year-old boy captive, in southern Arizona. Blunders lead to Cochise's escape, the murders of hostages on both sides, and a war between Apaches and whites that lasts 25 years.
October 24, 1861	The Transcontinental Telegraph is completed, putting the Pony Express out of business.
January 1, 1863	Daniel Freeman becomes the first person to submit a claim under the Homestead Act, signed into law in 1862 by President Abraham Lincoln, when he files a claim on 160 acres near Beatrice, Nebraska.
November 29, 1864	Col. John Chivington's volunteer cavalry troops launch a surprise attack on an Indian village at Sand Creek, Colorado, massacring more than 230 Cheyenne and Arapaho Indians, including roughly 150 women, children, and elderly.

July 21, 1865

James Butler "Wild Bill" Hickok shoots Davis K. Tutt dead on the town square of Springfield, Missouri, in one of the few documented walk-down gunfights. Hickok is acquitted of manslaughter on August 6.

December 21, 1866

An alliance of Lakota, Cheyenne, and Arapaho Indians wipe out Capt. William J. Fetterman and his command of 80 soldiers near Fort Phil Kearny in Wyoming Territory. Fetterman had allegedly bragged earlier: "Give me eighty men and I can ride through the whole Sioux nation."

September 5, 1867

Joseph G. McCoy's Great Western Stock Yards begin shipping cattle to markets by rail, establishing Abilene, Kansas, as a cattle town and opening a route from southern Texas that becomes known as the Chisholm Trail.

October 21–27, 1867

At Medicine Lodge Creek in Kansas, representatives of the Arapaho, Comanche, Kiowa, Kiowa-Apache, and Southern Cheyenne tribes meet with U.S. officials and agree to treaties in which the tribes agree to surrender traditional territories for smaller reservations in present-day Oklahoma.

November 27, 1868

At dawn, Lt. Col. George Custer leads a surprise attack on a Cheyenne village on the Washita River in present-day Oklahoma, killing more than 100 Indians, including Black Kettle, a Cheyenne peace chief, and his wife. Many call the attack a massacre, but it gives Custer credentials as an "Indian fighter."

May 10, 1869

Central Pacific locomotive "Jupiter" and Union Pacific's No. 119 meet at Promontory Summit in northern Utah, where the Transcontinental Railroad is completed.

February 17, 1870

Esther Morris is appointed justice of the peace in South Pass City, Wyoming Territory, becoming the first woman to hold a public office in the United States—just months after the territory approved women's suffrage.

June 28, 1870

Sgt. Emanuel Stance of the 9th Cavalry is awarded the Medal of Honor for gallantry in action the previous month while campaigning against Indians at Kickapoo Springs, Texas. Stance becomes the first African American to win the Medal of Honor.

July 5, 1871

Kiowa Indians Satanta and Big Tree are convicted by an all-white jury in Jacksboro, Texas, for their roles in a raid on a wagon train at Salt Creek, which left seven teamsters dead.

October 5, 1871

In Abilene, Kansas, Marshal "Wild Bill" Hickok mortally wounds gunman-gambler Phil Coe in a gunfight outside of the Bull's Head Saloon, but then he mistakenly shoots and kills a deputy, Mike Williams, who was running to assist the lawman.

June 27, 1874

Armed with long-range, large-caliber rifles, 28 men, mostly buffalo hunters, and a woman hold off a large war party of Comanche, Cheyenne, Kiowa, and Arapaho Indians at a trading post in the Texas Panhandle known as Adobe Walls.

September 28, 1874

Col. Ranald Mackenzie's 4th Cavalry launches a surprise attack on a large Indian encampment in Palo Duro Canyon in the Texas Panhandle, the last major battle of the Red River War that ends the Southern Plains tribe's resistance against white settlement.

May 4, 1875

Thirty-six-year-old Isaac Parker, the West's youngest federal judge, presides over the U.S. Court for the Western District of Arkansas for the first time in Fort Smith, Arkansas. Over the next 21 years, Parker sentences 160 men to death and earns the nickname of "Hanging Judge."

June 2, 1875

Quanah Parker, a son of Comanche Peta Nocona and white captive Cynthia Ann Parker, surrenders the last band of Comanche Indians at Fort Sill in present-day Oklahoma.

June 25–26, 1876

Defending their encampment, a large body of mostly Lakota and Cheyenne Indians defeat Lt. Col. George Custer's command of the 7th Cavalry at the Little Big Horn River in southern Montana Territory. Custer and more than 250 of his men are killed.

August 2, 1876	Jack McCall kills Wild Bill Hickok with a bullet to the back of the head while the latter is playing poker at the Saloon No. 10 in Deadwood, Dakota Territory. Although a "miner's court" acquits McCall of murder, McCall is arrested later and tried, convicted, and executed in Yankton in 1877.
September 7, 1876	The James-Younger Gang's attempted bank robbery in Northfield, Minnesota, leaves two outlaws and two citizens dead. The six surviving outlaws flee, kicking off the largest manhunt in U.S. history. On September 21, brothers Cole, Bob, and Jim Younger are captured at Hanska Slough and later sent to prison in Stillwater. Only Jesse and Frank James manage to escape.
September 5, 1877	Lakota leader Crazy Horse dies after being bayoneted in the back by an army soldier during a fight with soldiers who were attempting to place him in a guardhouse at Fort Robinson, Nebraska.
October 5, 1877	Chief Joseph surrenders his Nez Perce followers to army forces in the Bear Paw Mountains of Montana, ending a desperate flight for freedom that covers more than 1,170 miles but is stopped less than 40 miles from the Canadian border.
February 18, 1878	A sheriff's posse murders transplanted Englishman John Henry Tunstall in Lincoln County, New Mexico Territory, touching off the Lincoln County War, which leads to more violence and propels a young cowboy and killer known as Billy the Kid into legend.
May 12, 1879	In *Standing Bear et al. v. Crook*, Judge Elmer Dundy of the U.S. Circuit Court for the District of Nebraska rules in Omaha "That an Indian is a PERSON" and that "Indians have the inalienable right to life, liberty, and the pursuit of happiness."
July 14, 1881	Lincoln County Sheriff Pat Garrett shoots and kills Henry McCarty, alias William H. Bonney, Kid Antrim, and Billy the Kid, in Pete Maxwell's house in Fort Sumner, New Mexico Territory.

October 26, 1881	John "Doc" Holliday and brothers Virgil, Wyatt, and Morgan Earp kill Billy Clanton and brothers Tom and Frank McLaury in a gunfight in a vacant lot in Tombstone, Arizona Territory, an event that goes down in history as the Gunfight at the O.K. Corral.
April 3, 1882	Gang member Robert Ford kills an unarmed Jesse James at James's rented home in St. Joseph, Missouri.
May 19, 1883	William F. "Buffalo Bill" Cody debuts his Wild West show in Omaha, Nebraska. Cody goes on to take his various exhibitions across the world before his death in 1917.
September 4, 1886	Apache leader Geronimo surrenders to General Nelson Miles at Skeleton Canyon in Arizona Territory, ending years of bloodshed in the Southwest and becoming the last Native American leader to formally surrender to U.S. forces.
January 9, 1887	A severe blizzard with driving winds dumps more than 16 inches of snow over the Great Plains and drops temperatures to roughly 50 degrees below zero. Coupled with a severe drought the previous summer, the "Hard Winter" or "Great Die Up" leaves millions of cattle dead, wipes out many ranches, and ends the open-range cattle era.
April 22, 1889	At noon, thousands of settlers dash to stake claims after nearly two million acres are opened for settlement in Oklahoma Territory.
December 29, 1890	In the final clash between U.S. soldiers and Native Americans, members of the 7th Cavalry massacre at least 150 Lakotas at Wounded Knee, South Dakota. Almost half of the dead are women and children.
April 5, 1892	Several armed men leave Cheyenne, Wyoming, by train for Casper, where they mount horses and ride north with orders from cattle barons to shoot or hang 70 small ranchers, beginning the Johnson County War.

October 5, 1892	The Dalton Gang's attempt to rob two banks simultaneously in their hometown of Coffeyville, Kansas, leaves brothers Bob and Grat Dalton, gang members Dick Broadwell and Bill Powers, and four townsmen dead and Emmett Dalton badly wounded. Emmett recovers and is sentenced to life in prison, but he receives a parole after 14 years.
November 3, 1892	After being wrongly accused of killing a federal marshal in 1887, Cherokee Indian Ned Christie is finally killed by a posse that uses a cannon and dynamite to blast him out of his fort and guns him down as he flees the smoking ruins, ending "Ned Christie's War."
July 12, 1893	During an American Historical Association meeting at the World Columbian Exposition in Chicago, Frederick Jackson Turner reads his "The Significance of the Frontier in American History," which cites an 1890 Census report that the American frontier has vanished and theorizes that the conquest of the Western frontier shaped America's character and values.
September 16, 1893	More than 100,000 settlers rush into Oklahoma's Cherokee Strip after more than 8 million acres are opened, the largest land run in American history.
August 19, 1895	Seventeen months after being released from the Texas State Penitentiary in Huntsville, gunfighter John Wesley Hardin, now a practicing attorney, is shot and killed by John Selman while rolling dice in an El Paso saloon. Selman's trial ends with a hung jury, and he is killed by lawman George Scarborough on August 6, 1896.
May 28, 1902	The Macmillan Company publishes the novel *The Virginian* by Owen Wister. The best-selling novel transforms the image of the cowboy and inspires four theatrical films, one made-for-television movie, and a long-running TV series.
November 20, 1903	Tom Horn is hanged in Cheyenne, Wyoming, after being convicted of murdering a 14-year-old boy while working as a hired killer for cattlemen.

December 1903	Edison Mfg. Co. releases director Edwin S. Porter's one-reel Western film *The Great Train Robbery*. Filmed in New Jersey, the movie helps establish techniques and a narrative storytelling approach in motion pictures.
November 6, 1908	American bank and train robbers Robert Leroy Parker and Harry Longabaugh, better known as Butch Cassidy and the Sundance Kid, are reportedly killed in a shootout with Bolivian soldiers near San Vicente.
November 1, 1924	William "Bill" Tilghman, a city marshal in Dodge City in the 1870s, federal marshal in Oklahoma in the 1890s, and filmmaker (*The Passing of the Oklahoma Outlaws*) in the early twentieth century, is killed while serving as a special investigator in Cromwell, Oklahoma, at age 70.
November 18, 1932	RKO Radio's *Cimarron* is awarded the Academy Award for outstanding production of 1931, becoming the first Western to receive the Oscar for Best Picture.

Chapter 1

Union Pacific (1939)

Hollywood's greatest year, according to most historians and movie buffs, was 1939. Historian Mark A. Vieira wrote, "What year before or since has yielded as many masterpieces? . . . In 1939, every week was a cinematic cornucopia" (Vieira 2013, 5). That year saw the releases of classics such as *Gunga Din, The Wizard of Oz, Mr. Smith Goes to Washington, The Hunchback of Notre Dame*, and *Gone with the Wind*. It was also the year in which Western movies, typically relegated to low-budget programmers during the Great Depression (1929–1939), returned to big-budget, A-list status: 20th Century Fox's *Jesse James*, United Artists' *Stagecoach*, Warner Bros.' *Dodge City*, Universal's *Destry Rides Again*, and Paramount's *Union Pacific* all had big budgets, scored big in the box office, and helped propel the Western into one of the most popular film genres for the next three decades.

Jesse James was the year's top Western at the box office, *Stagecoach* made John Wayne (1907–1979) a major star, *Dodge City* turned swashbuckler Errol Flynn (1909–1959) into a Western player (he made seven more Westerns over the next 11 years), and *Destry Rides Again* gave James Stewart (1908–1997) his first taste in the genre, in which he became an icon beginning in the 1950s. But *Union Pacific* was one of the most ambitious. Filmed at an estimated $1.45 million, it grossed $3.2 million domestically, making it among the year's top moneymakers.

Union Pacific opens toward the end of the Civil War (1861–1865) in Washington, D.C., with senators debating the merits of undertaking the construction of a railroad from Omaha, Nebraska, to the California coast. The bill wins support, and President Abraham Lincoln signs the bill into law. The Central Pacific Railroad will lay track eastward to the California state line, while the Union Pacific will build west from Omaha. After

Lincoln's assassination on April 14, 1865, financiers debate the undertaking, but Asa M. Barrows (played by Henry Kolker, 1870–1947), "the biggest moneybags in Chicago," sees a profit by supporting the enterprise. The Central Pacific has no plans to stop in California, and if the Central Pacific reaches Ogden, Utah, first, the Union Pacific, which by law can build only until it reaches the Central Pacific's rails, "will have a thousand miles of track and a gopher hole for its western terminal." By selling Union Pacific stock short and buying Central Pacific stock, Barrows can bust the Union Pacific and make millions.

In St. Louis, Barrows hires crooked gambler Sid Campeau (Brian Donlevy, 1901–1972) and his partner, Dick Allen (Robert Preston, 1918–1987), to run gambling operations at the Union Pacific's "end of track" (the name given to a railroad's temporary terminus) with orders to delay the railroad's westward progress. Three years later, the Union Pacific is moving west with Irish engineer Monahan (J. M. Kerrigan, 1884–1964) piloting his locomotive and his daughter Mollie (Barbara Stanwyck, 1907–1990) serving as postmistress, but Campeau's men, including crooked gambler Jack Cordray (Anthony Quinn, 1915–2001) and thug Al Brett (Harry Woods, 1896–1970), delay progress by enticing the workers with prostitutes, gambling, and whiskey galore. General Dodge (Francis McDonald, 1891–1968), the Union Pacific's chief engineer, hires Jeff Butler (Joel McCrea, 1905–1990) as a troubleshooter to stop Campeau's treachery. Allen and Butler are old friends, having served together in the Union Army, and though they know they are on opposite sides this time, they remain cordial. However, the two pals are also both attracted to Mollie.

When Brett, to win a bet, shoots a Native American who is racing the train, Butler beats up the killer, throws him off the train, and refuses to let the conductor stop. After Cordray kills a railroad worker who caught him cheating, Butler kills Cordray. Meanwhile, General Ulysses S. Grant (Joseph Crehan, 1883–1966), soon to become president of the United States, asks Barrows to loan the Union Pacific money. Barrows agrees but hires Campeau to get that money back. Under Campeau's orders, Allen robs the payroll, killing a guard, but Butler follows him to Mollie's railroad car, where Allen has hidden the money. Mollie agrees to marry Allen, but only if he returns the money. He does, but when Butler threatens Campeau into confessing that Allen robbed the payroll, Mollie helps Allen escape and is fired by the railroad. Butler's men destroy Campeau's end-of-track gambling parlor and run the thugs out of Cheyenne.

Native Americans derail a train as it heads to the next end-of-track, Laramie; and all are killed except Mollie, Allen, and Butler. A makeshift telegraph is used to send word to Cheyenne, and soldiers arrive to drive off the attackers, but not before Mollie is wounded. Butler lets Allen go, and without the treachery of Campeau and his men, the railroad continues westward, laying track over snow in the mountains in order to beat the Central Pacific to

Ogden. The first train wrecks when the rails collapse under the train's weight, killing Monahan, but the Union Pacific goes on to reach Ogden first, after two of Butler's associates, Fiesta (Akim Tamiroff, 1899–1972) and Leach (Lynne Overman, 1887–1943), kidnap Barrows and force him to help lay track. At the celebration after the two railroads meet at Promontory Summit, Utah, Campeau tries to murder Butler but kills Allen by mistake; he is then shot dead by one of Butler's comrades, allowing Mollie and Butler to be together.

Having finished *The Buccaneer* (1938), about pirate Jean Lafitte (ca. 1780–ca. 1823) and the War of 1812, director-producer Cecil B. DeMille (1881–1959) was considering a movie about the early fur trade in Canada but dropped that project upon learning that another studio planned a movie about the very subject; Irving Pichel (1891–1954) wound up directing *Hudson's Bay* (1941) for 20th Century Fox. Martin Quigley (1890–1964), publisher of the trade journal *Motion Picture Herald*, suggested a movie about the building of the United States' First Transcontinental Railroad, an idea DeMille liked. Film rights were bought for *Trouble Shooter* (1936), a Western novel by Ernest Haycox about a Union Pacific Railroad troubleshooter's adventures during the last months of construction of the Transcontinental Railroad; Haycox's short story "Stage to Lordsburg" was turned into *Stagecoach*.

DeMille sent his writers to work. "I want train wrecks," DeMille said. "I want to see the explosions of steam and bursting boilers! Iron guts! I want to smash through the barricades of mountain ranges and ice! I want a love story that nobody has ever got on the screen. I want human drama! Suspense. Not just 'Will they make it, or won't they make it?' which any damn fool can write. I want a snake under every bed!" (DeMille and Vieira 2014, 286).

Jack Cunningham (1882–1941) adapted Haycox's novel, and Walter DeLeon (1884–1947), C. Gardner Sullivan (1884–1965), and Jesse Lasky Jr. (1910–1988) earned screenplay credits, but Stuart Anthony (1891–1942), Frederick Hazlitt Brennan (1901–1962), Harold Lamb (1892–1962), Jeanie Macpherson (1886–1946), and Stanley Rauh (1898–1979) also worked on the script. "DeMille used writers like a general who counted no costs and spared no feelings," Lasky said. "Some writers were quite literally driven to drink, or into massive sulks or sudden resignations" (DeMille and Vieira 2014, 286).

DeMille wanted Gary Cooper (1901–1961) and Claudette Colbert (1903–1996) for the two lead roles, but Cooper had too many projects, and Colbert turned down DeMille's offer. Vivien Leigh (1913–1967) was then offered the part, but she sought (and later landed) the part of Scarlett O'Hara in *Gone with the Wind*, so she asked for $20,000 for six weeks and a one-picture option—too pricey for DeMille, who signed Stanwyck to play the female lead. McCrea landed Cooper's part. "No one writes things for me," McCrea said. "They write them for Gary Cooper and if they can't get him, they use me" (Nott 2000, 30).

For research, DeMille already had a connection with the Union Pacific Railroad. In 1930, his daughter, Cecilia (1908–1984), married Frank Calvin (1898–1972), son of retired Union Pacific Railroad president Edgar Eugene Calvin (1858–1938). The railroad's current president, William M. Jeffers (1876–1953), "put all the resources of the railroad at our disposal," DeMille said. "He assigned two railroad superintendents and a roadmaster to us as advisers. He opened the company's archives . . . and they proved a mine of information for the authenticity we were seeking, even if we could not use all the intriguing material in them, such as the letters from proprietresses of certain establishments who complained to the railroad that some of its workmen had taken their pleasures without paying the tariff customary in those ladies' line of work" (DeMille 1959, 363).

The railroad lent "its fastest track-laying crew" as extras for some scenes, with footage from the filming later used in government training films during World War II (DeMille 1959, 363). Locations included Cedar City and Iron City in Utah for second-unit work and, in California, Sonora, Woodland Hills, and an icehouse in Los Angeles. Much of the film was shot on Paramount's sound stages with second-unit process shots serving as the background—a film technique that wasn't even convincing in 1939.

In late March 1938, DeMille had emergency prostate surgery and was recovering when *Union Pacific* went into production that fall, but he directed in spite of the pain. "I had my stretcher fixed to the camera boom," DeMille recalled, "and for ten days swung with it up in the air and down again, for whatever camera angles were required" (DeMille 1959, 364–365).

Union Pacific provided a train from Los Angeles to Omaha to send De-Mille, cast members, and other celebrities to the movie's April 28 world premiere. "At the head of the train is a tiny, wood-burning locomotive, pushed by a new steam electric engine, which pulls modern coaches and five others built in the Civil war days" (Associated Press 1939b, 7). An estimated crowd of 50,000 packed Omaha's streets for the movie's debut.

Reviews were mostly positive. "There is an epic quality to this saga of rails, laid with the sweat and brawn of Irish immigrants," wrote the *New York Daily News*'s Kate Cameron, who said the movie ran about 30 minutes too long. "Some of the speech-making scenes might have been cut effectively" (Cameron 1939, 52). "In his much heralded railroad saga 'Union Pacific' Cecil B. DeMille has again this week demonstrated on the screen his special art of the epic with an action tale on the big canvas of the American West and its romantic, dramatic tradition," Joseph F. Coughlin wrote for *Motion Picture Herald*—the journal owned by Quigley, who suggested the idea to DeMille. "Excitement is the dominant emotion, with swift succession of contrasting materials and episodes, grim and gay, often furious, sometimes funny. The narrative and action take hold at the start and never let go" (Coughlin 1939, 51). Ada Hanifin of the *San Francisco Examiner* called the movie "as American as the Rocky Mountains and as undaunted in courage as the Stars and Stripes that waves over it" (Hanifin 1939, 18). DeMille liked it, too. "Union Pacific was Grandfather's favorite of all his American history films," DeMille's granddaughter said (DeMille and Vieira 2014, 288).

HISTORICAL BACKGROUND

In 1855, 59 years before the Panama Canal opened, Panama completed a railroad that linked the Atlantic and Pacific oceans, which helped refuel interest in the United States to join the Pacific coast with the Atlantic by rails. "The dream that a great transcontinental railroad would one day cross the Mississippi and link the Atlantic and Pacific coasts of North America was neither new nor novel in the early 1850s, but it was becoming more urgent and, in the minds of both businessmen and politicians, increasingly inevitable" (McGinty 2015, 34).

As early as the 1840s, New York promoter and merchant Asa Whitney (1797–1872) had seen the need to link the coasts. Whitney's interests were fueled by profit; he was focusing on trading with China, and the current route meant sailing around the tip of South America, across the Pacific. He proposed a route for a railroad from Lake Michigan in Illinois to South Pass in Wyoming, where the route split, one connecting with San Francisco and the other to the Columbia River in Oregon. Whitney's demands for a large land grant didn't help his cause; Congress rejected the plan.

At the time, although Northern and Southern states hotly debated the question of slavery, there was no political divide regarding the railroad—although the South, naturally, preferred the financial rewards a Southern route would bring. For the most part, both North and South wanted a railroad that connected the West with the East.

In 1853–1854, the U.S. Army began surveying possible routes for such a railroad. One went from St. Paul, Minnesota, to Puget Sound on the Washington coast. Another followed the 38th parallel, which crossed southern Kansas, Colorado, Utah, and Nevada into California. The third followed the 35th parallel heading west from Fort Smith, Arkansas. The fourth started from Fort Washita in present-day Oklahoma and moved west along the 32nd parallel and east from Fort Yuma, Arizona. Surveys were also conducted for a route from Oregon to California as well as four possible passes in the southern Sierra Nevada, the rugged mountain range along the California-Nevada border. Ironically, the eventual route of the first Transcontinental Railroad, which ran along the 41st parallel, had been surveyed earlier. The preliminary report, released in 1855, recommended the Southern route—probably no surprise, considering that Secretary of War Jefferson Davis (1808–1889) of Mississippi oversaw the surveys. Final reports became available between 1856 and 1861, when several Southern states seceded from the union and the Civil War began. The war ruled out any hope in the South that the Southern route would be chosen.

President Lincoln knew about railroads. As a lawyer in Illinois, Lincoln had taken cases representing railroads as well as going up against them, and while running for the Illinois State Senate at age 23—an election he lost—he said in a campaign speech that "no other improvement . . . can equal in utility the rail road" despite the "heart-stopping cost" it took to build a railroad (Ambrose 2001, 27).

On January 31, 1862, U.S. Congressman Aaron A. Sargent (1827–1887), newly elected from California, brought up the proposed Transcontinental Railroad during what had been a discussion about the issue of slavery, saying that the "railroad is a necessity of the times—and a great war measure—to be inaugurated now" (Bain 1999, 110). That sparked action, and Congress's railroad committee formed a subcommittee, which appointed Sargent as chair and Theodore Judah, an engineer, lobbyist, and promoter for California's Central Pacific Railroad, as clerk to draft a railroad bill. Judah, who had also mapped a route through the Sierra Mountains, was appointed secretary of both House and Senate railroad committees. "All of this, though hardly proper then or today, firmly put Judah and the Central Pacific into the center of things" (Bain 1999, 110).

Debates continued as the war dragged on with bloody battle after bloody battle. Lobbyists promoted their railroads. Senators and Congressmen fought for their states or territories. After lengthy debate, the Central Pacific was given the right to build across California, beginning either in San Francisco or Sacramento. After more fine-tuning, the Senate passed the bill by a 35-to-5 vote on June 20—the same day Congress also prohibited slavery in the U.S. territories—and the House concurred with the Senate's amendments, and passed the measure on June 24. On July 1, 1862, Lincoln signed the Pacific Railway Act into law.

The original bill awarded the Union Pacific and Central Pacific free land— 10 alternating sections of land (totaling 6,400 square miles) per mile near each railroad's right-of-way—an amount later doubled so that the railroads received 19 million acres of public land, which the railroads could then divide up and sell to settlers. Railroads were also issued stock and awarded government grants. Each railroad was paid $16,000 per mile across flat country, $32,000 per mile across foothills, and $48,000 per mile across the Rocky and Sierra mountain ranges.

When Judah would not certify the foothills east of Sacramento as mountains, denying the Central Pacific $16,000 per mile, the railroad's leaders— Collis P. Huntington (1821–1900), Mark Hopkins (1813–1878), Charles Crocker (1822–1888), and Leland Stanford (1824–1893)—excluded him from any other decisions, so Judah and his wife left California for New York, hoping to secure investors in an attempt to buy out the Central Pacific's "Big Four." But while crossing Panama by land, Judah contracted either yellow fever or typhoid fever and died in New York City on November 2, 1863, at age 37. "The stakes for building the railroad were high," historian Jeremy Agnew wrote. "The prize was great and the potential profits immense" (Agnew 2012, 20).

The Union Pacific's biggest problem came from its inability to sell much stock, but financier Thomas Durant (1820–1885) became vice president and general manager of the Union Pacific in 1863 and created Crédit Mobilier of America, a construction and finance company that was nothing more than a fraudulent moneymaking scheme. Historian Stephen E. Ambrose explains:

> The Union Pacific awarded construction contracts to dummy individuals, who in turn assigned them to Crédit Mobilier. The UP paid the Crédit Mobilier by check, with which the Crédit Mobilier purchased from the UP stocks and bonds—at par, the trick to the whole thing—and then sold them on the open market for whatever they could fetch, or sued them as security for loans. The construction contracts brought huge profits to the Crédit Mobilier, which in turn was owned by the directors and principal stockholders of the UP. In short, it didn't matter if the UP ever got up and running and made a profit, because the Crédit Mobilier would make a big profit on building it. Profit that it would pay out to its stockholders in immense amounts. (Ambrose 2001, 93)

But with hundreds of thousands of men fighting for the Union and Confederate armies during the war, labor was short—even in California, "where the mines seductively beckoned" (Williams 1989, 94). Construction west and east remained slow. Building railroads proved to be hard labor, and workers frequently quit. By the middle of 1864, the Central Pacific had laid less than 50 miles of track. Earlier that year, the Central Pacific brought in Chinese workers from mining communities. Toward the end of the following year, Chinese workers for the Central Pacific numbered in the thousands. The Union Pacific, which employed Irish immigrants and, after the Civil War, a number of war veterans, even tried to recruit some of the Central Pacific's Chinese workers.

In 1864, Congress amended the Pacific Railway Act, inserting a provision that awarded the westbound construction of the Transcontinental Railroad to the first company that laid track to the 100th meridian near present-day Cozad, Nebraska, where a Pony Express station had been established for that short-lived mail enterprise of 1860–1861. The Union Pacific's competitor, the Leavenworth, Pawnee & Western Railroad (later the Union Pacific Eastern Division), had already started laying track from Kansas City, Kansas, in September 1863, whereas the Union Pacific did not start until 1865 and had managed only 40 miles by the end of the year—the minimum number of completed track needed to qualify to continue in the race.

On May 1, 1866, the Union Pacific hired former Union General Grenville M. Dodge (1831–1916) as its chief engineer, and Dodge recommended that John S. "Jack" Casement (1829–1909), who had been breveted a brigadier general during the Civil War, and his brother Daniel T. Casement

(1831–1881) be contracted for the Union Pacific's track laying. Durant persisted in demanding that a circuitous route be used—and thus increase his profits—and hired Silas Seymour (1817–1890) as a consulting engineer to make sure that happened. But Dodge and the Casement brothers were honest. "Seymour was a constant thorn in Jack Casement's side, issuing orders contradictory to Dodge's plans," said historical novelist Robert Lee Murphy, author of a series of novels about the building of the railroad. "'General' Jack was astute enough to maneuver around most of the distractions while also overcoming environmental and technical difficulties. Today, the Union Pacific Railroad largely follows the route 'General' Jack built" (Robert Lee Murphy, interview with author, May 15, 2019).

On October 6, 1866, the Union Pacific reached the 100th meridian, winning the race and the right to continue building the railroad westward to meet the Central Pacific, which had to build 15 tunnels in the Sierra Nevada, where winter storms of 1866–1867 slowed progress. Twenty workers died in an avalanche. Six were killed when nitroglycerine, a volatile explosive, accidentally detonated. On June 19, 1867, another tunnel explosion killed six crewmen—five Chinese and one white crewman. That was enough for the Chinese, who were being paid less than their white counterparts, had to work longer hours, and had to pay for their own food (white workers for both railroads were not charged for meals).

On June 24, 1867, 3,000 Chinese workers stopped work between Cisco and Truckee, almost 30 miles, in an organized labor strike. "It was disciplined and methodical," historian Gordon Chang wrote. "How they planned, communicated, and coordinated with one another, however, is not known at all" (Chang 2019, 151). Neither do historians know what the workers demanded, though it appears to have included equal pay and shorter hours. After eight days, railroad officials, accompanied by a sheriff and deputies, refused to concede to any demands, and the Chinese workers went back to work.

During interrogation in 1876 by a special committee of congressmen and senators investigating Chinese immigration, Crocker explained how the strike was broken:

> I stopped the provisions on them, stopped the butchers from butchering, and used such coercive measures. I then went up there and made them a little war speech and told them they could not control the works, that no one made laws there but me. I talked to them so that they could comprehend what the rules and regulations were, and that if they did not choose to obey they could go away from the work, but under no circumstances would I give way to them. I gave them until the next Monday morning at six o'clock to come back, and told them that every man who went to work then should be forgiven for the week's strike, but that all others should be fined. (Report of the Joint Special Committee to Investigate Chinese Immigration, 1877)

In the long run, though, the strike was not a failure. With workers still hard to find, and the Chinese skilled at what they did, the experienced Chinese

HELL ON WHEELS

The Transcontinental Railroad's ever-moving "end-of-track" gave birth to sometimes temporary towns known as Hell on Wheels, places where railroad workers could unwind, as depicted in *Union Pacific*, by getting drunk, carousing, and gambling.

A newspaper correspondent described one such Hell on Wheels, Benton, which was boomed in present-day Wyoming, in the summer of 1868:

> When the editors visited the town it was two weeks old. Its population was fifteen hundred. It was entirely formed of large tents. Every other tent was either a gambling den, or a "drinking saloon," or a dancing hall—with adjoining chambers that go down to hell. There were sixty woman [sic] in the town, not one of them virtuous[,] all of them belonging to the vilest grade of criminal life. Every night in the large tents . . . there are lewd dances, and drinking and gambling, and every variety of obscene and criminal indulgences. Every man goes armed; every man and every woman drinks; every one of both sexes gambles; and, of course, fights are frequent and murders not uncommon. (*N.Y. Independent* 1868, 1)

Some of these towns—including North Platte, Nebraska; Julesburg, Colorado; and Cheyenne and Laramie, Wyoming—survived. Benton, located roughly 11 miles east of present-day Rawlings, Wyoming, did not. "It was not a country where people are disposed to linger," a surveyor said (Williamson 2011, 97). By December, Benton had all but vanished.

workers saw their wages increase slightly, and when the Central Pacific was moving through the harsh Nevada desert in the summer, Crocker rewarded the workers with a bonus.

Construction picked up. So did the competitive rivalry between the two railroads. When the Central Pacific set a record by laying more than six miles of track on September 3, 1868, the Union Pacific paid track layers triple time to lay eight miles of track in a day.

The Central Pacific cleared the mountains in the summer of 1867, and the Union Pacific had reached Wyoming, and both companies raced for Utah. However, the heads of the railroads preferred to keep laying track and earning more money until President Ulysses S. Grant (1822–1885) became president in 1869 and withheld money from both companies until they picked a meeting point. Huntington and Dodge picked Promontory Summit, a desolate location north of Utah's Great Salt Lake—roughly 690 miles from Sacramento and 1,086 miles from Omaha. They chose April 27, 1869, for the joining of the two railroads, but when the Central Pacific's locomotive derailed, the date was pushed back to April 28, when the country's first Transcontinental Railroad was all but completed—seven years ahead of schedule—except for the final celebration.

The Transcontinental Railroad, however, didn't exactly connect the two coasts. "On the Union Pacific's half of the new so-called Pacific Railroad, there was no bridge over the Missouri River until March 1872," Murphy said. "Prior to that date, passengers had to be ferried across the river between Council Bluffs, Iowa, and Omaha, Nebraska, before they could continue their journey by rail. On the Central Pacific's half, no tracks existed between Sacramento and San Francisco, California. Passengers traveled by steamboat on the Sacramento River to make connection to or from the Pacific Ocean" (Robert Lee Murphy, interview with author, May 16, 2019).

Regardless, the official dedication and driving of the last railroad spike was held on May 10, 1869, complete with railroad dignitaries, hundreds of railroad workers, and some 20 newspaper reporters. "One lone tie also remained. It was a length of beautifully polished laurel, with silver straps and a silver commemorative plaque bearing the names of the Central Pacific's leaders. A gift from the company's chief tie contractor, West Evans, the tie had spike holes already drilled so that the precious ceremonial spikes would not be damaged" (Williams 1989, 265).

After the Reverend John Todd of Pittsfield, Massachusetts, opened with a prayer, two rails—one for each railroad—were placed opposite the other, and Stanford and Durant were presented golden spikes. Both men gently tapped their spikes with a silver maul, before the gold spike was replaced with an iron one. After the last spike was driven, the Union Pacific's Engine No. 119 and the Central Pacific's locomotive named Jupiter slowly moved forward until their cowcatchers touched.

In San Francisco the following day, the *Daily Morning Chronicle* reported: "At precisely forty-six minutes past eleven o'clock yesterday morning one of the great guns at Fort Point thundered forth the announcement that the greatest materialistic achievement of this generation, and of the nineteenth century, was an accomplished fact" ("A GREAT FEAT" 1869, 1). Roughly 3,000 miles east, the *New York Herald* reported: "The long-looked for moment has arrived. The construction of the Pacific Railroad is un fait accompli. The inhabitants of the Atlantic board and the dwellers of the Pacific slope are henceforth emphatically one people" ("The Celebration at Promontory" 1869, 3).

"With the driving of the golden spike, Manifest Destiny became a reality," Murphy wrote. "The Overland Trail that had required six months to traverse in a wagon could now be crossed in six days by train. The western lands that had been home to Indian tribes for centuries were rapidly taken from them" (Murphy 2019, 18).

DEPICTION AND CULTURAL CONTEXT

The Union Pacific's cooperation gave the film production a certain amount of realism. Jeffers allowed DeMille to use six locomotives and 55 railroad cars, all from the 1860s or 1870s, and also provided a right-of-way of 15 miles of track for location filming. DeMille also hired actors who resembled the historical figures shown in the movie: Jack Casement (his brother Daniel is left out), Grenville Dodge, and especially Ulysses S. Grant. Crehan played Grant for the 41st time, then played him again in *Geronimo* (1939). "Crehan," film historian Jon Tuska wrote, "made almost a career out of playing Grant, to whom he bore a striking resemblance, although he was reputed to dislike cigars, which, to make is characterization accurate, the role invariably demanded he smoke" (Tuska 1976, 359).

The screenwriters even used a historical figure as the basis of Stanwyck's Mollie Monahan. Hanna Maria Strobridge (1843–1891) was the wife of the Central Pacific's construction manager, James Harvey Strobridge (1837–1921), who managed to have Hanna—and their six children and reportedly a pet canary—travel with him by converting a railroad car into a three-bedroom home. Hanna Strobridge likely was the only woman who saw the completion of the railroad from roughly the start to the celebration at Promontory Summit.

Union Pacific opens with a senate floor debate over the need for a cross-country railroad. After calling the idea "the most monumental folly," a senator (Morgan Wallace, 1881–1953) begins to quote a speech delivered in the senate chambers years earlier by the late Daniel Webster (1872–1852): "What do we want with this vast, worthless area, this region of savages and wild beasts, of deserts and endless mountain ranges? What can we ever hope to do with 3,000 miles of cheerless, rockbound coast, and not a harbor on it?"

Considering the access the Union Pacific provided DeMille's writers and researchers, it's possible that the speech was found in an editorial in the *Union Pacific Magazine*'s March 1931 issue. The magazine attributed Webster's quote to an 1852 debate over a proposal for government aid to construction of a transcontinental railroad.

That speech has also been attributed to Webster during an 1824 debate against expanding the United States into the Great Plains, an 1844 debate about buying the land base that makes up California, an 1844 debate over establishing a mail route from Missouri to the Pacific coast, and other debates from the 1830s to the 1850s. The speech has been quoted by President John F. Kennedy (1917–1963) and in the *Washington Post* and *Time* magazine. But Webster likely never said it.

In his Pulitzer Prize–winning 1947 book *Across the Wide Missouri*, Bernard DeVoto wrote: "Mr. Webster has been libeled, he never made that speech—but the point is that the speech was so common in and out of Congress that any expansionist could believe he had" (DeVoto 1998, 3).

The source of the speech was journalist Ben Perley Poore (1820–1887), who mentioned the speech in his memoir published in 1886. Poore gave no date or year, but he said the speech came when Webster denounced a proposal for a mail route from Independence, Missouri, to the Columbia River in Oregon:

What do we want with this vast, worthless area? This region of savages and wild beasts, of deserts of shifting sands and whirlwinds of dust, of cactus and prairie dogs? To what use could we ever hope to put these great deserts, or those endless mountain ranges, impenetrable and covered to their very base with external snow? What can we ever hope to do with the western coast, a coast of three thousand miles, rock-bound, cheerless, uninviting, and not a harbor on it? What use have we for this country? (Poore 1996, 213–214)

After Poore's book was published, newspapers frequently quoted the speech. In a 1902 book, Henry M. Field added a few sentences to Poore's version and dated Webster's alleged speech at 1844, saying, "Mr. Clay and Mr. Calhoun," presumably Henry Clay (1777–1852) and John C. Calhoun (1782–1850), "and other leaders of the Senate were of the same mind" (Field 1902, 173). Neither Clay nor Calhoun served in the Senate in 1844, and no Senate records mention such a speech by Webster. In the early 1900s, scholars began questioning Poore and White's veracity. But Webster's alleged speech continues to be quoted.

In 1998, Byron L. Dorgan (1942–), a Democratic senator from North Dakota, quoted Webster's alleged speech during a debate over a farming crisis. Dorgan then said, "Daniel Webster is not considered thoughtless because he made this statement. But is quite clear, I suppose, to all of us now that he missed the mark some" ("THE FARM CRISIS" 1998, 20,082). According to Dorgan, though, Webster made the speech when President Thomas Jefferson (1743–1826) was proposing the Louisiana Purchase (1803). In 1803, Webster, a recent graduate from Dartmouth College, was reading law, a nineteenth-century type of apprenticeship, with Thomas Thompson in Salisbury, New Hampshire. Webster didn't take office in Congress until 10 years later as a member of the House of Representatives.

Union Pacific also gives President Lincoln credit for the railroad bill. "I think Lincoln gets too much credit for the Transcontinental Railroad and the Homestead Act [of 1862]," said Daniel W. Stowell, director and editor of The Papers of Abraham Lincoln at the Abraham Lincoln Presidential Library and Museum in Springfield, Illinois. "I say this because [the railroad and Homestead Act] were part of the Republican Platform for 1860. He completely supported that platform, but it would be really inaccurate and unfair to others in Congress to say that he spearheaded those" (Boggs 2015, 6). More importantly, however, *Union Pacific* begins with the senators debating pros and cons for such a railroad in 1865. Lincoln actually signed the act into law three years earlier.

But *Union Pacific* is right in letting Sargent (Russell Hicks, 1895–1957) champion the railroad's cause. Sargent, editor of the *Nevada City Morning Transcript*, supported the Central Pacific Railroad, and after his election to the House of Representatives, he introduced a railroad bill in October 1861. The Central Pacific's first locomotive built in California was named the *A. A. Sargent*. The biggest problem in the film's version is that Sargent was not a senator at that time but rather was serving as one of California's congressmen in the U.S. House of Representatives. He was not a U.S. senator until 1869.

The fictional character of Frank Butler is introduced in *Union Pacific* during a meeting with Dodge and Jack Casement, when the heroic trouble-shooter tells Dodge that his meeting with Lakota leader Red Cloud went well. "Red Cloud says the Indians'll lay off the railroad if the whites will lay off the Indians," Butler says in the film.

In 1868, treaty agreements were reached with tribal leaders, but Red Cloud of the Lakotas proved to be a tough negotiator. He demanded that the Bozeman Trail, which linked the Oregon Trail to the gold-mining camps in Montana, be closed and that three forts in Lakota country (Reno and Phil Kearny in Wyoming and C. F. Smith in Montana), established to protect white settlers traveling to the gold camps, be abandoned. None of those military posts had been effective, and Phil Kearny had lost more than 80 soldiers when Captain William Fetterman (1833–1866) led his command into an ambush by Lakotas and Cheyennes in 1866. Those three remote military installations had been difficult to man, were constantly harassed by Native Americans, and, located too far north, provided no protection to the Union Pacific.

Red Cloud became "the first Indian leader to force the federal government to back down in a truly major controversy," wrote historian Robert W. Larson. "It was not a sign of weakness on the part of the government, for the army was stronger than ever; it was merely a matter of priorities. The federal government could not occupy the South and protect the Union Pacific at the same time it was defending the Powder River Road, in the opinion of an economy-minded Congress" (Larson 1999, 217). Under terms of the Treaty of 1868, the Bozeman Trail was closed and the three army posts abandoned; the Lakotas promptly burned the forts. The Lakotas were granted land west of the Missouri River in present-day South Dakota and allowed to hunt in "unceded Indian territory," which included parts of Wyoming, Montana, Kansas, and Nebraska. Red Cloud himself made his mark on the treaty in November. "The whites assumed the buffalo would only last a few more years, and soon the tribes would move peacefully onto the reservation and start farming. The Indians, and especially the Oglala [Lakota], assumed they had won the war and protected their traditional hunting ground. Both would turn out to be very, very wrong" (Rea 2014).

Other Native American tribes signed similar treaties that allowed for railroad construction, but none could have predicted the impact railroads would have. They changed the migratory patterns of American bison, commonly called buffalo, which were soon hunted by white hide hunters until the bison stood at the brink of extinction. The railroads also brought in vast number of white settlers to what had once been Native American lands.

In one of *Union Pacific*'s most spectacular scenes (presented effectively despite the use of miniature models, long before computer-generated imagery, commonly known as CGI), Native Americans on horseback attack the train carrying Butler, Allen, and Mollie. While the white travelers fire back at the mounted attackers, other Native Americans begin chopping the support posts on a water tower and then use ropes to pull the weakened posts and topple the tower onto the engine, causing a massive wreck. Lakotas, Cheyennes, and Arapahos often harassed Union Pacific construction crews in Nebraska and present-day Wyoming, and one of the Cheyennes' biggest successes, though not as elaborate as the wreck staged by DeMille, proved effective.

The area around Plum Creek, near present-day Lexington, Nebraska, had seen bloodshed before the Union Pacific began grading. On August 8, 1864, a party of roughly 100 Lakotas and Cheyennes attacked a wagon train, killing all 10 men and capturing a woman and a nine-year-old boy. In August 1867, three and a half miles west of the station at Plum Creek, Cheyennes cut down the telegraph wire, pried up one end of two rails, and covered the tracks with several railroad ties the workers had abandoned. The Cheyennes then built a bonfire in a ravine close to the tracks, and waited in the darkness.

When workers realized that the telegraph line was dead, employee William Thompson, a native of England, and four or six others loaded tools, weapons, and replacement wire onto a hand-pumped car, and, guided by lamps, drove the car west, watching for the reflection of the light from the telegraph line to discover the break's location. When they saw the bonfire, they pumped frantically, fearing an ambush by Indians, but they didn't see the barricade and loosened rails. The car wrecked, spilling the men, who then tried to run. Early reports said all but one of the railroad workers were killed, but most historians today believe all but one survived. Wounded, Thompson feigned death and was scalped. "It just felt as if the whole head was taken right off," he said (Miller 2012, 77). The Indian dropped the scalp, which Thompson found. After hiding, he headed for the Willow Creek station, 15 miles west.

About 90 minutes later, a westbound train came. The train left Omaha on August 6 and passed Plum Creek at 12:25 a.m. on August 7. As it neared the ambush site, Cheyennes rode alongside the train, shooting at it—accurately depicted in the movie—and the engineer, "Bully" Brooks Bower, increased the speed. When Bower saw the barricade, he signaled for the brakes, but the train, pulling several cars (reports range from 5 to as many as 25) and reportedly traveling at 35 miles per hour, struck the barricade, flew into the air, and derailed. "The cars were literally jammed into a mass, while their contents were crushed and scattered about in great confusion," the *Omaha Republican* reported. "No sooner were the cars off the track than about one hundred Indians leaped out of the darkness, surrounding the entire train, making it almost impossible for any one to escape" (*Omaha Republican* 1867, 1). The conductor, brakeman, and two other men managed to jump

---

GOLDEN SPIKE STARS IN FILM

One of the actual golden spikes from 1869 was used in *Union Pacific*. For the scene depicting the driving of the golden spike, the Union Pacific Railroad sent its spike from San Francisco to Hollywood for close-ups only. "Even De Mille dared not hammer home the Union Pacific railroad's most precious possession," United Press reported. "He ran in a ringer of iron" (Othman 1939, 10). That iron spike was painted gold for that scene.

Source

Othman, Frederick C. 1939. "EARTH PAINTED AT FILMING OF 'GOLDEN SPIKE': DeMille Exacting as U.P. Rail Epic Scenes Reenacted." *Ogden Standard-Examiner*, p. 10.

---

from the caboose. The fireman was killed in the wreck; Bower was reportedly thrown through the engine's window, disemboweled, and was sitting up on the ground when a Cheyenne shot and killed him. The conductor and other crewmen escaped.

In *Union Pacific*, Butler, Mollie, and Allen, having survived the derailment, splice the telegraph wire and strike it against a rifle barrel to send a telegraph for help, and soldiers come to the rescue on a train. Such technology might have worked. After all, the idea at Promontory Summit during the final ceremony was that the metal maul would strike the iron spike, wired to the telegraph, and this would let the world know that the railroad had been completed. It might have worked if Stanford had been able to actually strike the spike with his sledgehammer. In 1867, the conductor of the wrecked train, William Kinney, ran east down the track. Kinney knew that a second train was coming, and he flagged it down. That train quickly reversed its way back to Plum Creek station, where word was spread of the ambush.

As in many Western movies, the cavalry arrives in the nick of time to drive off the attackers in *Union Pacific*. Usually, the cavalry rides to the rescue on horses, but in DeMille's movie, the train brings them. Trains also brought the relief party in 1867. A special train was loaded at Plum Creek and sent to the site, while Major Frank North (1840–1885), in charge of Pawnees scouting for the army, gathered several detachments west of Plum Creek at Julesburg, then the end-of-track. At Julesburg, men, horses, and wagons were loaded on a train that then steamed east. But there was no resounding victory for the Union Pacific or the army in 1867. By the time, the avengers arrived, the Cheyennes had left and torched the train cars. Pursuits proved to be in vain.

DeMille did a moderately authentic recreation of the celebration at Promontory Summit. Two golden spikes (a third failed to arrive in time); a silver spike; and a spike made of gold, silver, and iron were used in 1869. These ceremonial spikes were tapped into the laurel wood tie with predrilled holes. After this ceremony, iron spikes and a real tie were used.

In the movie, Stanford and Durant are given the honor of driving the last spike, and both men miss with the sledgehammer. Then the fictional character of Barrows, "whose financial aid came to us in a time of great need," is then called upon—and, having been kidnapped by Butler's cronies and forced to help complete the railroad, he easily drives in the last spike.

In 1869, after the ceremonial tie and spikes were removed, replaced by a regular tie, the first three spikes were driven into place by railroad workers. Stanford was given the honor to strike the last spike with a sledgehammer. That iron spike had been wired to the telegraph "so that the big blow from the iron spike hammer could be heard from coast to coast." When Stanford's swing missed the spike and hit the rail, railroad workers "yelled with delight," a witness said. "Everybody slapped everybody else on the back and yelled 'He missed it. Yee'" (Hart 2018). The telegraph operator then tapped out the message: "Done." Durant took the hammer and tried, but his attempt missed, too. Others taking turns included Dodge and Jack Casement before Hanna Strobridge took the final swing. Not present at the ceremony was Anna Judah, the widow of Theodore Judah, who had died before seeing his dream of a transcontinental railroad completed. Anna was in Greenfield, Massachusetts, but she later recalled: "The spirit of my brave husband descended upon me, and together we were there unseen" (Sandler 2015, 172).

CONCLUSION

Like director John Ford's silent epic *The Iron Horse* (1924), DeMille loosely combined history with melodrama in creating a sprawling historical adventure. DeMille's writers and researchers "discovered the vernacular names for the service lines used to construct the road, found the actual prayer spoken as dignitaries drove home the golden spike, established the physical size of the principle historical figures, and authenticated the tools, store fronts, saloons, and locomotives used throughout the film," David Blanke wrote (Blanke 2018, 151).

Like most Westerns, *Union Pacific* did not faithfully follow history, and despite DeMille's name recognition, *Union Pacific* is likely the least remembered of the string of major Western hits in 1939; arguably it has not aged as well as *Stagecoach*, *Dodge City*, and *Jesse James*. Many of the year's Westerns led to changes in the genre. *Union Pacific*'s success paved the way for more historical Westerns, such as *Dark Command*, *Kit Carson*, *Santa Fe Trail*, *Brigham Young*, and *The Westerner*, all in 1940, as well as *Western Union* and *They Died with Their Boots On* in 1941. Likewise, *Stagecoach* led to more adult-themed Western movies in the next three decades (1943's *The Ox-Bow Incident* and *The Outlaw*, 1946's *Duel in the Sun*, and 1947's *Ramrod*); *Dodge City* rekindled an interest in big-budget, traditional

Westerns (1940's *Virginia City*, 1941's *Texas*, 1945's *Along Came Jones*); and *Jesse James* brought about a renewal in movies about Western outlaws (1940's *When the Daltons Rode*; 1941's *Belle Starr* and *Billy the Kid*). After a drought caused by the Great Depression, Westerns were back in favor among studios and moviegoers because of the success of *Union Pacific* and 1939's other hit Western features.

FURTHER READING

Agnew, Jeremy. 2012. *The Old West in Fact and Film: Hollywood versus History.* Jefferson, NC: McFarland & Company, Inc.

Ambrose, Stephen E. 2001. *Nothing Like It in the World: The Men Who Built the Transcontinental Railroad, 1863–1869.* New York: Touchstone.

Associated Press. 1938. "OGDEN TO SEE OLD TRAIN ON WAY TO ZION'S: Chinese Queques [sic] Will Be Missing in Movie Union Pacific." *Ogden Herald-Examiner*, October 13, 1938, p. 4-B.

Associated Press. 1939a. "OMANA OUTDOES FILM CAPITAL IN PREMIERE: DeMille Says It Is Greater Than Anything Hollywood Ever Attempted." *Evening State Journal*, April 29, 1939, p. 3.

Associated Press. 1939b. "TRAIN HEADS FOR OMAHA." *Evening State Journal*, p. 7.

Bain, David Haward. 1999. *Empire Express: Building the First Transcontinental Railroad.* New York: Penguin Books.

Ball, Edward. 2013. *The Inventor and the Tycoon: A Gilded Age Murder and the Birth of Moving Pictures.* New York: Doubleday.

Baxter, Maurice G. 1984. *One and Inseparable: Daniel Webster and the Union.* Cambridge, MA: The Belknap Press of Harvard University Press.

Blanke, David. 2018. *Cecil B. DeMille: Classical Hollywood, and Modern American Mass Culture: 1910–1960.* Cham, Switzerland: Palgrave Macmillan.

Blashfield, Jean F. 2002. *The Transcontinental Railroad.* Minneapolis: Compass Point Books.

Boggs, Johnny D. 2015. "Abraham Lincoln Presidential Library and Museum." *Roundup Magazine*, April 2015, p. 6.

Cameron, Kate. 1939. "'Union Pacific' Is an Epic of Steel Trails." *New York Daily News*, May 11, 1939, p. 52.

Carter, Charles Frederick. 1909. *When Railroads Were New.* New York: Henry Holt and Company.

Chang, Gordon. 2019. *Ghosts of Gold Mountain: The Epic Story of the Chinese Who Built the Transcontinental Railroad.* New York: Houghton Mifflin Harcourt.

Chang, Gordon H., and Shelley Fisher Fishkin, eds. 2019. *The Chinese and the Iron Road: Building the Transcontinental Railroad.* Stanford, CA: Stanford University Press.

Coughlin, Joseph F. 1939. "Epic on Wheels." *Motion Picture Herald*, April 29, 1939.

DeMille, Cecil B. 1959. *The Autobiography of Cecil B. DeMille.* New York: Prentice Hall.

DeMille, Cecilia, and Mark A. Vieira. 2014. *Cecil B. DeMille: The Art of the Hollywood Epic.* Philadelphia, PA: Running Press.

DeVoto, Bernard. 1998. *Across the Wide Missouri*. New York: Mariner Books.

"EDITORIAL: Page Daniel Webster!" 1931. *The Union Pacific Magazine*, X, no. 3 (March): 16.

Etulain, Richard W. 2017. *Ernest Haycox and the Western*. Norman, OK: University of Oklahoma Press.

Eyman, Scott. 2010. *Empire of Dreams: The Epic Life of Cecil B. DeMille*. New York: Simon & Schuster.

"THE FARM CRISIS." 1998. *Congressional Record: Proceedings and Debates of the 105th Congress Second Session: Volume 144-Part 14: September 9, 1998 to September 21, 1998*. Washington, DC: United States Government Printing Office, p. 20,082.

Field, Henry M. 1902. *Our Western Archipelago: Third Edition*. New York: Charles Scribner's Sons.

From the N.Y. Independent. 1868. "Christianity on Wheels." *Alexandria Gazette*, August 17, 1868, p. 1.

From the Omaha Republican. 1867. "THE MASSACRE ON THE PACIFIC RAILROAD. Several Men Killed and Others Badly Wounded. HORRIBLE TORTURES COMMITTED BY THE SAVAGES." *The Cincinnati Daily Enquirer*, August 14, 1867, p. 1.

"A GREAT FEAT. The Gun That Announced the Completion of the Trans-Continental Road—How It Was Fired by Telegraph—The Process Described." *The Daily Morning Chronicle*, May 11, 1869, p. 1.

Hanifin, Ada. 1939. "'UNION PACIFIC' DEPICTS BATTLE TO LINK NATION." *San Francisco Examiner*, May 1, 1939, p. 18.

Hart, Louis. 2018. "A Few Good Points about the Golden Spike." *Wild West*, October 4, 2018. https://www.historynet.com/good-points-golden-spike.htm

Johnson, C. T. 1913. "DID DANIEL WEBSTER EVER SAY THIS?" In *The Washington Historical Quarterly*, pp. 191–193. Seattle, WA: The Washington University State Historical Society.

"Key Questions." 1913. *Chinese Railroad Workers in North America Project*, Volume IV. https://web.stanford.edu/group/chineserailroad/cgi-bin/website/faqs

Lamar, Howard R., ed. 1998. *The New Encyclopedia of the American West*. New Haven, CT: Yale University Press.

Larson, Robert W. 1999. *Red Cloud: Warrior-Statesman of the Lakota Sioux*. Norman: University of Oklahoma Press.

Mann, May. 1938. "'UNION PACIFIC' FILM TO EMPLOY BEEHIVE EXTRAS: DeMille Production Set to Start Near Cedar City in October." *The Ogden Standard-Examiner*, September 28, 1938, p. 8.

McGinty, Brian. 2015. *Lincoln's Greatest Case: The River, the Bridge, and the Making of America*. New York: Liveright Publishing Corporation.

Miller, Eugene Arundel. 2012. *Railroad 1869: Along the Historic Union Pacific through Nebraska*. Mill Valley, CA: Antelope Press.

Murphy, Robert Lee. 2019. "RACES WITHIN A RACE: The building of the Transcontinental Railroad." *Roundup Magazine*, April 2019, pp. 15–18.

Nott, Robert. 2000. *Last of the Cowboy Heroes: The Westerns of Randolph Scott, Joel McCrea, and Audie Murphy*. Jefferson, NC: McFarland & Company, Inc.

"PERLEY'S BOOK. GOSSIPY AND INTERESTING MEMOIRS OF WASHINGTON LIFE. Recollections of Ben: Perley Poore, the Celebrated Journalist and

Government Clerk—The Public Man Who Figured at the Capital from 1825 to 1860—Celebrated Ladies and Other Characters." 1886. *St. Louis Post-Dispatch*, October 25, 1886, p. 4.

Pitts, Michael R., compiler. 1984. *Hollywood and American History: A Filmography of over 250 Motion Pictures Depicting U.S. History.* Jefferson, NC: McFarland & Company, Inc.

Poore, Ben Perley. 1886. *Perley's Reminiscences of Sixty Years in the National Metropolis.* Philadelphia, PA: Hubbard Brothers, Publishers.

Public Documents Printed by Order of The Senate of the United States, First Session of the Twenty-Ninth Congress, Begun and Held at the City of Washington, December 1, 1845, and in the Seventieth Year of the Independence of the United States, Volume IV, Containing Documents from No. 44 to No. 195. Washington, DC: Ritchie & Heiss.

Rea, Tom. 2014. "Peace, War, Land and a Funeral: The Fort Laramie Treaty of 1868." *Wyoming History*, November 8, 2014. https://www.wyohistory.org/encyclopedia/peace-war-land-and-funeral-fort-laramie-treaty-1868

Report of The Joint Special Committee to Investigate Chinese Immigration. http://cprr.org/Museum/Chinese_Immigration.html

Sandler, Martin W. 2015. *Iron Rails, Iron Men, and the Race to Link the Nation: The Story of the Transcontinental Railroad.* Somerville, MA: Candlewick Press.

Smith, Ella. 1974. *Starring Miss Barbara Stanwyck.* New York: Crown Publishers, Inc.

Smith, J. Gregg. 1962. "Keeping Early Nebraska Trains Running Could Be Hair-Raising," *Sunday Journal and Star*, August 12, 1962, pp. 1B, 9B.

Special Collections of the Sacramento Public Library. 2019. *Images of America: Sacramento.* Charleston, SC: Arcadia Publishing.

Tuska, Jon. 1976. *The Filming of the West.* Garden City, NY: Doubleday & Company, Inc.

Vieira, Mark A. 2013. *Majestic Hollywood: The Greatest Films of 1939.* Philadelphia, PA: Running Press.

Williams, John Hoyt. 1989. *A Great and Shining Road: The Epic Story of the Transcontinental Railroad.* New York: Times Books.

Williamson, G. R. 2011. *Frontier Gambling: The Games, the Gamblers & the Great Gambling Halls of the Old West.* Kerrville, TX: Indian Head Publications.

Wilson, Victoria. 2013. *Barbara Stanwyck: Steel-True: 1907–1940.* New York: Simon & Schuster.

Chapter 2

The Ox-Bow Incident (1943)

Premiering May 21, 1943, *The Ox-Bow Incident* became a victim of timing and subject matter. Flooding in the Midwest, a strike at three Chrysler plants in Detroit, and war news from Europe and the Pacific dominated headlines. Western movies made during World War II (1939–1945) ended with the villains defeated and heroes winning the girl; and in a year that saw the release of feel-good movies like *Coney Island, Star Spangled Rhythm, This Is the Army*, and the Academy Award–winning *Casablanca*, few wanted to watch a movie about the lynching of three innocent men. Darryl F. Zanuck (1902–1979), 20th Century Fox's vice president of production, knew that when he agreed to make the movie, telling director William A. Wellman (1896–1975): "You can do it, but it won't make a cent" (Thompson 1983, 209).

A modern-day law calls "lynching" the attempt to free a prisoner from police custody during a riot, but historically lynching means the illegal execution of a person or persons, typically by hanging, for an alleged crime without a legal trial. Common in the nineteenth century and even late into the 1900s, lynching was often depicted in Western cinema and fiction, including Owen Wister's 1902 novel *The Virginian*. As in the novel, the three film versions of *The Virginian* in 1914, 1923, and 1929 (it was later filmed in 1946 and as a made-for-television movie in 2000) justified lynching in a lawless West. *The Ox-Bow Incident* took another approach.

Based on a best-selling 1940 novel by Walter Van Tilburg Clark, *The Ox-Bow Incident* opens with cowboys Gil Carter (Henry Fonda, 1905–1982) and Art Croft (Harry Morgan, 1915–2011) riding into Bridger's Wells, Nevada, in 1885. Local ranchers have been hit hard by rustlers, so when news arrives that Larry Kincaid has been murdered and his cattle rustled,

Kincaid's best friend, Jeff Farnley (Marc Lawrence, 1910–2005), wants revenge. Town drunk Monty Smith (Paul Hurst, 1888–1953) and others are quick to form a posse, while pleas from town merchant Arthur Davies (Harry Davenport, 1866–1949) and Judge Daniel Tyler (Matt Briggs, 1883–1962) cannot silence the demand for vengeance; even "Ma" Grier (Jane Darwell, 1879–1967), a big woman who dresses in men's clothing, is eager to help. Major Tetley (Frank Conroy, 1890–1964), who dresses in a Confederate uniform, agrees to lead the posse, forcing his timid son Gerald (William Eythe, 1918–1957) to join the group, which is sworn in by cruel deputy sheriff Butch Mapes (Dick Rich, 1909–1967), even though he has no authority to do so. Accompanied by Sparks (Leigh Whipper, 1876–1975), an African American lay preacher, Davies, and a reluctant Carter and Croft, the posse pursues the suspected rustlers.

In the Ox-Bow Valley that night, the mob captures three sleeping men who have been herding cattle wearing Kincaid's brand. The leader of the three, Donald Martin (Dana Andrews, 1909–1992), says Kincaid sold him the cattle but was too busy to write a bill of sale. Martin also says he has just bought a place at Pike's Hole, but no one in the posse knows him. With Martin are an addled old man called "Dad" (Francis Ford, 1881–1953) and a Mexican named Francisco Morez (Anthony Quinn, 1915–2001), who is recognized as a gambler sought by vigilantes. Tetley agrees to wait until morning to give Martin time to write a letter to his wife and young children before hanging the three for murder and rustling.

During the night, Davies tries to persuade Carter and others to read Martin's letter, saying that a man who can write such beautiful words cannot be capable of murder and rustling, but no one will do it. When Morez is wounded in the leg trying to escape, Kincaid's gun is discovered. Morez says he found the gun, but no one believes him. With dawn breaking, Tetley calls for a vote.

Only seven men, including Sparks, Carter, Croft, Davies, and Gerald Tetley, vote against hanging, and Tetley orders his son to whip Martin's horse from underneath him so that Martin's neck will be broken during the hanging. The timid Gerald Tetley cannot do that deed, and Farnley shoots the strangling Martin with his rifle.

After leaving the men hanging, the mob meets Sheriff Risley (Willard Robertson, 1886–1948), who says Kincaid is not dead and that the men who committed the crime have been caught. Learning that all but seven participated in the lynching, Risley rips off Mapes's badge and tells the lynchers, "God better have mercy on you. You won't get any from me."

Back in Bridger's Wells, Major Tetley kills himself with a self-inflicted gunshot wound, and Carter reads Martin's letter aloud inside the quiet saloon before Carter and Croft ride away to help Martin's widow and children.

Born in Maine, Walter Van Tilburg Clark (1909–1971) moved with his parents to Reno, Nevada, in 1917 after his father was hired as president of the University of Nevada. After the younger Clark earned bachelor's and master's degrees in English from the university, he taught and lectured around the country before he was hired to teach high school English in Caze-novia, New York. His first published novel was *The Ox-Bow Incident*—a manuscript Clark almost burned in frustration before a literary agent asked to see it. Random House offered a $450 advance, and *The Ox-Bow Incident* became an instant success upon publication. Reviewer John Shelby called the novel "a 'Western' which will be read years hence as an example of what an honest writer can do with standard material used honestly" (Shelby 1940, 4).

Former Paramount producer Harold Hurley (1895–1946) bought the film rights for $6,000 and approached Wellman about directing the movie. Wellman was interested until Hurley revealed his vision of casting actress Mae West (1893–1980) in the movie: "When the posse and the tired cow-boys gather in the saloon, Mae will cheer them up with song and dance" (Wellman 2015, 381). Wellman declined the offer but couldn't stop thinking about the novel's potential as a film. Six months later, when Hurley said no studio wanted to turn *The Ox-Bow Incident* into a movie, Wellman bought the film rights from Hurley for $6,500. Every studio rejected Wellman, too, until he met with Zanuck, "the only one with guts to do an out-of-the-ordinary story for the prestige, rather than the dough" (Wellman 1974, 28). Wellman agreed to Zanuck's terms to make two films for Zanuck—without reading the scripts first—after directing *The Ox-Bow Incident*.

Other studio executives tried to terminate the project, but Zanuck backed Wellman, although the budget was kept low, $565,000, and most of the filming occurred on a sound stage. Other scenes were shot on the studio's back lot and Western town set, with minimal second-unit filming done near Lone Pine, California.

Andrews, hoping for a breakout role, landed the part of the doomed rancher Donald Martin. "It gave me a chance to try to do something I've always wondered whether I could manage—playing a character who was sensitive without making him seem weak," Andrews said (Meyer 1979, 136). Sara Allgood (1879–1950) was first cast as Ma Grier, but was replaced—the reasons unrecorded—by Florence Bates (1888–1954). After Bates was injured horseback riding, Darwell, Academy Award winner for Best Sup-porting Actress in *The Grapes of Wrath* (1940), took the unsympathetic role of Ma Grier, one of the executioners during the lynching. Wellman insisted on casting Fonda, "perhaps the best actor I have ever directed," as Gil Carter. Before filming started, Wellman recalled, Fonda "wardrobed himself, had me okay it, and then lived and probably slept in it. The boots, the Levi's, the hat, the shirt, the bandanas, became a part of Gil Carter . . . not Hank Fonda because Hank had become Gil. He looked it, talked it, felt it, and, by the time we were ready to shoot the picture, smelled it, and his performance was perfection" (Wellman 1974, 205–206).

"I wanted the picture to be the book," Wellman said (Thompson 1983, 209), and screenwriter Lamar Trotti (1900–1952), also a producer, remained relatively faithful to Clark's novel. There were some significant changes, however; most importantly, Martin's letter is never read in the novel but is in the film. Still, Clark liked the film version.

First, the script had to be approved by the Production Code Administration (PCA). Since 1934, the PCA required all films to be approved before release. The PCA "devoted most of its attention to morality and vulgarity" but also created a "lack of innovation and aversion to serious subjects" (Schatz 1997, 262). The Code's power began fading in the 1950s and was eliminated in 1968 with the implementation of the Motion Picture Association of America's film rating system.

In a May 12, 1942, letter to 20th Century Fox's director of public relations, the PCA objected to several scenes, including one in which the sheriff excused the lynching, as he does in Clark's novel; the "Code" always demanded that criminals be punished for their actions. After changes were made, the PCA approved the film on September 11, 1942. "If nobody else sees it," Wellman told a journalist, "my kids are going to" (Carroll 1942, 6).

After previewing *The Ox-Bow Incident* in 1942, syndicated film critic Sara Davis wrote: "The drama had a positively stunning effect on Hollywood previewers. But western fans who are looking for a formula film story and a manufactured happy ending will not find them in 'The Ox-Box Incident.' It is a truly grim and uncompromisingly dramatic photoplay" (Davis 1942, 13). Years later, Morgan recalled that while leaving the theater after the preview, actor-director Orson Welles (1915–1985) explained the moviegoers' silence: "They don't realize what they just saw" (Wellman 2015, 380).

Most critics raved about the movie when it was released the following spring. "'The Ox-Bow Incident' is one of the most powerful indictments [against] mob lynching ever offered on the screen," Edgar Price wrote in *The Brooklyn Citizen*. "It's a real horror picture, something that will make strong men flinch; weaklings and adolescents should give it a wide berth. Its truthfulness will positively amaze you for it pulls no punches" (Price 1943, 10). Writing for the *San Francisco Examiner*, Moira Wallace said, "'Ox-Bow Incident' uses the medium of the motion picture so beautifully that it is an impertinence to try to transpose it back into words—it is an experience to share deeply only with one's own conscience" (Wallace 1943, 9).

"It took two years for Hollywood to muster the courage to film 'Ox-Bow Incident' and, from the looks of it, the result is well worth while," John M. Sturdevant wrote for *American Weekly*. "The film would never have been made had it not been for the convictions of [Wellman and Fonda] and it is to the credit of Twentieth Century-Fox that they finally produced it" ("OX-BOW INCIDENT" 1943, 11).

However, *The Atlanta Constitution*'s Paul Jones disliked the portrayal of Tetley as a former Confederate soldier, as he is in Clark's novel. "Hollywood, or a certain producer, went out of its way to put the south in a bad light by dressing the leader of a lynch-mad mob in a Confederate uniform for the hanging scene" because "it seems that the uniform of the Confederacy had little bearing on the content of the story and could have been left out entirely" (Jones 1943, 12-C).

The National Board of Review named *The Ox-Bow Incident* the best film drama of 1943, Wellman best director, and Morgan one of the best actors. The movie was also nominated for Best Picture in the Academy Awards, losing to *Casablanca*. But Zanuck had been right. Commercially, *The Ox-Bow Incident* "had been a flop. In spite of its significance and its dramatic value, our records showed that it had failed to pay its way. In fact, its pulling power was less than that of a Laurel and Hardy comedy we made about the same time" (Behlmer 1993, 75).

HISTORICAL BACKGROUND

Vigilantes—people taking the law into their own hands—had been a part of the American frontier since the colonial era. In the years before the American Revolution (1775–1783), a group of vigilantes known as Regulators succeeded in punishing outlaws who had been terrorizing the settlement of Ninety Six, South Carolina, but when the Regulators got out of hand, local residents organized another group of vigilantes to stop them. Even the Boston Tea Party, where American colonists threw 342 chests of tea into Boston Harbor on December 16, 1773, could be called an act of vigilantism. Almost every state witnessed some form of vigilantism or lynching. "When judges, juries, the state, or any other authority reached a point where its effect on the system led to too much or too little vigor, sometimes 'the people,' or the self-appointed 'people' took the law into their own hands," legal historian Lawrence M. Friedman wrote. "Vigilantes and lynch mobs were pathologies of a system with too many checks and balances to satisfy at least some members of the public" (Friedman 2007, 214).

While vigilantes and mob rule were often decried in most regions of the United States, Western states and territories seemed more sympathetic to such tactics. Historian Hubert H. Bancroft wrote that vigilantes served as "the keen knife in the hands of a skillful surgeon, removing the putrefaction with the least possible injury to the body politic" (Bancroft 1887, 11).

"The need for vigilantism in the Old West is much debated today," said Gregory J. Lalire, editor of the Vienna, Virginia-based *Wild West* magazine. "At the time, many people believed vigilantes were necessary to keep the peace in areas that were remote and lawless, that is to say beyond the grasp of legal governance. It was a way for a community to deal with—get rid of, sometimes with warnings to leave town instead of something as drastic as hangings—not only criminals but also gamblers, drunks, immigrants—Chinese or other—and vagrants" (Gregory J. Lalire, interview with author, April 25, 2019).

According to Richard Maxwell Brown, Nevada had seven deaths at the hands of vigilantes in the 1800s; by comparison, Texas had 140 and Montana 101. California, considered the birthplace of vigilantism in the Old West, had 109 victims of vigilantes.

Hangings in California's mining camps became commonplace. "The miners showed a determination to administer swift and decisive justice in communities that were without jails and formal courts," historian Wayne Gard wrote. "Improvised courts sprang up in nearly all the early California diggings, not so much from choice as from necessity" (Gard 1981, 150). Miner's courts, or people's courts, were the law of the land in such remote regions, even though few, if any, of those officiating the proceedings had legal training.

In January 1849, five men were captured after trying to rob a gambler at a California mining camp called Dry Diggings. With no jail, the roughly 200 miners ordered an immediate trial, selected 12 men as jurors and another as judge, and proceeded with a trial. The defendants were found guilty, and each was given 39 lashes. Three of the robbers, however, were then tried for robbery and attempted murder, having been suspected of committing the crime that autumn on the Stanislaus River. Those three were found guilty. One miner said the three should be hanged, and although another objected, he was overruled, and the three men were hanged from the branches of a tree in camp. After that, Dry Diggings became known as Hangtown until it was renamed Placerville when the city was incorporated in 1854.

In May 1851, two men were captured on the Cosumnes River in northern California and charged with horse theft. A motion was made to allow the two men a trial by jury, but miners rejected that idea and declared that the prisoners should be hanged immediately. The two prisoners were told to confess and given a half hour to prepare to die. "When the half hour had elapsed, they were told their time had come," the *Sacramento Transcript* reported. "Lariats were brought, nooses were made, and the guilty wretches hung up. This took place at 12 o'clock last night (Friday), and the bodies were still suspended this morning when our informant left, although persons were engaged in digging two graves" ("LYNCHING IN CALIFORNIA" 1851, 4).

On August 2, 1876, Jack McCall (ca. 1852–1877) shot and killed James Butler "Wild Bill" Hickok (1837–1876) in the back of the head while Hickok played poker in a saloon in the gold-mining camp of Deadwood in present-day South Dakota. Vigilantes captured McCall the following day and assembled a miner's court. The miners appointed residents as judge, sheriff, prosecutor, and defense lawyer; they selected a jury; and the trial began after Hickok's funeral. Claiming that Hickok had killed his brother, McCall was acquitted and fled the Black Hills for Wyoming Territory. But Deadwood had been founded illegally in land belonging to the

Lakota Indians, and a miner's court has no legal standing in the eyes of the federal government. "Double jeopardy" (where defendants cannot be tried for a crime for which they have previously been acquitted) was not in effect. McCall was arrested in Wyoming, transported to Yankton, Dakota Territory, and tried for murder. This time, a legal jury found McCall guilty, and McCall was hanged on March 1, 1877.

Founded in the 1850s—some say in Clark County, Missouri; others say in Fort Scott, Kansas—the Anti Horse Theft Association protected honest folks from having their horses stolen during the Kansas-Missouri Border War, a series of violent encounters between proslavery Missourians and antislavery Kansans. The organization proved successful enough that it spread to other states and territories, having bylaws, a national constitution, and more than 30,000 members by 1906. "The Anti Horse Theft Association is in no sense a vigilance committee, and the organization has never found it necessary to adopt the mysterious methods of 'Regulators,' 'White Caps' or kindred organizations. Its deeds are done in the broad open light of the day" (Blackmar 1912, 88). But on February 27, 1865, in Nemaha County, Kansas, a mob took suspected horse thief Miles N. Carter out of jail and hanged him. "It was generally conceded that the Anti Horse Theft Association, composed of our best citizens, dealt out the punishment Carter so richly deserved" (Tennal 1916, 212).

During the 1860s, boomtowns of Bannack and Virginia City in what is now Montana, outlaws murdered more than 100 men, according to reports, helped by the fact that their leader was Henry Plummer, who had been elected sheriff in May 1863. Before that, Plummer had been acquitted of the killing of Jack Cleveland, a horse dealer. After Plummer assumed office, robberies and murders increased, and residents began to suspect their new sheriff. By early January 1864, citizens had organized a group of law enforcers, complete with regulations and bylaws that required recordkeeping and trial of anyone accused with a crime. "In this case, the regulations stipulated only one punishment—death" (Gard 1981, 178). "These men, who did not hide their identities behind masks or by operating only at night, executed hard cases, often with military procession, and were praised for that effort by most citizens," Lalire said (Gregory J. Lalire, interview with author, April 25, 2019).

The vigilantes caught "Erastus Red" Yeager, whom they suspected of being one of the bandits; he confessed, naming Plummer and other gang members before the vigilantes hanged him. Shortly after that, Plummer and five men were captured, tried, and hanged. In six weeks, the vigilantes hanged 22 men, banished others from the territory, and frightened several into fleeing. "Seventy-two names are still on the list in the hands of the vigilance committee, who will be treated in the same manner as the others when caught," a Salt Lake City newspaper correspondent reported ("From the Southwest" 1864, 1).

Another vigilante group was the Bald Knobbers, who were formed in southern Missouri's Ozark Mountains to stop outlaw raids and got their name from holding meetings on barren hilltops. The first group was formed in Taney County, with another organized in Christian County. Before long, the Bald Knobbers were accused of murder and intimidation, which led to the formation of the Anti-Bald Knobbers. After Bald Knobbers killed two men during a raid in Christian County, sentiment moved against those vigilantes. More than a dozen of the vigilantes were arrested, and in May 1889, three Bald Knobbers, convicted of murder, were hanged in the town of Ozark.

In addition to vigilantes, the American frontier witnessed many actions of mob rule. There is a difference, though often blurred, between vigilantes and mobs. Hubert Howe Bancroft wrote: "The vigilance committee is not a mob; it is to a mob as revolution is to rebellion, the name being somewhat according to its strength. Neither is a tumultuous rabble a vigilance committee. . . . The vigilance committee will itself break the law, but it does not allow others to do so. It has the highest respect for law" (Bancroft 1887, 8).

As the frontier became settled, vigilantes and lynch mobs were often condemned. "Bald Knobbers, Klu [sic] Klux regulators, vigilantes, white caps, or whatever name they may bear, invariably become worse terrors and greater violators of law, order, decency and morality than the criminals they seek to punish," the *Seneca Courier-Democrat* editorialized. "They imagine the law is insufficient and not sufficiently stringent, and they themselves attempt to make up the loss, and the result is violence, outrage and murder" (Untitled Article 1889, 2). "If lynching is tacitly conceded to be a necessary evil, there is no telling what dimensions it may assume," *The Galveston Daily News* commented after two men were lynched in Tarrant County in 1880. But the settlers and newspapers of the West did not always agree.

In the early morning of April 19, 1909, an estimated 30 to 40 masked men broke into the county jail in Ada, Oklahoma, and hauled four prisoners to a downtown barn. The men were accused of murdering Allen Augustus "Gus" Bobbitt, a local rancher and former deputy U.S. marshal. One of the prisoners was "Deacon Jim" Miller (1861–1909), a notorious hired gunman also suspected of murdering New Mexico lawman Pat Garrett (1850–1908). Before he was hanged, Miller said, "Just let the record show that I've killed fifty-one men" (Shirley 1970, 115). The mob left the four men hanging from the rafters.

"Lynchings are to be deplored," the Ada newspaper commented the following day, "but—Oklahoma juries are permitting too many murderers to escape the penalty of their crimes, while procedure in the courts, with the importance given to trifling technicalities, is making it easy for criminals to escape punishment" ("WHERE PLACE THE BLAME?" 1909, 3).

Lynchings continued into the twentieth century across the country. One of the ghastliest crimes happened on September 28, 1919, in Omaha, Nebraska.

Will Brown, an African American about 40 years old, was arrested for the rape of a 19-year-old white girl. Late that afternoon, a crowd estimated at 4,000 to 5,000 began throwing rocks at the courthouse. City Commissioner Harry B. Zimmerman tried to talk to the throng but was shouted down. That evening, Mayor Ed Smith confronted the mob and was savagely beaten into unconsciousness, and the courthouse was set afire. Police retreated, and somehow—reports vary—the rioters captured Brown.

> Before a rope was touched, Brown had died, his body riddled with a hundred bullets. When he was lowered from the court house the fury of the mob had reached such a pitch his clothes were torn from him. After Brown's body had been hanging in the air for a few minutes, the bullet from a rifle cut the rope and it dropped among the crowd. An automobile was requisitioned and then the mob started to drag the corpse along the streets. At last a fire was started, gasoline taken from nearby automobiles and poured on the blaze. Pieces of the rope were used for the lynching were retailed by small boys for 10 cents apiece. Men and women alike made attempts to mutilate Brow[n]'s body for souvenirs. (Moody 1919, 1)

A teenager leading the rioters and a businessman walking two blocks away were killed by gunfire, and several others were injured. Army troops were called in from several Midwestern states to restore peace, and although a grand jury issued 189 indictments, only two men were charged with murder; both were acquitted.

One 14-year-old boy witnessed the lynching when his father drove him from their home to the plant where his father worked. There the boy and father stood at an upstairs window to view the gruesome scene. The boy later recalled:

> They took him, strung him up to the end of a lamppost, hung him, and while his feet were still dancing in the air, they riddled his body with bullets. It was the most horrendous sight I'd ever seen. Then they cut down the body, tied it to an auto, and dragged it through the streets of Omaha. Aside from the lynching, there was something else. It was my father. He never said a word to me. He didn't preach, he didn't make a point, he just made sure I saw it! We locked the plant, went downstairs, and drove home in silence. My hands were wet and there were tears in my eyes. All I could think of was that young man dangling at the end of the lamppost, the shots, and the revulsion I felt. I could not sleep that night and a lot of other nights after that. (Fonda 1981, 24–25)

The boy was Henry Fonda. Biographer Scott Eyman called that night "the beginning of Henry Fonda's fierce hatred of bigotry and intolerance" (Eyman 2017, 13). Twenty-three years after witnessing that lynching, Fonda made *The Ox-Bow Incident*.

DEPICTION AND CULTURAL CONTEXT

Strong resentment against cattle thieves was accurately depicted in *The Ox-Bow Incident*. Rustling—the theft of livestock such as cattle, horses, and/or sheep—was common on the American frontier. "Most rustlers of the open-range era were cowboys who had drifted into dubious practices," historian Wayne Gard wrote. "They knew the cattle country and were adept at roping, branding, and trailing. One needed only to buy a few cows, register a brand, and begin branding strays. Many cowboys' herds increased so rapidly that some ranchmen refused to hire any hand who had stock of his own" (Gard 2017). Film, fiction, and even popular belief say cattle rustling and horse theft were hanging offenses. "There was that old saw, 'A man left afoot is the same as murder,' was the reason given for lynching," historian Marshall Trimble said (Marshall Trimble, interview with author, April 26, 2019). But legally, cattle rustling and horse theft were never capital crimes in any Western state or territory.

Many film historians say *The Ox-Bow Incident* correctly captured the lynch-mob mentality of the American frontier. Richard W. Etulain, an Old West and Western film scholar, said that such spur-of-the-moment violence contained the same familiar ingredients: "Regular sheriff—established law and order—not on the scene. Inadequate opposition from non-lynchers, the two wandering cowboys and Davies, and the detrimental influences of Major Tetley" (Richard W. Etulain, interview with author, April 19, 2019). Etulain drew a comparison between the events of *Ox Bow* and the Plummer lynchings in Montana in the early 1860s, as well as lynchings in several other towns. According to Etulain, while Southern lynchings focused specifically on racism against African Americans, "lynchings of Hispanics, Chinese, and Indians were in high percentages on the Western frontier. And you see that ethnic hatred in this movie in the casting of Anthony Quinn as a troubled Mexican, who seems guilty of everything. I think the film follows fairly closely what we know about lynchings in the Old West" (Richard W. Etulain, interview with author, April 19, 2019).

Montanans, who had formed vigilantes in the gold camps of the 1860s, formed a new group in the 1880s, this time to combat the theft of cattle and horses in central Montana and western Dakota Territory. Cattleman Granville Stuart, later known as Mr. Montana, led a meeting of ranchers, cowboys, and stock detectives. "No memoir tells what transpired at this conference, but from it emerged a determined little company which became known as 'Stuart's Stranglers.' Stuart himself preferred to call it a 'Vigilance Committee.' It had fourteen members" (Howard 1943, 127). During that spring and summer, the Stranglers began a series of raids against rustling outfits, killing several in gunfights and lynching others. Estimates of the dead vary, from 19 to as high as 75, though most historians put the dead at around 20. While defenders said the Stranglers killed rustlers, thieves, and outlaws, others said they also killed squatters and nesters. According to President Theodore Roosevelt, who ranched in present-day North Dakota in the 1880s: "The vigilantes or stranglers, as they were locally known, did their work thoroughly; but, as always happens with bodies of the kind, toward the end they grew reckless in their actions, paid off private grudges, and hung men on slight provocation" (Roosevelt 1913, 20).

The Ox-Bow Incident also depicts a woman assisting in the lynching. A woman actively lynching a man on the Western frontier is hard to verify, but there are several documented cases of women being lynched, including one famous incident in Wyoming in 1889. The six cattleman who hanged her said she was a prostitute and a cattle rustler called Cattle Kate who "had to be killed for the good of the country" (Bommersbach 2014). A woman named Kate Maxwell received nationwide attention in likely highly exaggerated newspaper articles as "Cattle Kate" or "the 'Belle Starr' of Wyoming" (Associated Press 1889, 1). But the woman hanged on July 21, 1889, was not Kate Maxwell, was never known as "Cattle Kate," and was neither a rustler nor a prostitute.

The oldest daughter of a Scottish family that had settled in Kansas, Ellen L. Watson (1860–1889) drifted West after a failed marriage, where she eventually settled on the Sweetwater River in Wyoming, perhaps because women had the right to vote in the territory and land was still available to claim under the Homestead Act of 1862. In 1886, Watson married James Averell (1851–1889)—or at least the two were granted a marriage license—and filed a claim on 160 acres adjacent to Averell's claim, which blocked rancher A. J. Bothwell (1854–1928) from watering his cattle on a creek until he bought an easement from Watson.

In the fall of 1888, Watson and Averell bought 28 cattle, some of which were pregnant, from a Nebraska immigrant, and when the calves were born, she bought a registered brand from a neighbor and branded the calves. A range detective (a person hired by ranchers to prevent rustling but with no legal authority) saw the cattle and calves and reported his findings to Bothwell, who alerted other ranchers. Bothwell and five others rode to Watson's ranch. Watson explained that she had a bill of sale in a bank in Rawlings, but the ranchers refused to believe her. They brought her to Averell's place, captured him, and took Averell and Watson to "a stunted pine growing on the summit of a cliff fronting the Sweetwater," where "[c]ommon cowboy lariats" were placed over their necks ("HOW THEY WERE HANGED" 1889, 3).

With the ropes secured to a tree limb, the condemned, with their feet and arms unbound, were placed on a rock. One of Averell's friends shot at the lynch mob, but was driven off by rifle fire. Watson and Averell were shoved off the rock. "The hanging were not clean executions by a skilled hangman, ones that would have resulted in quick deaths from a broken neck, but stranglings in which the victims became exhausted and slowly asphyxiated," historian John W. Davis wrote. "Eventually, inevitably, Ellen and Jim lost their fight with the ropes" (Davis 2010, 75). The six killers were never indicted.

In theory, when a person is hanged, the drop snaps the neck, resulting in instantaneous death, but hangings did not always work as planned. *The Ox-Bow Incident* accurately depicts that when Gerald Tetley does not whip the horse from underneath Donald Martin. The horse slowly walks away, leaving Martin strangling. Farnley then kills Martin with two rounds from his Winchester. To get around the PCA's standards against graphic violence, Wellman filmed this without showing the lynched men. Only shadows are depicted after the three men are dead.

Historically, even legal hangings had problems. In 1889, a newspaper correspondent covering the execution of three Bald Knobbers in Ozark, Missouri, described the botched hanging:

> John Matthews fell praying. The stretch of the rope let all fall to the ground. The rope broke and William Walker fell loose and lay there struggling and groaning. He talked for three minutes when he was taken up by the Sheriff and deputies on the scaffold. Dave Walker was drawn up and died in about fifteen minutes. Matthews lived about thirteen minutes and died with his feet on the ground. The scene was horrible in the extreme. Matthews and Dave Walker were cut down at 10:10. The trap was again adjusted and Wm. Walker lifted helpless and groaning and gurgling and almost insensible and the rope again adjusted and the trap again sprung. This time the descent came to a sudden stop with his feet full thirty inches from the ground, and he died without a struggle. ("By Telegraph to the POST-DISPATCH" 1889, 1)

George Maledon (1830–1911) served as executioner for Judge Isaac Parker (1838–1896) in Fort Smith, Arkansas, until retiring in 1894. When asked if he feared being haunted by the men he had hanged, he answered, "No, I never hanged a man who came back to have the job done over. The ghosts of men hanged at Fort Smith never hang around the old gibbet" (Harrington 1996, 150). A newspaper described Maledon's attention to detail:

> The ropes, manufactured for that express purpose and strictly according to the hangman's orders, are given the same careful testing as the scaffold. The men to be executed are carefully measured and weighed, and from these calculations are made with the uttermost exactness as to what drop will be just enough to accomplish the work required, making sure that it be neither too much nor too little. Each rope is then furnished with its noose and is adjusted according to the man it is expected to kill, so that he may know when he stands within its deadly loop that everything has been done with mathematical precision to insure his instant destruction. ("MANDATES OF DEATH" 1890, 8)

Not all of the 60 men Maledon executed, however, died instantly. Fort Smith's gallows could hold as many as eight, but no more than six were ever executed simultaneously, and five were hanged on April 21, 1876. Of the condemned men—Orpheus McGee, William Leach, Isham Seely, Gibson Ishtanubbee, and Aaron Wilson, all convicted of murder—only McGee died quickly. Wilson's violent convulsions tore the crucifix from the ribbon around his neck; Seely moaned before finally strangling; Ishtanubbee and Leach took nine and ten minutes, respectively, to die. "Despite Maledon's skillful preparation and technique, hanging remained an inexact 'science'" (Tuller 2001, 61).

Other types of gallows were developed in an attempt to make hangings more humane. When Constable Milton Yarberry was sentenced to hang for murder in Albuquerque, New Mexico, in 1883, his friend, Bernalillo County Sheriff Perfecto Armijo, used a model he had read about in *Scientific American*. The *Santa Fe New Mexican* described the apparatus:

> There is no trap—nothing but the platform, two uprights and cross beams, as a scaffold. The condemned man stands upon the scaffold, the noose encircling his neck, the rope runs over a pulley when it reaches the crossbeam, leaving two feet of slack between the beam and the noose; thence it runs along the beam to the upright and over another pulley down to six feet from the ground, where it ends with a 400 pound weight. A smaller cord holds the weight until the last moment; then it is cut, the weight falls six feet to the ground, the main is jerked six feet into the air and falls back two feet. (Tórrez 2008, 34–35)

In theory, the jerk up or the fall down would snap the neck, causing instant death. A cruder method of this "jerk" apparatus had been used in a September 12, 1870, execution in Las Vegas, New Mexico, but Yarberry's hanging did not go smoothly. The *Albuquerque Morning Journal* reported that when the rope to the weight was cut, "Yarberry shot into the air. The jerk was so sharp and sudden that his head struck the cross beam of the scaffold and he again dropped until he took up the slack of the rope, and remained dangling in the air. The man's neck was broken by the shock and the cracking of the joints could be plainly heard" ("THE LAST CHAPTER" 1883, 4). Doctors, however, found that Yarberry still had a pulse, and he was left hanging until he was declared dead nine minutes later. "This gruesome development may have caused officials to wonder whether Yarberry was killed by the jerking action of the rope or by the impact of his head against the crossbeam. This may also explain why the 'jerk' device was never again used in an execution in New Mexico" (Tórrez 2008, 35).

Another special gallows was used in 1903 when range detective Tom Horn, convicted of murdering a teenage boy, was hanged in Cheyenne, Wyoming, on "this weird-looking device" that "allowed the accused to literally hang himself" (Herzberg 2013, 221). Cheyenne architect James P. Julian designed the device in 1892, which eliminated the need of a hangman. "When the condemned man steps on the trap his weight opens a valve in a vessel of water under the scaffold, and when the vessel becomes empty the counterbalance operates and jerks the plug under the trap, letting the drop fall and shooting the condemned man into eternity," the *Chicago Tribune* noted (*Chicago Tribune* 1903, 9).

At 11:07 a.m. on November 20, two officers placed Horn on the trap door, and a click sounded, followed by the noise of running water. "You aren't getting nervous, are you, boys?" Horn asked the men holding him in place. When the running water stopped, a silence followed—31 seconds, according a *Denver Republican* reporter—and many witnesses looked away. Finally, the trap door sprung open, Horn dropped, "turned slightly and then hung still" at 11:08 a.m. (Ball 2014, 420–421). Doctors pronounced Horn dead 16 minutes later.

The electric chair, gas chamber, and lethal injection eventually replaced hanging as the preferred form of capital punishment in the United States, although it remains an option, along with lethal injection, in New Hampshire. The last person executed by hanging in the United States was Bill Bailey in 1996 in Delaware, which dismantled its gallows in 2003. Washington allowed hanging as an option over lethal injection until the state Supreme Court declared capital punishment unconstitutional in 2018.

Lynchings, however, were much in the news when *The Ox-Bow Incident* was released in 1943. The Tuskegee Institute, founded in Alabama in 1881 by Booker T. Washington (1856–1915) to train teachers, announced that three African Americans were lynched that year in separate incidents in Florida, Georgia, and Illinois for "resisting arrest, killing a white man in a robbery attempt and insulting white women over the telephone" (Associated Press 1943d, 1). The institute said five persons had been lynched in 1942, four in 1941, and five in 1940. In July 1942, a federal grand jury in St. Louis failed to return indictments for the January lynching of an African American man accused of assaulting a white woman in Sikeston, Missouri. In April 1943, five white men were acquitted in federal court in Hattiesburg, Mississippi, for the 1940 lynching of an African American farm hand who had been convicted of murdering his employer but had been sentenced to life imprisonment. The five white men had been charged for violating the murdered man's civil liberties. In August, 13 white farmers were indicted for violating the civil rights of James Edward Person, an African American World War II veteran found dead from exposure and gunshot wounds near Paris, Illinois, in November 1942. In 1946, nine of those men were found guilty and each fined $200. Race riots also broke out in 1943 in Detroit, New York City, and Los Angeles.

The Ox-Bow Incident was timely enough that the *Evening Huronite* of Huron, South Dakota, ran a short editorial about the movie on its front page:

> Once in a blue moon there comes along a moving picture of such unusual merit that you feel like shouting about it from the house tops. Such a picture is "The

Ox-Bow Incident," showing the second and last day locally at the Bijou Theatre. "The Ox-Bow Incident" is not a war picture. In fact, it is a western, horse opera. The scene is Nevada. The time is 1885. And yet, despite the fact that the narrative is based upon an actual incident that occurred nearly 60 years ago, the show is as timely as today's newspaper. Every American living in a land which has only this summer witnessed widespread lawlessness in Los Angeles, Detroit, New York and elsewhere should see "The Ox-Bow Incident." ("An Editorial" 1943, 1)

Columnist Walter Winchell praised the National Board of Review of Motion Pictures for choosing *The Ox-Bow Incident* as the best picture of 1943, writing, "This is a powerful drama, but (more important) it pictured lynching as the criminal, senseless business it has always been. At a time when so many lunatic fringers want a hand in the government—most of them lynchers in spirit—this was a swell pick" (Winchell 1944, 6).

But *The Ox-Bow Incident* remained a box-office failure.

CONCLUSION

Today, *The Ox-Bow Incident* is regarded as one of the few, and perhaps the only, adult-themed westerns produced during World War II—a remarkable accomplishment during the era of the PCA. "It is interesting in this era when Mexicans and African Americans often played stereotypical and unflattering roles, that arguably the two most admirable men with the most integrity in the whole film are the religious African-American Sparks, the first to step up and vote against the hanging, and the Mexican-American Martinez, who speaks 11 languages and faces his death with great dignity," wrote William Hampes, professor emeritus of psychology and sociology at Black Hawk College (Hampes 2019, 127).

It was a movie that accurately depicted lynch-law mentality on the American frontier, but, despite its accolades when released, it took decades before American movie fans recognized what the movie had accomplished. As critic Gene Farmer wrote: "Yet the film seems to indicate that the same Hollywood is developing a social perspective as she comes of age. For it is 60 years after 'The Ox-Bow Incident,' and America has yet to wipe its shirt front clean of the atavistic coffee stain of lynching" (Farmer 1943, 7).

That *The Ox-Bow Incident* was ahead of its time is an understatement. Etulain said, "The lynching, the lack of shoot-outs, the absence of definite 'White hats' like John Wayne, and little or no romance—those were noted but seemed not to influence later films" (Richard W. Etulain, interview with author, April 19, 2019). Etulain further said that audiences in 1943 hadn't seen anything like *The Ox-Bow Incident*, especially not from powerful Western stars of the day like John Wayne or Gary Cooper. Films that challenged the "Western framework" put into place by the 1950s didn't emerge until the 1960s. Etulain said, "So, the movie broke from traditions, but did not shape or influence later Westerns—at least not that I can see. And even though the film got primarily positive salutes as a strong Western, it did not make the company much money, taking in only $750,000" (Richard W. Etulain, interview with author, April 19, 2019).

FURTHER READING

Associated Press. 1889. "PLUCKY 'CATTLE KATE.' She Closes up a Cattle Ranch, Seizes the Money, and Saves the Men from Lynching." *Buffalo Times*, February 21, 1889, p. 1.

Associated Press. 1919. FOUR INFANTRY UNITS SPEED TO OMAHA BY SPE-CIAL TRAIN; GENERAL WOOD IN COMMAND: Baker Orders Central Department Commander to Proceed with Troops to Quell Future Race Rioting. Two Killed, 45 to 60 Are Injured When Mob Burns Courthouse and Lynches Negro—Mayor is Critically Wounded." *Lincoln Daily Star*, September 29, 1919.

Associated Press. 1943a. "Governor's Death, Draft Board Indictments, 'Lynching' Trial Headline Highlights for '43." *Greenwood Commonwealth*, December 31, 1943, pp. 1, 6.

Associated Press. 1943b. "'Ox-Bow Incident' Judged Best Film." *The Troy Record*, December 24, 1943, p. 1.

Associated Press. 1943c. "THREE MEN ARE ACQUITTED: Group Was Charged with Lynching a Negro Last October." *Lawrence Daily Journal-World*, April 24, 1943, p. 2.

Associated Press. 1943d. "THREE NEGROES LYNCHED 1943, REPORTS SHOW." *Manhattan Mercury-Chronicle*, December 31, 1943, p. 1.

Associated Press. 1943e. "Trio Is Freed in Mississippi Lynching Case." *Kingsport Times*, April 25, 1943, p. 8.

Associated Press. 1943f. "U.S. JURY INDICTS 5 IN MISSISSIPPI LYNCHING INQUIRY: Action under Civil Liberties Statutes Is 'Based on Theory' Not Yet Passed on by Courts. JAILER IS ONE OF MEN ACCUSED: Other Four Named as Leaders of Mob That Took Negro from Cell and Hanged Him." *St. Louis Post-Dispatch*, January 13, 1943, p. 1, 10.

Associated Press. 1943g. "Zoot Suit Riots 'Near Anarchy,' Says Prosecutor." *Boston Daily Globe*, June 11, 1943, p. 1.

Ball, Larry D. 2014. *Tom Horn: In Life and Legend*. Norman: University of Oklahoma Press.

Bancroft, Hubert Howe. 1887. *The Works of Hubert Howe Bancroft. Volume XXXVI. Popular Tribunals, Vol. 1*. San Francisco, CA: The History Company, Publishers.

Bass, Robert D. 1978. *Ninety Six: The Struggle for the South Carolina Back Country*. Orangeburg, SC: Sandlapper Publishing Co., Inc.

Behlmer, Rudy, ed. 1993. *Memo from Darry F. Zanuck: The Golden Years at Twentieth Century-Fox*. New York: Grove Press.

Benson, Jackson J. 2004. *The Ox-Bow Man: A Biography of Walter Van Tilburg Clark*. Reno: University of Nevada Press.

Berg, Manfred. 2011. *Popular Justice: A History of Lynching in America*. Chicago, IL: Ivan R. Dee.

Blackmar, Frank Wilson, ed. 1912. *Kansas: A Cyclopedia of State History, Embracing Events, Institutions, Counties, Cities, Towns, Prominent Persons, Etc., Volume 1*. Chicago, IL: Standard Publishing Company.

Boardman, Mark. 2017a. "The Anti Horse Thief Association." *True West*, January 13, 2017, https://truewestmagazine.com/anti-horse-thief-association

Boardman, Mark. 2017b. "Stuart's Stranglers." *True West*, September 1, 2017, https://truewestmagazine.com/stuarts-stranglers

Boggs, Johnny D. 2003. *Great Murder Trials of the Old West*. Plano: Republic of Texas Press.

Bommersbach, Jana. 2014. "Dead Wrong about Cattle Kate: The Truth Is More Titillating Than the Legend." *True West*, October 9, 2014, https://truewestmagazine.com/dead-wrong-about-cattle-kate

Brown, Richard Maxwell. 1975. *Strain of Violence: Historical Studies of American Violence and Vigilantism*. New York: Oxford University Press.

Bryan, Howard. 2006. *Albuquerque Remembered*. Albuquerque: University of New Mexico Press.

"By Telegraph to the POST-DISPATCH." 1889. "A HORRIBLE SIGHT. Bungling Work at the Execution of the Bald Knobbers. William Walker Hanged Twice on Account of the Rope Breaking. All Three Men Met Their Fate Bravely—How They Passed Their Last Night on Earth—Divine Services in the Jail—Reading the Death Warrant—An Orderly Crowd at Ozark—A Statement from Matthews—Horrible Scenes at the Gallows—Bald Knobberism Wiped Out." *St. Louis Post-Dispatch*, May 10, 1889, p. 1.

Carroll, Harrison. 1942. "Behind the Scenes in Hollywood." *Fairfield Daily Ledger*, July 25, 1942, p. 6.

Chicago Tribune. 1903. "His Own Executioner." *Nashville American*, October 17, 1903, p. 9.

Davis, John W. 2010. *Wyoming Range War: The Infamous Invasion of Johnson County*. Norman: University of Oklahoma Press.

Davis, Sara. 1942. "REVIEWS OF PREVIEWS." *Alton Evening Telegraph*, October 31, 1942, 13.

DeArment, R. K. 2007. "Gang Crackdown: When Stuart's Stranglers Raided the Rustlers." *Wild West*, June 7, 2007. https://www.historynet.com/gang-crackdown-when-stuarts-stranglers-raided-the-rustlers.htm

Dimsdale, Thomas J. 1988. *The Vigilantes of Montana*. Norman: University of Oklahoma Press.

"An Editorial." 1943. *Evening Huronite*, August 16, 1943, p. 1.

"EXCESSIVE PUBLIC SPIRIT." 1880. *Galveston Daily News*, May 12, 1880, p. 2.

Eyman, Scott. 2017. *Hank & Jim: The Fifty-Year Friendship of Henry Fonda and James Stewart*. New York: Simon & Schuster.

Farmer, Gene. 1943. "Story of Lynching Violence at State Outstanding Film." *Cedar Rapids Gazette*, August 13, 1943, p. 7.

"Federal Government Indicts Thirteen for Illinois Lynching." 1943. *Gazette and Daily*, August 18, 1943, p. 1.

"Federal Jury Raps Lynching at Sikeston: 'Deplorable Blot' On State, But No U.S. Indictment Is Returned," *St. Louis Star-Times*, July 30, 1942, p. 1.

Fonda, Henry, as told to Howard Tiechmann. 1981. *Fonda: My Life*. New York: New American Library.

Friedman, Lawrence M. 2007. *A History of American Law: Third Edition*. New York: Touchstone.

"From the Southwest." 1864. *Buffalo Commercial Advertiser*, February 24, 1864, p. 1.

Gard, Wayne. 1981. *Frontier Justice*. Norman: University of Oklahoma Press.

Gard, Wayne. 2017. "Cattle Rustling." *Handbook of Texas Online*. https://tshaonline .org/handbook/online/articles/jbc01

Gevinson, Alan, ed. 1997. *American Film Institute Catalog: Within Our Gates: Ethnicity in American Feature Films*. Berkeley: University of California Press.

Hampes, William. 2019. *Cowboy Courage: Westerns and the Portrayal of Bravery*. Jefferson, NC: McFarland & Company, Inc.

Harrington, Fred Harvey. 1996. *Hanging Judge*. Norman: University of Oklahoma Press.

Herzberg, Bob. 2013. *Hang 'Em High: Law and Disorder in Western Films and Literature*. Jefferson, NC: McFarland & Company, Inc.

"HOW STATES EXECUTE." 2007. *Tampa Tribune*, September 2, 2007, p. 6.

"HOW THEY WERE HANGED." 1889. Further Details of the Lynching of 'Cattle Kate' and Her Companion—A Number of Vigilantes Arrested." *Topeka Daily Capital*, July 27, 1889, p. 3.

Howard, Joseph Kinsey. 1943. *Montana: High, Wide, and Handsome*. New Haven, CT: Yale University Press.

Jones, Paul. 1943. "Backstage." *Atlanta Constitution*, June 20, 1943, p. 12-C.

Krakel, Dean F. 1988. *The Saga of Tom Horn: The Story of a Cattlemen's War*. Lincoln: University of Nebraska Press.

Lang, Marissa. 2015. "Woman Accused of 'Lynching' Appears in Court." *Sacramento Bee*, April 9, 2015, https://www.sacbee.com/news/local/crime/article17965127 .html

"THE LAST CHAPTER in Milton J. Yarberry's Eventful Career. HE SHOWS THEM HOW TO DIE GAME. The Trip from Santa Fe to Albuquerque on a Special Train. HIS LAST MOMENTS ON EARTH. His Speech Delivered from the Gallows Just Before the Death Signal. His Denial of Ever Killing Anyone before Living in Albuquerque. LAST NIGHT ON EARTH." *The Albuquerque Morning Journal*, February 10, 1883, p. 4.

Lindsey, Ellis. 2012. "The Lynching of Assassin Jim Miller." *Wild West*, August 18, 2012, https://www.historynet.com/the-lynching-of-assassin-jim-miller.htm

"LYNCHING IN CALIFORNIA." 1851. *Freeman's Journal*, May 23, 1851, p. 4.

"MANDATES OF DEATH. Issued by the United States Court at Fort Smith, Ark. The Foremost Criminal Tribunal in the World. Sixty-Nine Men Who Have Dropped to Death—The Judge and Executioner." 1890. *Daily American*, January 30, 1890, p. 8.

McCormick, Mike. 2012. "HISTORICAL PERSPECTIVE: Unsolved Homicides from 70 and 140 Years Ago." *Tribune-Star*, October 21, 2012, https://www .tribstar.com/news/lifestyles/historical-perspective-unsolved-homicides-from -and-years-ago/article_931e2b38-f004-51e4-91e8-06b100d74020.html

Menard, Orville D. 2010. "Lest We Forget: The Lynching of Will Brown, Omaha's 1919 Race Riot." *Nebraska History*, Fall/Winter 2010, pp. 152–165.

Meyer, William R. 1979. *The Making of the Great Westerns*. New Rochelle, NY: Arlington House.

Moody, R. R. 1919. "MORE OR LESS PERSONAL." *Nebraska State Journal*, October 8, 1919, p. 8.

"'MY, GOD, I NEVER DID IT; NEGRO CRIES AS MOB SEEKS TO FORCE HIS SURRENDER." *Lincoln Daily Star*, September 29, 1919, p. 1.

O'Shea, Kathleen A. 1999. *Women and the Death Penalty in the United States, 1900–1998*. Westport, CT: Praeger.

"OX-BOW INCIDENT." 1943. http://digitalcollections.oscars.org/cdm/compound object/collection/p15759coll30/id/11419/rec/2

"'Ox-Bow Incident' Being Made into Motion Picture." 1943. *The Nevada State Journal*, February 14, 1943, p. 11.

Pettengill, Samuel B. 1943. "Northern Reformers Can Look at Record in Own Territory." *San Antonio Express*, August 17, 1943, p. 4.

Price, Edgar. 1943. "Reel Review: 'The Ox-Bow Incident,' a Picture with a Terrific Wallop, Moves into the Rivoli—Henry Fonda, Dana Andres, William Eythe and Frank Conroy, Head an Exceptionally Fine Cast." *Brooklyn Citizen*, May 10, 1943, p. 10.

Rafferty, Milton D. 2001. *The Ozarks: Land and Life: Second Edition*. Fayetteville: University of Arkansas Press.

Roosevelt, Theodore. 1913. "Chapters of a Possible Autobiography: EIGHTH INSTALLMENT: THE WESTERN SPIRIT." *Butte Miner*, July 6, 1913, p. 20.

Schatz, Thomas. 1997. *Boom and Bust: American Cinema in the 1940s*. Berkeley: University of California Press.

Shelby, John. 1940. "The Literary Guidepost." *Sandusky Register*, October 8, 1940, p. 4.

Shirley, Glenn. 1968. *Law West of Fort Smith*. Lincoln: University of Nebraska Press.

Shirley, Glenn. 1970. *Shotgun for Hire: The Story of "Deacon" Jim Miller, Killer of Pat Garrett*. Norman: University of Oklahoma Press.

Tennal, Ralph. 1916. *History of Nemaha County, Kansas*. Lawrence, KS: Standard Publishing Company.

Thompson, Frank T. 1983. *William A. Wellman*. Metuchen, NJ: The Scarecrow Press, Inc.

Tórrez, Robert J. 2008. *Myth of the Hanging Tree: Stories of Crime and Punishment in Territorial New Mexico*. Albuquerque: University of New Mexico Press.

Tuller, Roger H. 2001. *"Let No Guilty Man Escape": A Judicial Biography of "Hanging Judge" Isaac C. Parker*. Norman: University of Oklahoma Press.

United Press. 1942. "Fonda, Power in U.S. Services: Henry Enlists in Navy, Tyrone Joins Marines." *Moorhead Daily News*, August 25, 1942, p. 2.

Untitled Article. 1889. *Seneca Courier-Democrat*, May 17, 1889, p. 2.

"U.S. Grand Jury Found No Federal Offense in Sikeston Lynching." 1943. *St. Louis Post-Dispatch*, January 13, 1943, p. 10.

"U.S. Indicts 13 in Ill Lynching." 1943. *Baltimore Afro American*, July 17, 1943, pp. 1–2.

VIGILANTES. 2011. *Encyclopedia of the Great Plains*, http://plainshumanities.unl .edu/encyclopedia/doc/egp.law.051

Vigilantism. n.d. *Crime Museum*, https://crimemuseum.org/crime-library/other -crime-topics/vigilante

Waldrep, Christopher, ed. 2006. *Lynching in America: A History in Documents*. New York: New York University Press.

Wallace, Moira. 1943. "'Ox-Bow Incident' at Warfield Tells Human Interest Story."
    San Francisco Examiner, June 11, 1943, p. 9.
Wellman, William A. 1974. *A Short Time for Insanity: An Autobiography.* New
    York: Hawthorn Books, Inc.
Wellman, William, Jr. 2015. *Wild Bill Wellman: Hollywood Rebel.* New York: Pan-
    theon Books.
"WHERE PLACE THE BLAME?" 1909. *Evening News*, April 20, 1909, p. 3.
Winchell, Walter. 1944. "Walter Winchell." *Jones County Observer*, January 28,
    1944, p. 6.

Chapter 3

Red River (1948)

While cowboys had long been featured in Hollywood Westerns, movies focusing on cattle drives were rare, partly because of the expenses and difficulty in shooting such a movie. *North of 36* (1924), *The Conquering Horde* (1931), and *The Texans* (1938), all based on Emerson Hough's novel *North of 36*, used footage originally filmed for the 1924 version—"an obvious inducement to remake the film" (Tuska 1988, 24). Those films chronicled a post–Civil War cattle drive from Texas to Abilene, Kansas, and *Red River* blazed that same trail. But while the film adaptations of Hough's novel are all but forgotten, *Red River*'s reputation had endured as one of the best movies about cattle drives as well as one of the best films of the Western genre.

John Wayne (1907–1979) plays pioneer Tom Dunson, who leaves a California-bound wagon train with his friend Groot (Walter Brennan, 1894–1974). Planning to start a cattle herd in Texas, Dunson won't allow his lover, Fen (Coleen Gray, 1922–2015), to accompany them, and heads south toward the Red River, which separates Indian Territory (present-day Oklahoma) from Texas. Smoke over the plains reveals that Native Americans have attacked the wagon train, and Dunson and Groot wait on the river's edge, expecting the tribe to send warriors after them. That night, Dunson and Groot kill the warriors, including one wearing the bangle Dunson gave Fen. Fen's death haunts Dunson for the rest of his life.

The next morning, a young boy who avoided the wagon-train massacre arrives in camp, leading a cow. Teenager Mathew Garth (Mickey Kuhn, 1932–) is incoherent from shock, but Dunson revives him with a hard slap, and when the kid draws a pistol, Dunson easily disarms him. The adults take the orphan with them. Near the Texas-Mexico border, Dunson decides to start his ranch, with his bull and Garth's cow, claiming the land from the owner of a hacienda south of the Rio Grande. Dunson brands his bull and Garth's cow with "the Red River D." When Garth points out that there's no "M" (for Matt) on the brand, Dunson says he'll add an "M" when Garth earns it.

Fourteen years later, Dunson has carved a cattle empire in south Texas— but he's broke. The Civil War (1861–1865) has stripped Texas of cash, meaning Dunson must drive cattle to the railroad in Sedalia, Missouri. An older Garth (Montgomery Clift, 1920–1966), just home from fighting in the war, joins him; Groot will drive the chuckwagon. Missouri bandits have stopped other trail herds from reaching Sedalia, and Dunson refuses to believe that the railroad has reached Abilene, Kansas—far west of Missouri.

After cowboy Bunk Kenneally (Ivan Parry, 1915–2001) accidentally causes a stampede in which young Dan Latimer (Harry Carey Jr., 1921–2012) is trampled to death, Dunson orders Bunk whipped. Bunk draws his revolver in self-defense, and Garth wounds Bunk in the shoulder before Dunson can kill him. Despite more evidence that the railroad has reached Kansas, the tyrannical Dunson refuses to change direction. When three cowboys threaten to quit unless they head for Abilene, Dunson, reluctantly assisted by Garth and gunfighter Cherry Valance (John Ireland, 1914–1992), kills them. Three more men desert, and Dunson sends Valance to bring them back. Drinking heavily, refusing to sleep, Dunson pushes his men and cattle north. Valance returns with two of the quitters—the third he killed—and Dunson threatens to hang them. But Garth leads a mutiny, takes control of the herd, and abandons Dunson, who vows to kill Garth.

After saving a wagon train from an attack by Comanches, Garth falls in love with gambler Tess Millay (Joanne Dru, 1922–1996). Dunson, backed by hired gunmen, pursues Garth, who reaches Abilene safely and sells Dunson's herd, but Dunson still plans to kill Garth. Knowing that Garth won't shoot his surrogate father, Valance attempts to stop Dunson, and the two men wound each other with pistol shots. Dunson keeps walking, firing several shots at Garth, who refuses to draw his revolver. A vicious fistfight follows before Tess stops them, saying it's obvious that they love each other. Reconciled, Dunson tells Garth that an "M" will be added to the "Red River D" brand. "You've earned it," Dunson says.

Early in 1946, director-producer Howard Hawks (1896–1977) bought "The Chisholm Trail," a *Saturday Evening Post* story by Borden Chase (1900–1971) about the first cattle drive up that cattle trail. Hawks's Monterey Productions Inc., founded with his wife, actress Lauren Bacall (1924–2014) and partner Charles Feldman (1905–1968), financed the movie, with United Artists handling distribution. Hawks paid Chase $50,000 for the story and $1,250 a week to write the screenplay.

Born Frank Fowler, Chase—who reportedly used Borden milk and Chase-Manhattan Bank to come up with his pen name—moved from New York to Los Angeles in 1935 after his novel *Sandhog* was turned into the movie *Under Pressure*. His first screenplays were war stories, but he became best known for Westerns, including *Winchester '73* (1950) and *Bend of the River* (1952). "He once told a colleague that regarding Westerns he had rewritten the same story eight different times; each version was then made into a movie," historian Larry Len Peterson said (Larry Len Peterson, interview with author, January 22, 2019). Hawks took Chase's script and then hired Charles Schnee (1920–2009), a law-school dropout who took up screenwriting, for a rewrite. Chase's story and script had Dunson killing Valance but being mortally wounded in the gunfight. Garth and Tess take Dunson across the Red River so that he can die in his beloved Texas. Chase despised the new ending, but Hawks hated killing off characters he liked. Schnee also added Fen to the screenplay.

Hawks wanted Gary Cooper (1901–1961) to play Dunson and Cary Grant (1904–1986) to play Valance. Cooper declined because of Dunson's brutality; Grant wouldn't take a role that small. But Wayne, who was represented by Feldman, signed on after Hawks convinced Wayne that he could play an older man. "Duke, you're going to be one pretty soon, why don't you get some practice?" Hawks told him (McCarthy 1997, 412). Cast as Fen, Gray got permission from 20th Century Fox, which owned her contract, by telling studio mogul Darryl F. Zanuck (1902–1979): "You're hurting yourself by not lending me to Howard Hawks so that I can prove that I have talent" (Hopper 1947, 7). Hawks cast Los Angeles native Margaret Sheridan (1926–1982) as Tess, but Dru replaced her, roughly six weeks after production began in Tucson, Arizona, when Sheridan revealed she was pregnant.

For Mathew Garth, Hawks landed Clift, a 25-year-old Broadway star being courted for various movie roles; *Red River* would be his first film production. When Clift asked if it was hard to act in a Western, Hawks replied, "Well, first you'll have to forget everything you learned from the Lunts," referring to the noted Broadway team of Alfred Lunt (1892–1977) and Lynn Fontanne (1887–1983) (Lyons 1948, 4). Clift and Kuhn, a 14-year-old whose credits included *Gone with the Wind* (1939), shared a dressing room. "He talked to my mother about the industry," Kuhn recalled. "He picked her brain" (Mickey Kuhn, interview with author, January 23, 2019).

How the climactic fight between Wayne, roughly six inches taller than Clift, would play out on film concerned the cast and crew. So did how Wayne, an instinctive actor, would take to Clift's Method style, developed by Konstantin Stanislavsky (1863–1938), in which actors immerse themselves emotionally into their roles. They pulled it off, Kuhn said, because "[t]hey played off each other. They were smart enough to do that. And John Wayne did it his way, Montgomery Clift did it another way, but it just seemed to hold together" (Mickey Kuhn, interview with author, January 23, 2019).

The production, with a budget of $1.75 million, faced bigger problems. Filming began southeast of Tucson in the fall of 1946, with a company of 200, 300 extras, and thousands of cattle and horses. A centipede bit Hawks on the first day of shooting; Dru replaced Sheridan; and Carey got his part because Hawks fired the original actor who, while drinking in Tucson, called in sick. Ireland was unprofessional and unreliable, Hawks complained. Scenes took longer to shoot than had been expected. The stampede sequence, filmed over 13 days, injured 7 men, 13 horses, and 69 steers. Worst was the weather. Flash floods washed out roads, filled arroyos, and threatened the company camp, where 75 tents (with electricity and running water) had been erected. Kuhn was on and off the set for 10 weeks. "They'd send me home for a week, 10 days, then fly me back down, then back home again," he said. "The good thing about it was they were all paid" days (Mickey Kuhn, interview with author, January 23, 2019).

By the time production ended, roughly a month longer than expected, Monterey had to obtain bank loans, as the film's production totaled $2,836,661. When Hawks left Arizona in November, he announced that the movie would be released in March, but two years passed before the film premiered. *The Search*, Clift's second movie, was filmed during the second half of 1947 but released in March 1948, five months before *Red River* opened.

In December 1947, United Artists threatened prosecution for breach of contract and demanded immediate delivery of *Red River*. Yet Hawks, who was going through a divorce with Bacall, soon faced another obstacle. Before the movie's scheduled opening on August 26, 1948, Howard Hughes (1905–1976) filed an injunction, accusing Hawks of lifting a scene from Hughes's *The Outlaw* (1943)—which Hawks had directed before either quitting or being fired by Hughes, who finished directing the picture. Hughes demanded that Hawks cut the scene where Dunson tries to get Garth to draw his pistol. On August 20, Hawks agreed to Hughes's terms and *Red River* opened to rousing business—taking in $69,810 in four days in New York City—and excellent reviews.

"It is great because it treats the old west with at least some semblance of realism," Betty French wrote in the *Akron Beacon Journal*. "It strips away the phony trappings that usually come with westerns—at least, most of them" (French 1948, 8B). The *New York Daily News*'s Kate Cameron called it "thrilling, absorbing entertainment" and said Clift "is definitely star material" (Cameron 1948, 72), while the *Los Angeles Times*'s Philip K. Scheuer wrote that "an adult, three-dimensional quality . . . lifts it entirely out of the conventional 'horse opera' class" (Scheuer 1948, 18).

Praise wasn't confined to the United States. In Vancouver, British Columbia, Clyde Gilmour of the *Sunday Sun* called it "[o]ne of the best westerns in years, palatable even to people who usually 'can't stand them'" (Gilmour 1949, 15). In Australia, a critic for the *Sydney Morning Herald* said *Red River* "might very well become a classic among Hollywood's finest frontier epics" ("NEW FILMS" 1949, 10), alluding to advertisements that compared *Red River* to *The Covered Wagon* (1923) and *Cimarron* (1931).

Red River was nominated for Academy Awards for screenplay and Christian Nyby's editing; Hawks received a Directors Guild of America Award nomination; and the script was nominated for the Writers Guild of America's Best Written American Western Award. Clift was on his way to stardom, and Wayne began to be taken seriously as an actor—and a box-office draw. A year after *Red River's* release, Wayne debuted at No. 4 in Quigley Publishing's Top 10 Money Making Stars Poll. In 1950, Wayne was No. 1, and from 1949 to 1974, he made the top 10 a record 25 times.

HISTORICAL BACKGROUND

The beginnings of the cowboy era in the American West can be traced to the second voyage to the New World led by Christopher Columbus (1451–1506) in 1493, when Columbus took horses, cattle, and other animals to Hispaniola to help establish Spanish ranches. By 1521, cattle had been transported to Mexico, and 20 years later Spanish explorer Francisco Vásquez de Coronado (1510–1554) is believed to have brought the first cattle into what became the state of Texas. Cattle soon ran wild by the thousands, but early settlers found their value not in meat but in hides and tallow. Over time, the breed that emerged was the longhorn, with curving, powerful, pointed horns that could reach five feet or longer in length from tip to tip. These long-legged animals "were the cow brutes for the open range, the cattle of the hour," Texas folklorist J. Frank Dobie wrote. "They suited the wide, untamed land and the men that ranged it" (Dobie 1941, 42). In the early 1800s, ranching (raising animals) and farming (raising crops) were combined in the Mexican colony of Texas, but by the time Texas entered the union in 1845, ranching became a separate enterprise along the state's frontier. Cattle could be found across America—the Revolutionary War battle site of Cowpens, South Carolina (January 17, 1781) took its name from an overnight stop for cattle drovers who traveled by foot—but ranching was different in the arid Southwest where cattle had to graze over unfenced pastures that might cover several sections (640 acres, one square mile) of land.

The new ranchers and their hired hands quickly adapted methods and dress used by *vaqueros*, the Spanish cattle herders who rode horses and used long ropes at Mexican ranches, and modified the wardrobe into a style that identified the wearer as a cowboy. The line from the traditional cowboy song "Streets of Laredo"—"I see by your outfit, that you are a cowboy"—wasn't an exaggeration. Styles and material varied regionally, but cowboy hats served as protection from rain and sun and could be used as a pillow or to hold water. In 1865 John B. Stetson opened a hatmaking

operation in Philadelphia, and his "Boss of the Plains"—flat-brimmed with
a low, uncreased crown—became one of the most popular styles for cowboys. Bandanas (scarves of silk, cotton, or linen) were worn loose around
the neck and served "as a towel, personal or dish; bronc blind; tourniquet;
pigging string; sling; water filter ear muff; hot handle pad" (Mora 1994, 50)
or pulled up over nose and mouth for protection against dust. Gauntlets
were leather gloves that extended past the wrist for protection from brush
and rope burns. Leather cuffs, developed in the late 1880s, replaced gauntlets in the 1890s but faded out of popularity after 1910. Leather chaps were
worn over pants legs for extra protection against thorns, brush, and potential saddle sores. Vests, usually of wool, provided an extra layer of clothing
and, as most shirts came without pockets, offered places to store tobacco
and other items.

What became known as the cowboy boot, made of heavy cowhide with
a square toe and higher heel suited for a saddle's stirrup, was developed in
Coffeyville, Kansas, in the 1870s, and boot shops sprung up in cattle towns.
In 1877, a barber loaned H. J. "Big Daddy Joe" Justin $35 to open a one-
room boot shop in Spanish Fort, Texas, on the Chisholm Trail near the Red
River. He took orders from cowboys heading to the Kansas trail towns, and
when the cowboys returned south, they paid for and picked up their boots.
Spurs, made of a metal shank, pronged rowels, and leather strap, were worn
on the boot heels to help control horses. Some spurs came with "jingle bobs"
or "clinkers," small metal accouterments that hit the rowel and made a jin-
gling noise when the cowboys walked.

An *Austin State Gazette* correspondent wrote:

> The "Cow-Boy" of Texas was a peculiar institution. No other State in the Un-
> ion produced his like. Most of them brave, generous and free-handed, hale,
> healthy and hearty, as from the nature of his exercise he was bound to be. Fear-
> less and intrepid riders, they roam throughout the year over the broad prairies
> of Texas, riding half-broke horses, fiery and vicious, and naturally become what
> is commonly called a dare-devil, the very material to make gallant soldiers.
> ("MIDDLE TEXAS" 1869, 1)

In 1876, a salesman in Fort Worth, Texas, noted that a cowboy "has but
little, if any, taste for reading. He enjoys a coarse, practical joke, or a smutty
story; loves danger but abhors labor of the common kind; never tires of riding, never wants to walk" (Worcester 1994, 84).

That was a generalization. What one cowboy didn't like, another one
might love—including reading. New Mexico cowboy Eugene Manlove
Rhodes, who later became a writer of Western fiction and nonfiction, often
read books while working, even in the saddle. Once, the horse Rhodes rode
became frightened and jumped, with Rhodes still mounted, into a ravine.
Found bruised and bleeding, Rhodes was asked if he were badly hurt. "No,"

he answered. "But dammit, I lost my place in the story" (Boggs and Reed 2012).

The real boost in the cattle market came at the end of the Civil War when Americans developed a taste for beef, and railroads could ship cattle to packinghouses in Kansas City, Chicago, or New York. Though infrequent, long drives had been completed before the war. In 1854, Thomas Candy Ponting (1824–1916) managed to drive a herd of 600 longhorns from northeastern Texas all the way to Muncie, Indiana. From there, Ponting transported the cattle to New York by railroad. Other herds were trailed to Chicago, St. Louis, and Kansas. In the Civil War, Texas rancher John Chisum (1824–1884), later a cattle baron in New Mexico, organized trail drives to feed Confederate troops to Louisiana. After the war, cattle were hard to find in the northeastern United States, and sirloin steaks cost 25 cents to 35 cents a pound, a high price for that time. Cattle in Texas, on the other hand, numbered roughly 3.5 million, according to the 1860 U.S. census—and maybe 4.5 million—more than one-eighth of all cattle in the United States. All any ambitious Texan had to do was figure out how to get cattle to the markets.

Cattle were shipped from the Texas ports of Indianola and Galveston to New Orleans, but herding cattle to the railheads north seemed more profitable, so around 1866, some Texans began gathering longhorns and driving them up the Shawnee Trail to Baxter Springs, Kansas, or Sedalia, Missouri, but local farmers complained that Texas longhorns were killing their cattle with Texas (or Spanish or Mexican) fever. Ticks spread the deadly disease that rarely killed longhorns. Outbreaks of fever and complaints from local farmers led to quarantine laws that prohibited or restricted the trailing of cattle from Texas or Indian Territory into Missouri, Kentucky, Illinois, Nebraska, and Colorado. In 1867, Kansas enacted a law outlawing the transporting of Texas or Indian cattle into the state between March and December. That quarantine line extended west of the sixth meridian and south of a line that ran from near present-day McPherson, Kansas west to the Colorado border. That meant cattle could be trailed the entire year in the south-central and southwestern part of the state. As the quarantine line moved west over the years, cattle towns like Abilene, Newton, Ellsworth, Wichita, Dodge City, and Caldwell—briefly boomed.

After spending months on the dusty trail from Texas, cowboys were ready to party when they reached the trail towns and had been paid, typically, in cash money. "Suddenly they felt free, uninhibited, and rich by cowboy standards, with anywhere from $50 to $90 in accumulated wages" (Dary 1982, 201). The cowboys, generally young and unmarried, could get a hot bath and a shave and buy new clothes. Gambling, drinking alcoholic beverages, and other forms of entertainment usually followed.

In Kansas, operating a brothel and being a prostitute were both misdemeanors with fines as high as $1,000 and sentences to up to six months in jail. Gambling that required a device or table was also a misdemeanor, punishable by a jail sentence of no less than 24 hours and no more than one year, and by a fine of not more than $1,000. Cattle towns, however, tended to ignore those statutes or at least keep fines low. The carrying of weapons, including firearms, Bowie knives, and dirks, was also prohibited. Men were usually told to leave weapons at a police station, hotel, restaurant, saloon, or other business and pick them up before leaving town. In Wichita, special policemen were hired to greet cowboys at the Chisholm Trail bridge and exchange a token for a weapon from travelers entering town. Dodge City passed an ordinance that made the railroad tracks what was called the "deadline"; north of the tracks, firearms were prohibited, but south of the deadline, weapons were allowed. Other cattle towns had similar policies where laws were enforced in the city proper, but practically anything was allowed in the sections that catered to seamier businesses. In 1880, Kansas banned alcohol, but "Dodge City and Prohibition just didn't mix" (Smarsh 2010, 31). Cattle towns weren't the only municipalities ignoring the prohibition statute. A *New York Times* correspondent noted that in Topeka, the state capital, "30 or 40 saloons are open day and night, and it is just as easy to get a glass of whisky or beer in Topeka as at any time of the past" ("KANSAS PROHIBITION LAW" 1882, 3).

Although Easterners and newspapers were prone to exaggerate the wildness of cowboys and cattle towns, violence did break out. In Newton, four men were killed and another four, including two bystanders, were wounded in an 1871 gunfight called the "General Massacre" and led to the town's nickname, "Bloody Newton." Gunfights claimed lives in Abilene, Ellsworth, Wichita, Caldwell, and Dodge City, too. The dilemma the trail towns faced "was not to rid themselves of visitors prone to violence, but to suppress the violence while retaining the visitors" (Dykstra 1983, 116).

Because of the quarantine laws, economics and/or better advertising, locations, or offerings from competing towns, the cow-town era rarely lasted longer than five years for most towns. Baxter Springs and Caldwell, because of their location on the state's southern border, dealt in cattle longer, and Dodge City, located in the western part of the state, reigned as "Queen of the cowtowns" from 1877 to 1885.

Most cattle towns were glad to be rid of the cowboys and the gamblers, saloonkeepers, and prostitutes that followed the cattle trade. "The shade of the cow-boy's sombrero has fled, and the jingle of his spurs are no longer heard on our streets," the *Wichita Eagle* opined in 1873. "With the fading of one and the silence of the other, the flight of soiled doves for other and more wicked towns has been precipitous" ("State Items" 1873, 8).

Later trails reached Ogallala, Nebraska, a cattle town on the Union Pacific Railroad line, or brought cattle to stock ranches in New Mexico, Colorado, Wyoming, or Montana.

Cowboys, however, did more than just drive cattle to the markets. They worked on ranches, sometimes drifting from job to job, season to season.

"They were loyal to their outfit and to one another," Montana rancher Granville Stuart (1834–1918) recalled (Dary 1982, 278). Ranch cowboys typically lived in bunkhouses—"bachelor living quarters on a ranch" (Dary 1982, 284)—where they could sleep, relax, and eat. At larger ranches, a hired cook typically fed the cowboys, whereas cowboys might cook for themselves at smaller outfits. Although ranchers knew that the better the food, the longer good cowboys were likely to stay employed, the quality of the grub wasn't always exceptional. Lee D. Leverett, who worked on a ranch in Indian Territory in the 1880s, recalled:

> I want to say right here that the belly-cheater didn't learn to bake bread from the teaching of Mr. John Bun, the inventor of the bun. Sometimes the bread would come up in fair shape, and then not so anyone would hanker for it. The bread was a hit and miss proposition, with more misses than hits. . . . But, kick as we may about the chuck, there was always all that we wanted, and none of us lost any loaf lard from eating it. Facts is, we were all as strong as a hoss in power, and smell as well. (Leverett 1941)

On roundups and cattle drives, food was often served near a chuckwagon. Texan cattleman Charles Goodnight (1836–1929) created the chuckwagon in 1866, buying a government wagon and having a woodworker rebuild it with bois d'arc, a local tree species known for its hardness and durability. Iron axles replaced the original wooden ones, and tallow instead of tar was put in an underneath bucket to be used for greasing. At the rear of the wagon, a chuck-box was built with compartments and drawers to hold supplies and cookware. Sloping outward from top to bottom, a hinged lid covered the box so that when it was opened, it swung down to serve as a worktable.

Depending on the season and the location of the ranch, calves had to be branded, and cattle had to be fed, watered, doctored, or moved, while fences—when there were fences—had to be mended or cattle separated to be shipped to market or allowed to grow fatter. During winter months, some cowboys might be shipped to remote locations of the ranch, where they would stay in line shacks to look after cattle. Horses were important for cowboys, and many cowboys disliked doing any work they couldn't do on horseback.

Most Western ranches in the 1800s operated on the open range. Fences were rare, but the invention of barbed wire by Joseph Glidden in 1873 began to change ranching and the life of the cowboy. Ranchers had used public lands to graze their livestock. Some cattlemen began to fence in pastures and water holes. So did homesteading farmers, but many ranchers and cowboys resisted barbed wire. Fences, one Texan remarked in 1884, "are the curse of the country" (Dary 1982, 319). The biggest change came after the harsh winter of 1886–1887, which killed hundreds of thousands

---

BRANDING CATTLE

Tom Dunson describes the mark, or brand, he plans to put on his first bull and cow in *Red River*: "It'll be two lines. Like this. Like the banks of a river. It'll be the Red River brand." The "D" beside the wavy lines turns the brand into the "Red River D."

Brands were (and remain) a way for stock raisers to show ownership once the brand had been registered in a state or territory, although thieves (rustlers) using "running irons" could alter brands.

Branding typically occurred during roundups when new calves were caught, brought to a fire, and thrown on their sides. Another cowboy would pull a hot branding iron from the fire and place it on the calf's flank. "The calf balls. The smell of burning hair and flesh drifts skyward in a puff of white smoke. Seconds later the branding is over" (Dary 1982, 156). As cattle being shipped to market often came from various ranches, those cattle would receive a "road brand" for identification.

Unbranded cattle were called mavericks. The name came from Texan Samuel Maverick (1803–1870), who neglected to brand his cattle. "A maverick was a big calf that had been missed in a roundup and gotten weaned away from its mother before it had any brand," E. C. "Teddy Blue" Abbott wrote, "so there was no way of telling who owned it, but that did not prevent a lot of people from using a rope and a running iron for their own benefit" (Abbott 1955, 86).

---

of cattle and financially ruined many ranchers. Realizing the need for better land management, ranchers began to modernize with smaller herds and more fenced-in pastures. The cowboy, however, did not vanish. Ranchers and cowboys remain prominent fixtures in the American West today, still riding horses (or in pickup trucks), and still working cattle.

In 1902, a Harvard University graduate named Owen Wister, a friend of President Theodore Roosevelt—who, as a rancher in what's now North Dakota, had suffered great losses during the 1886–1887 winter—published a romantic novel titled *The Virginian*. That novel, selling more than 1.5 million copies in its first 50 years in print, reinvented the cowboy as the prototypical western hero.

DEPICTION AND CULTURAL CONTEXT

Like most westerns of the 1940s, *Red River* stretches geography and history. Groot's voiceover narration tells viewers that in August 1851, Tom Dunson decided to pull out of a wagon train bound for California. Fourteen years later, Groot's narration informs the viewer, on August 14, 1865, Mathew Garth completed "the first drive up the Chisholm Trail." That's more than two years before the first cattle were shipped from Abilene.

Dunson's need for driving cattle to market, however, is fairly accurate. Though far removed from the major Civil War battlefields, Texas felt the financial stress like the rest of the South at the war's end, and owning a lot of cattle or land did not necessarily mean wealth. Even today, it's not uncommon to hear ranchers say they are "cattle-poor."

> Texas was cattle poor and land poor when the drives started. The Carpet Baggers had issued land certificates which came to be worth next to nothing. In some parts of the State, land was not worth more than twenty cents an acre. Probably the average value throughout the State was about one dollar an acre. ("OLD TEXAS CATTLE TRAILS" 1927, 3)

When Garth reaches the town, he finds a small town with a railroad. Moviemakers had transformed the "[s]leepy and peaceful" community of Elgin, Arizona, roughly 65 miles south of Tucson, into an Abilene of "[f]alse-front hotels, provision stores and saloons" (Kalil 1946a, 10). A railroad spur was already there. Garth and Dunson would not have found that much in Abilene in 1865; the railroad did not reach Abilene until the spring of 1867.

A decade before the events of *Red River* are said to take place, in 1856, a man from Illinois built a cabin near the Smoky Hill Trail on Mud Creek, marking the earliest settlement in what would become Abilene. In 1860, Charles Thompson claimed 40 acres on which he planned to start the town of Abilene, taking the name from the Bible's Luke 3:1. Seven years later, with the Union Pacific Railroad Company, Eastern Division (later the Kansas Pacific Railway) running past the settlement, Joseph McCoy came with plans to start a cattle-shipping point. Despite serving as the Dickinson County seat, Abilene "was a very small, dead place, consisting of about a dozen log huts—low, small rude affairs, four-fifths of which were covered with dirt for roofing" (McCoy 1986, 116). "A plank on a sawhorse served as a railroad station until 1868" one historian observed (Verckler 1961, 3). Even when the first cattle arrived for sale and shipment in 1867, Abilene was nowhere near the rollicking cowtown it came to be. Photographs taken in 1867 by Alexander Gardner (1821–1882), documenting the railroad's progress, "showed little more than a creek, a prairie-dog town, a newly built three-story building, and a stockyard with stock cars sitting on a rail siding" (Sherow 2018, 32).

While Abilene was a small town in 1865, accurately portrayed in *Red River*, it grew into a larger and livelier town by 1869. McCoy was a 29-year-old from Illinois who, like his two older brothers, had pursued a career in transporting livestock to packing centers. Realizing that New York and other northern cities needed beef, and that beef was abundant in Texas, McCoy envisioned the riches available for someone who could link Texas cattle to northern markets. After failing to convince Junction City, Solomon City, and Salina of the wealth stockyards and a shipping facility could bring,

McCoy came to Abilene, where he and Thompson agreed to terms, and McCoy started work. The only problem was that Abilene fell within the Kansas quarantine line, but McCoy and Thompson persuaded the governor to grant an exception, helped by a $50,000 bond from Texas cattlemen to cover livestock losses from Texas fever incurred by Kansans.

McCoy realized that he needed more than just his "Great Western Stock Yards" to hold and load cattle onto trains, so he invested roughly $18,000 in a hotel to lure cattle buyers and cattlemen. Christened the Drovers Cottage, the 50-room hotel had a billiard room, saloon, and dining hall. McCoy hired James and Louise Gore from St. Louis to manage the Drovers Cottage, which served Kentucky bourbon, Baltimore oysters, and French wines and brandies. By 1869, Gore began enlarging the hotel and McCoy started construction on "a very handsome residence ... an ornament to this Western country" ("Abilene Items" 1869, 3).

In *Red River*, the cattle buyer (Harry Carey Sr., 1878–1947) is accurate when he tells Garth that Abilene's pens can't hold anywhere near the more than 9,000 longhorns Garth has brought from Texas. When completed, McCoy's Great Western Stock Yards could hold 1,500 head of cattle, and the railroad could transport 40 stock cars per day.

Once Abilene had been established as the shipping point, McCoy sent a rider south to alert drovers and point them to the new mecca. Having faced unfriendly farmers and bandits in Missouri and Kansas, the first trail bosses "were not ready to credit the proposition that the day of fair dealing had dawned for Texan drovers, and the era of mobs, brutal murder, and arbitrary proscription ended forever" (McCoy 1986, 121). The Texans cautiously turned their cattle toward Abilene. So Dunson would have been right to keep driving his herd to Sedalia in 1865, and if he had delayed his drive two years, he likely would have been greeted by a rider encouraging him to go to Abilene or followed other crews that were bound for Abilene.

While *Red River* credits Garth with completing the first cattle drive up the Chisholm Trail in 1865, in reality, the first cattle drivers didn't arrive in the town until two years later. On September 4, 1867, canvas tents were set up in Abilene along the railroad tracks. Wine and food were served, speeches made, and songs sung. The next day, 400 longhorns were loaded onto 20 stock cars bound for Chicago. The first cattle leaving Abilene could have belonged to Californians Oliver Wolcott Wheeler (1830–1890) and his two partners, often credited for being the first to follow the Chisholm Trail with 2,400 steers from San Antonio. Or they could have belonged to a herd that a drover named Thompson trailed from Texas to Indian Territory, where he sold his cattle to three men named Smith, McCord, and Chandler, who drove the herd to Abilene.

Red River even places Garth's cattle drive prior to two historical cases that didn't follow the Chisholm Trail. In 1866, a year after Garth's fictitious drive in *Red River* and a year before the first cattle departed from the Abilene stockyards, Charles Goodnight and Oliver Loving (1812–1867) drove cattle from northern Texas to Fort Sumner, New Mexico, over part of what became known as the Goodnight-Loving Trail; and Nelson Story (1838–1926) led a herd of cattle from Texas to the gold-mining town of Virginia City, Montana.

Navajos and Mescalero Apaches were imprisoned at the Bosque Redondo reservation near Fort Sumner, New Mexico Territory, and Goodnight thought that he could drive cattle west from Belknap, Texas, sell the herd to the U.S. Army for beef to feed the captured Navajo and Mescalero. He discussed his idea with Loving, a native Kentuckian who came to Texas in 1843. Having driven herds to Denver in 1860 and to Confederate forces on the Mississippi River during the Civil War, Loving warned Goodnight of the dangers of attempting such a drive, but when Goodnight refused to change his mind, Loving offered to join him. Goodnight readily agreed, saying, "I not only need the assistance of your force, but I need your advice" (Haley 1949, 127).

Joining forces, Goodnight and Loving struck the trail 25 miles west of Belknap with 2,000 head of cattle on June 6, 1866, and 18 men. At first they followed what had been the Butterfield Overland Mail route, which had operated from St. Louis to San Francisco from September 15, 1858, until March 1, 1861, before the threat of Civil War caused the U.S. government to move the mail route out of the South. The Goodnight-Loving group "trailed out into a tried, but still an uncertain, land" (Haley 1949, 128).

The herd included steers and cows, and some cows birthed calves on the drive. Goodnight tried to haul the newborns in a wagon, but when that didn't work, he gave African American cowboy Jim Fowler the grim job of killing calves unable to finish the drive. After crossing dry country, the herd reached the Pecos River, where weary cattle drowned or became mired in quicksand. The cowboys left more than 100 cattle in the bogs to die.

They followed the Pecos River toward New Mexico, but the bleak country proved no easier. Eventually, Goodnight and Loving reached Fort Sumner, having lost 400 of the original 2,000 head. The contractors at the fort, however, were willing to buy only steers, at eight cents a pound on the hoof, leaving Goodnight and Loving with 700 to 800 head of cows. Goodnight returned to Texas to start forming another herd, while Loving led the rest of the cattle north to near Denver, Colorado, where he sold the longhorns to rancher John W. Iliff.

A number of cattle are killed or lost during the drive in *Red River*, too. Dunson points out that they lost 300 to 400 steers during the stampede that killed Dan Latimer. While swimming the Red River, Garth's men lose 30 or 40 steers out of some 9,000—a much lower percentage than what Goodnight and Loving lost on the Pecos River. After reaching Abilene, Garth tells the cattle buyer that they have lost 600 or 700 head during the drive. Losing cattle was expected on a lengthy drive, although stray cattle from farms and ranches near the cattle drives sometimes might join the passing herd, accidentally or with some encouragement, and help reduce those losses.

Ohio-born Nelson Story led the other historic cattle drive of 1866. Rich from his business ventures in Kansas, Colorado, and western Montana, Story headed to Texas to buy cattle. In Fort Worth (some say Dallas), Story bought 600, 1,000, or as many as 3,000 head of cattle, with plans to either drive them to the market in Kansas City—Abilene, in 1866, was a year away from shipping cattle—or to Montana. He reportedly ran into trouble in Kansas, where he was fined $75 for violating the quarantine law. If Story had planned on selling the beef in Kansas City, that incident changed his mind. He outfitted his men with breech-loading Remington rifles, bought 150 head of oxen and three (reports go as high as 15) freight wagons, which he filled with provisions, and turned north toward Nebraska.

Picking up the Oregon Trail in Nebraska, Story led his party to Fort Laramie, Wyoming. Army officers warned the adventurer of the dangers; Arapaho, Cheyenne, and Lakota tribes along the Bozeman Trail were causing trouble after the army began building new forts along the trail. The tribes refused to sign a new treaty and launched Red Cloud's War, named after the Lakota leader Red Cloud (1822–1909). Two freighters also bound for Montana joined Story's group, which moved on toward Fort Reno. Near there, Native Americans attacked the party, stampeded the herd, and stole cattle. Story "hunted a fight and when he found it he knew how to handle it," recalled one of the new freighters, John B. Catlin (1837–1917), who said Story and his men tracked the Native Americans into the badlands and "took the cattle back" (Boggs 2016).

That attack, though, is certainly different than the one depicted in *Red River*, in which Garth and his men drive off Comanches that have pinned down the Nevada-bound wagon train carrying Tess Millay and others. Story was moving cattle through country where indigenous tribes were fighting against white encroachment on their lands. Garth was herding cattle through land predominantly controlled by some of the Five Civilized Tribes (Cherokee, Chickasaw, Choctaw, Creek, and Seminole) that had been removed from the southeastern states into Indian Territory in the 1820s and 1830s. Trail crews did encounter Native Americans along the Chisholm Trail, sometimes in Kansas but more often in Indian Territory, but armed conflict proved rare.

Typically, Native Americans requested some cattle for payment to cross their land, or merely because they were hungry. Denied, the tribes might steal stock, stampede the herd, or set fire to prairie grass. On the Shawnee Trail in 1867, the Cherokee National Council began charging a toll of ten cents a head for all cattle crossing tribal land. In 1871, the Creeks began charging 27.5 cents for each head passing through and 25 cents a month for each head of cattle grazing. "One effect of these new levies was to dry up the use of the old Shawnee route in favor of the Chisholm Trail" (Gard 1954, 131).

Cowboy L. D. Taylor recalled this 1869 encounter with some 400 Comanches on a drive to Abilene:

> When they came up to our herd they began killing our beeves without asking permission or paying any attention to us. Some of the boys of our herd went out to meet them, but the boys of the other herds hid out in the grass, and only one man from the other outfit came to us. They killed twenty-five of our beeves and skinned them right there, eating the flesh raw and with the blood running down their faces, reminding me of a lot of hungry dogs. . . . We were powerless to help ourselves, 'for we were greatly outnumbered. Every time we would try to start the herd the Indians would surround the herd and hold it. Finally they permitted us to move on, and we were not slow in moving, either. (Hunter 1992, 501)

Once Story reached newly built Fort Phil Kearny, north of Buffalo, Wyoming, Colonel Henry Carrington (1824–1912) stopped Story, ordering him to graze his animals three miles from the fort—so they wouldn't be eating army grass. After about a week, Story called for a vote to determine if they would wait or sneak out. According to legend, one man voted to stay. Story drew his pistol, disarmed the dissenter, took him prisoner, and forced him along when they left at night. When Story returned the dissenter's revolver, the frightened man agreed to finish the drive with Story rather than travel alone to the fort. The departure allowed Story's group to miss one of the key events of Red Cloud's War. On December 9, Captain William J. Fetterman (1833–1866) led 80 men from the fort on a relief detail, but Native Americans lured the command into an ambush, where all 81 men were killed.

Native Americans also attacked Story's party, which began traveling only at night. A snowstorm struck near the Big Horn River, but the men rounded up the cattle that had drifted in the storm and pushed on toward present-day Columbus, Montana, and into the Gallatin Valley. Story ordered some of his men to cut down trees for a ranch house and corral, which became Story's ranch near present-day Bozeman. After leaving most of his men and enough cattle at his ranch, Story and other cowboys drove some steers into Virginia City on December 9, 1866.

The first gunfight between Dunson and three "quitters" in *Red River* is precipitated by a conversation with a cowboy wounded by Missouri outlaws who tells them about a trail blazed by Jesse Chisholm, an Indian trader, to Abilene. First published in 1924, *The Trail Drivers of Texas*, a collection of former cowboys' narratives of their experiences "on the Range and on the Trail," mentions several cowboys quitting during drives, but no one cites any cowboy ever getting killed for trying to quit. But *Red River* gets some of the facts right about the Chisholm Trail.

Jesse Chisholm (1805–1868) moved to Indian Territory in 1820, began trading with various Native American tribes and established a trading post near present-day Wichita, Kansas. The trail he blazed around 1864 ran from near the Indian Territory-Texas border to Wichita. Wheeler reputedly followed Chisholm's wagon tracks into southern Kansas and worked his way to Abilene. At first, the trail was called the Kansas Trail, Abilene Trail, McCoy's Trail, the Great Cattle Trail, Texas Cattle Trail, Great Texas Cattle Trail, and the Wichita Trail. Within a few years, however, the Chisholm Trail referred to not just the trail Chisholm blazed but also trails from south Texas to Abilene, or Ellsworth, or other cattle towns. Later, the Western Trail linked the Texas cattle country with Dodge City, although some drovers used the Chisholm Trail before taking the "cutoff" to Dodge City. The "Chisholm trail," a correspondent for a Topeka, Kansas, newspaper noted in 1871, "is, perhaps, as hot a meridian as any that transects the western country" ("NEWTON" 1871, 2).

"Most of the men who used the trail probably had never heard of Jesse Chisholm or his wagon road," historian Don Worcester wrote (Worcester 1994, xx). And Jesse Chisholm never learned of his namesake cattle trail. He died on March 4, 1868, of cholera morbus after eating bear grease that had been contaminated after being melted in a brass kettle.

Another stretch in *Red River* is the herd's size. When Dunson and Garth start, they have between 9,000 and 10,000 cattle—a staggering number that likely would have required four trail crews. Trail herds typically numbered from 2,000 to 2,500, requiring a trail boss, 10 to 12 cowboys, and a cook. A wrangler was in charge of the extra horses, which could number up to 150. The two most experienced cowboys typically rode at the head of the herd, called point. Where the herd began to widen, called the swing, two more cowboys rode on each side of the cattle; farther back, at the flank, rode another two men. Trailing the herd were two to four usually inexperienced cowboys riding drag, of which cowboy E. C. "Teddy Blue" Abbott said: "I have seen them come off herd with the dust half an inch deep on their hats and thick as fur in their eyebrows and mustaches, and if they shook their head or you tapped their cheek, it would fall off them in showers" (Abbott 1955, 62–63).

Often overlooked in film and fiction were minority cowboys; however, *Red River* depicts a Native American and a Hispanic working on Dunson's drive. African American or Hispanic cowboys made up roughly one-third of 35,000 cowboys that pushed cattle up the trails from 1868 to 1895. "All the real cowboys—black, brown, red and white—shared the same jobs and dangers," historians Philip Durham and Everett L. Jones wrote. "They ate the same food and slept on the same ground" (Durham and Jones 1983, 1).

For an occupation and lifestyle that many people found glamorous, being a cowboy was a low-paying job of hard work. A *Louisville Courier-Journal* correspondent wrote:

Nor is cattle herding an easy life.—Think of driving wild, fierce brutes from the Rio Grand[e] to Kansas, compelled to watch them day and night.—If they stampede, as they often do, the cow-boy must ride after or before them, and the dangerous race is most frequently made during dark nights, thro' drenching storms, over ya[w]ning barrancas [ravines] and in the midst of tangled thickets that fearfully test the strength of the leather fenders on his arms and the cow-skin leggings which protect his lower limbs. ("TEXAS COW BOYS" 1873, 1)

Red River accurately captures the hardships of life on a cattle trail. While battles with Native Americans were rare, lightning claimed many lives, river crossings could be treacherous, hailstorms could injure horses and cowboys, and stampedes were extremely dangerous. *Red River*'s cowboys are disappointed after Dunson gives orders to keep pushing the cattle north, robbing his men of a chance to bathe in a watering hole. And the search for Latimer shows dead cattle before they find the young cowboy's remains. "Dan was wearing checkered pants, wasn't he?" Dunson asks. "Yeah," Garth replies, "and he was riding a little buckskin mare."

Abbott described finding the remains of a cowboy and horse killed during a stampede in 1879: "The horse's ribs was scraped bare of hide, and all the rest of horse and man was mashed into the ground as flat as a pancake. The only thing you could recognize was the handle of his six-shooter" (Abbott 1955, 37).

But "the worst hardship" on a trail drive, Abbott said, "was loss of sleep" (Abbott 1955, 67).

CONCLUSION

The history isn't always reliable in *Red River*, often called a *"Mutiny on the Bounty* Out West," but the movie looks authentic. That's one reason Hawks elected to film in black and white rather than color. Hawks also hired Joe De Yong (1894–1975), a protégé of Western artist Charles M. Russell (1864–1926), known for his authenticity, to draw costume sketches for each character. De Yong left before filming began, but his touches can be seen in most of the costumes, although Clift's modern hat is an exception. Hawks gave that hat, which once belonged to Gary Cooper, to Clift.

Red River marked the first Western film Hawks finished as a director, having either been fired from or quit *Viva Villa!* (1934) and *The Outlaw* (1943). Hawks went on to direct *The Big Sky* (1942), *Rio Bravo* (1959), *El Dorado* (1967), and *Rio Lobo* (1970), the latter three also starring Wayne, whom Hawks credited for *Red River*'s success, saying that Wayne's "strong character and integrity, plus a vast knowledge of western pictures, made him a tower of strength in helping me get the film done" (Johnson 1948, 4).

But *Red River*'s biggest claim to fame is for elevating Wayne's status in Hollywood. "For the first time," *Akron Beacon Journal* theater editor Betty

French wrote, Hawks "makes an actor out of John Wayne" (French 1948, 8B). Wayne's performance even surprised Wayne's mentor and friend, director John Ford, whose *Stagecoach* (1939) turned Wayne into a major star. After seeing *Red River*, Ford remarked, "I never knew that big son of a b— could act" (Davis 1998, 125). Said Wayne: "*Stagecoach* established me as a star. *Red River* established me as an actor" (Eyman 2000, 179).

FURTHER READING

Abbott, E. C. ("Teddy Blue"), and Helena Huntington Smith. 1955. *We Pointed Them North: Recollections of a Cowpuncher*. Norman: University of Oklahoma Press.

"Abilene Items." 1869. *Western Home Journal*, October 21, 1869, p. 3.

AP (Associated Press). 1947. "Delivery of Films Sought." *Los Angeles Times*, December 10, 1947, p. Part II, 11.

Bailey, Jack. 2006. *A Texas Cowboy's Journal: Up the Trail to Kansas in 1868*. Edited by David Dary. Norman: University of Oklahoma Press.

Boggs, Johnny D. 2016. "North to Montana: Nelson Story's Epic Cattle Drive 150 Years Ago Is the Perfect Road Trip from Texas to Montana in 2016." *True West*. https://truewestmagazine.com/north-to-montana

Boggs, Johnny D. 2018. "These Boots Aren't Made for Walking." *Roundup Magazine*, April 2018, pp. 15–16.

Boggs, Johnny D., and Ollie Reed Jr. 2012. "28 Moments of Entrapment in New Mexico's Pre-Statehood History." *True West*. https://truewestmagazine.com/28 -moments-of-entrapment

Cameron, Kate. 1948. "Capitol's 'Red River' Spectacular Feature." *New York Daily News*, October 1, 1948, p. 72.

Cushman, George L. 1940. "Abilene, First of the Kansas Cattle Towns." *Kansas Historical Quarterly*, August 1940. https://www.kshs.org/p/abilene-first-of-the -kansas-cow-towns/12833

Dary, David. 1982. *Cowboy Culture: A Saga of Five Centuries*. New York: Avon Books.

Davis, Ronald L. 1998. *Duke: The Life and Image of John Wayne*. Norman: University of Oklahoma Press.

Dobie, J. Frank. 1941. *The Longhorns*. New York: Bramhall Books.

Drago, Harry Sinclair. 1960. *Wild, Woolly & Wicked: The History of the Kansas Cow Towns and the Texas Cattle Trade*. New York: Clarkson N. Potter, Inc./ Publisher.

Durham, Philip, and Everett L. Jones. 1983. *The Negro Cowboys*. Lincoln: University of Nebraska Press.

Dykstra, Robert R. 1983. *The Cattle Towns*. Lincoln: University of Nebraska Press.

Etulain, Richard W. 2006. *Beyond the Missouri: The Story of the American West*. Albuquerque: University of New Mexico Press.

Eyman, Scott. 2000. *Print the Legend: The Life and Times of John Ford*. Baltimore: The Johns Hopkins University Press.

Fidler, Jimmie. 1948. "Jimmie Fidler in Hollywood." *Joplin Globe*, October 13, 1948, p. 9.

"Film-Making Is Commenced." 1946. *Tucson Daily Citizen*, September 6, 1946, p. 14.

French, Betty. 1948. "'Red River,' 'Johnny Belinda' Films to Renew Faith of Fans." *Akron Beacon Journal*, October 24, 1948, p. 8B.

Gard, Wayne. 1954. *The Chisholm Trail*. Norman: University of Oklahoma Press.

Gilmour, Clyde. 1949. "SCREENING the FILMS." *Sunday Sun*, March 5, 1949, p. 15.

Groves, Melody. 2018a. "I See by Your Outfit . . . : Cowboys Donned Functional Styles." *Roundup Magazine*, April 2018, pp. 17–18.

Groves, Melody. 2018b. "A Tip of the Hat: 10-Gallon Salute to This Cowboy Trademark." *Roundup Magazine*, April 2018, pp. 14–15.

Haley, J. Evetts. 1949. *Charles Goodnight: Cowman and Plainsman*. Norman: University of Oklahoma Press.

"Heavy Rains Hamper Red River Production." 1946. *Arizona Daily Star*, October 2, 1946, p. 16.

Hopper, Hedda. 1947. "A Mystery Yard for Spencer Tracy." *Shreveport Times*, June 9, 1947, p. 7.

Hunter, J. Marvin, compiler and editor. 1992. *The Trail Drivers of Texas*. Austin: University of Texas Press.

INS (International News Service). 1946. "Marriage on Rocks for Howard Hawks." *Miami Daily News*, October 29, 1946, p. 13-A.

Johnson, Erskine. 1948. "'Jolson Story' May Be Serial." *Rhinelander Daily News*, November 15, 1948, 4.

Kalil, Dorothy. 1946a. "ELGIN ENJOYING OVERNIGHT BOOM: Tiny Community Captured by Movie Unit; Is Now Abilene." *Arizona Daily Star*, September 6, 1946, p. 10.

Kalil, Dorothy. 1946b. "Elgin Locale for Hawks' Production No Accident: Texas Got Every Break in 15,000-Mile Location Search." *Arizona Daily Star*, September 22, 1946, p. 14.

Kalil, Dorothy. 1946c. "STARS AT ELGIN: Director Seeks to Elevate Two to Stardom in 'Red River.'" *Arizona Daily Star*, September 11, 1946, p. 5.

"KANSAS PROHIBITION LAW. GOV. ST. JOHN CLAIMING CREDIT WHICH HE DOES NOT DESERVE. THE HISTORY OF THE PASSAGE OF THE AMENDMENT—THE GOVERNOR'S LOFTY AMBITION—A LAW WHICH IS NOT EN FORCED—SOME OTHER KANSAS MATTERS." 1882. *New York Times*, February 19, 1882, p. 3.

Leverett, Lee D. 1941. U.S. Works Projects Administration Interview Transcript by Sheldon F. Gauthier, February 11, 1941. Folklore Project, Life Histories, MSS55715: BOX A734, Library of Congress. https://www.loc.gov/resource/wpalh3.35020608/?sp=1

Lyons, Leonard. 1948. "The Lyons Den: Disney Atones for Erroneous Charge." *Fort Myers News-Press*, July 29, 1948.

Manns, William, and Elizabeth Clair Flood. 1997. *Cowboys & Trappings of the Old West*. Santa Fe, NM: Zon International Publishing Company.

McCarthy, Todd. 1997. *Howard Hawks: The Grey Fox of Hollywood*. New York: Grove Press.

McCoy, Joseph G. 1986. *Historic Sketches of the Cattle Trade of the West and Southwest*. Lincoln: University of Nebraska Press.

"MIDDLE TEXAS." 1869. *Galveston Daily News*, p. 1.

Mora, Jo. 1994. *Trail Dust and Saddle Leather.* Ketchum, ID: Stoecklein Publishing.

"NEW FILMS." 1949. *Sunday Herald.* April 3, 1949, p. 10.

"NEWTON. A Description of the Gold Room. PEN PORTRAITS OF THE PRO-FESSIONAL GAMBLERS. PREACHING MIXED WITH MONTE AND DOG FIGHTING." 1871. *Kansas Daily Commonwealth*, September 17, 1871, p. 2.

"OLD TEXAS CATTLE TRAILS." 1927. *Bryan Daily Eagle*, June 15, 1927, p. 3.

Raymond, Ken. 2017. "The Chisholm Trail at 150: Remembering the greatest cattle migration in American history." *Oklahoman*, August 20, 2017, https://newsok .com/article/5560635/the-chisholm-trail-at-150-remembering-the-greatest -cattle-migration-in-american-history

"RED RIVER FILM SHOOTING ENDED. Hawks, Stars Leave Elgin Site for Hollywood; Worked 10 Weeks." 1946. *Arizona Daily Star*, November 5, 1946, p. 3.

"'Red River' Location Shots Near End." 1946. *Arizona Daily Star*, October 18, 1946, p. 9.

Reynolds, William. 2018. *Joe De Yong: A Life in the West.* Santa Ynez, CA: Alamar Media, Inc.

Sandoz, Mari. 1958. *The Cattlemen: From the Rio Grande Across the Far Marias.* New York: Hastings House.

Sarris, Andrew. 1969. *Interviews with Film Directors.* New York: Avon.

Scheuer, Philip K. 1948. "'Red River' Powerful, Sweeping Saga of West." *Los Angeles Times*, October 15, 1948, p. 18.

Sheaffer, Lew. 1948. "Hawks' 'Red River' at the Capitol Belongs with the Great Western Films." *Brooklyn Eagle*, October 1, 1948, p. 8.

Sherow, James E. 2018. *The Chisholm Trail: Joseph McCoy's Great Gamble.* Norman: University of Oklahoma Press.

Smarsh, Sarah. 2010. *It Happened in Kansas: Remarkable Events that Shaped History.* Guilford, CT: Globe Pequot Press.

"State Items." 1873. *Kansas Tribune*, December 4, 1873, p. 8.

Taylor, Irwin. 1889. *General Statutes of Kansas.* Topeka, KS: Geo. W. Crane & Co., Law Book Publishers.

"TEXAS COW BOYS." 1873. *Ellsworth Reporter*, August 28, 1873, p. 1.

Thomas, Bob. 1947. "Hollywood Gossip." *Bryan Daily Eagle*, November 28, 1947, p. 7.

Tuska, Jon. 1988. *The American West in Film.* Lincoln: University of Nebraska Press.

U.P. (United Press). 1948. "Hughes Wins Fight over Movie Scene." *Bakersfield Californian*, August 20, 1948, p. 4.

Verckler, Stewart P. 1961. *Cowtown—Abilene: The Story of Abilene, Kansas, 1867–1875.* New York: Carlton Press.

Wellman, Paul I. 1988. *The Trampling Herd: The Story of the Cattle Range in America.* Lincoln: University of Nebraska Press.

Worcester, Don. 1994. *The Chisholm Trail: High Road of the Cattle Kingdom.* New York: Indian Head Books.

Zolotow, Maurice. 1975. *Shooting Star: A Biography of John Wayne.* New York: Pocket Books.

Chapter 4

High Noon (1952)

When United Artists released Stanley Kramer Productions, Inc.'s *High Noon* in July 1952, few could have predicted the movie's success that year or its lasting legacy decades later. There was little reason to think the movie would be a hit. Producer Stanley Kramer (1913–1991) said, "I had my share of worries" (Kramer 1997, 69). *High Noon* starred actor Gary Cooper (1901–1961), but the former box-office favorite's last hit movie was *Unconquered* in 1947. "Cooper needed a hit," film historian Robert Nott wrote, "and it's fair to say that had *High Noon* not come along, he would have ended up riding the B-Western trail" (Nott 2013, 40). Costar Grace Kelly (1929–1982) became a major star but was unknown in 1952, hired because Kramer "couldn't afford anyone else" (Nott 2013, 40). The distribution company, United Artists, "was navigating itself through the shoals of bankruptcy" (Kramer 1997, 69).

The movie was filmed over 32 days with a final budget of $786,600.01; in comparison, RKO's *The Big Sky* and MGM's *Lone Star*, both 1952 releases, had budgets of roughly $1.7 million and $1.6 million, respectively. More modestly budgeted 1952 Westerns such as Warner Bros.' *Carson City* and Republic's *Ride the Man Down* cost about $750,000 and $665,000, respectively. "*High Noon*," Nott wrote, "might be the cheapest Western film classic ever made" (Nott 2013, 40).

High Noon opens on a Sunday morning as Jim Pierce (Robert Wilke, 1914–1989), Jack Colby (Lee Van Cleef, 1925–1989), and Ben Miller (Sheb Wooley, 1921–2003) ride into Hadleyville a few minutes after 10:30 a.m., just as town marshal Will Kane (Cooper) and Amy Fowler (Kelly) are being married in a ceremony performed by Justice of the Peace Percy Mettrick (Otto Kruger, 1885–1974). Immediately after the wedding, when Kane has reluctantly turned in his badge—his replacement won't arrive until the following day—he learns that Ben Miller's brother Frank (Ian MacDonald, 1914–1978) has been pardoned and that Pierce, Colby, and Ben Miller are at the depot, where they asked about the noon train. Five years ago, Frank Miller was sentenced to hang for murder, but the sentence was commuted. Now it looks like Miller's coming back to fulfill his vow to kill Kane in revenge. With much encouragement, Kane leaves town with Amy in a buggy but quickly turns around. He has never run from anyone, and he thinks Miller and his bunch will come after him no matter how far he runs. It's better, he tells his new bride, to face them where he has friends. Amy, however, is a Quaker, staunchly opposed to violence after seeing her father and brother gunned down, and threatens to leave on the noon train. "I've got to stay," he tells her, and Amy leaves, buys a train ticket, and waits at the hotel for the train to arrive, first in the lobby and later with Helen Ramirez (Katy Juarado, 1924–2002), Kane's former lover who once was Frank Miller's girl. Ramirez is leaving town, too, telling deputy Harvey Pell (Lloyd Bridges, 1913–1998), her most recent lover, that when Kane dies, "this town dies too."

By swearing in special deputies, Kane hopes that a violent confrontation against Miller and his bunch can be avoided. Mettrick thinks otherwise. After packing his belongings, Mettrick urges Kane to run, too. "There isn't time," Kane says. "What a waste," Mettrick responds and rides away.

Kane attempts to recruit deputies. Pell agrees to help Kane only if Kane will use influence with Hadleyville's board of selectmen to appoint Pell as the new marshal. "Sure I want you to stick, but I'm not buying it," Kane says. "It's gotta be up to you." Pell tosses away his badge. Another selectman, Sam Fuller (Harry Morgan, 1915–2011), hides inside his house and makes his wife (Eve McVeagh, 1919–1997) lie to Kane about Fuller's whereabouts. Kane finds no help in the town's saloon or church, the latter where, after a lengthy debate among worshipers, Mayor Jonas Henderson (Thomas Mitchell, 1892–1962) says Kane should leave town because if potential town investors "read about shooting in the streets. . . . They'll think this is just another wide-open town, and everything we worked for will be wiped out." Former marshal Martin Howe (Lon Chaney Jr., 1906–1973) cites busted knuckles and arthritis when he turns down Kane's plea for help. A deputy named Baker (James Millican, 1911–1955) is ready to go—until learning just before noon that Kane hasn't been able to find any assistance; then he leaves. Kane's only volunteers are a 14-year-old boy (Ralph Reed, 1931–1997) and the town drunk (William Newell, 1894–1967), but Kane declines those offers. As the train arrives, he finishes writing his last will and testament, steps onto the deserted street and walks toward the depot.

Kane kills Ben Miller first, and, hearing that gunshot, Amy runs from the train she has boarded, finds the dead gunman in the dirt, and waits in Kane's office. Chased into a livery stable's barn, Kane guns down Colby. When the killers set the barn on fire, Kane flees on horseback and takes shelter in an empty building near his office. Pierce and Frank Miller pin down Kane inside the building, but Amy finds a loaded pistol and kills Pierce with a bullet to his back. Frank Miller then takes Amy hostage, ordering Kane out of the building. As soon as Kane steps outside, Amy claws Miller's face, giving her new husband time enough to shoot the killer dead. With the fight over, citizens rush to celebrate and congratulate Kane. A disgusted Kane tosses his badge in the dirt and leaves town in his buggy with his new wife.

Kramer, an independent producer, and screenwriter Carl Foreman (1914–1984) joined together in the late 1940s and made critically acclaimed movies, including *Champion* (1949), *The Men* (1950), and *Cyrano De Bergerac* (1951). Foreman had an idea for a movie that would be told in real time—a minute of the story relatively equal to a minute of film. *Rope* (1948), directed by Alfred Hitchcock (1899–1980), and *The Set-Up* (1949), directed by Robert Wise (1914–2005), used similar concepts. Foreman wanted to write a Western as a parable to the United Nations, the international organization founded in 1945 to maintain peace and security while tackling global issues. Foreman's agent, however, found Foreman's plot too similar to "The Tin Star," a short story by John M. Cunningham (1915–2002) published by *Collier's* in 1947. Stanley bought the film rights for Cunningham's story, and Foreman wrote the screenplay, borrowing some names and dialogue from "The Tin Star." Soon Foreman changed the story to an allegory about the Red Scare and the Hollywood blacklist.

Kirk Douglas (1916–) and Henry Fonda (1905–1982) were among the actors considered for the starring role. Gregory Peck (1916–2003) turned it down. Bruce Church (1900–1958), a lettuce producer and financier in Salinas, California, who had invested in *The Men* and *Cyrano De Bergerac*, and was putting in $200,000 for *High Noon*, pushed for Cooper. To Kramer's surprise, Cooper—ailing from ulcers, hernias, marital problems, and a fading career—was willing to take a major salary cut from roughly $275,000–$295,000 to $50,000–$60,000 and a percentage of profits.

Austria-Hungary–born Fred Zinnemann (1907–1997) had been directing movies for MGM since the late 1930s, garnering an Oscar nomination for *The Search* (1948) before signing with Kramer and Foreman. The trio's first collaboration was *The Men*. After reading Foreman's first draft of *High Noon*, Zinnemann was eager to direct. "Friends were puzzled by my enthusiasm over what they thought to be the script for just another Western," he recalled, "but when I told the story to [wife] Renée, who is a good movie audience, she immediately said, 'You must do it'" (Zinnemann 1992, 96). Zinnemann changed the marshal's name from Doane, the name of the lawman in Cunningham's story, to Kane, reportedly because Juarado had trouble pronouncing Doane.

Zinnemann and cinematographer Floyd Crosby (1899–1985) decided to film without filters or soft-focus lenses in an attempt to copy the types of

Civil War photographs taken by Mathew Brady (1822–1896), an "approach that ran counter to the then fashionable style of Western—the pretty clouds in a filters sky, the handsome, magnetic figure of the fearless young hero" (Zinnemann 1992, 101). When filming ended, the editors went to work. Kramer tried to supervise the cutting of the film but handed it over to Elmo Williams (1913–2015), who "felt the emphasis should be on Cooper and his problem, and anything that didn't contribute to this should be eliminated" (Blake 2003, 35). *High Noon* ran a taut, tense 85 minutes. Who came up with the idea of adding a ballad to the finished film has been debated, but the theme song, written by Dimitri Tiomkin (1894–1979) and Ned Washington (1901–1976) and sung by Tex Ritter (1905–1974), became a key to the movie's success—recorded by dozens of artists over the years.

The movie opened to tremendous box office and rave reviews. *New York Daily News* critic Kate Cameron singled out Cooper's "fine performance, one of his best," and Tiomkin's "haunting melody" (Cameron 1952, 40). The *Los Angeles Times*' Philip K. Scheuer said: "The phenomenon of a scared Cooper is only one of several that transform this Stanley Kramer production into a western distinguishable from most others" (Scheuer 1952, Part III, 8). "This isn't exactly a Hollywood type of movie," Henry Ward of the *Pittsburgh Press* wrote, "It's the kind that Stanley Kramer believes in—one of those meticulously planned, expertly directed, minutely detailed sort of film that leaves you with the same satisfaction of a well balanced meal" (Ward 1952, 6). The *Newark Advocate*'s Hazel Kirk wrote that "it takes ingenuity to make one [Western film] stand out from others. Fred Zinnemann . . . has been able to do this" (Kirk 1952, 9).

In 1953, John Wayne (1907–1979), who later called *High Noon* "the most un-American thing I've seen in my whole life" (Blake 2003, 41), accepted the Best Actor Academy Award for his friend Cooper, who was filming a movie in Mexico. *High Noon* also won Oscars for editing, original song, and musical score, and was nominated for best picture, director, and screenplay. After a rerelease in 1956, the movie earned domestically more than $3.9 million.

HISTORICAL BACKGROUND

Much as in today's legal system, Old West law-enforcement officers had various titles and jurisdictions. A sheriff was an elected position for a state (often appointed in a territory) with jurisdiction limited to one county. The sheriff could hire deputies and had the authority to deputize civilians. In addition to maintaining the county jail, the sheriff often served as a tax collector—sometimes earning a percentage of collected taxes—and had to carry out executions before states assumed that job. A U.S. marshal, who oversaw a district, was appointed by the U.S. president and confirmed by the Senate. Since the marshal was basically a political appointment, he selected deputies for most of the police work. As enforcers of federal laws, U.S. marshals and their deputies only worked on local crimes when requested by local authorities or when ordered by superiors. Some deputy marshals served in local law enforcement in a county sheriff's or town police or marshal's office. "Up through 1870, marshals also carried out the mundane chore of taking the census every ten years," historian Monty McCord said (Monty McCord, interview with author, April 11, 2019). Town or city marshals (or constables or police chiefs) were appointed by the mayor or council or were elected. They had the right to hire a certain number of deputies or policemen to keep the peace within the town or city limits. "He could be anyone, the owner of the general store, livery man, etcetera," McCord said. "A town of any size would usually prefer to hire someone that was ex-military, or had any prior experience as a lawman. Some crossed the line back and forth between lawman and outlaw" (Monty McCord, interview with author, April 11, 2019).

"When I die, I hope they have something better to say about me than to tell how many men I've killed," Texas lawman Jeff Milton (1861–1947) said (Cain 2000, 115). But most Old West lawmen are remembered for officer-involved shootings.

One of the most famous gunfights involving a county sheriff occurred in 1887 in Holbrook, Arizona Territory. Commodore Perry Owens (1852–1919), newly elected sheriff of Apache County, wore his hair long, sported a mustache, cut a dashing figure, and was known as a crack shot with pistol and rifle. Andy Blevins, a Texas ruffian who moved to Arizona in 1884, was a murderer and thief who took the name Cooper for an alias. In a feud known as the Graham-Tewksbury War, Cooper, siding with the Graham faction, and others murdered John Tewksbury and Bill Jacobs on September 2, 1887, in retaliation for the deaths of Cooper's father and brother. With a warrant for Cooper's arrest for horse theft, Owens arrived in Holbrook on Sunday, September 4, and asked where Cooper was. Told that the killer was in his house on the north side of town, Owens said, "I am going to take him in" (Trimble 2016). One citizen volunteered to accompany Owens, but the sheriff rejected the offer.

Around 4:00 p.m., Owens walked to the Blevins house where Cooper cracked the house's east-facing door open. Told of the warrant, Cooper reportedly tried to slam the door, but Owens put a foot in the doorway. Seeing Cooper raise a revolver, Owens fired his Winchester. The bullet hit Cooper in the stomach. Cooper's brother, John, opened the west-facing door and fired his revolver, missing Owens, who seriously wounded John with a rifle shot. One account says the wounded Cooper tried to raise his pistol, but Owens shot Cooper in the hip. Owens backed away from the house as Mote Roberts, one of Cooper's accomplices, tried to escape from a side window but was mortally wounded by another round from Owens's rifle. Finally, Sam Houston Blevins, another one of Cooper's brothers, came through the door and aimed a revolver at Owens, who shot the 15-year-old in the chest as Blevins's mother tried to pull him back inside the house. "I see no other man," Owens said, "so I left the house" (Ball 1992, 44).

The gunfight was over in three minutes, and Owens's actions were ruled justifiable. Of the Blevins faction, only John survived and was charged with attempted murder. As Owens walked away, a resident asked him, "Have you finished the job?" Owens answered, "I think I have" (Trimble 2016).

On September 24, 1789, President George Washington signed the Judiciary Act into law, creating the U.S. Marshals Service. On January 1, 1794, U.S. Marshal Robert Forsyth of the District of Georgia became the first federal marshal killed in the line of duty when he was serving civil papers. Since then, more than 250 members of the service—most of them deputy marshals but also including five other U.S. marshals—have been killed. Among the most famous deputy marshals were Bill Tilghman (1854–1924), Chris Madsen (1851–1944), and Heck Thomas (1850–1912), dubbed the Three Guardsmen of Oklahoma; Pat Garrett (1850–1908) of New Mexico Territory; and brothers Virgil (1843–1905) and Wyatt Earp (1848–1929) of Arizona Territory. The most respected, however, might have been Bass Reeves (1838–1910).

Born into slavery in Arkansas, Reeves escaped into Indian Territory (present-day Oklahoma) during the Civil War (1861–1865), where he became familiar with the land and the custom of some of the Native American tribes. Freed by the 13th Amendment, Reeves was recruited by U.S. Marshal James Fagan (1828–1893), who operated under federal Judge Isaac C. Parker (1838–1896) in the Western District of Arkansas, which included Indian Territory.

Roughly 200 federal lawmen were responsible for policing 74,000 square miles and 60,000 people. Sixty-five of those lawmen were killed. "That Judge Parker's administration was stern to the extreme is attested by the fact that he sentenced 160 men to die and hanged 79 of them" (Shirley 1968, ix).

A strong man standing six feet, two inches tall, Reeves was deputized in 1875. He reportedly arrested more than 3,000 people and killed 14 outlaws during his career. An uncompromising lawman, he once arrested one of his sons for the murder of the son's wife. When the marshal suggested that another lawman take responsibility for arresting Reeves's son, Reeves answered: "Give me the writ" ("BLOODY RECORD OF BASS REEVES" 1910, 4). Reeves served 32 years as a federal deputy and then became a police officer in Muskogee, Oklahoma, in 1907, where he worked for two years before retiring.

In the early 1890s, Reeves finally caught up with Bob Dozier (or Dosser or Dossay), an outlaw who robbed banks, stores, cattlemen, stagecoaches, and poker games; rustled cattle and horses; dabbled in confidence games and land swindling; fenced stolen goods; and killed people, but "Because of his diversified actions, he never enraged any one particular group of people" (Burton 2006, 168). In 1890, Reeves had first sworn out a warrant for Dozier, who was arrested in 1892 but charges were dismissed. Sometime after that, Reeves closed in on the outlaw, who sent word to the marshal that if Reeves didn't stop pursuit, he would be dead. Reeves allegedly responded

BOUNTY HUNTERS AND "DEAD OR ALIVE"

Other types of peace officers on the Western frontier were bounty hunters and bail bondsmen, both hired to track down and bring in wanted criminals or bail jumpers.

Bail bondsmen got jurisdictional freedom when the 1872 Supreme Court decision in *Taylor v. Taintor* made a warrant unnecessary to arrest bail jumpers, and allowed a person to enter another person's home to make an arrest. Movies like *The Naked Spur* (1953) and *The Bounty Hunter* (1954) typically depicted Old West bounty hunters as scavengers neither liked nor respected by most settlers, but Stuart H. Traub wrote that "the bounty hunter was neither highly respected nor much remembered in his own time" (Traub 1988, 300).

"As romantic as the notion is of freelance bounty hunters bringing in their prey 'dead or alive,' there's not much historical evidence for this," journalist Max McCoy said. "The problem is that the idea of being pre-authorized to kill rather than attempt a capture goes contrary to our system of law, even in the Old West. That said, there was an understanding then – as today – that lawmen could use deadly force in defending themselves and others while executing an arrest warrant, and in practical terms this often came down to a 'dead or alive' scenario" (Max McCoy, interview with author, April 16, 2019).

Source

Traub, Stuart H. 1988. "Rewards, Bounty Hunting, and Criminal Justice in the West: 1865–1900." *Western Historical Quarterly* 19, no. 3 (August): 287–301.

that Dozier would have to stop running to kill Reeves, and Reeves "was ready at any time to give Dozier his chance" (Burton 2006, 169). During a thunderstorm in the hills of the Cherokee Nation, Dozier tried to ambush Reeves and his posse. Reeves's posse fled, but Reeves shot one of the outlaws, and when Dozier returned fire, Reeves fell to the ground, feigning death with a cocked weapon in his hand. Dozier laughed and approached the fallen lawman. Biographer Art T. Burton wrote:

> Bass waited till Dozier was only a few yards away before he raised up and ordered him to stop. Dozier stopped laughing, his eyes wide with surprise. He hesitated for a moment, then dropped into a crouch and attempted to shoot once again as Bass lay stretched out ready and waiting in the mud before him. Before he could level his gun, Bass shot first, hitting him in the neck and killing him instantly. (Burton 2006, 170)

After Reeves died of Bright's Disease on February 15, 1910, the *Muskogee Phoenix* praised his life and service:

> He was buried with high honors, and his name will be recorded in the archives of the court as a faithful servant of the law and a brave officer. And it was fitting

that such recognition was bestowed upon this man. It is fitting that, black or white, our people have the manhood to recognize character and faithfulness to duty. And it is lamentable that we as white people must go to this poor, simple old negro to learn a lesson in courage, honesty and faithfulness to official duty. (Burton 2006, 301)

One of the most beloved frontier town marshals was Dodge City, Kansas's Ed Masterson (1852–1878), brother of "Bat" Masterson (1853–1921). In December 1877, a month after Bat was elected Ford County sheriff, Ed, who had been serving as assistant marshal, was appointed city marshal after the town council voted to fire the current marshal. Ed Masterson "was a natural gentleman, a man of good judgment, cool and considerate," town merchant Bob Wright wrote. "He had another very important qualification, that of bravery" (DeArment 1989, 101). As assistant marshal, the *Dodge City Times* noted in August 1877, Masterson "seemed to be always on time to quell the disturbance" and "made a remarkable record during the month as the docket of the Police Court will bear testimony" ("The Judge and the Coons" 1877, 1).

Around 10 p.m. on April 10, 1878, Masterson and policeman Nat Haywood stepped inside a saloon, where several trail hands were drinking. One of the cowboys had a revolver in a shoulder holster, so Masterson approached him and explained that carrying firearms was against the law, and the revolver had to be checked. The cowboy, Jack Wagner, surrendered the weapon without argument, and Masterson gave the revolver to trail boss Alf Walker, asking him to make sure the gun was checked with the bartender. The lawmen stepped outside, and a short while later, Wagner and Walker followed. Masterson spotted a revolver again in Wagner's shoulder holster. When Masterson attempted to take the revolver from the drunken cowboy, Wagner resisted. Haywood started to help, but more armed cowboys rushed outside. One aimed a pistol in Haywood's face and pulled the trigger, but the weapon misfired. While Masterson and Wagner struggled, Wagner's revolver discharged, sending a bullet through Masterson's abdomen, the closeness of the shot igniting Masterson's clothes. Somehow Masterson kept his feet and fired four shots, hitting Wagner in the stomach and Walker twice in the right arm and once through his left lung. Masterson staggered two hundred yards to Hoover's Saloon, where he told George Hinkle, "George, I'm shot," and slumped to the floor, his clothes still smoldering. Less than 40 minutes later, Masterson died. He was 26.

"Everyone in the City knew Ed Masterson and liked him," the *Ford County Globe* reported. "They liked him as a boy, they liked him as a man, and they liked him as an officer" ("SAD NEWS" 1878, 2).

The following morning, businesses in Dodge City closed from 10:00 a.m. until 6:00 p.m. Black crepe hung from most doors. "Never before was such an honor show in Dodge, either to the living or dead" ("SAD NEWS" 1878, 2). The city fire department, of which Masterson was a member, paid for the entire funeral, which began at 3:00 p.m. Masterson was buried in the cemetery at nearby Fort Dodge. "Riders, wagons and buggies, it is said, covered the entire five-mile funeral procession to the cemetery," said Brent Harris, a spokesman for Dodge City's Boot Hill Museum, adding that Masterson's funeral was the biggest in the town's history (Brent Harris, interview with author, April 9, 2019).

Wagner, who admitted to shooting Masterson, died that evening and was buried on Boot Hill the following afternoon. Four cowboys were arrested as accessories, but Judge R. G. Cook released them, "as it was established that they were to blame only for being in bad company" ("SAD NEWS" 1878, 2). Alf Walker was taken home by his father to Kansas City, where, according to Wyatt Earp, Walker died of pneumonia.

"As an officer he was vigilant, courageous and conscientious of the important trust in his hands," the *Dodge City Times* eulogized. "As we knew him he was kind, civil and steadfast—combined with those qualities that make the brave man, the true friend and good citizen" ("THE MURDER" 1878, 1).

In 1879, the city fire department reinterred Masterson's remains in the new Prairie Grove Cemetery, which was established "for 'respectable people'" (DeArment 1989, 108). Years later, the bodies at Prairie Grove were moved to the new Maple Grove Cemetery, and Masterson's grave was lost.

DEPICTION AND CULTURAL CONTEXT

Astute observers of *High Noon* have suggested that the setting of the film is circa 1898, pointing out that the "WAR IS DECLARED" volunteer recruitment flyer on Will Kane's office wall is from the 1898 Spanish-American War and that the year on a town building's facade reads 1888 (courthouses, opera houses, and other buildings often had the year of their construction painted or chiseled into the structures). That would help explain why Kane has trouble finding help; most of town's bravest men might have been fighting in Cuba or the Philippines at the time. Film historian Michael F. Blake believes otherwise. Blake's father, Larry Blake (1914–1982), played the bartender Kane hits in the saloon for offering odds that Frank Miller will kill Kane five minutes after arriving on the noon train. "The war declaration was just set dressing, has no meaning," Michael F. Blake said, adding that the producers were "too cheap to change" the year on the building. "Yes," Blake said, "the budget was that tight" (Michael F. Blake, interview with author, December 31, 2018). Besides, in the script, "Foreman sets things up with a synopsis of the town, characters, etcetera, before starting the actual script. He expressly writes: 'The time is 1870 or 1875'" (Michael F. Blake, interview with author, March 26, 2019). Zinnemann backs that up in his autobiography, saying that he and Crosby wanted the movie to "look like a newsreel of the period, if newsreels had existed around 1870" (Zinnemann 1992, 101).

No matter the year, Percy Mettrick is the town's justice of the peace and officiates the marriage of Will Kane and Amy Fowler, but he flees Hadleyville because he sentenced Frank Miller to hang. That a justice of the peace, basically a local magistrate, would try a capital case in a Western state or territory is highly unlikely, because although a county sheriff might also have a commission as a deputy U.S. marshal, a district judge would not also serve as a justice of the peace.

In organized territories of the American West, the U.S. government appointed at least one district judge to try federal crimes (counterfeiting, mail theft, selling whiskey to Native Americans, train robbery, etc.) and also major crimes (armed robbery, murder, rape, etc.) while minor crimes were left to local justices of the peace or police court judges, who were elected or appointed. Regarding the legal training of Western judges and justices, historian Jeremy Agnew wrote:

> There were no minimal standards of performance for being a judge. District judges were supposed to have some formal legal training, but the men appointed in the West were those who were often not as capable as those who received assignments in the East. Justices of the peace or police court justices required few qualifications to secure their positions, and did not necessarily need knowledge of the law or any legal training. They often had no training at all, but merely demonstrated a willingness to do the job. Thus the legal expertise of those administering the lower courts was uneven at best. (Agnew 2017, 179)

One of the West's most famous justices of the peace was Roy Bean (ca. 1825–1903), whose exploits were highly fictionalized in the movies *The Westerner* (1940) and *The Life and Times of Judge Roy Bean* (1972). After the Kentucky-born adventurer arrived in Vinegarroon, Texas, Pecos County commissioners appointed him justice of the peace in August 1882, a position Bean held, except when voted out of office in 1886 and 1896, until he retired in 1902. Bean considered himself the "Law West of the Pecos" despite his only lawbook being the 1879 *Revised Statutes of Texas*. He set up his courtroom in his saloon and is said to have dismissed a case against a white man charged with killing a Chinese railroad worker because he could find no statute that prohibited the killing of a Chinese person. He also reputedly fined a corpse $40 (the amount the found on the dead body, along with a pistol) for carrying a concealed weapon. "Roy Bean did have authority to conduct inquests, collect fines and things like that," historian Marshall Trimble said. "Despite what some people think, Bean never hanged anybody. He did fake a hanging one time to scare the dickens out of a guy who smarted off. It's a great story, and the guy returned to Langtry many years later and credited Bean with making him change his ways" (Marshall Trimble, interview with author, April 4, 2019).

After the legendary Gunfight at the O.K. Corral, a preliminary hearing began on October 31, 1881, in Tombstone, Arizona Territory, overseen by Wells Spicer, the mining town's justice of the peace. The following day, defense attorney Thomas Fitch, representing Morgan, Virgil, and Wyatt Earp, objected that Spicer, as a justice of the peace and not a judge, was not qualified to rule on what testimony could be admitted or disallowed. Spicer ruled in favor of himself and later declared that the Earp brothers and Doc Holliday were justified in killing Billy Clanton and Frank and Tom McLaury. In December, a Cochise County grand jury voted against indicting the Earps and Holliday. If the hearing had turned out differently, Jeff Guinn, author of *The Last Gunfight: The Real Story of the Shootout at the O.K. Corral—And How It Changed the American West*, said, "Spicer would never have handled the trial. He forwarded the big stuff to higher pay grades" (Jeff Guinn, interview with author, April 10, 2019).

Regarding the fictional trial of Frank Miller in *High Noon*, Trimble agrees that Justice of the Peace Percy Mettrick would not have tried that case. "A capital offense would have to go to a higher court," Trimble said (Marshall Trimble, interview with author, April 4, 2019).

One factor overlooked by many film scholars and critics is that Kane is no longer Hadleyville's marshal; even the town mayor has asked Kane to leave town to avoid a gunfight on the streets. While facing down Frank Miller's bunch, Kane "is, in effect, a vigilante: a private man assuming the power of the law without submitting himself to the democratic process" (Slotkin 1993, 392).

Also in the movie, one churchgoer points out that Kane and Miller have a personal feud because of past relationships with Helen Ramirez. One of the most famous officer-involved gunfights in Old West history might have been on account of a love triangle.

On October 5, 1871, as the cattle season was ending in Abilene, Kansas, dozens of cowboys and others, filled with liquor and good spirits, went through town, demanding that citizens buy them drinks. They even approached town marshal James Butler "Wild Bill" Hickok (1837–1876), who "treated, but told them that they must keep within the bounds of order or he would stop them" ("SHOOTING AFFRAY" 1871, 3). When the group reached the Alamo saloon, gambler Phil Coe (1839–1871) fired a shot in the air. Hickok hurried to the saloon, where, despite being outnumbered by some 50 revelers, he demanded to know who had fired the shot, a violation of the town's ordinance against the carrying of weapons. After saying he had shot at a stray dog, Coe fired at Hickok. Coe's bullet missed, but Hickok shot Coe twice in the abdomen, and Coe died four days later. Mike Williams, one of Hickok's deputies, rushed around a corner to assist

Hickok, who didn't recognize his friend and shot and killed Williams and then ordered the revelers out of Abilene. Realizing that he had killed Williams, Hickok carried his deputy's body into the saloon, laid it on a poker table, reloaded his guns, grabbed a shotgun, and took to the streets, running gamblers and other cowboys out of town.

Coe was "a gambler," the *Abilene Chronicle* reported, "but a man of natural good impulses in his better moments" but also "had a spite at Wild Bill and had threatened to kill him" ("SHOOTING AFFRAY" 1871, 3). One rumored reason for that "spite" was that both men were involved with Jessie Hasel (or Hazell), usually identified as a prostitute or owner of an expensive brothel. Historian Tom Clavin, author of *Wild Bill: The True Story of the American Frontier's First Gunfighter*, said that Hasel likely spent time with Coe, Hickok, and perhaps other men, too.

> In frontier towns in the 1860s and '70s, especially ones booming from cattle or ore strikes, there could be 50 or more men to every woman, and "love triangles" were unavoidable. Women of flexible virtue had a better chance of survival. With Hickok's easy-going history with [women], it's more likely that any involvement with Hasel drove Coe crazy while Hickok took things in stride. Coe could not have been in his right mind when he decided to take on Wild Bill single-handedly, and jealousy had as much or more to do with that suicidal act as alcohol. (Tom Clavin, interview with author, April 9, 2019)

That's all conjecture, however. No record of Jessie Hasel/Hazell has ever been located.

A better documented case happened in 1881 when Milton J. Yarberry, an alias of Arkansas-born John Armstrong (1849–1883), shot to death an express agent in Albuquerque, New Mexico Territory. Appointed constable (but considered Albuquerque's first marshal), Yarberry reportedly arrived in town with Sadie Preston and her young daughter. Preston's husband and Yarberry had been partners in a Cañon City, Colorado, saloon. When Harry Brown (ca. 1857–1881) arrived in Albuquerque, Sadie began seeing him. On March 27, 1881, Brown, Sadie and her four-year-old daughter arrived in a hack (the equivalent of today's taxicab) at a restaurant, where Yarberry waited. After escorting the mother and child into the restaurant, Yarberry talked to Brown. Moments later, shots rang out. The hack driver testified that he saw Brown reel from a bullet wound to the chest and fall to the sidewalk before Yarberry shot him twice more. Yarberry was charged with murder but was acquitted. Three months later, Yarberry shot and killed another man, 32-year-old Charles D. Campbell, who was unarmed, and again Yarberry was charged with murder. This time the charge stuck, and on February 9, 1883, Yarberry was hanged in Albuquerque. "You are going to hang Milt Yarberry," Yarberry said before he was executed. "You are going to hang him not for the murder of Campbell, but for killing Brown" ("THE LAST CHAPTER" 1883, 4).

Film historian Jon Tuska noted that before *High Noon*, "town marshals were generally honest and capable, or dishonest, or just inept. When they were honest and capable, their heroics more often than not took on a quality of the superhuman. HIGH NOON attacked this premise, showing a law man to be human and deeply troubled" (Tuska 1988, 36).

One historical reversal of the *High Noon* plot occurred in Ingalls, Oklahoma Territory, on September 1, 1893, when U.S. Marshal Evett Dumas "E. D." Nix (1861–1946) led a posse of federal lawmen into the town where "a gang of bandits, murderers, horse-thieves and train robbers [the Doolin-Dalton Gang] was making its headquarters . . . where they had many sympathizers and secret assistants" (Special Correspondent of the Daily Eagle 1893, 1).

Around 9:00 a.m., more than a dozen lawmen entered Ingalls in a buggy and two covered wagons—unlikely to arouse suspicion with homesteaders coming into the territory during the Boomer land rush. The lawmen hoped to capture or kill gang leaders Bill Doolin (1858–1896) and Bill Dalton (1866–1894) and outlaws "Tulsa Jack" Blake, "Dynamite Dick" Clifton, "Arkansas Tom" Jones, "Bitter Creek" Newcomb, "Red Buck" Weightman, and others.

When Newcomb rode to investigate one of the wagons, deputy Dick Speed fired a round from his rifle, the bullet ricocheting off Newcomb's rifle into the outlaw's leg and groin. Newcomb turned his horse and fled. From a hotel window, Jones shot Speed in the shoulder, then in the chest. A teenage bystander, mistaken for a lawman by Jones, was mortally wounded. Most of the gang remained in Ransom's saloon, where lawmen directed their fire. As bullets peppered the building, resident Leamon Myers hid in saloon's icebox. Myers recalled that "it sounded like a hail storm when the marshals turned loose on the place. The sawdust in that ice box saved my life" (Bell 2003). The outlaws inside the saloon ran to the livery, mounted their horses and galloped out of town. The marshals then focused on Jones, who, "had a complete survey of the entire town and every time a man exposed himself he picked him off. Proof is complete that Jones killed Speed and [bystander Del] Simmons and fatally wounded [deputies Tom Hueston] and [Lafe] Shadley" (Special Correspondent of the Daily Eagle 1893, 1).

The *Wichita Daily Eagle* reported the killed and wounded as: "Richard Speed, marshal, killed; Dallas Simmons, spectator, killed; T. J. Houston, marshal, killed; L. J. Shadley, marshal, killed; Owen Walker, spectator, fatally wounded; N. D. Murray, bartender in Ransom's saloon, shot in right arm; large bone fractured. . . . William Ransom, spectator, shot in calf of leg; flesh wound. . . . Frankie Briggs, a boy 14 years old, spectator, wound in left shoulder, flesh wound" (Special Correspondent of the Daily Eagle 1893, 1). Seven or eight horses and mules were reportedly killed.

"It is estimated that at least 500 shots were exchanged," the *Eagle* reported. "Ransom's saloon is riddled with bullets, and the portion of the town where the conflict occurred looks like a scene of battle" (Special Correspondent of the Daily Eagle 1893, 1). The gunfight became known as the Battle of Ingalls.

Jones, whose real name was Roy Daugherty, was sentenced to prison in Guthrie, Oklahoma. In 1915, he appeared in the movie *The Passing of the Oklahoma Outlaws*, made by former Deputy U.S. Marshal Bill Tilghman. On August 16, 1924, police officers in Joplin, Missouri, shot and killed Daugherty, suspected of robbing a bank in Asbury, Missouri. The man "whose crimes had stretched over three states . . . in the last two decades, died . . . with his boots on" at age 54 (Special to the Post-Dispatch 1924, 1).

While most Western historians like *High Noon* as a movie, they fault its premise that a lawman could find no volunteers to help him fight a gang of killers. "They knew fully well what the town was like when Frank Miller and his cohorts were having their way," Trimble said. "Many of these were Civil War veterans or had dealt with hostile Indians, and they could handle firearms" (Marshall Trimble, interview with author, April 4, 2019). Citing bank robberies in Northfield, Minnesota, by the James-Younger Gang in 1876, and in Coffeyville, Kansas, by the Dalton Gang in 1892, Trimble said: "Those farmers and town folk took down the most notorious outlaws of their time" (Marshall Trimble, interview with author, April 4, 2019). In Northfield and Coffeyville, the local lawmen didn't even have to deputize townsmen to help fight the invaders.

In the twentieth century, Americans began to fear a new kind of invader. During the Red Scare of 1919–1920, labor unrest and the immigration of southern and eastern Europeans into the United States fueled concern that communists, socialists, and anarchists might threaten the United States democracy. That hysteria was short-lived, but the end of World War II (1939–1945) and the beginning of the Nuclear Age resurrected a more intense terror.

With the Cold War (1947–1991) between the United States and the Soviet Union intensifying, the U.S. government instituted the Federal Employee Loyalty Program aimed at making sure communists, known as "Reds" for the color of the Soviet Union's flag, were not involved in the government. Joseph McCarthy (1908–1957), a Republican senator from Wisconsin, fueled fears across the nation with unsubstantiated allegations of subversive communist activity so much that the term "McCarthyism" was associated with many anti-communist tactics. Anti-communist movies such as *The Iron Curtain* (1948), *The Red Menace* (1949), *The Woman on Pier 13* (1949), and *I Was a Communist for the F.B.I.* (1951) were released, but the House of Representatives' Un-American Activities Committee began investigating communist activity in the film community. Hollywood remained "a mere sideshow in the larger struggle. No atomic secrets were sold or stolen in Beverly Hills. No acts of sabotage or espionage were alleged to have taken place" (Frankel 2017a, xi). But repercussions of what happened in Hollywood during the 1950s would be felt for a long time. Ten Hollywood veterans—writers, producers and directors—who refused to answer questions were charged with contempt, fined, sentenced to prison, and were blacklisted, unable to work in Hollywood, although some writers got around this by having other writers take credit for their screenplays. Roughly 500 people in the entertainment business, including radio and television, were blacklisted, or denied work.

In September 1951, Foreman, a former member of the American Communist Party, testified before the House committee, saying that his current movie was about "a town that died because it lacked the moral fiber to withstand aggression" (Hoberman 2011, 176). Foreman took the Fifth Amendment to avoid self-incrimination and refused to answer other questions.

Foreman began to see *High Noon* as an allegory that became "perfectly recognizable to people in Hollywood . . . because I was using dialogue that was in spirit the same thing that I was hearing—'Don't do that; the town has so much trouble; go away'" (Hoberman 2011, 207). The church scene in *High Noon* was based on Foreman's meetings with lawyers, partners, and others. "As I was writing the screenplay, it became insane," Foreman later said, "because life was mirroring art and art was mirroring life . . . I became the Gary Cooper character" (Frankel 2017b).

Staunchly conservative actor John Wayne lambasted Foreman during a private meeting between the two and then pleaded with Cooper not to back a communist like Foreman. "It was horrible to walk down Hollywood Boulevard and have acquaintances turn away to avoid the stigma of speaking to you," Foreman said (Brown 1981, 5).

Kramer reportedly bought out Foreman's interest in Kramer's production company, stripping the screenwriter of a producer's credit on *High Noon*. They never spoke again. Foreman moved to London, living there for 25 years and writing several screenplays—without receiving credit until decades after the blacklist—including for *The Bridge on the River Kwai* (1957), cowritten with the blacklisted Michael Wilson. "Foreman's screenplay for that film won an Oscar, but his name was nowhere near the screen. His official credit wasn't restored until June 1984—the day before he died" (Gray 2018).

Zinnemann didn't see *High Noon* as a Red Scare parable but as "the story of a man who must make a decision according to his conscience," he wrote. "It is a story that still happens everywhere, every day" (Zinnemann 1992, 97).

Maybe, but Wayne and director Howard Hawks (1896–1977) didn't believe that kind of story would have happened in the American West. "I didn't think a good sheriff was going to go running around town like a chicken with his head off asking for help, and finally his Quaker wife had to save him," Hawks said (McCarthy 1997, 548–549). Hawks and Wayne teamed up to make *Rio Bravo*, "an enduring cinematic rebuttal" (Frankel 2017a, 256) to *High Noon* that Warner Bros. released in 1959. In *Rio Bravo*, Wayne plays a sheriff who doesn't want help from "well-meaning amateurs" when going against a bunch of gunmen, but finds plenty of helpers, including from his gimpy old jailer, a drunken deputy, a woman gambler, and a hotel owner. "We did . . . the exact opposite of what annoyed me in *High Noon* and it worked," Hawks said, "and people liked it" (McCarthy 1997, 549).

Rio Bravo's "suspense, strong and sustained, grows out of a reverse 'High Noon' situation," *Detroit Free Press* critic Helen Bower wrote, adding that "As a 'different' Western when every possible variation would seem to have been used, 'Rio Bravo' rates bravos all around" (Bower 1959, 27).

Rio Bravo earned $5.75 million at the box office, and in 2008, Western Writers of America voted it the 24th greatest Western of all time. But while highly regarded, *Rio Bravo* didn't tarnish *High Noon's* badge of honor.

CONCLUSION

High Noon wasn't Hollywood's last word on the blacklist. In 1954, RKO released *Silver Lode*, a Western in which a killer poses as a lawman and stirs up resentment and paranoia against one of the town's leading citizens—"the parallels with McCarthyism would be clear even if the film's villain wasn't named McCarty" (Lombardi 2013, 290). Screenwriter Karen De Wolf (1909–1989), reputedly blacklisted, never had another big-screen film credit. Eventually, exposes by journalist Edward R. Murrow (1908–1965) helped lead to McCarthy's downfall, and the blacklist ended in the early 1960s. *High Noon* endured. In 2008, both the American Film Institute (AFI) and Western Writers of America (WWA) voted *High Noon* the second-best Western film of all time, with the AFI putting it behind *The Searchers* (1956) and WWA placing it behind *Shane* (1953). In *Western Movie References in American Literature*, Henryk Hoffman called *High Noon* "the most frequently quoted title among all westerns" (Hoffman 2012, 35), citing at least 15 examples, ranging from dialogue as early as 1958 in Robert Travers's novel *Anatomy of a Murder* to the title of Elmore Leonard's 1980 novel *City Primeval: High Noon in Detroit*.

High Noon remains popular for reasons beyond its political parable or its cinematic achievements.

"We have all been Will Kane at one time or another in our lives, whether it was standing up to the schoolyard bully or standing up for one's personal beliefs," Blake wrote. "*High Noon* is very much part of the American culture and American film history" (Blake 2003, 46).

FURTHER READING

Agnew, Jeremy. 2012. *The Old West in Fact and Film: History Versus Hollywood.* Jefferson, NC: McFarland & Company, Inc.

Agnew, Jeremy. 2017. *Crime, Justice and Retribution in the American West, 1850–1900.* Jefferson, NC: McFarland & Company, Inc.

Ball, Larry D. 1992. "COMMODORE PERRY OWENS: The Man behind the Legend." *The Journal of Arizona History* 33, no. 1 (Spring): pp. 27–56.

Bell, Bob Boze. 2003. "Ingalls Onslaught Turns Bloody! The Doolin-Dalton Gang vs Stillwater Marshals. *True West,* January 1, 2003. https://truewestmagazine.com/ingalls-onslaught-turns-bloody/

Blake, Michael F. 2003. *Code of Honor: The Making of Three Great American Westerns: High Noon, Shane, and The Searchers.* Lanham, MD: Taylor Trade Publishing.

"BLOODY RECORD OF BASS REEVES: FEDERAL OFFICERS MOURN THE DEATH OF DEPUTY MARSHAL, WHO KILLED 14 MEN." *Daily Ardmoreite,* January 18, 1910, p. 4.

Bower, Helen. 1959. "'Rio Bravo' Rates Big Bravo." *Detroit Free Press,* March 18, 1959, p. 27.

Brown, Peter H. 1981. "BLACKLIST: THE BLACK TALE OF TURMOIL IN FILM-LAND," *Los Angeles Times Calendar,* February 1, 1981, pp. 3–5.

Bryan, Howard. 2006. *Albuquerque Remembered.* Albuquerque: University of New Mexico Press.

Burton, Art T. 2006. *Black Gun, Silver Star: The Life and Legend of Frontier Marshal Bass Reeves.* Lincoln: University of Nebraska Press.

Cain, Del. 2000. *Lawmen of the Old West: The Good Guys.* Plano, TX: Republic of Texas Press.

Calhoun, Frederick S. 1989. *The Lawmen: United States Marshals and Their Deputies, 1789–1989.* Washington, D.C.: Smithsonian Institution Press.

Cameron, Kate. 1952. "Suspense Pervades Cooper's 'High Noon.'" *New York Daily News,* July 25, 1952, p. 40.

Clavin, Tom. 2019. *Wild Bill: The True Story of the American Frontier's First Gunfighter.* New York: St. Martin's Press.

DeArment, Robert K. 1989. *Bat Masterson: The Man and the Legend.* Norman: University of Oklahoma Press.

Dungan, Ron. 2016. "The Real Deal: Commodore Perry Owens Didn't Talk Tough, but He Was Fast with a Gun." *Arizona Republic,* April 28, 2016. https://www.azcentral.com/story/news/local/arizona-best-reads/2016/04/21/inglorious-arizona-commodore-perry-owens-arizonas-toughest-sheriff/82963496/

Ernst, Robert. 2006. *Deadly Affrays: The Violent Deaths of the US Marshals.* No City Listed: ScarletMask Enterprises.

Frankel, Glenn. 2017a. *High Noon: The Hollywood Blacklist and the Making of an American Classic.* New York: Bloomsbury.

Frankel, Glenn. 2017b. "*High Noon's* Secret Backstory: In this adaptation from his new book, *High Noon: The Hollywood Blacklist and the Making of an American Classic* (Bloomsbury), Pulitzer Prize-winning reporter Glenn Frankel reveals how power and politics shaped—and almost scuttled—a cinematic landmark." *Vanity Fair*, February 22, 2017. www.vanityfair.com/hollywood /2017/02/high-noons-secret-backstory

Gray, Chris. 2018. "Story behind 'High Noon' as Gripping as the Film Itself." *Houston Chronicle*, May 5, 2018. www.houstonchronicle.com/entertainment/books /article/Story-behind-High-Noon-as-gripping-as-the-12888793.php

Groves, Melody. 2017. "Jerked to Jesus: Albuquerque's First Town Marshal Met His Maker on an Unusual Gallows." *True West*, November 17, 2017. https:// truewestmagazine.com/jerked-old-west-outlaw/

Guinn, Jeff. 2011. *The Last Gunfight: The Real Story of the Shootout at the O.K. Corral—And How It Changed the American West*. New York: Simon & Schuster.

Hoberman, J. 2011. *An Army of Phantoms: American Movies and the Making of the Cold War*. New York: The New Press.

Hoffman, Henryk. 2012. *Western Movie References in American Literature*. Jefferson, NC: McFarland & Company, Inc.

"Judge and the Coons, The." 1877. *Dodge City Times*, August 11, 1877, p. 1.

Kirk, Hazel. 1952. "Suspense Well Sustained in Film 'High Noon.'" *Newark Advocate*, September 8, 1952, p. 9.

Knowlton, Christopher. 2017. *Cattle Kingdom: The Hidden History of the Cowboy West*. New York: Houghton Mifflin Harcourt.

Kramer, Stanley. 1997. *A Mad, Mad, Mad, Mad World: A Life in Hollywood*. New York: Harcourt Brace.

"THE LAST CHAPTER in Milton J. Yarberry's Eventful Career. HE SHOWS THEM HOW TO DIE GAME. The Trip from Santa Fe to Albuquerque on a Special Train. HIS LAST MOMENTS ON EARTH. His Speech Delivered from the Gallows Just before the Death Signal. His Denial of Ever Killing Anyone before Living in Albuquerque. LAST NIGHT ON EARTH." *Albuquerque Morning Journal*, February 10, 1883, p. 4.

Lombardi, Frederic. 2013. *Allan Dwan and the Rise and Decline of the Hollywood Studios*. Jefferson, NC: McFarland & Company, Inc.

Lubet, Steven. 2004. *Murder in Tombstone: The Forgotten Trial of Wyatt Earp*. New Haven, CT: Yale University Press.

McCarthy, Todd. 1997. *Howard Hawks: The Grey Fox of Hollywood*. New York: Grove Press.

Morgan, Thad. 2018. "Was the Real Lone Ranger a Black Man? The amazing true story of Bass Reeves, the freed slave who protected the Wild West." *Wild West*, February 1, 2018. https://www.history.com/news/bass-reeves-real-lone-ranger -a-black-man

"MURDER, THE." 1878. *Dodge City Times*, April 13, 1878.

Murray, Robert K. 19. *Red Scare: A Study in National Hysteria, 1919–1920*. Minneapolis: University of Minnesota Press.

Nott, Robert. 2013. "High Noon, Low Budget." *Roundup Magazine*, December 2013, p. 40.

Rosa, Joseph G. 1974. *They Called Him Wild Bill: The Life and Adventures of James Butler Hickok*. Norman: University of Oklahoma Press.

"SAD NEWS. Marshal Masteston [sic] Hurried Hence by a Murderer's Hand. A PUBLIC CALAMITY." 1878. *Ford County Globe*, April 16, 1878, p. 2.

Scheuer, Philip K. 1952. "GARY HITS TARGET ON STROKE OF NOON." *Los Angeles Times*, August 14, 1952, p. Part III, 8.

Schillinberg, Wm. B. 2009. *Dodge City: The Early Years, 1872–1886*. Norman: The Arthur H. Clark Company.

Shirley, Glenn. 1968. *Law West of Fort Smith: A History of Frontier Justice in Indian Territory, 1834–1896*. Lincoln: University of Nebraska Press.

"SHOOTING AFFRAY. Two Men Killed." 1871. *Abilene Chronicle*, October 12, 1871, p. 3.

Slotkin, Richard. 1993. *Gunfighter Nation: The Myth of the Frontier in Twentieth-Century America*. New York: Harper Perennial.

Sonnichsen, C. L. 2015. "Bean, Roy." *Handbook of Texas*. https://tshaonline.org /handbook/online/articles/fbe08

Soodalter, Ron. 2018. "The Day the Bad Guys Won: Echoes from the Battle of Ingalls Continue to Reverberate throughout History." *Oklahoma Today Magazine*, July/August 2018.

Special Correspondent of the Daily Eagle. 1893. "THE BATTLE OF INGALLS. Details of the Conflict Between Federal Marshals and Outlaws." *Wichita Daily Eagle*, September 5, 1893, p. 1.

Special to the Post-Dispatch. 1924. "BANK ROBBER, ALLEGED SLAYER OF 18 MEN, KILLED: Roy Daugherty, with Record of Crime in Three States, Shot in Hiding Place in Joplin." *St. Louis Post-Dispatch*, August 17, 1924, p. 1.

Thomas, Bob. 1953. "Gary Cooper, Shirley Booth Win '52 Hollywood 'Oscars.'" *Florence Morning News*, March 20, 1953, p. 1.

Trimble, Marshall. 2016. "The Shoot Out in Holbrook." *True West*, August 4, 2016. https://truewestmagazine.com/the-shoot-out-in-holbrook/

Tuska, Jon. 1988. *The American West in Film: Critical Approaches to the Western*. Lincoln: University of Nebraska Press.

Ward, Henry. 1952. "'High Noon' Classed Tops among Westerns: Gary Cooper in Best Role in Gripping Harris Film." *Pittsburgh Press*, July 28, 1952, p. 6.

Weinraub, Bernard. 2002. "'High Noon,' High Dudgeon." *New York Times*, April 18, 2002. www.nytimes.com/2002/04/18/movies/high-noon-high-dudgeon .html

Zinnemann, Fred. 1992. *Fred Zinnemann: An Autobiography*. London: Bloomsbury.

Chapter 5

The Searchers (1956)

In 1956, with the civil rights movement heating up and filmmakers pushing the boundaries of what movies could depict, Warner Bros. released *The Searchers*, a hard-edged film in which the Comanche leader and the white Texas hero are driven by hatred. Since the silent era, most Hollywood Westerns depicting fights between warring Native Americans and white settlers or soldiers followed the tropes shown in *The Battle of Elderbush Gulch* (1913), directed by D. W. Griffith (1875–1948): savage, drunken, scalping Native Americans who murder mothers and babies; courageous whites fighting to protect innocent women and children; when all looks lost, a gun placed against a woman's head to save her from that fate worse than death; the U.S. cavalry charging to the rescue; and the happy ending with the warriors defeated. *The Searchers*, however, was vastly different, rarely sympathetic to white settlers or Native Americans. More than 60 years after its release, *The Searchers* remains dark, raw, and intense.

The movie opens in 1868, when Confederate veteran Ethan Edwards (John Wayne, 1907–1979) returns to his brother's Texas ranch after end of the Civil War (1861–1865). When Texas Rangers led by Reverend Captain Samuel Johnston Clayton (Ward Bond, 1903–1960) arrive the next morning, needing volunteers to pursue Native Americans who have stolen cattle, Edwards volunteers and rides out with young Martin Pauley (Jeffrey Hunter, 1926–1969), a part-Cherokee orphan who has been living with the Edwards family after Comanches killed his parents. The theft of the cattle, however, is a ruse to pull men away from the ranches, and the Comanches attack and burn the Edwards ranch, murdering Ethan's brother, sister-in-law, and nephew and abducting the two daughters. Clayton leads a party in pursuit, but after being attacked by the large force of Comanches, Clayton tells Edwards, "This is a job for a company of Rangers, or it's a job for one or two men. Right now we're too many, an' not enough."

Edwards, Pauley, and Brad Jorgensen (Harry Carey Jr., 1921–2012), beau of the kidnapped Lucy Edwards (Pippa Scott, 1935–), continue the search, but when Jorgensen learns that the Comanches have raped and murdered Lucy, he charges after the Comanches in a camp and is killed. Edwards is a hard man. Driven by revenge and hatred, he shoots out a dead Comanche's eyes, takes scalps, and even kills buffalo just so the meat won't feed the Native Americans during the winter. Pauley is the movie's conscience: young, emotional, and "wonderfully callow" (Crowther 1956, 21). Together, the two keep searching for five years before finding the younger daughter, Debbie (Natalie Wood, 1938–1981), in a Comanche camp. Now in her teens, Debbie has become one of the wives of the white-hating chief named Scar (Henry Brandon, 1912–1990). By this time, the Indian-hating Edwards is ready to kill his niece, believing that she has been disgraced after living with the Comanches all these years. Pauley thinks differently, even though Debbie does not want to leave with them. Before Edwards can murder Debbie, he is wounded by Comanches, and Pauley saves Edwards's life. Debbie's mind changes, however, after Pauley sneaks into another Comanche camp some time later just before Clayton, Edwards, and a party of Rangers and U.S. Army soldiers attack the Comanches. Pauley kills Scar just before the attack. In the confusion of battle, Debbie spots Edwards, who chases her into a cave. But unable to kill his blood kin, he returns Debbie to the Jorgensen home, where the door closes as Edwards wanders away.

Late in 1954, millionaire Cornelius "Sonny" Vanderbilt Whitney (1899–1992) and filmmaking pioneer Merian C. Cooper (1893–1973), creator of *King Kong* (1933), formed C. V. Whitney Pictures, Inc., with Cooper becoming vice president in charge of production. Whitney, who had invested in *Gone with the Wind* (1939), wanted to turn *The Valiant Virginians*, a Civil War novel by James Warner Bellah (1899–1976), into a movie. Cooper had helped produced *Fort Apache* (1947), *She Wore a Yellow Ribbon* (1949), and *Rio Grande* (1950), the "Cavalry Trilogy" directed by John Ford (1894–1973), starring Wayne and based on Bellah's short stories. Cooper talked Whitney into starting with a movie that would be less expensive than a Civil War epic like *The Valiant Virginians*, and the two men agreed to make *The Searchers*, based on a novel published by Harper & Bros. that the *Saturday Evening Post* was serializing as *The Avenging Texans*. Author Alan LeMay (1899–1964), burned out from his dealings as a screenwriter and never a fan of Hollywood's collaborative approach to screenwriting, facetiously told his son that he sold the film rights "with the stipulation that he didn't have to write the screenplay and he didn't have to see the film" (LeMay 2012, 164). Former *New York Times* film critic Frank Nugent (1908–1965), who had often worked with Ford, was hired to write the script.

LeMay's first Western novel, *Painted Ponies* (1927), had been sympathetic to the Northern Cheyenne Indians. LeMay took a different approach in *The*

Searchers, writing a high school student: "I thought it was time that some-body showed that in the case of the Texans, at least, there were two sides to it, and that the settlers had understandable reasons to be sore" (LeMay 2012, 171). Set after the Civil War, *The Searchers* follows Amos Edwards and young Martin Pauley on their five-year quest to rescue Edwards's niece, Debbie, kidnapped by Comanches during a murder raid in Texas. Scoring stellar reviews, *The Searchers* seemed to be the kind of Western Ford needed after a string of misfires that had followed his Academy Award–winning *The Quiet Man* (1952). "He needed a hit badly," film historian Michael F. Blake wrote, "something that would prove him to be at the top of his game" (Blake 2003, 142).

Wayne, who had made several films directed by Ford, was cast as Ethan (a name change from the novel's Amos) Edwards. Wood, who had received an Oscar nomination for best supporting actress in *Rebel Without a Cause* (1955), played Debbie Edwards as a young teen. When Walt Disney (1901–1966) would not loan *Davy Crockett* star Fess Parker (1924–2010) to play Martin Pauley, Ford hired Hunter. Robert Wagner (1930–) asked to play Martin, but Ford mercilessly told him no.

More characters' names were changed, and Nugent strayed from LeMay's novel in other areas. Amos Edwards is killed when he mistakes a young Comanche woman for Debbie in the novel, but Ethan Edwards survives in the film. Debbie is adopted as Scar's daughter in the novel but becomes one of the chief's wives in the film. LeMay also bluntly stated that Amos Edwards had been in love with his brother's wife, while Nugent took a subtle approach such as when Martha (Dorothy Jordan, 1906–1988) lovingly strokes Ethan's Confederate greatcoat before storing it. LeMay and Nugent both have Ethan remaining silent when he first reaches his brother's burning ranch. In the movie, though, Wayne shouts Martha's name. It is unclear if Wayne ad-libbed the line or whether Ford changed the script before shooting the scene. Ford "very often created a scene right at the moment," Carey said. "He was always changing the script. . . . So I'm not positive, but I'm pretty sure that's what happened" (Harry Carey Jr., interview with author, May 15, 2006).

Wayne definitely ad-libbed the final scene in which Ethan, outside the house, watches the celebration of Debbie's return. Spotting Olive Carey (1896–1998), Harry Carey Jr.'s mother who played Brad Jorgensen's mother, behind the camera, Wayne grabbed his right elbow with his left hand, a pose Olive's husband and Carey's father, actor Harry Carey Sr. (1878–1947), was known for in his Western movies. When the younger Carey saw the finished film, "I started to cry," he said (Harry Carey Jr., interview with author, May 15, 2006).

Principal photography began in mid-June 1955 at Monument Valley in the Navajo Nation on the Utah-Arizona border. Navajo Indians were hired to play Comanche extras and for other off-camera jobs, earning the tribe $35,000. Other locations included Mexican Hat, Utah; Edmonton, Alberta;

Aspen and Gunnison, Colorado; Bronson Canyon near Hollywood; and RKO-Pathe Studios in Culver City, California. The budget was $2.5 million.

Unlike other Ford Westerns, the mood on *The Searchers* set turned serious. "Duke [Wayne's nickname] was into that role so much that even off the screen he seemed to carry the part of Ethan with him," Carey recalled. "He didn't kid around as much, and he didn't joke and tease around" (Harry Carey Jr., interview with author, May 15, 2006). Shooting ended August 13 after 56 days, a week over schedule.

The Searchers opened in May 1956 to mostly positive reviews. Leonard Mendlowitz of the *Pittsburgh Sun-Telegraph* called it "far and away the best Western the stalwart Wayne has ever made" (Mendlowitz 1956, 10); and the *Cincinnati Enquirer's* E. B. Radcliffe said, "It is the best Western of them all, not excepting 'Shane,' 'High Noon,' 'The Westerner,' 'Stagecoach,' 'Cimarron' and 'The Covered Wagon'" (Radcliffe 1956, 18).

"The New York film critics are not among John Wayne's most avid fans, but he took them completely into camp in 'The Searchers,'" the *Los Angeles Times'* Richard Griffith reported (Griffith 1956, Part I, 36). But the movie didn't receive all raves. While the *New York Times'* Bosley Crowther said it was "as brashly entertaining as they come," he also wrote, "Episode is piled upon episode, climax upon climax and corpse upon corpse until the whole thing appears to be taking a couple of turns around the course" (Crowther 1956, 21). *Variety's* Ronald Holloway called it "eyefilling and impressive" but also found it "[o]verlong," "repetitious," and "somewhat disappointing. There is a feeling that it could have been so much more" (Holloway 1956). Gee Mitchell of the *Dayton Daily News* said *The Searchers* "doesn't come up to expectations" (Mitchell 1956, 21).

The Searchers earned more than $5 million, becoming one of the top 20 moneymakers of 1956, but it received no big awards and just one major nomination from the Directors Guild of America (Ford lost to George Stevens for *Giant*). C. V. Whitney Pictures never made *The Valiant Virginians* and produced only two other movies, *The Missouri Traveler* (1958) and *The Young Land* (1959), "not financial triumphs, but they had a modest critical success, and they helped to appease [Whitney's] desire to glorify the early pioneer spirit" (Wright 1961).

The Searchers soon faded from memory, "exiled," historian Glenn Frankel noted, "by the early 1960s to the relatively new medium of television, where it received an occasional sowing, cut and pasted to coexist with commercials inside a two-hour frame" (Frankel 2014, 316). That did not surprise Harry Carey Jr. "I wasn't sure about *The Searchers* because it was so heavy and dark in spots," he said (Harry Carey Jr., interview with author, May 15, 2006).

In the 1970s, however, the movie's reputation underwent reevaluation. Younger filmmakers such as Martin Scorsese (1942–) and Steven Spielberg (1946–) cited its influence on their careers. French critics began praising it.

The National Film Preservation Board added *The Searchers* to the National Film Registry in 1989, and in 2008, the American Film Institute voted it the best American Western. Over the years it has continued to be polled as one of, and often the, best Western movie ever made, "revered as one of the great American films," Ford and Wayne biographer Scott Eyman wrote, "with a resonance that dwarfs the official classics of its year—*Around the World in 80 Days* and *Giant*" (Eyman 2000, 450).

"It's held in great esteem, and it's a marvelous film," Carey said. "Wayne said it's the best thing [Ford] ever did, and he was a pretty good judge of pictures" (Harry Carey Jr., interview with author, May 15, 2006).

HISTORICAL BACKGROUND

Conflicts between European settlers and indigenous peoples of what is now the United States began as early as 1622, when Powhatan Indians rose up against English colonists on the James River in Virginia, killing roughly 347 white settlers, and the Peqout War (1636–1638) in New England might have claimed as many as 1,000 casualties among the colonists and Native American allies, with more than 1,500 Pequots killed or enslaved. Conflicts in the American Southwest and Mexico began even earlier, during the Spanish campaign against the Aztecs in 1519–1521. Even focusing only on the period of the westward expansion of the United States from 1850 to 1890, the "Indian Wars," as they came to be known, had extensive casualties. In a study by historian Gregory Michno, the number of killed, wounded, and captured for that period totaled 21,586—and that was just for military engagements (6,596 civilians and military personnel; 14,990 Native Americans). Other figures, including nonmilitary engagements, have placed the number of combined deaths anywhere from 5,000 to 500,000.

Before white settlement, native tribes often went to war, and the reasons often were similar to what led to the Native Americans' later wars against whites. A Cheyenne leader once explained why his people fought the Crows: "We stole the hunting grounds of the Crows because they were the best. We wanted more room" (Cozzens 2016, 9).

In August 1854, a Mormon settler's cow was killed and butchered at a Lakota encampment near Fort Laramie, Wyoming. The Mormon said the Lakotas stole the cow. Lakota leader Conquering Bear said the puny cow had stampeded into the village and was killed by Straight Foretop, a visiting Minneconju who had killed the cow as it ran wildly through the camp. The settler complained to soldiers at Fort Laramie. Conquering Bear pleaded on behalf of his own people and his guest. Satisfactory terms could not be met, so Conquering Bear returned to his village. Second Lieutenant J. L. Grattan, a recent graduate from the U.S. Military Academy at West Point, was ordered to arrest Straight Foretop and get payment for the cow. Grattan left with a force of 29 soldiers, two cannon, and a drunken interpreter who was nowhere close to being fluent in Lakota.

On August 19, 1854, Conquering Bear met the party outside the camp and offered to give the Mormon a mule for the cow, but Grattan insisted on arresting Straight Foretop. The offer was increased to five horses. As Conquering Bear walked back to the village, soldiers opened fire with rifles and cannon, killing and wounding a number of Lakotas. Conquering Bear fell mortally wounded. Enraged Lakotas swarmed the command, killing all 31 men. That incident led to an on-and-off war between whites and Lakotas that ended with the massacre at Wounded Knee in present-day South Dakota on December 29, 1890, in which roughly 150 Lakotas—almost half women and children—were killed and 14 U.S. soldiers were awarded the Medal of Honor.

In January 1861, Apaches stole 20 cattle and kidnapped a 12-year-old boy, whose stepfather accused Cochise, leader of the Chiricahua Apaches, of the crime. Second Lieutenant George Bascom and 54 soldiers were ordered to find Cochise and return the cattle and boy. When word reached Cochise, he met with Bascom and even brought members of his family with him. Bascom demanded the return of the beef and boy, and when Cochise said he had neither but would see what he could do to find them, Bascom said he would hold Cochise and his family hostage. Cochise was slightly wounded after a daring escape, but his family remained Bascom's prisoners. Cochise took his own hostages, but when negotiations failed, and more soldiers arrived, Cochise ordered the hostages killed, and he left. In retribution, the army executed six male Apache prisoners and left them hanging from tree limbs to rot. "Thus the seeds were sewn for twenty-five years of intermittent and hideous warfare between Whites and the Apache, all of it fueled by perpetual acts of deceit" (Blake 2006, 24).

In 1864, Colorado Governor John Evans (1814–1897) picked a Methodist elder nicknamed the "Fighting Parson," John Chivington (1821–1894), a Union hero at the 1862 Civil War battle at Glorieta Pass in New Mexico, to lead a volunteer regiment and follow Evans's proclamation that gave citizens the right to "kill and destroy hostile Indians" (Blake 2006, 32). Chivington reportedly said, "I . . . believe it is right and honorable to use any means under God's heaven to kill Indians. Kill and scalp all, big and little; nits make lice" (Boggs 2014b). On November 29, 1864, Chivington's troops attacked a Cheyenne and Arapaho encampment in which Cheyenne peace chief Black Kettle had raised a U.S. flag and a white flag for protection. When the volunteer soldiers attacked, White Antelope, nearly 80 years old, and Standing in the Water, thought to have been in his 60s, walked out to meet the soldiers, only to be shot down. The massacre that followed left about 200 Native Americans dead. Historian Louis Kraft said:

> Volunteer troops used small children for target practice, an unborn child was cut from its dead mother's body and scalped, three women and five children

prisoners were executed by a lieutenant as their guards backed away in horror and while they begged for their lives. . . . Penises, vaginas and breasts were cut from the dead and displayed as ornaments and trophies. (Boggs 2014b)

Black Kettle survived the attack only to be killed with his wife during George Armstrong Custer's surprise attack on a village on the Washita River in what is now western Oklahoma in 1868. Although Chivington and his men were praised as heroes in Denver and elsewhere in Colorado, the Sand Creek massacre was condemned in Washington, D.C., and other places.

Other Native American tribes suffered experiences similar to those of the Lakotas, Apaches, and Cheyennes. Even General George Crook (1828–1890), who led military campaigns against several Native American tribes, sympathized with the Native Americans, saying:

> [W]hen Indians see their wives and children starving and their last source of supplies cut off, they go to war. And then we are sent out there to kill them. It is an outrage. All tribes tell the same story. They are surrounded on all sides, the game is destroyed or driven away, they are left to starve, and there remains one thing for them to do—fight while they can. Our treatment of the Indian is an outrage. (Cozzens 2016, 7)

In Texas, the main setting for *The Searchers*, the Comanches had been the dominant tribe long before the United States brought what had been an independent republic into the Union in 1845. "No tribe in the history of North America had more to say about the nation's destiny," historian S. C. Gwynne wrote (Gwynne 2010, 12). Typically small and short, the Comanches "were not handsomely proportioned" (Fehrenbach 1994, 33). But few Native American tribes could match their horsemanship. They controlled much of the Southwestern territories and consistently fought off incursions from Mexican, Spanish, French, Texan, and U.S. forces.

Never a large tribe—the highest estimate at roughly 20,000 at their peak in the mid-1800s and other estimates at between 5,000 and 7,000—the Comanches controlled much of western Texas, eastern New Mexico, what is now western Oklahoma, southern Kansas, and southeastern Colorado before the 1860s—a region the Spanish called *Comanchería*. "We probably held this place for almost 200 years ourselves," said Comanche Nocona Burgess, great-great grandson of Quanah Parker (ca. 1845–1911), the last chief of the Comanches (Nocona Burgess, interview with author, February 24, 2004). They were also a tribe of warriors, leading raids across the Southern Plains and into Mexico. "Comanches are fun-loving and real happy-go-lucky people, but they're aggressive almost to a fault sometimes," Burgess said (Nocona Burgess, interview with author, February 24, 2004).

Sarah Ann Horn, an Englishwoman kidnapped by Comanches in 1836, saw how loving her captors were to each other but how brutal they could be to non-Comanches. "The strength of their attachment to each other, and the demonstration they give of the same, even to the dividing of the last morsel with each other upon the point of starvation, might put many professed Christians to blush," she recalled. "But they are just the reverse of all this to all the world outside" (Frankel 2014, 41). Typically, the Comanches showed no mercy.

> The dead were mutilated horribly. Arms and legs were severed, genitals invariably smashed or amputated. Female breasts were sliced off, and corpses of both sexes were eviscerated and decapitated. Bloody entrails were burned if there was time. (Fehrenbach 1994, 77)

But much of what white settlers would consider barbaric butchery was, to the Comanches, not only vengeance but also a way to hurt their enemies in the afterlife. Mutilations would be carried with the dead throughout eternity, and those terribly mutilated would be destroyed, becoming ghosts, "ominous shades who came out with the rising moon" (Fehrenbach 1994, 54).

Their downfall came after the Civil War when the U.S. Army pushed back hard against Comanche resistance, disease began to take its toll, and white hunters slaughtered vast herds of American bison, more commonly known (and misidentified) as buffalo, for their hides.

Military forts on the Texas frontier that had been abandoned during the Civil War were reoccupied. Other posts, such as Fort Richardson near Jacksboro, Fort Concho in San Angelo, and Fort Griffin near Albany, were built and manned with troops. Civil War veterans serving in regiments out west were battle-hardened, and Ulysses S. Grant (1822–1885), William T. Sherman (1820–1891), and Philip Sheridan (1831–1888)—"these grim warriors who beat the South" (Boggs 2010)—commanded that army. Four army regiments, often ignored by Hollywood filmmakers, were manned with African Americans. After the Civil War, the 9th and 10th Cavalry and the 24th and 25th Infantry were filled with African American enlisted men and almost always commanded by white officers. In 1877, former slave Henry Ossian Flipper (1856–1940) became the first African American graduate of West Point and served as a second lieutenant with the 10th Cavalry in Texas and Indian Territory but was court-martialed and dismissed from the service in 1882.

With the swelling of white migration across Native American lands, diseases such as cholera, smallpox, and measles took a deadly toll on the Comanches and other tribes. According to Burgess, "They didn't beat us on the battlefield. They beat us with smallpox" (Nocona Burgess, interview with author, February 24, 2004). Gwynne noted:

> So you had disease, and the sheer U.S. military capabilities and the death of the buffalo. But to me, once the last buffalo is shot, there's no such thing as a Plains Indian. There can't be. What are they supposed to do? They are then forced to trade cattle for white man's goods. That's all they can do, and increasingly it

was going to be harder for them to steal cattle. It's the end of the Plains warriors. (Boggs 2010)

After the 1867 Treaty of Medicine Lodge, some Comanche bands began moving onto reservations in the western part of Indian Territory (now Oklahoma), but not all Comanches were willing to give up their way of life. Before signing the treaty, Comanche chief Ten Bears said:

> You said that you wanted to put us upon a reservation, to build us houses and make us medicine lodges. I do not want them. I was born upon the prairie, where the wind blew free and there was nothing to break the light of the sun. I was born where there were no enclosures and everything drew a free breath. I want to die there and not within walls. . . . When I was at Washington the Great Father told me that all the Comanche land was ours, and that no one should hinder us in living upon it. So, why do you ask us to leave the rivers, and the sun, and the wind, and lie in houses? Do not ask us to give up the buffalo for the sheep. (Wallace and Hoebel 1986, 283)

Once numbering in the tens of millions, the American bison began to be hunted by white men after developments in the leather industry made bison hides valuable. In the 1870s, 40,000 hides left Dodge City, Kansas, daily. By the turn of the century, bison were on the verge of extinction. Comanches and other tribes on the Great Plains depended on bison for clothing, shelter, food, and tools. Seeing their livelihood being slaughtered, the tribes retaliated. In 1874, a large force of Comanches, Cheyennes, and Kiowas attacked a camp of hide hunters at Adobe Walls in the Texas Panhandle but was driven off by the hunters' high-powered, long-range buffalo rifles. The U.S. Army sent out forces commanded by Nelson A. Miles (1839–1925) and Ranald S. Mackenzie (1840–1889) to push the warring tribes back onto the reservations. A surprise attack on a large Native American camp in Palo Duro Canyon, south of present-day Amarillo, Texas, drove off the tribes, and Mackenzie ordered the slaughter of some 1,400 to 2,000 captured ponies. Slowly, the warring tribes began to surrender. On June 2, 1875, 407 of the last warring Comanches, led by Quanah, surrendered to Mackenzie a few miles west of Fort Sill. Historian T.R. Fehrenbach quotes the Smithsonian Institute's W. T. Hornaday as saying "perhaps the most gigantic task ever undertaken on this continent in the line of game slaughter was the extermination of the bison in the great pasturage region by the hide-hunters" (Fehrenbach 1994, 522).

Some Comanches left the reservation to fight buffalo hunters, and a few joined Apache bands in Mexico, but the Comanche wars were over in Texas. By 1900, after the 1892 Jerome Agreement had broken up the reservations in Oklahoma by allotting each Comanche, Kiowa, and Apache man, woman, and child 160 acres, the Comanche population was 1,499.

DEPICTION AND CULTURAL CONTEXT

In *The Searchers*, when Samuel Johnston Clayton, part-time clergyman and full-time captain of the Texas Rangers, first arrives at the Edwards ranch, he's recruiting volunteers to ride with him to track down cattle stolen by Native Americans. Ethan Edwards agrees to ride the place of his brother, Aaron, but after refusing to be sworn in, Clayton asks if Edwards is wanted for any crime, noting, "You fit a lot of descriptions" on warrants. That sounds accurate enough, except that the year is 1868.

Texas Ranger historian Mike Cox explained that while the Texas Rangers were well known at the time, for the first half-century of their existence, they were not the law enforcement agency that everyone remembers today. At first, the Rangers solely focused on combatting Native Americans and Mexican raiders. The Rangers received their official law enforcement powers in 1874, "So, in the case of *The Searchers*, while it is entirely plausible that the captain would be seeking volunteers to go after Indians and the cattle they stole, he wouldn't have worried about someone on the dodge. All he cared about was whether a fellow could ride, shoot straight and, as they used to say, 'hand sand'" (Mike Cox, interview with the author, March 26, 2019).

When Stephen F. Austin (1793–1836) led Anglo-American settlers into the Mexican province of Texas in 1821, he realized that the newcomers needed more than the small company of men the Mexican government provided for protection against hostile Native Americans. On August 23, 1823, Austin authorized the formation of a unit of "ten men . . . to act as rangers for the common defense" that would be paid $15 a month in land, not cash (Cox 1991, 2). In 1835, lawmakers authorized a Rangers force of 56 men in three companies. After Texas won its independence from Mexico in 1836, the Rangers fought several battles against the Comanches, and when Texas joined the United States, Rangers fought with distinction in the ensuing Mexican War (1846–1848).

After the Civil War, the Rangers were shoved aside as the State Police and U.S. troops were in charge of law enforcement and protection against hostile Native Americans until 1874. At that time, with Texas officially back in the Union and the Democrats returning to power in the state capital, the Texas Rangers were reorganized. A Special Force of Rangers led by Captain Leander H. McNelly (1844–1877) was recruited to put an end to lawlessness in Dewitt County and then in the Nueces Strip. Another Ranger force, the Frontier Battalion, led by Major John B. Jones (1834–1881), used six companies, each with 75 Rangers, to fight Native Americans and outlaws. In 1935, the Rangers became part of the Texas Department of Public Safety. Today, the division includes 166 commissioned Rangers and 68 support personnel. The Rangers "left an indelible mark on history," historian Robert M. Utley wrote. "They fully merit their niche in the annals of Texas and the nation" (Utley 2002, 302).

THE TEXAS RANGERS BADGE

Ward Bond's costume as the Texas Rangers captain in *The Searchers* includes a shield badge. Today, the Rangers are known for a "star-in-wheel" badge, but badges did not become official until 1900. At some point before that, Rangers started cutting a star into a Mexican silver coin that was soft enough that it could be carved by hand. In the 1800s, the badge had "double symbolism: Since Texas had just been wrested from Mexico by Anglo-Americans and native-born Tejanos, a star cut from a Mexican coin represented a near perfect metaphor" (Cox 1997, 269).

Source

Cox, Mike. 1997. *Texas Ranger Tales: Stories That Need Telling*. Plano: Republic of Texas Press.

Texas Rangers in *The Searchers* wear no uniforms, and few have badges—all accurate depictions for the time. In the novel and film, the Rangers are respected by most of the community. "Rangers were a good thing," LeMay wrote, "and there ought to be more of them. Sometimes you needed a company of them badly" (LeMay 1956, 132). That's certainly how most law-abiding citizens felt in post–Civil War Texas. "One company of Texas rangers is worth two regiments of U.S. troops," the *Texas Republican* in the east Texas town of Marshall declared ("TEXAS ITEMS" 1868, 2).

Raids like the one Scar leads on the Edwards ranch, in which three family members are killed and two girls abducted, were not uncommon. The most famous of these happened at Parker's Fort near present-day Groesbeck, Texas, on May 19, 1836, less than a month after the Texas army under General Sam Houston (1793–1863) had defeated the Mexican army of Antonio López de Santa Anna (1794–1876) at the Battle of San Jacinto near present-day Houston to win Texas's independence. Late in 1833, John Parker and three of his sons, part of a group of Illinois Baptists who had been granted permission to settle in Texas, then part of Mexico, began constructing a wooden stockade in a remote region near the Navasota River. Named Parker's Fort, the palisade structure was completed in March 1834. Parker family members and others moved into the fort, which included corner blockhouses and log cabins, and began clearing the land to farm. Gwynne noted that the region was a dangerous place in 1836.

On that fateful morning, most of the men were working in the cornfields when a large party of mostly Comanches, with some Kiowas and Caddoes, rode up to the fort. One of the Indians waved a dirty white flag. Benjamin Parker walked through the open gate, unfathomably left unsecured, to talk to the Native Americans. Returning, he told his brother Silas that the visitors said they wanted meat and directions to the nearest watering hole. Benjamin didn't believe them, but by that time, there was no time to close the gate. He walked back to the warriors in a vain attempt to negotiate or to buy time for those left inside the fort. Almost immediately, he was clubbed, pierced with lances, riddled with arrows, and scalped. With "voices that seemed to reach the very skies," the attackers rushed inside the compound (Gwynne 2010, 23).

Silas Parker managed to fire one shot before he was overwhelmed, killed, and scalped. Elderly John and Sallie Parker and a widow named Elizabeth Kellogg fled through a low exit at the back of the fort. Samuel Frost and his son Robert were killed at the gate. Rachel Plummer, running with her 14-month-old son, James, in her arms for the back exit, was captured. Others managed to hide in the woods, but outside the fort, raiders rode down the fleeing Parkers and Kellogg, and they stripped them, beat the man to death, cut off his genitals, and scalped him. They pinned his wife to the ground with a lance and threw Kellogg on the back of a horse. By that time, the settlers working the cornfields came running with their rifles. The Native Americans rode away with five captives: Kellogg, Plummer and her young son, and six-year-old John Parker and his sister, nine-year-old Cynthia Ann. Left behind were five dead men and several wounded women, including Sallie Parker, who pulled the lance out of her body. She "was of a tough breed, and lived" (Fehrenbach 1983, 450).

Elizabeth Kellogg and Rachel Plummer were ransomed after three months and eighteen months in captivity, respectively. Rachel Plummer died in 1839. James Plummer and John Parker were ransomed in 1842, by then 8 and 13 years old and speaking no English. James Plummer died of pneumonia in 1862 while serving with the Confederate army in Little Rock, Arkansas. John Parker, according to legend, had trouble readapting to living with whites and, by one account, was sent by his mother in the early 1850s to find his sister. He might have died of smallpox while living with the Comanches, or he might have died in 1915 in Mexico, where he had become a rancher.

Cynthia Ann Parker's story grew into one of Texas's most enduring stories. Living with the Comanches, she married Peta Nocona, chief of the Noconi band, and bore him two sons, Quanah and Pecos, and a daughter, Topsannah. On December 18, 1860, Texas Rangers attacked a Comanche village on the Pease River, and discovered that one of the captives had blue eyes. Her uncle, Isaac Parker, identified her and brought her home. Parker had long searched for Cynthia and John, as had James Parker, Rachel Plummer's father, with neither having any success. Cynthia Ann Parker died most likely around 1870, and her oldest son, Quanah, become leader of the last band of Comanches to surrender to white authorities, and as the last chief of the Comanches, he helped his people adjust to reservation life. He also took his mother's last name, becoming known as Quanah Parker.

Although many historians compare *The Searchers* with the Cynthia Ann Parker story, LeMay's son argued that the abductions of Sarah White, Anna

Brewster Morgan, and Susanna Alderdice "were better prototypes for Debbie Edwards than Cynthia Ann Parker" (LeMay 2012, 171). After all, Cynthia Ann was taken from a palisade fort that housed many families when Texas was a republic—more than 30 years before *The Searchers* was set. Cheyenne Indians took White, 17, off her farm in Cloud County, Kansas, in September 1868—the same year *The Searchers* opens. About a month later, Lakotas abducted Morgan, a newlywed, off her farm in Ottawa County, Kansas. Both were exchanged for captured tribal chiefs, but Morgan gave birth to a son, fathered by an Native American, a few months after the exchange and is said to have died in an asylum. "After I came back," Morgan told a neighbor in 1872, "the road seemed rough, and I often wished they had never found me" (Stratton 1982, 125).

Alan LeMay, whose grandparents settled in Kansas in the 1870s, researched more than just the Parker raid of 1836 before writing *The Searchers*. "I have dug up some 64 cases of white children kidnapped in this period," he wrote, "but I believe these to be only a small minority of the actual total" (LeMay 2012, 171).

Alderdice was staying with friends with her baby daughter and three sons while her husband, Tom, was away, when Tall Bull led several Cheyennes on a raid in western Kansas. Alderdice tried to flee with her family, but she and her eight-month-old daughter were captured; two of the boys were killed and the third gravely wounded. Tom Alderdice began searching for his wife and daughter and eventually met George Armstrong Custer at an army post. Custer's wife, Libbie, described Alderdice "as nearly a madman as can be" with "eyes wild, frenzied, and sunken with grief, his voice weak with suffering" (Custer 1890, 224). Alderdice provided a description of the captives and continued his search, eventually finding the body of his baby daughter, who had been strangled to death with a bowstring. On July 11, 1869, Major Eugene Carr of the 5th Cavalry led a charge of soldiers and civilian and Pawnee scouts into Tall Bull's camp at Summit Springs near present-day Sterling, Colorado. The battle, which lasted less than three hours, left 52 Indians, including Tall Bull, dead; and 17 Indian women and children were captured. When the fight started, the Indians tried to kill their white captives. So in *The Searchers*, when Pauley tells Clayton before the final battle that if they charge into the Indian camp, the Comanches will certainly murder Debbie, historically he's correct. At Summit Springs, one hostage, Maria Weichel, was found with a serious bullet wound, but she survived. Susanna Alderdice was less fortunate. She had been shot in the head, and her skull was crushed by a tomahawk.

Like most Native Americans in most Western films, the Comanches scalp their victims in *The Searchers*. When Edwards and Pauley finally come face-to-face with Scar in the Comanche village in New Mexico Territory, they are told that Scar takes scalps because his sons are dead, presumably killed by whites. That seems accurate enough, for Burgess says, "I think that's why

[Comanches] fought so hard. They were so devoted to the family" (Nocona Burgess, interview with author, February 24, 2004). Scar has one of his wives, Debbie, show a collection of scalps—one of which, Ethan later points out, belonged to Pauley's mother—hanging from Scar's lance. That's fairly accurate, too. In *The Comanches: Lords of the South Plains*, authors Ernest Wallace and E. Adamson Hoebel point out, "A warrior returning from a successful raiding party set his lance upright before the door of his lodge with the scalps of his victims dangling from it" (Wallace and Hoebel 1986, 111).

Comanches usually scalped all their victims, regardless of age or sex. After cutting deeply around the hairline with a knife, the hair was jerked off the head. "Sometimes the whole scalp, sometimes only a centerpiece was retained, to be tanned carefully and stretched and preserved as a permanent trophy" (Fehrenbach 1994, 77). Comanches had another reason for scalping, though: the act denied the victim entrance into heaven.

Native Americans practiced scalping before Christopher Columbus arrived in the New World in 1492, but scalping was not confined to Native American peoples, and not all Indians scalped; Apaches, who avoided contact with the dead, rarely took scalps. Ethan Edwards scalps the dead Chief Scar in the movie, but not in LeMay's novel. Western heroes rarely took scalps in Hollywood movies, but in reality, colonists were scalping Indians in the seventeenth century. During King Philip's War (1675–1678), Connecticut and Massachusetts offered 30 shillings for an enemy's "Head" (Nichols 1986, 59); Massachusetts in 1704 agreed to pay 100 pounds for scalps of adult men or youths old enough to carry weapons but only 10 pounds for the scalps of children or women 10 years or older, and no reward for children under 10 years old, although they could be sold as slaves. In 1837, the Mexican government instituted a plan to pay 100 pesos for the scalp of each Indian man, 40 pesos for each scalp of an Indian woman, and 25 pesos for the capture of each Indian 12 years old or younger.

Showman and frontier scout William F. "Buffalo Bill" Cody (1846–1917) took one of the most famous scalps. On July 17, 1876, Cody, dressed in a *vaquero* stage costume he had worn in a play back East, was scouting for the 5th Cavalry near Warbonnet Creek in Nebraska when the U.S. forces and Cheyenne met in a brief engagement weeks after George Custer and most of his command had been killed at the Little Big Horn in Montana. On horseback, Cody and a Cheyenne named Yellow Hair, often mistranslated as Yellow Hand, fired at each other. Most of the fight would be embellished over the years, but Cody killed the Cheyenne in a heroic charge by both men. As soldiers rode by, Cody took the Indian's scalp, about 2 inches in diameter and about 14 inches long. He raised it in his hand and yelled to the cheering soldiers, "The first scalp for Custer" (Hedren 2001). Later he wrote his wife:

We have had a fight. I killed Yellow Hand a Cheyenne Chief in a single-handed fight. You will no doubt hear of it through the papers. I am going as soon as

I reach Fort Laramie the place we are heading for now send the war bonnet, shield, bridal whip, arms and his scalp to Kerngood [a Rochester, New York, clothing-store owner] to put in his window. I will write Kerngood to bring it up to the house so you can show it to the neighbors. (Russell 1960, 230)

The next year, Cody reenacted the event onstage in a new play written by Prentiss Ingraham (1843–1904), *Red Right Hand, or Buffalo Bill's First Scalp for Custer*, often displaying the scalp and other souvenirs taken from the dead Cheyenne in theater lobbies. "Yellow Hair's scalp became Cody's trademark," biographer Louis Warren wrote, "distinguishing him in the scout business so effectively that other scouts' attempts to mark their own authenticity always seemed to mimic his" (Warren 2005, 272–273).

Late in *The Searchers*, a Mexican trader named Emilio Gabriel Fernandez y Figueroa (Antonio Moreno, 1887–1967) leads Edwards and Pauley to Scar's camp in New Mexico "for a price . . . always for a price." The implication is that Figueroa is a Comanchero, typically a Hispanic trader who dealt with the Comanches, trading firearms and other goods for (sometimes) stolen cattle. In Nugent's screenplay—but not in the finished film—a soldier recommends that Edwards seek out "those Mexican traders along the border."

In 1873, a Texas cattleman blamed horse and cattle theft by Comanche and Kiowa Indians on "certain merchants and traders in New Mexico. They employ a low set of vagabonds styled Comancheros, who operate with the Indians. These Comancheros are generally half-breeds, and so they have much influence with the roving tribes" ("Stock-Raising in Texas" 1873, 1). Texas settlers and army soldiers despised Comancheros. During the search for the Comanche camp in the Texas Panhandle in 1874, Mackenzie's troops caught a Comanchero named José Piedad Tafoya. When Tafoya denied knowing the location of the village, Mackenzie ordered the Comanchero hanged from an upright wagon tongue, the pole connected to the front axle that extends between horses or mules, allowing the wagon to be pulled. After nearly strangling, Tafoya told Mackenzie where the Comanches were camped, leading to the army's successful attack at Palo Duro Canyon.

For a Comanchero, *The Searchers'* Figueroa has morals. When he realizes that Scar knows the real reason Edwards and Pauley have come to the camp, the trader returns the reward Edwards has paid him. "I do not want blood money," Figueroa says before galloping away. "*Vaya con Dios*" (Spanish for "Go with God").

In *The Only Good Indian: The Hollywood Gospel*, authors Ralph and Natasha Friar theorize that with the movie's climax, with Ethan Edwards sweeping Debbie into his arms and returning her home, "we know that they will live happily ever after. The old man is taking her home to family and civilization" (Friar and Friar 1972, 165–166). That's an optimistic view. Earlier in the film, Martin's sweetheart, Laurie (Vera Miles, 1929–), sister of the slain Brad Jorgensen, calls Debbie "the leavin's of Comanche bucks, sold time an' again to the highest bidder," and tells Martin: "Do you know what Ethan will do if he has a chance? He'll put a bullet in her brain. And I tell you Martha would want him to." Debbie's eventual fate might have played out more like that of Cynthia Ann Parker.

In 1861, the Texas legislature passed two bills to provide relief for the mother and daughter, granting each one league of land and each a pension of $100 a year. That much is known, but the rest of Parker's life is mostly legend. Returned to relatives in 1860 with her daughter, she reportedly tried to escape back to the Comanches with whom she had lived for 24 years until her family had to put her under guard. When her young daughter died in 1863 or 1865 or 1870, the grieving mother mourned her loss the Comanche way, self-mutilating her body, eventually starving herself to death or dying of a broken heart. No newspapers ran her obituary, though the *Daily Herald* in Dallas reported in 1874 that Cynthia "died some four years ago" ("Untitled Paragraph" 1874, 2), which makes 1870 seem a better guess of when she died. No matter when she and her young daughter died, historian Glenn Frankel writes, "Cynthia Ann was not the hardy survivor but rather the ultimate victim of the Texan-Comanche wars, abducted and traumatized by both sides" (Frankel 2014, 87).

In 1875, after Quanah surrendered, Texas newspapers published excerpts of a letter from Mackenzie seeking information on behalf of a Comanche who had recently surrendered who was "very desirous of finding out the whereabouts of his mother, if still alive, who was captured by the Indians, near the falls of the Brazos, nearly forty years ago, while yet a girl, and recaptured by the United States troops eighteen years ago, since which time she has remained in Texas" ("Sequel to a Remarkable History" 1875, 1).

On December 5, 1910, the remains of Cynthia Ann Parker were reinterred at the Post Oak Cemetery in Cache, Oklahoma, after Quanah Parker persuaded an Oklahoma congressman to sponsor a bill to have the chief's mother's remains moved from Texas. Several hundred whites and even more Comanches attended the funeral, where Quanah gave a short speech, first in Comanche, then in broken English, beginning: "Forty years ago my mother died. She was captured by Indians when nine years old. Love Indian so well no want to go back folks. I love my people anyway, God say. I love my mother" ("CYNTHIA PARKER REBURIED" 1910, 2).

On February 23, 1911, Quanah Parker died of rheumatism-induced heart failure. He was buried beside his mother.

CONCLUSION

The late 1950s saw several westerns addressing white bigotry against Native Americans: *The Last Hunt* (1956), known for an uncompromising performance by Robert Taylor (1911–1969) as an Indian-hating buffalo hunter; and *Fort Massacre* (1958), in which Joel McCrea (1905–1990), usually typecast as a good guy, played a racist sergeant on an Apache-killing vendetta. But *The Searchers* remains the best known, partly because of Wayne's performance, which Wayne liked enough to name his youngest son Ethan. "He is likable, but turns vicious as an Indian-hating bigot," wrote Dan LeMay (LeMay 2012, 172), who also pointed out the scene in which Ethan Edwards shoots down Indian trader James Futterman and two associates in the back after they tried to ambush Edwards and Pauley. "The more typical Hollywood characterization would have contrived a face-to-face gunfight. But this is frontier reality" (LeMay 2012, 172). For these reasons and others, *The Searchers* remains a powerful movie and a grim portrait of a violent, uncompromising, and racist West.

FURTHER READING

Blake, Michael. 2006. *Indian Yell: The Heart of an American Insurgence*. Flagstaff, AZ: Northland Publishing.

Blake, Michael F. 2003. *Code of Honor: The Making of Three Great American Westerns: High Noon, Shane, and The Searchers*. Lanham, MD: Taylor Trade Publishing.

Boggs, Johnny D. 2010. "Interview with Author S.C. Gwynne." *Wild West*, December 3, 2010. https://www.historynet.com/interview-with-author-s-c-gwynne.htm

Boggs, Johnny D. 2014a. "Quanah Parker Rides Again: *Empire of the Summer Moon* Has Taken American Readers by Storm." *True West*, February 14, 2012. https://truewestmagazine.com/quanah-parker-rides-again/

Boggs, Johnny D. 2014b. "Trail of Tragedy: The Road to the Sand Creek Massacre 150 Years Later Is Filled with Heartache—And Hope." *True West*, October 9, 2014. https://truewestmagazine.com/trail-of-tragedy/

Boulton, Richard N. 1954. "'Deep in the Heart of—.'" *The Hartford Courant Magazine*, October 31, 1954, p. 18.

Broome, Jeff. 2003. "Death at Summit Springs: Susanna Alderdice and the Cheyennes." *Wild West*. https://www.historynet.com/death-at-summit-springs-susanna-alderdice-and-the-cheyennes.htm

Carey Jr., Harry. 1996. *Company of Heroes: My Life as an Actor in the John Ford Stock Company*. Lanham, MD: Madison Books.

Chamberlain, Kathleen P. 2007. *Victorio: Apaches Warrior and Chief*. Norman: University of Oklahoma Press.

Cox, Mike. 1991. *The Texas Rangers: Men of Action & Valor*. Austin, TX: Eakin Press.

Cozzens, Peter. 2016. *The Earth Is Weeping: The Epic Story of the Indian Wars for the American West*. New York: Alfred A. Knopf.

Crowther, Bosley. 1956. "Screen: 'The Searchers' Find Action: Entertaining Western Opens at Criterion." *New York Times*, May 31, 1956, p. 21.

Custer, Elizabeth Bacon. 1890. *Following the Guidon*. New York: Harper & Brothers.

"CYNTHIA PARKER REBURIED: Chief Speaking at Grave Urges His People to Follow 'After White Way.'" 1910. *Wichita Eagle*, December 6, 1910, p. 2.

Davis, Ronald L. 1995. *John Ford: Hollywood's Old Master*. Norman: University of Oklahoma Press.

Davis, Ronald L. 1998. *Duke: The Life and Image of John Wayne*. Norman: University of Oklahoma Press.

Eyman, Scott. 2000. *Print the Legend: The Life and Times of John Ford*. Baltimore: The Johns Hopkins University Press.

Fausz, J. Frederick. 1998. "Powhatan Uprising of 1622." *American History*, March 1998. https://www.historynet.com/powhatan-uprising-of-1622.htm

Fehrenbach, T. R. 1983. *Lone Star: A History of Texas and the Texans*. New York: American Legacy Press.

Fehrenbach, T. R. 1994. *Comanches: The Destruction of a People*. New York: De Capo Press.

"FILM COMPANY HEADS FOR RESERVATION." 1955. *Arizona Daily Sun*, June 15, 1955, p. 1.

Ford, Dan. 1998. *Pappy: The Life of John Ford*. New York: De Capo Press.

Frankel, Glenn. 2014. *The Searchers: The Making of an American Legend*. New York: Bloomsbury.

Friar, Ralph E., and Natasha A. Friar. 1972. *The Only Good Indian: The Hollywood Gospel*. New York: Drama Book Specialists/Publishers.

"GOD IN THE CONSTITUTION." 1861. *Dallas Herald*, April 17, 1861, p. 1.

Griffith, Richard. 1956. "John Ford's 'Searchers' Wins Eastern Critics," *Los Angeles Times*, June 11, 1956, Part I, p. 36.

Gwynne, S. C. 2010. *Empire of the Summer Moon: Quanah Parker and the Rise and Fall of the Comanches, the Most Powerful Indian Tribe in American History*. New York: Scribner.

Hagan, William T. 1990. *United States-Comanche Relations: The Reservation Years*. Norman: University of Oklahoma Press.

Hedren, Paul L. 2001. "Buffalo Bill's First Scalp for Custer." *True West*, July 1, 2001. https://truewestmagazine.com/buffalo-bills-first-scalp-for-custer/

Holloway, Ronald. 1956. "The Searchers." *Variety*, March 13, 1956. https://variety.com/1956/film/reviews/the-searchers-1200418123/

"Indian Wars." http://www.newworldencyclopedia.org/entry/Indian_Wars#cite_note-1

Joyner, C. Courtney. 2013. "Searching for The Searchers: Glenn Frankel's book is a superb record of the complex journey behind the American Classic." *True West*, June 10, 2013. https://truewestmagazine.com/searching-for-the-searchers/

LeMay, Alan. 1956. *The Searchers*. New York: Popular Library.

LeMay, Dan. 2012. *Alan LeMay: A Biography of the Author of The Searchers*. Jefferson, NC: McFarland & Company, Inc.

Malham, Joseph. 2013. *John Ford: Poet in the Desert*. Chicago: Lake Street Press.

McBride, Joseph. 2004. *Searching for John Ford: A Life*. London: Faber and Faber Limited.

Mendlowitz, Leonard. 1956. "Stanley's Western a 'Real Epic.'" *Pittsburgh Sun-Telegraph*, June 4, 1956, p. 10.

Michno, Gregory F. 2009. *Encyclopedia of Indian Wars: Western Battles and Skirmishes, 1850–1890*. Flagstaff, AZ: Mountain Press Publishing Company.

Mitchell, Gee. 1956. "A Hero Nobody Loves—That's John Wayne's Lot in 'Searchers.'" *Dayton Daily News*, June 4, 1956, p. 21.

"Monument Area to Be Film Site." 1955. *Arizona Daily Sun*, June 8, 1955, p. 1.

"Movie Reviews." 1956. *Staunton News-Leader*, June 10, 1956, p. 16.

Neeley, Bill. 1995. *The Last Comanche Chief: The Life and Times of Quanah Parker.* New York: John Wiley & Sons, Inc.

"New Fiction Revives Old West." 1954. *Oakland Tribune*, December 26, 1954, p. 2-C.

Nichols, Roger L., ed. 1986. *The American Indian Past and Present: Third Edition.* New York: Alfred A. Knopf.

Nye, Colonel W. S. 1988. *Carbine & Lance: The Story of Old Fort Sill.* Norman: University of Oklahoma Press.

O'Neal, Bill. 2008. *Reel Rangers: Texas Rangers in Movies, TV, Radio & Other Forms of Popular Culture.* Waco, TX: Eakin Press.

Parsons, Louella O. 1954. "Multi-Millionaire Sonny Whitney Forms New Film Company; Will Screen Best Seller." *San Francisco Examiner*, November 12, 1954, p. 27.

Radcliffe, E. B. 1956. "The Best Western What Is (Albee)." *The Cincinnati Enquirer*, May 30, 1956, p. 18.

Rand, Yardena. 2006. "The Searchers at 50: Classic Film Spurs New Historical Research, Too." *True West*, April 1, 2006. https://truewestmagazine.com/the-searchers-at-50/

"Remnant of Comanche Tribe Pay Last Honors to Chief's Mother." 1910. *Houston Post*, December 11, 1910, p. 10.

Robinson, Charles M., III. 1986. *Frontier Forts of Texas.* Houston, TX: Lone Star Books.

Robinson, Charles M., III. 1993. *Bad Hand: A Biography of General Ranald S. Mackenzie.* Austin, TX: State House Press.

Robinson, Charles M., III. 1995. *The Buffalo Hunters.* Austin, TX: State House Press.

Russell, Don. 1960. *The Lives and Legends of Buffalo Bill.* Norman: University of Oklahoma Press.

Sagala, Sandra K. 2002. *Buffalo Bill, Actor: A Chronicle of Cody's Theatrical Career.* Bowie, MD: Heritage Books, Inc.

Scheuer, Philip K. 1954. "Vanderbilt-Cooper Bow Due with Searchers;' Barry Saves Day at 20th." *Los Angeles Times*, November 12, 1954, p. Part III, 7.

"Sequel to a Remarkable History." 1875. *Dallas Weekly Herald*, June 5, 1875, p. 1.

Smith, Harrison. 1955. "Stirring Tale of West Is No 'Western': Central Theme of Epic Heroic." *Sunday Journal and Star*, March 6, 1955, p. 3D.

Smith, Ralph Adam. 1999. *Borderlander: The Life of James Kirker, 1793–1852.* Norman: University of Oklahoma Press.

"Stock-Raising in Texas." 1873. *Chippewa Herald*, May 31, 1873, p. 1.

Stratton, Joanna L. 1982. *Pioneer Women: Voices from the Kansas Frontier.* New York: Touchstone.

"TEXAS ITEMS." 1868. *Texas Republican*, January 25, 1868, p. 2.

"Texas Rangers." n.d. Texas Department of Public Safety. http://www.dps.texas.gov/texasrangers

"Untitled Paragraph." 1874. *The Daily Herald*, May 19, 1874, p. 2.

Utley, Robert M. 2002. *Lone Star Justice: The First Century of the Texas Rangers.* New York: Oxford University Press.

Wallace, Ernest, and E. Adamson Hoebel. 1986. *The Comanches: Lords of the South Plains.* Norman: University of Oklahoma Press.

Warren, Louis. 2005. *Buffalo Bill's America: William Cody and the Wild West Show.* New York: Alfred A. Knopf.

Webb, Walter Prescott. 1982. *The Texas Rangers: A Century of Frontier Defense.* Austin: University of Texas Press.

Wilbarger, J. W. 1985. *Indian Depredations in Texas*. Austin, TX: Eakin Press/Statehouse Books.

Wilkins, Frederick. 1999. *The Law Comes to Texas: The Texas Rangers, 1870–1901*. Austin, TX: State House Press.

Wright, Alfred. 1961. "Sonny Whitney: A Success in Spite of His Money." *Sports Illustrated*, September 4, 1961. https://www.si.com/vault/1961/09/04/588168 /sonny-whitney-a-success-in-spite-of-his-money

Zolotow, Maurice. 1975. *Shooting Star: A Biography of John Wayne*. New York: Pocket Books.

Chapter 6

The Magnificent Seven (1960)

Produced by the Mirisch Company, Inc., and distributed by United Artists, *The Magnificent Seven* ranks among the most successful Western movie franchises in Hollywood history, spawning three sequels, a television series, a 2016 remake, and many unofficial remakes. *The Magnificent Seven* itself was a remake, not of a Western, but of a 1954 Japanese-made film, *Seven Samurai*, set in sixteenth-century Feudal Japan (1165–1603). A Broadway musical based on *The Magnificent Seven* was considered in the mid-1960s, and the movie's popular musical score remains easily recognized today.

Set in the 1880s or 1890s, *The Magnificent Seven* brings six out-of-work professional gunfighters (instead of samurai) and a young man, the son of Mexican peasants who wants to become a gunfighter, to a poor Mexican village. With villagers terrorized by a gang of bandits and Mexican law enforcement unable to stop the pillaging, three farmers head to the U.S. border with hopes of buying guns for the villagers to use to defend themselves. Told that men come much cheaper than firearms, the farmers agree to hire experienced gunfighters to train the villagers and help them fight the bandits.

A black-clad gunfighter named Chris (Yul Brynner, 1920–1985) leads the recruitment, having been won over by the fact that the village has sold everything of value to buy guns/gunmen. "I've been offered a lot for my work," Chris says, "but never everything." Although the villagers can pay little, Chris hires young Vin (Steve McQueen, 1930–1980), who can fire witticisms as fast as he can a revolver; Chris's old friend Harry Luck (Brad Dexter, 1917–2002), who takes the job because he believes there is more than just a piddling $20 to be earned; the Irish-Hispanic Bernardo O'Reilly (Charles Bronson, 1921–2003), who has been reduced to chopping wood for food and shelter; a lanky cowboy named Britt (James Coburn, 1928–2002), who can throw a knife faster than a man can draw and fire a revolver; dapper-dressed Lee (Robert Vaughn, 1932–2016), who secretly has lost his nerve; and, eventually, the Hispanic wannabe-gunfighter named Chico (German actor Horst Buchholz, 1933–2003).

While training the village men in combat, most of the hired gunmen grow fond of the villagers. When roughly 40 bandits return, the seven gunmen drive them off. Later, however, the bandits, led by the ruthless Calvera (Eli Wallach, 1915–2014), capture and disarm the seven gunmen. Illogically, Calvera doesn't execute his captives but sends them back toward the United States.

Gunmen, however, have pride. "Nobody throws me my own guns and says run," Britt says. All seven return to the village to fulfill their contract and destiny by attacking Calvera's men. Seeing the Americans fighting—and dying—for them inspires the farmers to join the attack. Calvera is killed, as are most of his men. Four American mercenaries also die, but Chico hangs up his gun and returns to the village to farm, leaving Chris and Vin to ride away. "Only the farmers won," Chris tells Vin. "We lost. We always lose."

The genesis of *The Magnificent Seven* can be traced to Japanese director Akira Kurosawa (1910–1998), whose *Rashomon* (1950) brought him and Japanese filmmaking international recognition; *Rashomon* won an honorary Academy Award in 1952. In 1954, Kurosawa directed and cowrote *Seven Samurai*, about a poor farming village in the sixteenth century that recruits out-of-work samurai to defend it against bandits.

When *Seven Samurai* reached North American theaters in 1956, playing under the title *The Magnificent Seven*, reviewers quickly pointed out the film's similarities with American Westerns. "What Hollywood's 'Shane' did for the gunfighter of the Old West, 'Seven Samurai' attempts to do for the samurai, professional fighter of his day," United Press reported. "Both strive to strip these fighting men of false glamor and legend and show them as human beings. Kurosawa points out that his own script was written before he knew anything about 'Shane'" (United Press 1954a, 36). *Los Angeles Times* critic Richard Griffith praised *Seven Samurai's* "touches that would do honor to Fred Zinnemann [director of the Oscar-winning *High Noon*] or John Ford [director of iconic Westerns including *Stagecoach*, *My Darling Clementine* and *The Searchers*]" (Griffith 1956, 10, Part II).

After seeing *Seven Samurai* during its U.S. run, Lou Morheim (1922–2013), a story editor at Columbia Pictures best known for helping script *The Beast from 20,000 Fathoms* (1953), paid $250 for American remake rights for *Seven Samurai*. Morheim thought the movie could be remade as a Western. So did Brynner and two other two popular actors, Anthony Quinn (1915–2001) and Kirk Douglas (1916–).

After decades of legends, lawsuits, points and counterpoints, the rest of the filming process often boils down to cases of He Said/He Said. In short,

Brynner sold the project to the Mirisch Company; John Sturges (1910–1992), who wanted to be credited as the film's only producer, was hired as director; and Morheim took credit as associate producer and was no longer involved in the production.

It took some persuading from Sturges before Walter Mirisch agreed to cast Wallach as the bandit leader Calvera, a choice that Mirisch said came out of nowhere. The bandit leader of *Seven Samurai* was menacing, but the screenplay gave depth to Calvera, and Wallach expanded on that. Wallach explained:

> In all the cowboy pictures I saw as a boy, the bandits held up trains, robbed banks, stole cattle, but no one ever knew what they did with the money. That was the key I needed to create my character; I would be a dandy spendthrift. I asked Sturges and he smilingly agreed, if I could have a beautiful horse, a silver-studded saddle, red silk shirts, silver rings on all my fingers and two gold caps for my teeth. (Eliot 2011, 77)

According to Mirisch, various composers were discussed before Sturges and Mirisch agreed on Elmer Bernstein (1922–2004), but another report said Bernstein "lobbied" for the job (Lovell 2008, 208). Bernstein received an Academy Award nomination for *The Magnificent Seven*, and received 12 other nominations for score or song during his career, winning for scoring *Thoroughly Modern Millie* (1967). One of those nominations came for *Return of the Seven* (1966), for which "he was adapting his own music, written for the earlier film, 'The Magnificent Seven'" (Campbell 1967, 2).

Brynner rejected Morheim's original script. Walter Bernstein (1919–), Robert Alan Aurthur (1922–1978), Walter Newman (1916–1993), and William Roberts (1913–1997) apparently worked on the script, which included scenes and some dialogue from *Seven Samurai's* screenwriters Kurosawa, Shinobu Hashimoto (1918–2018), and Hideo Oguni (1904–1996), but Roberts wound up with sole credit. The script was originally titled *The Magnificent Six* to avoid confusion with *Seven Samurai's* U.S. title. At some point, the *Six* became *Seven*.

With a budget set at $2 million, filming began in late February 1960 in Mexico; exteriors were primarily shot in Tepoztlán and Oacalco and interiors at Estudios Churubusco in Mexico City, with some reshoots staged at Old Tucson in Tucson, Arizona. The Western *Vera Cruz* (1954), which had also been filmed in Mexico, infuriated Mexican officials, leading to a government crackdown on foreign productions. Mexican censor Jorge Ferretis objected to several parts of *The Magnificent Seven* script that showed, in his view, unflattering portrayals of the Mexican population. Rewrites were demanded so that instead of traveling to the United States to hire gunmen to fight for them, the villagers try to buy guns, only to be told that gunmen are cheaper. Bits of dialogue were changed, and the censor demanded that villagers be outfitted in clean white pants and shirts—"Tide clean," Sturges called it (Lovell 2008, 200). The roles of Chico and O'Reilly had to be expanded, although the development of the latter character improved the movie. Still, a furious Sturges complained: "If it weren't for this censor, Mexico would be a wonderful country for making movies. But as it is now, it is okay only so long as you are making movies about Americans or about a boy and his dog" (Schumach 1960, 25).

Rosenda Monteros (1935–2018), the Mexican actress who played Petra, Chico's love interest, said, "The script had to be checked and revised very carefully to make sure that there were no images that denigrated the country. Because of the importance of the coproduction, we had to get the film off the ground one way or another. It was good for the country" (Slotnik 2019).

Conflicts aside, the film wrapped in early May and was released on November 23. Some critics praised it, with Theresa Loeb Cone noting in the *Oakland Tribune* that "[i]t has a good strong script, characterizations that make sense and a point of view which suggests that by actions, not words, we can properly judge a man" (Cone 1960, 31). But overall reaction tended to be unsupportive. The *New York Times'* Howard Thompson called it "a pallid, pretentious and overlong reflection of the Japanese original. . . . Mr. Brynner just is not a cowboy" (Thompson 1960, 48). The *Los Angeles Times'* Philip K. Scheuer said the movie "is likely to frighten, thrill and perplex most movie-goers, not necessarily in that order" (Scheuer 1960, 3). James Powers of the *Hollywood Reporter* wrote: "*The Magnificent Seven* has the stars and the production values to open big, and probably will. But it is not a success, as a story or as entertainment," and he went on to make a few predictions, including, "McQueen, if he can get sprung from TV, where he is learning nothing and only getting older, is going to be a great big star" and "Elmer Bernstein's music is truly memorable; the theme will stick" (Powers 1960).

Powers proved to be right about Bernstein's score, among the most recognized in film history, and about McQueen, who had been starring in a TV Western, *Wanted: Dead or Alive*, but soon skyrocketed to movie stardom; but Powers was wrong about the movie opening big. Larry Cohen (1941–), who wrote the film's first sequel, *Return of the Seven*, said *The Magnificent Seven* "never played in a decent theater" (Lovell 2008, 211). Vaughn saw it for the first time in an empty theater. Distributor United Artists tried to get Mirisch to cut 20 minutes out of the movie, but Mirisch refused. The movie found a following, however, in France. In Japan, *The Magnificent Seven* became the top-grossing imported film of 1961. The movie grossed five or six times more in foreign markets than it did in the United States, Mirisch said, and American audiences also started watching it—in second- and third-run theaters.

By the time Brynner signed a three-movie deal with Mirisch in 1961, *The Magnificent Seven* had grossed more than $9 million. Bernstein's score was used in a cigarette commercial. A TV series was discussed in the early 1960s but did not appear until running for 22 episodes from 1998 to 2000. Three movie sequels—*Return of the Seven* (1966), *Guns of the Magnificent Seven* (1969), and *The Magnificent Seven Ride!* (1972)—followed, although reviews were usually unkind. The sequels made a profit, however, while the original became one of the most-shown Westerns on television. European Westerns often used "Magnificent" or "Seven" in titles such as *7 Pistole per i MacGregor/Seven Guns for the MacGregors* (1966) and *Il Magnifico Texano/The Magnificent Texan* (1967). "Magnificent Seven" became a catchall phrase in the United States. Headlines touting sports teams borrowed the title. In Los Angeles in 1961, the Federal Bureau of Investigation busted a white-slave ring called the Magnificent Seven. "The title," Mirisch said, "has become part of our language" (Mirisch 2008, 113).

HISTORICAL BACKGROUND

Around 6 p.m. on July 21, 1865, Davis Tutt and James Butler "Wild Bill" Hickok, feuding over a poker debt, a gold watch, and/or a woman or women, stepped onto the town square in Springfield, Missouri, drew their revolvers, and fired. The two shots, witnesses said, sounded like one. The bullet from Davis's weapon flew over Hickok's head, but Hickok's round struck Davis in the chest despite an estimated 75 yards separating the duelists. Davis ran in and out of arches at the Greene County Courthouse and fell into the street. Within two minutes, he lay dead, and the legend of the gunfighter was born.

The Hickok-Tutt showdown is one of only a few documented walk-down, face-to-face gunfights. After a coroner's inquest, Hickok was arrested on a "charge of killing" (Rosa 1974, 76), later reduced to manslaughter, and jailed. After friends posted his $2,000 bail, he hired a lawyer. This wasn't Hickok's first time in court. In 1861, he had been tried for murder after a gunfight left three men dead at Rock Creek Station in Nebraska. In both cases, Hickok was acquitted.

After the Springfield verdict, Hickok was introduced to journalist George Ward Nichols (1831–1885), a New Englander, Union Army veteran, and correspondent for *Harper's New Monthly Magazine*. Hickok gave Nichols permission to publish an article, saying, "I am sort of public property" ("Wild Bill" 1867, 1). Ward's article, "Wild Bill," published in the February 1867 issue, contained exaggerated accounts of the Rock Creek and Springfield gunfights. How much Hickok made up or how much Ward embellished can't be divined, although *The Missouri Weekly Patriot* opined:

> In reading the romantic and pathetic parts of the article, "the undercurrent about a woman" in his quarrel and fatal fight with Dave Tutts; and his remarks

with "quivering lips and tearful eyes" about his old mother in Illinois, we tried to fancy Bill's familiar face while listening to the passages being read. We could almost hear his certain remark, "O! hell! What a d–d fool that Nichols is." We agree with "Wild Bill" on that point. ("'Wild Bill,' Harper's Monthly and 'Colonel' G. W. Nichols" 1867, 2)

The *Harper's* article, reprinted in newspapers across the country, made Hickok a national celebrity, and he became the prototype for the mythical gunfighter. "Bystanders pointed him out on the streets; eastern visitors sought interviews with him; and newspapers throughout the country reported his presence as he passed through their communities," one biographer wrote. (McLaird 2008, 16–17)

By almost all accounts, Hickok cut a striking figure, standing six feet tall or more, broad-shouldered, narrow-hipped, with curly auburn hair to his shoulders, a straw-colored mustached and occasional goatee. He also dressed fashionably. "But it was his eyes that commanded most attention," biographer Joseph G. Rosa wrote. "They were a translucent blue-gray in color, surprisingly gentle in normal conversation, but when he was aroused, they became coldly implacable" (Rosa 1974, 6).

Born May 27, 1837, in Homer, Illinois (later renamed Troy Grove), Hickok left home with an older brother in 1856 for Kansas, where Hickok was elected constable of Monticello Township in 1858. Later hired as a teamster for Russell, Majors and Waddell, Hickok was working for that company, which also ran the Pony Express, during the gunfight at Rock Creek Station. After serving in the Union Army on the Western frontier as a wagon boss, scout, spy, and detective during the Civil War (1861–1865), he was mustered out in June 1865.

After the Tutt gunfight, Hickok worked across Kansas as a special detective, army scout, deputy U.S. marshal, Ellis County sheriff, and Abilene town marshal. He survived two saloon gunfights in Hays City, Kansas, and killed gambler Phil Coe in a gunfight outside an Abilene saloon in 1871, in which Hickok also accidentally shot and killed a deputy who was running to help. In 1873–1874, Hickok toured with friends William F. "Buffalo Bill" Cody (1846–1917) and John Baker "Texas Jack" Omohundro (1846–1880) in a theatrical troupe back east, after which he made his living gambling in the West before he arrived in Deadwood, a mining boom town in present-day South Dakota. There, while playing poker, he was shot and killed by Jack McCall.

The gunfighter era is generally defined as between 1860 and 1900, although the word "gunfighter" did not come into usage until the late 1880s. Men skilled with handguns were more commonly called gunmen, man-killers, pistoleers, pistol men, or shootists. "Exactly how many men were gunfighters is debatable, but they really did exist in the Old West, and sometimes they were in demand as lawmen to tame towns or help settle feuds and range wars," said Gregory J. Lalire, editor of the Vienna, Virginia-based

Wild West, a Western history magazine (Gregory J. Lalire, interview with author, February 5, 2019).

Gunfighters, naturally, needed guns; Samuel Colt (1814–1862) helped on that end. In 1836, Colt began manufacturing revolving rifles and pistols at his factory in Paterson, New Jersey, and finding no interest from the army and no market in the East, Colt looked to Texas for customers. Equipped with a revolving cylinder that held five (later six) rounds, Colt's weapons could fire 30 shots in the time a single-shot muzzleloader could be loaded three times. In 1844, Texas Rangers Captain John Coffee "Jack" Hays (1817–1883) and 15 men, all armed with Colt revolvers, routed more than 60 Comanche Indians. The Paterson Colt, however, had flaws. The bore (.28, .31, .34 and .36 calibers) was too small, the folding trigger concerned the Rangers, who didn't like the pistol's balance, either. The weapon, Texas historian T. R. Fehrenbach noted, "was more an Easterner's toy" (Fehrenbach 1983, 481).

In 1846, Ranger Captain Samuel Walker (1817–1847) traveled east, met Colt and suggested improvements that resulted in the Walker Colt, a six-shot weapon in .44 caliber that weighed 4.5 pounds and could be used as a club on men "not worth shooting" (Fehrenbach 1983, 482). The new revolver came equipped with a trigger guard, was more durable than the Paterson and could be reloaded on horseback. Later Colt models included .44-caliber Dragoons and, during the Civil War, the 1851 .36-caliber Navy, and .44-caliber Army. These early cap-and-ball revolvers required a percussion cap to ignite gunpowder in the chamber and send a lead ball toward a target. By the 1870s, self-containing metallic cartridges had made cap-and-ball models antiquated, and six-shooters became easier and faster to reload.

Colt's first models were single-action, meaning the hammer had to be cocked before the revolver could be fired as opposed to double-action, or self-cocking revolvers, where the user only had to squeeze the trigger to fire the pistol. In 1873, the company sold the army its Single Action Army model, a .45-caliber revolver with a 7.5-inch barrel. When the revolver became available to the general public a few years later, at $13, the so-called "Peacemaker" became "as common as spittoons in a saloon" (Worman 2005, 151). A marketing campaign proclaimed: "God made all men, but Colonel Colt made them equal" (Anschutz 2015, 276).

The Peacemaker wasn't the only weapon used by gunfighters, and Colt wasn't the only manufacturer. Outlaw Frank James (1843–1915) preferred the .44-caliber Remington, calling it "the hardest and surest shooting pistol made" (Worman 2005, 180). Henry McCarty (1859–1881), also known as Billy the Kid, reportedly liked Colt's self-cocking .41-caliber Thunderer, while El Paso lawman Dallas Stoudenmire (1845–1882) favored single-action .44-caliber American models from Smith & Wesson. Development of these weapons, and relatively easy access to them, helped shape the gunfighter era in the post–Civil War West.

According to Lalire, many Civil War veterans traveled West after the war, carrying the violence of that conflict with them. Lalire noted that citizens could find land and opportunity in the West, but also presented alternative methods of questionably legality to obtain wealth. "The various gold rushes brought men to the West who found themselves in rough-and-tumble communities. Almost all were armed, mostly to shoot game and protect themselves, but it was easy enough for some men to turn their rifles and six-shooters on their fellow man to obtain gold—without digging for it—or to shoot those who offended them, often in a saloon," Lalire said. Fueled by alcohol and equipped with state-of-the-art weaponry, some men gained reputations as gunfighters (Gregory J. Lalire, interview with author, February 5, 2019). Newspapers, magazines, and novels sensationalized these gunmen long before motion pictures did. "There is no Western legend as enduring as that of the overrated gunfighter," historian Joseph G. Rosa wrote (Rosa 1969, 4).

Quick-on-the-draw contests might have been popular in fiction, but speed often was not best way to survive. As early as 1889, a San Francisco newspaper reported: "Anybody who tells about seeing frontiersmen shoot dimes in the air, perforate distant oyster cans with countless bullets while riding at full speed, drive nails off-hand and without taking careful sight, and all the other popularly accepted marvels, talks blue bosh" ("THE TRIGGERLESS GUN" 1889, 13). Hickok told Nichols: "Whenever you get into a row do not shoot too quick. Take time. I've known many a feller slip up for shootin' in a hurry" ("Wild Bill" 1867, 1). Famous lawman/gambler/journalist Bat Masterson (1853–1921) described a gunfight between Jim Levy and Charlie Harrison in Cheyenne, Wyoming, in 1877:

> They met on opposite sides of the principal street of the city and opened fire on each other without a moment's delay. Harrison, as was expected, fairly set his pistol on fire, he was shooting so fast and managed to fire five shots at Levy before the latter could draw a bead on him. Levy finally let go a shot. It was all that was necessary. Harrison tumbled into the street in a dying condition and was soon afterwards laid to rest alongside of others who had gone before in a similar way. (Masterson 1907, 26)

"Fanning" revolvers—keeping the finger pressed against the trigger while using the palm of their other hand to cock the hammer repeatedly, resulting in rapid firing—was also frowned upon. Famed lawman Wyatt Earp (1848–1929) said: "In all my life as a frontier peace officer, I did not know a really proficient gun-fighter who had anything but contempt for the gun-fanner or the man who literally shot from the hip" (Agnew 2012, p. 172).

As far as the best place to put a bullet in your opponent, Hickok recommended in the belly. "[Y]ou may not make a fatal shot," he reportedly said, "but he will get a shock that will paralyze his brains and arm so much that the fight is all over" (Rosa 1969, 120).

HICKOK VERSUS HARDIN

In June 1871, Wild Bill Hickok and John Wesley Hardin allegedly met outside a bowling alley in Abilene, Kansas, in a legendary confrontation between two of the West's most famous gunfighters.

Eighteen-year-old Hardin, wanted for murder in Texas, had recently finished a cattle drive. Hickok, 34, had been appointed city marshal earlier that year. Wearing two revolvers—in defiance of an ordinance prohibiting the carrying of weapons in the city limits—Hardin was "rolling ten pins and drinking" with other cowboys, he recalled (Hardin 1896, 45). When Hickok saw Hardin's weapons, he drew his revolver and attempted to arrest the Texan.

Hardin offered his pistols, butt forward, to Hickok, then "reversed them and whirled them over on him with the muzzles in his face, springing back at the same time. I cursed him for a long haired scoundrel" (Hardin 1896, 45). Hickok calmly invited the Texan to have a drink. "We went into a private room and I had a long talk with him and we came out friends," Hardin wrote (Hardin 1896, 45).

Hardin's alleged maneuver is known as a border roll, road agent's spin or the Curly Bill spin, the latter after gunfighter Curly Bill Brocious performed the move and pointed his revolver at Tombstone, Arizona, Marshal Fred White in 1880. When Virgil Earp grabbed Brocious from behind, the weapon discharged and White was shot. The dying White called the shooting accidental, and Brocious was acquitted in a "homicide by misadventure" (Trimble 2015, 127).

Many historians question the veracity of the Hickok-Hardin confrontation. The story did not surface until Hardin's posthumous autobiography was published in1896. Though Hickok's preeminent biographer, Joseph G. Rosa, called Hardin's autobiography "an attempt to vindicate himself and boost a rapidly fading ego" (Rosa 1974, 189), noted Hardin biographer Leon Claire Metz found "no evidence that Hardin lied" (Metz 1998, 53).

Sources
Hardin, John Wesley. 1896. *The Life of John Wesley Hardin, from the Original Manuscript, as Written by Himself.* Sequin, TX: Smith & Moore.

Metz, Leon. 1998. *John Wesley Hardin: Dark Angel of Texas.* Norman: University of Oklahoma Press.

Rosa, Joseph G. 1969. *The Gunfighter: Man or Myth?* Norman: University of Oklahoma Press.

Rosa, Joseph G. 1974. *They Called Him Wild Bill: The Life and Adventures of James Butler Hickok, Second Edition.* Norman: University of Oklahoma Press.

Trimble, Marshall. 2015. *Arizona Outlaws and Lawmen: Gunslingers, Bandits, Heroes and Peacekeepers.* Charleston, SC: The History Press.

These weren't the days of gentlemanly duels, the practice with codified rules and customs in which men met on the field of honor to settle their disputes complete with a choice of weapons. Drawing on the count of 3 or 10 went out with duels, and gunmen were not inclined to let the opponent draw first in life-or-death situations. The rule was to survive, at all costs. There was no typical gunfighter. Historian Eugene Cunningham noted that some gunfighters "were men of blind, bulldogged courage" while others were "almost arrant cowards" (Cunningham 1996, 5–6). Wearing a badge did not necessarily make a gunfighter a hero.

"I suppose I am called a red-handed murderer, which I deny," Hickok said. "That I have killed men I admit, but never unless in absolute self-defense, or in the performance of an official duty. I never, in all my life, took any mean advantage of an enemy" (Rosa 1974, 7).

Bat Masterson died of a heart attack in his New York City newspaper office in 1921. Wyatt Earp died in 1929 at age 80. But plenty of gunfighters died as they had lived. Hickok was shot in the back of his head while playing poker. John Wesley Hardin (1853–1895) was gunned down while rolling dice by John Selman (1839–1896), who was mortally wounded eight months later by lawman George Scarborough (1859–1900), who did not let Selman draw first. "Boys," Selman said, "you know I am not afraid of any man; but I never drew my gun" (O'Neal 1979, 279). Selman, shot four times, died after surgery. Billy the Kid, most of whose victims were killed from ambush or through chicanery, was shot without warning in a darkened bedroom.

"Attitudes of the gunfighter ranged from hatred to hero-worship," Joseph G. Rosa wrote, "with the latter feeling generally predominating, even though most people know that folk heroes are products of the imagination coupled with nostalgia and national pride" (Rosa 1969, 11).

The Magnificent Seven accurately depicts those ranges of feelings. Young Chico idolizes the six gunfighters hired to protect the farmers, but most villagers, especially in the beginning, fear, distrust, and even loathe the gunmen; young women and children are kept hidden from the gunfighters until Chico discovers Petra. The brutality of the gunmen's nature becomes clearer when Chris threatens to shoot any villager who tries to give up, and the gunfighters let Chico know what is in store for him if he follows their path. "Home, none," Vin says. "Wife, none. Children, none. Prospects, zero." After Calvera is killed and the bandits defeated, Chico hangs up his gun and returns to Petra. In *Seven Samurai*, the young woman spurns the villager-turned-samurai, but Hollywood opted for a happier ending.

DEPICTION AND CULTURAL CONTEXT

In Hollywood Westerns, Americans often crossed the border into Mexico for adventure, perhaps most famously in *The Wild Bunch* (1969). With the exception of *They Came to Cordura* (1959), set during the U.S. Army's expedition into Mexico after revolutionary Pancho Villa's 1919 attack on Columbus, New Mexico, and *Old Gringo* (1989), inspired by the disappearance of journalist Ambrose Bierce during the Mexican Revolution (1910–1920), those movies had little if any basis on actual history. Given that the story was originally set in 1500s Japan, *The Magnificent Seven* also offers no real history.

There are some documented cases of hired guns going into Mexico after the U.S. Civil War, when several Union and Confederate soldiers left the United States for Mexico. However, these were hired not by villagers but rather by governments. General Joseph O. Shelby (1830–1897) led 600 Confederate soldiers into Mexico, where Emperor Maximilian (1832–1867) allowed expatriates to found a colony near Vera Cruz. Union General George Armstrong Custer (1839–1876) was offered a job as adjutant general for the army of Benito Juárez (1806–1872), then fighting Maximilian's forces, and Custer likely would have gone had Secretary of State William H. Seward (1801–1872) not denied approval. Other former Union officers, however, helped Juárez in Mexico, and U.S. troops conveniently lost firearms near the border for Juárez's men to find.

The teaming of several top guns, however, has some historical basis. After the murder of theater performer Dora Hand in Dodge City, Kansas, in the fall 1878, legendary lawmen/gunfighters Wyatt Earp, Bat Masterson, and Bill Tilghman led a posse after James Kenedy, shooting Kenedy's horse and wounding Kenedy with gunfire before bringing him in to stand trial; the case was dismissed when no witnesses came forward. But hiring gunfighters for something other than a legal posse was not always for noble causes.

In 1892, Wyoming cattle barons said rustlers in Johnson County were robbing them of their livelihood and that since the legal system was not working, the cattlemen decided to handle the matter themselves. Buffalo, the county seat, was corrupt, the ranchers said. Residents of the county, on the other hand, accused the cattlemen of trying to drive off smaller ranchers who were legally homesteading on land the barons illegally claimed for their own cattle. The big ranchers dispatched stock detective Tom Smith to Paris, Texas, to hire gunmen. On April 5, 1892, a train arrived with 25 hired guns. According to former lawman George Tucker, "There were some good men, and some who were worse than no men at all" (Knowlton 2017, 270). Members of the Wyoming Stock Growers Association loaded another train with horses, rifles, wagons, and food. The train left Cheyenne that evening, with 75 animals, 52 men, and "enough ammunition to kill all the people in the state of Wyoming" (Davis 2010, 135). The cattleman funded this invasion with more than $100,000—more than $2.7 million today. Traveling with the gunmen were a surgeon, three teamsters, and two embedded journalists, Ed Towse of the *Cheyenne Daily Leader* and Sam T. Clover of the *Chicago Herald*.

After cutting telegraph lines near Douglas, the train stopped at Casper, where the invaders—as they would become known—unloaded and prepared to travel by horseback. The weather, however, did not cooperate.

PACKING IRON

Holsters and gun belts depicted in most sound western movies, including *The Magnificent Seven*, are often Hollywood creations. In the late 1800s, how a gunfighter carried his weapon was a matter of personal preference. Most photographs of Wild Bill Hickok show him carrying one or two revolvers holstered high, with the gun butts facing forward. John Wesley Hardin reportedly designed a vest with holsters for two revolvers, butts facing inward and barrels slanting toward the hips. This configuration required the wearer to cross their arms to grab the guns on the opposite side. Gunfighter Ben Thompson is said to have preferred a shoulder holster, which gave shootists more concealment for the weapons they carried. Most men, however, carried one revolver in a leather holster high on the hip.

Holsters typically slid over the belt in the nineteenth century. Some historians suggest that the Texas Rangers created the low-slung holster attached to the belt, commonly called a buscadero, in the late 1800s, but most call it a Hollywood creation from the 1920s.

"Old West holsters were designed to hold the pistol firmly in place no matter what you were doing," said Will Ghormley of Chariton, Iowa, who made leather belts and holsters for *The Assassination of Jesse James by the Coward Robert Ford* and *3:10 to Yuma* (both 2007). "You could run, ride a horse, chop wood, fall down, and in most cases the gun would stay in the holster. But then you would have to yank on it to get it out. So Hollywood's image of a fast gun is just that: a Hollywood invention" (Nott 2007, 58).

Source

Nott, Robert. 2007. "Hellbent for Leather." *Pasatiempo*, September 7, 2007, pp. 57–58.

April in Wyoming, the Texans soon learned, is still winter. A blizzard hit, but the invaders pushed on to the South Fork of the Powder River, where, on April 8, the gunmen learned that some men on their hit list, including alleged rustlers Nate Champion and Nick Ray, were at the KC Ranch. After arguing about whether they should attack the ranch or Buffalo, the invaders surrounded the ranch headquarters. On the morning of April 9, the invaders captured two trappers, who had spent the night with Champion and Ray and stepped outside to fetch water. When Ray went outside later, the gunmen shot him down, but Champion dragged his mortally wounded friend back into the cabin. For hours, Champion fought off the hired gunfighters, but when the invaders set the cabin on fire, Champion was gunned down while trying to escape.

Before torching the cabin, though, passersby had seen the attack and escaped to spread the alarm across the county, yet the gunmen tarried at the ranch after Ray and Champion were dead. Realizing that their raid was over, the invaders hurried for Fort McKinney, roughly three miles west of Buffalo, searching for army protection. Johnson County citizens, however, came out in force, and the killers took shelter at the T. A. Ranch near Buffalo; 200 to 400 angry men surrounded the gunmen. Before the Johnson County posse could dynamite the invaders into the open, soldiers from Fort McKinney arrived. Governor Amos Barber, in sympathy (and/or in the pockets) of the cattle barons, persuaded President Benjamin Harrison to send federal troops to save the invaders. The gunmen surrendered and were transported back to Cheyenne, where "a travesty of justice was played out eight months later" (Davis 2014). Unable to seat a jury or pay for further prosecution, Johnson County dropped all charges. The Texans returned home, and the Wyoming cattle barons "got away with murder" (Knowlton 2017, 290).

In *The Magnificent Seven*, Mexican peasants are forced to hire outsider gunfighters for protection from bandits, but in two documented cases of bandit attacks in the American West, townsmen not only fought the outlaws, they defeated them.

Around 2:00 p.m. on September 7, 1876, three members of the notorious James-Younger Gang (most likely Frank James, Charlie Pitts, and Bob Younger), wearing linen dusters and heavily armed, rode into Northfield, Minnesota, tethered their horses to hitching posts, and walked inside the First National Bank—a move that surprised two of their companions, Cole Younger and Clell Miller, because the town was crowded. The robbers inside the bank had not even closed the door, so Miller dismounted to do that while Younger swung off his horse and pretended to tighten the saddle's cinch. The strangers and the excellent horses they rode immediately attracted attention. "They didn't get suspicious because of dusters; they got suspicious of the horses, the equipment the horses had and the riders themselves," Northfield historian John J. Koblas (1942–2013) said (John J. Koblas, interview with author, April 24, 2012).

Resident J. S. Allen walked to the bank door and tried to look in, but Miller jerked him away, drew his pistol, and began cursing. Allen ran to a nearby store. "When the first cries of 'Robbers at the bank!' went up," historian T. J. Stiles said, Northfield residents went into action (T. J. Stiles, interview with author, April 24, 2012).

Younger and Miller mounted their horses while three other outlaws— Bill Chadwell and, most likely, Jesse James and Jim Younger—galloped down the street, shooting, cursing, and shouting—the method of operation the James-Younger Gang that had worked several times during their long career as outlaws. "Instead of panicking and running away in fear, several citizens went for their guns," said Mark Lee Gardner, author of *Shot All to Hell: Jesse James, the Northfield Raid, and the Wild West's Greatest Escape* (Mark Lee Gardner, interview with author, April 29, 2012). The outlaws were armed with revolvers, but the defenders did most of their damage with rifles. "Revolvers were fine for bushwhacker charges at close quarters, but the outlaws on Division Street, forced to wait for their cohorts in the bank, made for pretty easy targets in a real life shooting gallery," Gardner said (Mark Lee Gardner, interview with author, April 29, 2012).

Armed with a shotgun, Elias Stacy knocked Miller off his horse with a blast of birdshot into his face. Henry Wheeler, a medical student at the University of Michigan who was visiting home, borrowed a rifle and ran to a second-story hotel window. Taking careful aim, Wheeler shot and killed Miller. When Cole Younger ran to check on Miller, Anselm Manning wounded Younger and, moments later, shot Chadwell off his horse. Younger hurried to the bank door and yelled for his companions to hurry.

But things weren't going well for the robbers inside the bank, either. Frank Wilcox, Alonzo Bunker, and acting cashier Joseph Heywood refused to open the safe. Heywood lied and said that the safe was on a time lock. Even when he was hit in the head with a pistol, Heywood would not open the safe. When Bunker ran for the back door, Pitts shot him, but Bunker made it out and survived. Cole Younger's shouts and the gunfire outside persuaded the robbers to leave the bank. The last one out the door, presumably Frank James, cold-bloodedly shot and killed Heywood. Another resident, a Swedish immigrant named Nicolaus Gustavson who neither spoke nor understood English, was shot in the head on the street and died four days later.

The surviving six outlaws escaped Northfield with $27.60 for a robbery that lasted seven minutes. The largest manhunt in U.S. history up to that time began. At some point, the James brothers separated from the badly wounded Youngers and Pitts, and a posse from Madelia surrounded Pitts and the Youngers at Hanska Slough in western Minnesota on September 21. Pitts died in the ensuing gunfight, and the Youngers were captured. The brothers never implicated the James boys, pleaded guilty to avoid execution, and were sentenced to life in prison in Stillwater. Bob Younger died in prison of tuberculosis in 1889. After Cole and Jim were paroled in 1901, Jim died by suicide in 1902, and Cole, granted a conditional pardon the following year, returned to Missouri, where he died in 1916.

Heywood, who left behind a five-year-old daughter and young wife, was hailed and mourned across the nation. Other townsmen who fought off the outlaws were likewise heralded as heroes. They managed to do what Pinkerton detectives, lawmen, and other towns victimized by the bandits had failed to accomplish: they had defeated Jesse James and his gang. A festival, which originated in 1948, continues in Northfield on the weekend after Labor Day; now called "Defeat of Jesse James Days," this event includes accurate recreations of the raid. Though lesser known, the town of Madelia held an annual re-enactment of the Youngers' capture from 1996 through 2018. After the Madelia posse confronted the Youngers and Pitts, seven businessmen and farmers faced down the outlaws. Today, those volunteers are called the "Magnificent Seven" (Dougherty 2002, 3C).

Sixteen years after the Northfield raid, citizens in Coffeyville, Kansas, defeated the Dalton Gang when the outlaws brazenly attempted to rob two banks simultaneously in their hometown. On the morning of October 5, 1892, brothers Emmett, Grat, and Bob Dalton and gang members Dick Broadwell and Bill Power rode into Coffeyville. Although they might have worn theatrical facial hair, the disguises did not fool several townsmen. Coffeyville's streets were being paved, and the hitching rack where they planned to leave their horses had been removed, so the outlaws tied their horses along a fence in a narrow alley, 170 yards from the First National Bank, 130 yards from C. M. Condon & Company Bank.

"Looking east through the alley, which opened on the triangular central plaza, we could see the front of the First National Bank," Emmett Dalton wrote. "Adjoining it, and also plainly visible, was the Isham Brothers' hardware store. As events turned out we could not have placed the horses in a more dangerous spot" (Dalton 2012, 238). Grant, Power, and Broadwell entered the Condon bank; Emmett and Bob walked into the First National.

The brothers were three of Lewis and Adeline Dalton's 15 children. One brother, Frank, had been a deputy U.S. marshal in Fort Smith, Arkansas, but was killed in the line of duty in 1887. Grat and Bob Dalton also worked as deputy marshals, and Emmett sometimes rode with them in posses, before the brothers turned to crime. After stealing horses and transporting illegal whiskey into the Indian Territory (present-day Oklahoma), the Daltons began robbing trains in 1891. By the summer of 1892, the Daltons were wanted for robbery and murder. Another brother, Bill, also become an outlaw and was killed by lawmen in 1894 near his home in Ardmore, Oklahoma.

Inside the First National, Bob kept bank employees and customers covered while Emmett filled a grain sack with more than $20,000—but at the Condon, clerk Charles M. Ball lied that the safe had a time lock and could not be opened for three more minutes. Grat Dalton decided to wait, and during those minutes, weapons and ammunition were being passed out to citizens at Isham's store. Bob and Emmett forced the seven citizens through the First National's front door and started for the alley, but gunshots drove the brothers back inside the bank. Using teller W. H. Shepard as a shield, they ran out the back door. Lucious Baldwin, a 23-year-old clerk, armed himself with a pistol at Isham's store and met the Dalton brothers as they, and Shepard came outside. Baldwin called out for the Daltons to stop and was shot in the heart by Bob's Winchester. The brothers left Shepard and the dead clerk and ran for their horses in the alley. At a street corner, Bob killed George Cubine and Charles Brown; then he wounded First National cashier Tom Ayers, who had grabbed a rifle at Isham's, with a bullet that struck just below Ayers's left eye (Ayers later served as Coffeyville's mayor). Other defenders were wounded, while Grat, Power and Broadwell rushed out of the Condon bank. Grat and Power were wounded but kept their feet.

Meanwhile, Marshal Charles Connelly had crossed into the alley in an attempt to intercept the robbers, but Grat shot him in the back, killing him. Running for his horse, Grat was hit in the throat by a bullet that broke his neck. Broadwell made it to his horse, only to be mortally wounded by defenders. Hanging onto his saddle horn, Broadwell rode half a mile before falling dead. The wounded Power tried to seek shelter in a building in the alley, but the door was locked, and he was killed in the alley.

Bob and Emmett, somehow unwounded, dashed for their horses, but a bullet in the chest knocked Bob down. After firing fruitlessly, Bob rose, staggered toward a stable, was shot again in the chest, and fell into the alley. Emmett, despite being riddled with bullets, mounted his horse, but instead of trying to escape, he rode to his wounded brother in a vain attempt to lift him into the saddle. A shotgun blast knocked Emmett out of the saddle, and he also fell into what became known as "Death Alley." When citizens examined the outlaws' guns, they discovered that no revolver had been fired. "Unlike gunfights in the movies," *True West* magazine's Bob Boze Bell wrote, "this had been almost exclusively a rifle and shotgun contest" (Bell 2014).

In 12 minutes, some 500 shots had been fired, leaving four townsmen and four outlaws dead. Despite receiving 23 gunshot wounds, Emmett Dalton survived and spent 14 years in prison. Pardoned, he moved to California and wrote two books, *Beyond the Law* (1918) and *When the Daltons Rode* (1931), the latter being adapted into a popular—and highly whitewashed—1940 Western movie. The dead outlaws were buried in Coffeyville, though Broadwell's body was exhumed and reinterred in Hutchinson, Kansas. A hitching rail from Death Alley still marks the graves of the dead killers at Elmwood Cemetery.

Could 7 gunfighters beat a gang of 40 bandits as depicted in *The Magnificent Seven*? While Lalire said the movie's heroes "are a little too magnificent to believe," he pointed out that some gunfighters beat the odds. "In 1854 California, Jonathan Davis survived the Rock Canyon gunfight, killing seven bandits with his Colt revolver and four more with his bowie knife. Davis suffered only a couple of minor flesh wounds while 17 bullets passed through his clothing. But never did any real-life gunfighters face such lopsided odds as the 'heroes' in *The Magnificent Seven* and never was the body count higher" (Gregory J. Lalire, interview with author, January 1, 2019).

The Magnificent Seven might not accurately depict gunfighters in the Southwest of the late 1800s, but scholars have pointed out that the film reflects 1960s America. "*The Magnificent Seven* portrayed the activism that was the hallmark of American foreign policy throughout the 1960s," R. Philip Loy wrote. "Wallach is a bandit terrorizing his own people—and in Southeast Asia, Latin America and Africa of 1960 the American people saw more than a few twentieth century Wallachs" (Loy 2004, 78).

More comparisons have singled out the movie's similarities with what happened in Vietnam later in the decade. In the film, once the seven reach the Mexican village, they begin training the peasants in combat but are soon drawn into increasingly violent fights against Calvera's cutthroats, which some film historians have called a foreshadowing of U.S. military operations in Vietnam. To that end, the first gunfight against Calvera and his bandits might be compared to the 1964 Battle of Ia Drang in Vietnam, while the final attack is more reminiscent of later operations. Richard Slotkin likened the movie's plot to America's "nation-building" ideal: "When the Vietnamese displayed an unwillingness or inability to act up to American standards, the Americans felt they had to 'step in and take over,' substituting their own power and authority for the incompetent native policy" and that "The last assault in *The Magnificent Seven* is one step away from the terrible rationale associated with the nadir of the Vietnam War: 'We had to destroy the city in order to save it.' If such a scene had been filmed a few years later, it would have raised echoes of Mylai" (Slotkin 1992, 480–481 and 484).

CONCLUSION

As American West history, *The Magnificent Seven* is pure fantasy. "In the real West, such a collection of accomplished shootists joining forces for a noble cause—such as the one in the film: protecting a poor Mexican farming village from marauding bandits—is a stretch," Lalire said. "Could one picture the likes of Jesse James, Wyatt Earp, Wild Bill Hickok, John Wesley Hardin, Clay Allison, King Fisher and Tom Horn teaming up to save a village above or below the border when facing horrendous odds and without enough compensation to pay for their bullets? Well, only in the movies" (Gregory J. Lalire, interview with author, January 1, 2019).

On the other hand, the movie's success paved a path for other similar-themed movies, ranging from Westerns like *The Professionals* (1966) to war films including *The Guns of Navarone* (1961) and *The Dirty Dozen* (1967) to the science-fiction *Battle Beyond the Stars* (1980). The latter merely moved the plot into outer space and gave Robert Vaughn, one of the original Seven, another role as a mercenary. *¡Three Amigos!* (1986) was a "largely un-funny" (Weinberg 1987, 121) spoof of *Seven Samurai/The Magnificent Seven*, while Pixar's animated hit *A Bug's Life* (1998) reimagined much of *The Magnificent Seven*'s plot elements.

Yet *The Magnificent Seven* also reflects the early 1960s in America and the ideals of John F. Kennedy's New Frontier speech—a time of hope and excitement, which faded during a decade that brought assassinations, an escalating war, protests, and race riots. As Loy wrote: "The 1960s, which began on the optimistic note of *The Magnificent Seven* . . . defending a poor Mexican village from bandits, ends with Butch Cassidy and the Sundance Kid gunned down in a poor Bolivian village as outlaws by Bolivian soldiers" (Loy 2004, 216).

FURTHER READING

Agnew, Jeremy. 2012. *The Old West in Fact and Film: History Versus Hollywood.* Jefferson, NC: McFarland & Company, Inc.

Anschutz, Philip F. 2015. *Out Where the West Begins: Profiles, Visions & Strategies of Early Western Business Leaders.* Denver, CO: Cloud Camp Press.

AP (Associated Press). 1960. "Actor Files Breach of Agreement Lawsuit." *Wisconsin Rapids Daily Tribune*, February 3, 1960, p. 2.

Bandy, Mary Lea, and Stoehr, Kevin. 2012. *Ride, Boldly Ride: The Evolution of the American Western.* Berkeley: University of California Press.

Bell, Bob Boze. 2014. "Dalton Debacle: Dalton Gang vs The Town of Coffeyville." *True West*, June 17, 2014. https://truewestmagazine.com/dalton-gang-vs-the -town-of-coffeyville

Bischoff, Jane C. 2006. "The Buscadero Bio: Showcasing Authentic Old West– Style Gunleather." *True West*, June 2, 2006. https://truewestmagazine.com/the -buscadero-bio

Brynner, Rock. 1989. *Yul: The Man Who Would Be King: A Memoir of Father and Son.* New York: Simon & Schuster.

Campbell, Mary. 1967. "This Bernstein Writes Movie Music." *Chillicothe Constitution-Tribune*, April 19, 1967, p. 2.

Capua, Michelangelo. 2006. *Yul Brynner: A Biography.* Jefferson, NY: McFarland & Company, Inc.

Carter, Greg Lee, ed. 2012. *Guns in American Society: An Encyclopedia of History, Politics, Culture, and the Law, Second Edition.* Santa Barbara, CA: ABC-CLIO.

Cedrone, Lew. 1969. "Feliciano and the 'Guns.'" *Evening Sun*, June 12, 1969, p. A 14.

Clavin, Tom. 2019. *Wild Bill: The True Story of the American Frontier's First Gunfighter.* New York: St. Martin's Press.

Cone, Theresa Loeb. 1960. "'Magnificent 7' Makes a Point." *Oakland Tribune*, October 27, 1960, p. 31.

Connolly, Mike. 1959. "Mike Connolly." *Philadelphia Inquirer*, July 29, 1959, p. 17.

Crosby, Joan. 1967. "Groucho Makes His Marx." *Wausau Daily Record-Herald*, December 8, 1967, p. 7.

Cunningham, Eugene. 1996. *Triggernometry: A Gallery of Gunfighters.* Norman: University of Oklahoma Press.

Dalton, Emmett. 2012. *When the Daltons Rode.* Gretna, LA: Pelican Publishing Company.

Davis, John L. 2010. *Wyoming Range War: The Infamous Invasion of Johnson County.* Norman: University of Oklahoma Press.

Davis, John L. 2014. "The Johnson County War: 1892 Invasion of Northern Wyoming." https://www.wyohistory.org/encyclopedia/johnson-county-war-1892-invasion -northern-wyoming

"The Dead Cashier." 1876. *Minneapolis Tribune*, September 28, 1876, p. 1.

DeLay, Brian. 2013. "Mexico Benefitted from the Civil War." *New York Times*, July 2, 2013. https://www.nytimes.com/roomfordebate/2013/07/02/who-won-the -civil-war/mexico-benefitted-from-the-civil-war

Dougherty, Mike. 2002. "Madelia Celebrates Place in History." *St. Cloud Times*, September 12, 2002, p. 3C.

Editors of *Guns & Ammo*. 1982. *Guns and the Gunfighters*. New York: Bonanza Books.

Edwards, John N. 1964. *Shelby's Expedition to Mexico. An Unwritten Leaf of the War.* Austin, TX: The Steck Company.

Eliot, Marc. 2011. *Steve McQueen: A Biography*. New York: Crown Archetype.

Fehrenbach, T. R. 1983. *Lone Star: A History of Texas and the Texans*. New York: American Legacy Press.

Garavaglia, Louis A., and Charles G. Worman. 1997. *Firearms of the American West, 1866–1894*. Niwot: University Press of Colorado.

Garavaglia, Louis A., and Charles G. Worman. 1998. *Firearms of the American West, 1803–1865*. Niwot: University Press of Colorado.

Graham, Sheilah. 1958. "Deborah Kerr to Seek Custody of Children." *Odessa American*, June 17, 1958, p. 8.

Graham, Sheilah. 1960. "Apology Department." *Honolulu Advertiser*, June 13, 1960, p. 13.

Griffith, Richard. 1956. "New Japanese Picture Like American Western." *Los Angeles Times*, December 4, 1959, p. 10, Part II.

Guinn, Jeff. 2011. *The Last Gunfight: The Real Story of the Shootout at the O.K. Corral—And How It Changed the American West*. New York: Simon & Schuster.

Herzberg, Bob. 2015. *Revolutionary Mexico on Film: A Critical History, 1914–2014*. Jefferson, NC: McFarland & Company, Inc.

Hopper, Hedda. 1959. "Dean Jones Will Star in 'Magnificent Seven.'" *Tampa Tribune*, December 28, 1959, p. 9.

Hopper, Hedda. 1961a. "A Face of the Future with the 'Look of an Eagle': Horst Buchholz May Well become a Modern Matinee Idol in the Tradition of Young Barrymore or Tyrone Power." *Hartford Courant Magazine*, September 10, 1961, p. 12.

Hopper, Hedda. 1961b. "Yul Brynner Inks $12,000,000 Pact." *Shreveport Times*, July 11, 1961, p. 10-A.

Hopper, Hedda. 1965. "Marty Thinks This Is It." *New York Daily News*, May 17, 1965, p. 46.

Hughes, Howard. 2008. *Stagecoach to Tombstone: The Filmgoers' Guide to the Great Westerns*. London: I. B. Tauris & Co. Ltd.

Jackson, Matthew. 2016. "16 Epic Facts about Seven Samurai." April 6, 2016. http://mentalfloss.com/article/78097/16-epic-facts-about-seven-samurai

Johnson, Erskine. 1960. "Hidden Drama Highlights Tale of 'Magnificent Seven.'" *Corpus Christi Times*, April 8, 1960, p. 9-C.

Kennedy, Paul P. 1960. "SHOOTING A 'MAGNIFICENT SEVEN' IN MEXICO." *New York Times*, April 10, 1960, p. X 7.

Kleiner, Dick. 1964. "Hollywood Today." *Hazleton Standard-Speaker*, November 27, 1964, p. 31.

Knowlton, Christopher. 2017. *Cattle Kingdom: The Hidden History of the Cowboy West*. New York: Houghton Mifflin Harcourt.

Koblas, John J. 2001. *Faithful unto Death: The James-Younger Raid on the First National Bank: September 7, 1876: Northfield, Minnesota*. Northfield, MN: Northfield Historical Society.

Koblas, John J. 2005. *Minnesota Grit: The Men Who Defeated the James-Younger Gang*. St. Cloud, MN: North Star Press of St. Cloud, Inc.

Lovell, Glenn. 2008. *Escape Artist: The Life and Films of John Sturges*. Madison, WI: University of Wisconsin Press.

Loy, R. Philip. 2004. *Westerns in a Changing America, 1955–2000*. Jefferson, NC: McFarland & Company, Inc.

Marks, Paula Mitchell. 1996. *And Die in the West: The Story of the O.K. Corral Gunfight*. Norman: University of Oklahoma Press.

Masters, Dorothy. 1960. "'Magnificent Seven' Fine Entertainment." *New York Daily News*, November 9, 1960, p. 75.

Masterson, W. B. (Bat). 1907. *Famous Gunfighters of the Western Frontier: Wyatt Earp, Doc Holliday, Luke Short and Others*. Mineola, NY: Dover Publications Inc., 2009.

McLaird, James D. 2008. *Wild Bill Hickok & Calamity Jane: Deadwood Legends*. Pierre: South Dakota State Historical Society Press.

McLaughlin, Will. 1959. "Studio and Screen." *Ottawa Journal*, January 17, 1959, p. 44.

McLaughlin, Will. 2003. *The Encyclopedia of Lawmen, Outlaws, and Gunfighters*. New York: Facts on File, Inc.

Mirisch, Walter. 2008. *I Thought We Were Making Movies, Not History*. Madison: University of Wisconsin Press.

Morrell, David. 2016. *Stars in My Eyes: My Love Affair with Books, Movies, and Music*. Colorado Springs, CO: Gauntlet Press.

Murdoch, David Hamilton. 2001. *The American West: The Invention of a Myth*. Reno: University of Nevada Press.

NEA (Newspaper Enterprise Association). 1961. "'The Wild One' Simmers Down." *Racine Journal-Times Bulletin*, May 28, 1961, p. 17.

O'Neal, Bill. 1979. *Encyclopedia of Western Gunfighters*. Norman: University of Oklahoma Press.

Parsons, Louella O. 1960. "Mexicans to 'Censor' U.S. Films Shot There." *Indianapolis Star*, April 6, 1960, p. 26.

Powers, James. 1960. "THE MAGNIFICENT SEVEN A TOUGH PERIOD WESTERN." *Hollywood Reporter*, October 5, 1960. https://www.hollywoodreporter.com/review/magnificent-seven-1960-review-original-931098

Quinn, Anthony, with Daniel Paisner. 1995. *One Man Tango*. New York: HarperCollins.

Rosa, Joseph G. 1969. *The Gunfighter: Man or Myth?* Norman: University of Oklahoma Press.

Rosa, Joseph G. 1974. *They Called Him Wild Bill: The Life and Adventures of James Butler Hickok, Second Edition*. Norman: University of Oklahoma Press.

Rosa, Joseph G. 2001. *Wild Bill Hickok, Gunfighter: An Account of Hickok's Gunfights*. Norman: University of Oklahoma Press.

Scheuer, Philip K. 1960. "Swords of Bushido become Guns in 'Magnificent Seven.'" *Los Angeles Times Calendar*, October 30, 1960, p. 3.

Schumach, Murray. 1960. "PRODUCER SCORES MEXICAN CENSOR: John Sturges of 'Magnificent Seven' Says Official Is 'Confused, Petulant.'" *New York Times*, May 20, 1960, p. 25.

Skweres, Artur. 2017. *Homo Ludens as a Comic Character in Selected American Films*. Cham, Switzerland: Springer.

Slotkin, Richard. 1992. *Gunfighter Nation: The Myth of the Frontier in Twentieth-Century America*. New York: Harper Perennial.

Slotnik, Daniel E. 2019. "Rosenda Monteros, 83, Actress in 'The Magnificent Seven,' Dies." *New York Times*, January 7, 2019. https://www.nytimes.com/2019/01/07/obituaries/rosenda-monteros-dead.html

Smith, Robert Barr. 1996. *Daltons! The Raid on Coffeyville, Kansas*. Norman: University of Oklahoma Press.

Smith, Robert Barr. 2001. *The Last Hurrah of the James-Younger Gang*. Norman: University of Oklahoma Press.

"SPRINGFIELD, MISSOURI vs. HARPERS' MONTHLY. 'Wild Bill,' Harpers Monthly and 'Colonel' G.W. Nichols." 1867. *Leavenworth Daily Conservative*, February 7, 1867, p. 2.

Thompson, Howard. 1960. "Screen: On Japanese Idea: 'Magnificent Seven,' a U.S. Western, Opens." *New York Times*, November 24, 1960, p. 48.

"THE TRIGGERLESS GUN. Gun-Fighters' Rough-and-Ready Improvements in Revolvers. QUEER TRICKS WITH SMALL ARMS. How Cowboy Sinclair Fanned the Hammer at Mr. Riley—What Can and Cannot Be Done with Revolvers—Popular Fiction and Cold Fact about the Marksmanship of the Wild and Wooly Frontiersman." 1889. *Examiner*, December 1, 1889, p. 13.

UP (United Press). 1954a. "Japan Slates Feudal Film." *Windsor Daily Star*, April 2, 1954, p. 36.

UP (United Press). 1954b. "Japanese Movie to Compete in World Film Festival." *Tampa Sunday Tribune*, May 2, 1954, p. 22-C.

UP (United Press). 1961. "Malignant 7? White-Slave Operation Smashed in Los Angeles." *Courier-Journal*, August 13, 1961, p. 8.

UPI (United Press International). 1963. "Sally Rand to Star in NBC Special." *Courier-Post* (Camden, NJ), p. 5.

Utley, Robert M. 1988. *Cavalier in Buckskin: George Armstrong Custer and the Western Military Frontier*. Norman: University of Oklahoma Press.

Vaughn, Robert. 2008. *A Fortunate Life*. New York: Thomas Dunne Books.

Weinberg, Marc. 1987. "Only the Bad Ones Survived." *Orange Coast: The Magazine of Orange County*, January 2007.

"WESTERN BANDITTI. Remarkable Career of the James and Younger Brothers—The Band Broken Up after Fourteen Years of Crime." 1876. *Concordia Times*, November 3, 1876, p. 1.

Whitmer, Mariana. 2017. *Elmer Bernstein's The Magnificent Seven: A Film Score Guide*. Lanham, MD: Rowman & Littlefield.

"Wild Bill." 1867. *Green Mountain Freeman*, January 30, 1867, p. 1.

"'Wild Bill,' Harper's Monthly and 'Colonel' G. W. Nichols." 1867. *Missouri Weekly Patriot*, January 31, 1867, p. 2.

Worman, Charles G. 2005. *Gunsmoke and Saddle Leather: Firearms in the Nineteenth-Century American West*. Albuquerque: University of New Mexico Press.

Wright, Will. 1975. *Sixguns & Society: A Structural Study of the Western*. Berkeley: University of California Press.

Chapter 7

Butch Cassidy and the Sundance Kid (1969)

The year 1969 is often called the last great year of Western movies, a run that started in 1939 with the release of *Destry Rides Again*, *Dodge City*, *Jesse James*, *Stagecoach*, and *Union Pacific*—box-office hits that resurrected Westerns from B-list pot-boilers to A-list moneymakers. In 1969, director Henry Hathaway's *True Grit* premiered, which won iconic Western star John Wayne (1907–1979) the Best Actor Academy Award; and Sam Peckinpah's *The Wild Bunch* debuted, which transformed the way movies depicted violence, and is heralded as one of the greatest Westerns ever made. But the box-office champion for 1969 was another highly regarded Western, an elegiac ode to the end of the West, *Butch Cassidy and the Sundance Kid*, directed by George Roy Hill (1921–2002).

The film opens with bandit Butch Cassidy (Paul Newman, 1925–2008) amazed at the security measures being taken at a bank in some small Western town. "What happened to the old bank?" Cassidy asks a guard. "It was a beauty." Told that too many people robbed the bank, Cassidy says, "Small price to pay for beauty," and walks to a saloon to find his partner, the Sundance Kid (Robert Redford, 1936–), a well-known gunfighter. They ride to their outlaw hideout, known as the Hole in the Wall, where Butch is dismayed to learn that one of the gang, Harvey Logan (Ted Cassidy, 1932–1979), plans to take over the gang and has talked the other members into robbing a train. Flat Nose Curry, played by Charles Dierkop (1936–), says, "You always said one of us could challenge you."

Cassidy distracts Logan long enough to kick him in the groin, then knock him out, and when he hears about Logan's plan to hit the Union Pacific Flyer twice, Cassidy readily adopts that idea. They successfully rob the train and celebrate. Sundance joins his girlfriend, Etta Place (Katharine Ross, 1940–). When Cassidy runs out of money, the gang regroups to rob the Flyer again. But as they are gathering the money, another locomotive appears, pulling one car. When the train stops, men on horseback leap from the car, and the Hole in the Wall gang flees. Gang members News (Timothy Scott, 1937–1995) and Flat Nose are gunned down, and the remaining four split up, with Cassidy and Sundance riding out together. To their dismay, the small posse follows only Cassidy and Sundance. No matter what they try, they cannot shake this "Superposse."

They plead with a friendly lawman, Bledsoe (Jeff Corey, 1914–2002), that they can go straight and are even willing to serve in the Spanish-American War (1898) in exchange for amnesty; but though Bledsoe likes the two men, he tells them, "I never met a soul more affable than you, Butch, or faster than the Kid. But you're still two-bit outlaws on the dodge. It's over. Don't you get that? Your times is over, and you're gonna die bloody, and all you can do is choose where."

The Superposse—shown from a distance and played by uncredited actors or extras—continues to pursue the outlaws, who come to suspect that posse's tracker is a full-blooded Indian named Lord Baltimore who "could track anybody over anything day or night" and that the leader is lawman Joe Lefors (1865–1940), even though Lord Baltimore works only out of Oklahoma and Lefors operates in Wyoming. Cassidy and Sundance finally escape by jumping off a cliff into a river. They rejoin Etta, who tells them that the posse has been hired by the Union Pacific to kill Cassidy and Sundance. With nowhere else to turn to, Cassidy and Sundance head to Bolivia. Etta goes with them but says, "I'll do anything you ask of me except one thing. I won't watch you die."

In Bolivia, the two outlaws, sometimes assisted by Etta, rob a few banks, becoming known as *Bandidos Yanquis* (Yankee Bandits) before Etta returns to America. Attempting to go straight, Cassidy and Sundance find work as a payroll guard for a cranky American miner (Strother Martin, 1919–1980), and when he is murdered by bandits, the two outlaws retrieve the money, killing six bandits—the first men Cassidy has ever killed.

Cassidy and Sundance retire to a small Bolivian town, where they are recognized as the American bandits. The local law enforcement pins down the two outlaws, and, unbeknown to Cassidy and Sundance, a large patrol of Bolivian Army soldiers arrives. Wounded, Cassidy and Sundance make a break for their horses. As they dash onto the courtyard, the camera freezes on the pair as volleys of gunshots are heard.

Screenwriter William Goldman (1931–2018) learned about Butch Cassidy, an alias of Robert Leroy Parker (1866–1908), and the Sundance Kid, an alias of Harry Alonzo Longabaugh (ca. 1867–1908), in the 1950s. Intrigued, Goldman began researching the pair. "The more I read, the deeper my fascination became," Goldman recalled (Goldman 1984, 123). After years of research, Goldman, then teaching creative writing at Princeton University, wrote the first draft over the 1965–1966 Christmas break. After two revisions, Goldman pitched his script in Hollywood, which "aroused a quick no-interest, and a further re-write, which wasn't all that different but which, thank God, almost everybody wanted" (Goldman 1984, 292). Richard D. Zanuck (1934–2012), head of 20th Century Fox, paid Goldman $400,000 for the screenplay, plus a percentage of the film's net profit, news that "made a big flap and generated gleeful screenwriters into orbit (Gauguin 1968, 8). "And a lot of people wondered what the world was coming to," Goldman recalled, "a western selling for that" (Goldman 2001, 54).

After being hired to direct, Hill picked Conrad Hall (1926–2003) as cinematographer. Locations chosen were in Utah—including the ghost town of Grafton, which producer Harry Sherman (1884–1952) helped restore for *Ramrod*, a 1948 noir-like western—Los Angeles, Colorado, and New Mexico, plus Cuernavaca and Taxaco, Mexico, to sub for Bolivia. Redford, who had a home in Provo Canyon, helped bring the production to southern Utah.

Like many movies, how the casting came together becomes a matter of whom, or which version, one wants to believe. In one account, Newman wanted to do the movie as soon as he read the script, but he saw himself as Sundance, not Cassidy. According to that version, Hill told Newman he should play Cassidy, and when Newman reread the script later that night, he decided that "the parts are really about equal and they're both great parts. So I said, 'Okay, I'll be Butch'" (Levy 2009, 231). Goldman—or Newman—thought of Jack Lemmon (1925–2001) as Sundance, but that idea was quickly dismissed. The studio pushed for Warren Beatty (1937–), who reportedly said he would play Cassidy and could get Marlon Brando (1924–2004) to play Sundance, but when Brando read the script, he wanted to play Cassidy. That weeded out Beatty and Brando. Then Steve McQueen (1930–1980), according to one version, was sought out. McQueen wouldn't commit unless he received top billing. "I don't think that's nice," Newman said, and he refused McQueen's demand (Levy 2009, 232). McQueen was out. But Newman also reportedly said that McQueen and Newman talked about making the movie together before 20th Century Fox bought the screenplay, a plan that died because Goldman's agent was putting the script up for auction. "So that was the end of it for McQueen and me," Newman said. "I forgot about it. Then, out of the blue, Dick Zanuck had it and Hill was offering it to me, with no Steve attached" (Callan 2011, 145).

Stephanie "Steffie" Phillips, then an assistant to Redford's manager at Creative Management Associates, pushed for Redford, who won over Hill and Newman. Ross, who had gained notice in *The Graduate* (1967), was cast as Etta Place, and after two weeks of rehearsals, filming began in Durango, Colorado, on September 16, 1968.

Goldman had written a scene in which Cassidy takes Etta on a bicycle ride through a ghost town. Hill, a music major at Yale, "ran with it. He got the really remarkable notion that the bike ride not just be musicalized but should be a song" (Goldman 1997, 6). Hill hired Burt Bacharach (1928–) to write the score and an original song, "Raindrops Keep Falling on My Head"; Bacharach wrote the music; Hal David (1921–2012) wrote the lyrics. "While many moviegoers enjoyed watching this atypical Western," film historian Thomas D. Clagett wrote, "Burt Bacharach's bouncy musical score, particularly the song, 'Raindrops Keep Falling on My Head,' baffled, and even irritated, some" (Clagett 2018, 15). But the record became a hit record for singer B. J. Thomas (1942–), spending four weeks at No. 1 on the Top 40 charts beginning January 3, 1970.

Although Westerns were fading in popularity, Hill thought his film was different. "Ours is more than even an 'adult' Western; it's not a Western at all," he said. "It's a character study, and a retelling on the screen of the true adventures of a specific gang and their leader" ("New Type Western" 1969, 13).

After the film's preview, however, Hill became worried. "Everyone was pleased," associate producer Robert Crawford (1921–2016) recalled, "except George who said, 'They laughed at my tragedy; they don't get the end of my movie'" (Clagett 2018, 15). Too much laughter, Goldman said, "made the ending a problem. So [Hill] set about taking out laughs" (Goldman 2001, 54).

Things still did not bode well after the film premiered in late September 1969. "There is thus, at the heart of 'Butch Cassidy,' a gnawing emptiness that can't be satisfied," Vincent Canby wrote in the *New York Times*, adding that Newman, Redford, and Ross "succeed even if the movie does not" (Canby 1969, 54). Roger Ebert of the *Chicago Sun-Times* wrote that "Goldman's script is constantly too cute and never gets up the nerve, by God, to admit it's a Western" and that "we walk out of the theater wondering what happened to that great movie we were seeing until an hour ago" (Ebert 1969). The *Los Angeles Times*' Charles Champlin, however, called the movie "first and foremost a refreshing and tasty entertainment, a literate and sophisticated comedy, a western in which for once is adult not in its carnality but in its relative subtlety (Champlin 1969, Part VI, 1).

"All the New York and national magazine reviews were mixed to terrible," Goldman recalled. "You could not have reprinted one in its entirety. The reviews in the rest of the country were terrific, and in the rest of the world we soared" (Goldman 2001, 55). Indeed, the movie, which cost an estimated $6 million to film, earned more than $102 million at the box office to make it the No. 1 movie of the year. It won Academy Awards for Goldman's screenplay, Hall's cinematography, Bacharach's score, and Best Song ("Raindrops Keep Falling on My Head"). It was also nominated for Hill's direction as well as Best Picture and Best Sound.

Butch Cassidy and the Sundance Kid, however, did more than just reap money and rewards and help resurrect the western film genre. It made two almost-forgotten Old West outlaws household names.

HISTORICAL BACKGROUND

In 1866, Robert Leroy Parker was born in Beaver, Utah, the first of Max and Ann Parker's 13 children. His parents called their firstborn Leroy, but most people knew him as Bob. When he was 13, the family moved to a 160-acre plot in Circle Valley, Utah, and the young teen went to work at a ranch, where he fell under the influence of a good-natured cowboy named Mike Cassidy, who was also adept at rustling livestock. Young Bob had a couple of minor run-ins with the law, including one in which he broke into a store, stole a pair of pants, and left an IOU. At age 18, Bob left his home in search of a better life. He cowboyed; worked in the mines in Telluride, Colorado; and is said to have been as a butcher in Rock Springs, Wyoming. At some point, he adopted the alias of Cassidy, borrowing his rustling friend's surname. He became known as George Cassidy, and eventually Butch Cassidy, although how the "Butch" came about is anybody's guess; the butcher shop is often credited, but there's no consensus among biographers.

The locations are different, but Robert Leroy Parker's childhood isn't that much different than the early years of the boy who would become the Sundance Kid. The youngest of five children, Harry Longabaugh is believed to have been born in the spring of 1867 in Mont Clare or Phoenixville, two blue-collar towns on opposite banks of the Schuylkill River roughly ten miles north of Philadelphia. His mother was a devout Baptist; his father worked various jobs, moved the family from one rented house to another, and put Harry and another brother to work, including at an uncle's canal-boat service. At age 13, Harry was sent to be a servant 10 miles away for the Wilmer Ralston family, who farmed and bred and raised horses. On August 30, 1882, 14-year-old Harry left home to help a distant relative, George Longenbaugh, who had moved his family from Illinois to a homestead in Cortez, Colorado.

Harry helped out at the homestead and also hired on at neighbor's ranch, but he grew restless and rode north in 1886, working as a cowboy or wrangler in Wyoming and Montana, but the hard winter of 1886–1887, which killed thousands of cattle in the western United States, left Harry, and many cowboys, out of work. He sought employment in the Black Hills of present-day South Dakota, and wrote his sister that he wound up working "for my board . . . rather than to beg or steal" (Ernst 2009, 32), and then drifted back to the N Bar N Ranch near Miles City, Montana, where he had previously worked. On February 27, 1887, he stole a horse, revolver, and saddle from an employee of the Three V Ranch near Sundance, Wyoming. He was arrested in Miles City, and the sheriff set out to return him to Sundance, although the Miles City newspaper reported that "[t]he route taken by the sheriff would seem to be a long one; Miles City to St. Paul, St. Paul to the railroad terminus in the Black Hills and thence by state to Sundance, a distance in all of nearly 2,000 miles. Sundance is less than 300 miles across country from here" ("Local Items" 1887, 3).

Harry escaped by jumping off the train near Duluth, Minnesota, but returned to Miles City, where he was arrested again—and almost escaped again—before he landed in the new jail in Sundance on June 22, 1887. He was sentenced to 18 months of hard labor, but because of his age, he was confined in Sundance instead of the territorial penitentiary in Laramie. Although he attempted one escape, Harry, now known as "Kid" Longabaugh, was pardoned on February 4, 1889—a day before his scheduled release. Three months later, however, a sheriff and deputy found Harry in a dugout 35 miles south of Sundance with Buck Hanby and two other men. The lawmen were after Hanby, who was wanted for murder in Kansas. Hanby resisted arrest and was killed by the deputy. Harry apparently threatened the deputy, who swore out a complaint, but Harry either escaped or jumped bail. "Harry Alonzo Longabaugh had made the final transition to outlaw. He was now known as the Sundance Kid" (Ernst 2009, 44).

Robert Leroy Parker soon made that same transition. On June 24, 1889, the young man who would become known as Butch Cassidy robbed his first bank. On June 24, 1889, Cassidy, Matt Warner (1864–1938), and Tom McCarty (ca. 1855–ca. 1900)—and possibly another man who held the horses—robbed the San Miguel Valley bank in Telluride, Colorado, of a reported $20,750.

According to eyewitnesses, shortly after the bank's cashier had left, leaving only the teller inside, one of the robbers entered the building and asked to cash a check—one of the James-Younger Gang's methods of operation was to ask to change a bill or gold piece. When the teller bent down to examine the check, a gun barrel was pressed against his head. Two of the robbers' companions then came inside to gather up as much money as they could. After gathering the money, McCarty said, they warned the teller to "stay inside and keep quiet or his life would pay the penalty" (Patterson 1998, 25). The men reportedly fired guns as they spurred their way out of town, where they passed a rancher who recognized at least Warner and, according to most historians, Cassidy, although newspaper reports identified the suspects as "Thomas McCarty, Billy Madden [who might have held the horses during the robbery] and Matt Warner" ("Bank Robbers Recognized" 1889, 8). "Just that little incident made all the difference in the world to us the rest of our lives," Warner wrote. "It gave 'em a clue so they could trace us for thousands of miles and for years. Right at that point we broke with our half-outlaw past, became real outlaws, burned our bridges behind us, and had no way to live except by robbing and stealing" (Hatch 2014, 50–51). Some reports had the outlaws placing fresh horses along their escape route—a theory that Warner denied—that helped them get away.

Parker, Warner, and McCarty rode into Wyoming together but soon parted ways. Parker soon took upon the alias George Cassidy; "Butch" came later. Cassidy did honest work for a while before turning to rustling cattle and stealing horses. In 1892, Cassidy and his partner, Al Hainer, were arrested and charged with two counts of grand larceny for stealing a horse. The trial did not begin until January 1894; Hainer was acquitted, but Cassidy was convicted and sentenced to two years—he could have gotten as many as ten years—at the state penitentiary (Wyoming was granted statehood in 1890) in Laramie, where Cassidy joined "a brotherhood of hardened criminals who lived in an environment that offered little rehabilitation but plenty of schooling in the finer points of lawbreaking" (Hatch 2014, 133).

The Sundance Kid, meanwhile, had drifted into Canada, where he worked as an honest cowhand before returning to Montana. In a saloon in Malta, Montana, Sundance met Madden, whom he had known in Cortez and who was suspected of being involved in Cassidy's Telluride bank robbery, and another out-of-work cowboy named Harry Bass. Possibly on a whim, the three decided to hold up the Great Northern westbound express. On the morning of November 29, 1892, they robbed the train's express car of checks and packages worth a total of $63.80. The express company put up a reward of $500 for each of the robbers, and Montana's governor agreed to match the reward. Obviously "the railroads wanted to send a clear message that they would not tolerate train robbers" (Ernst 2009, 55). Madden and Bass were caught, tried, convicted, and sentenced to eight and ten years, respectively (Madden received less time for implicating Bass and Sundance) in the penitentiary in Deer Lodge. Though arrested and briefly jailed, Sundance was never rearrested or tried for the Malta robbery. He stayed out of trouble for three years.

On January 19, 1896, Cassidy, who had been a model prisoner during his stay at the Laramie penitentiary, was released about six months early, pardoned by Governor William A. Richards (1849–1912). Cassidy rode to Brown's Hole (called Brown's Park today), a rough, remote region near the Colorado-Utah-Wyoming border "where God turned back and the devil stepped in" (Horan 1970, 14). Cassidy reunited with Warner, now married and with no plans of returning to crime. Cassidy, on the other hand, had no plans to go straight. He bought a new .45-caliber Colt revolver in Vernal, Utah, and met another acquaintance, petty criminal William Ellsworth "Elzy" Lay (1869–1934).

In May 1896, Warner, gambler Bill Wall, and prospector E. B. Coleman were arrested for murdering miners Dave Milton and Dick Staunton. According to most historians, Coleman had conned Warner and Wall into helping him pack up some equipment at a mine he was closing when in reality he was hoping to scare off Milton and Staunton from a possible gold deposit. Milton and Staunton put up a fight and were killed. After the three killers were arrested, Warner pleaded with Cassidy that he needed money to hire a good lawyer. Cassidy said he knew where he could get that money.

That turned out to be from a bank in Montpelier, Idaho, which Cassidy, Lay, and a cowboy named Wilbur "Bob" (or "Bub") Meeks visited on August 13, 1896. "They dismounted and compelled six men who were standing in front of the bank to go inside," newspapers reported. "Two of the desperados then covered the men with revolvers, while the third went behind the counter and emptied all the cash in sight into three sacks. The robbers then mounted their horses and rode out of town. . . . The bank refuses to disclose the amount secured, but it is believed to be fully $10,000" ("BANK ROBBED IN DAYLIGHT" 1896, 2).

Defense attorney Douglas Preston denied that Cassidy had paid him. The jury convicted Wall and Warner of manslaughter—not first-degree murder— and both were sentenced to five years of hard labor; Coleman, who had organized the shootings, was acquitted. The following April, Cassidy and Lay robbed the Pleasant Valley Coal Company payroll in Castle Gate, Utah, of $7,000.

On June 28, 1897, five men—Flatnose George Currie (ca. 1864–1900), Tom O'Day, Harvey Logan (1865–1904), his brother Lonie (1871–1900), and Walt Punteney, or the Sundance Kid—robbed the Butte County Bank in Belle Fourche, South Dakota. It didn't go as planned. O'Day, sent in ahead to scout, reportedly went into a saloon and got drunk (some historians said he faked being intoxicated). The other four rode into town anyway and stepped into the bank. By chance, a businessman across the street looked up to see the people inside the bank raise their hands, and when he stepped outside to investigate, O'Day—reportedly out of the saloon and heading toward the bank—fired at the man. O'Day was caught and arrested; those inside the bank fled, with less than $100, for their hideout at Hole in the Wall, a "stronghold of silence and mystery" (Horan 1970, 13) in Johnson County, Wyoming, that had only one entrance and exit. Punteney was arrested later that summer with two other men who gave their names as Thomas Jones and Frank Jones (possibly Harvey Logan and the Sundance Kid), and all were indicted, along with O'Day, for the bank robbery. On October 31, the four escaped; O'Day and Punteney were recaptured, but Punteney was released because of insufficient evidence, and O'Day was acquitted.

At Hole in the Wall, outlaws came and went, and the gang rarely had more than 10 at a time and likely peaked at 25 or 30. Cassidy is said to have tried to get the robbers known as "Train Robbers' Syndicate." Another name, however, took hold, one "that would perfectly describe this elite corps of ruffians and manslayers. . . . No one knows its true origin, but the colorful moniker was destined to life in infamy—the Wild Bunch" (Hatch 2014, 162), though they were often still called the Hole in the Wall gang.

Members included Logan, who would become known as "Kid Curry," not to be confused with Flatnose George Currie; William "News" Carver (1868– 1901); Ben "the Tall Texan" Kilpatrick (1874–1912); Harry Tracy (1875– 1902); Punteney; O'Day; Lay; and others. "There does not seem to have been any clearly defined leader," historian Leon Claire Metz wrote, "although outlaws such as Butch Cassidy, the Sundance Kid, and the Tall Texan made most of the headlines and tended to be the spokesmen" (Metz 2003, 263).

WHO WERE THOSE GUYS?

Sheriffs, marshals, and vigilantes chased outlaws such as Butch Cassidy and the Sundance Kid, but the biggest threat to train robbers might have been Pinkerton's National Detective Agency.

Founded in Chicago by Allan Pinkerton (1819–1884), who led the Union Intelligence Service (a predecessor of the Secret Service) during the Civil War (1861–1865), Pinkerton and his male and female detectives "set the global standard for investigative and security excellence for generations to come" (Enss 2017, vii). America's first professional private-detective agency kept files of criminals, including mug shots, biographical files, newspaper clippings, and methods of operation.

By the mid-1850s, the company specialized in protecting shipments by railroads. When a train was robbed, Pinkertons might be called in. Among the outlaws pursued by Pinkerton's detectives were the Reno Gang, the James-Younger Gang, the Dalton Gang, and Butch Cassidy's Wild Bunch. After Pinkerton's death, his sons William and Robert took over operations. By the 1890s, the company employed approximately 2,000 detectives.

No longer chasing outlaws, the agency operates today as a security service and was acquired by Securitas AB, the world's largest security-service provider, in 1999.

Source

Enss, Chris. 2017. *The Pinks: The First Women Detectives, Operatives, and Spies with the Pinkerton National Detective Agency*. Guilford, CT: TwoDot.

Early in the morning on June 2, 1899, six members of the Hole in the Wall Gang/Wild Bunch robbed a Union Pacific express car near Wilcox, Wyoming. Three days later, a 14-man posse surprised three of the suspected robbers—supposedly Currie, Harvey Logan, and the Sundance Kid—at a water hole. In the ensuing gunfight, Converse County Sheriff Josiah Hazen was shot and killed. The three bandits escaped; the posse did not follow. The Pinkerton National Detective Agency was hired to track down the bandits. Other robberies followed—another Union Pacific train robbery near Tipton, Wyoming, on August 29, 1900; and the robbery of the First National Bank in Winnemucca, Nevada, on September 19, 1900. Many other crimes were attributed to the Wild Bunch, including a saloon hold-up in Elko, Nevada, on April 3, 1899. "The Wild Bunch holding up saloons? Maybe not. (Unsolved crimes are often attributed to famous outlaws.)," Wild Bunch historians Daniel Buck and Anne Meadows wrote (Buck and Meadows 2002).

Later that fall, five of the gang members—Cassidy, Sundance, Logan, Carver, and Kilpatrick—arrived in Fort Worth, Texas, to escape a tightening noose up north and/or to celebrate Carver's marriage to Callie May Hunt, also known as Lillie Davis.

On November 21, the five outlaws posed for a photograph at the Fort Worth studio of John Swartz. Each of the men got a print, and Swartz liked the photograph enough that he put a copy in his front window. "Cassidy showed uncharacteristic carelessness in going along with what was probably a lark," Logan biographer Mark T. Smokov said (Mark T. Smokov, interview with author, December 10, 2012). A detective—usually identified as Fred Dodge of the Wells Fargo & Company, but possibly Fort Worth police detective Charles R. Scott—saw the photograph, recognized one of the men, promptly ordered several copies of the photo, and began working on identifying the other men. Wanted posters soon included the likenesses of five of the most wanted outlaws in the West. "I think it at least helped to put pressure on the outlaws since the law now had good likenesses of five of the major members of the Wild Bunch that could be used in the circulation of wanted posters," Smokov said. "Before this, the only photo available, at least of any quality, was Cassidy's prison mug shot. [Logan] actually shaved off his thick mustache to change his appearance for the gang's next train robbery, the Great Northern in Montana" (Mark T. Smokov, interview with author, December 10, 2012).

With authorities closing in, Sundance and Cassidy left the United States for South America, accompanied by a woman usually known as Etta or Ethel Place. They sailed from New York City on the British ship *Herminius* to Buenos Aires, Argentina, and from there traveled by train to Patagonia and settled in sparsely populated southern Argentina under the names James "Santiago" Ryan and Mr. and Mrs. Harry "Enrique" Place. Between some honest jobs, they are believed to have participated in a few robberies before Etta returned to the United States. On November 6, 1908, Cassidy and Sundance rode into the mining village of San Vicente, Bolivia, where a resident agreed to put them up in a spare room. A village official then alerted a posse on the lookout for American bandits. Three members of the posse accompanied the villager to the building. A gunfight ensued and at dawn the following morning, the two American bandits were found dead.

The dead outlaws were believed to have been Butch Cassidy and the Sundance Kid, but William A. Pinkerton called the reports "a fake," and the Pinkertons "never officially called off the search for Butch and Sundance" (Meadows and Buck 1997). The files were finally closed in 1921.

DEPICTION AND CULTURAL CONTEXT

Western movies have rarely been known for getting facts right, but Goldman did his research for the screenplay. "Surprisingly," Thom Hatch said, "the movie did capture much of the known truth about Butch and Sundance. Obviously, they added dialogue in the 1969 movie to make them more lovable—Butch was happy-go-lucky; Sundance often moody—but the heists were factual, as far as we know" (Thom Hatch, interview with author, May 2, 2019).

Even the film's famous bicycle ride was put in a history book before the movie made it famous, although James D. Horan wrote that the ride was in San Antonio, Texas, outside of Fanny Porter's bordello, and some of Horan's facts have been questioned if not outright disproven. "The bicycle craze was sweeping the country at the time and Butch became an expert rider," Horan wrote. "It must have been a wonderful scene with Cassidy, his derby perched off to one side of his head, cycling up the street of the red-light district as Fanny and her girls shrilled encouragement" (Horan 1949, 243). In the movie, Cassidy takes Etta for a ride, but exactly who Etta Place really was continues to baffle historians.

The Pinkertons described her as "about 27 years old, five feet four inches in height, weighing about 110 pounds, medium complexion and wears her brown hair on the top of her head in a roll from forehead. She appears to be a refined type" (Hatch 2014, 169). Place was likely an alias; it was the maiden name of Sundance's mother, and Sundance sometimes used Harry A. Place as his alias. She was also called Ethel, Etta, Eva, and Rita. She might have married Sundance, or they—like many Westerners—could have been involved in a common-law relationship. She's a schoolteacher in *Butch Cassidy and the Sundance Kid*; some historians say she was likely a prostitute. Neither theory has been proven or disproven. A photograph of her and Sundance was taken at DeYoung Photography Studio on Broadway in New York City on February 3, 1901.

The movie has Etta assisting Cassidy and Sundance on some of their robberies, and on December 19, 1905, Etta and another person helped Cassidy and Sundance rob a bank in Villa Mercedes, Argentina, of about 12,000 pesos. They evaded posses and crossed the Andes into Chile. After that, she is believed to have left Cassidy and Sundance in South America, sailed to San Francisco on a ship, and "has eluded scholars with the same proficiency that Butch and Sundance eluded lawmen" (Hatch 2014, 170).

Redford had to fight to keep his mustache for the role, saying "that was the way those bandits looked at the turn of the century. It was authentic" (Callan 2011, 148). He was right. The Fort Worth and New York photographs of Sundance show him mustached. In the Fort Worth photograph, Logan and Cassidy also wear mustaches, but Newman remained cleanshaven. Phillips recalled the story of studio executive Darryl F. Zanuck's remark about the mustache Gregory Peck (1916–2003) grew for *The Gunfighter* (1950): "That facial hair is going to cost me $2 million." But Redford won out. The mustache stayed.

The Sundance Kid is portrayed as a fast-shooting and incredibly accurate gunfighter—so good he can shoot a gun belt off a gambler and then keep firing bullets to propel the gun belt and holster across a gambling den's floor. Most historians say Sundance was a gunman—one who "rarely had to pull his six-shooter because of his alleged reputation," Hatch said (Thom Hatch, interview with author, May 2, 2019). But it's hard to find contemporary accounts of his alleged expertise. "Harry Lonbaugh [sic], Cassidy's right hand and leading lieutenant, is almost as dangerous in criminal courage and intellect as the great 'Butch' himself," one newspaper reported ("OUTLAWS READY FOR DESPERATE WORK" 1902, 4). When another newspaper, the *Yellowstone Daily Journal* of Miles City, Montana, compared Sundance to the notorious robber and killer Jesse James (1847–1882), Sundance wrote a letter to the editor, calling the article "very sensational and partly untrue." Conceding that he had "done wrong and expecting to be dealt with according to the law," he said, "I have always worked for an honest living" before "my course of outlawry commenced" ("LONGABAUGH'S STATEMENT" 1887, 3). "Had Jesse James been in a position to post his own letter—he was not, having been killed some years earlier—he might have griped about being aligned with a callow horse thief," Buck and Meadows quipped (Ernst 2009, xiv).

The Sundance Kid is believed to have been involved in two incidents that resulted in deaths: the June 5, 1894, gunfight in Wyoming in which Converse County Sheriff Josiah Hazen was killed and the November 6, 1908, shootout with Bolivian officials in which soldier Victor Torres was mortally wounded, and the two American bandits, believed to be Cassidy and Sundance, were killed. But Logan is thought to have killed Hazen, and Cassidy is suspected of shooting Torres—which could make the Sundance Kid the greatest gunfighter who never killed anyone.

"They also got it right when showing that Butch and Sundance did not kill anyone during their robberies, and ordered their gang not to rob passengers or bystanders, just the bank or railroad," Hatch said. "How Butch managed to keep that killer Harvey Logan's finger off the trigger is beyond me" (Thom Hatch, interview with author, May 2, 2019).

Logan, alias Kid Curry, perhaps had the deadliest reputation among the Wild Bunch. "Logan was one of the most desperate bandits that ever infested the west or the country" ("Kid Curry Died Game" 1904, 3). But Logan biographer Mark T. Smokov argued that even Logan's reputation has been exaggerated, that he was not a cold-blooded homicidal maniac, and that only one killing can be directly attributed to Logan: the shooting of Powell "Pike" Landusky in Landusky, Montana, on December 27, 1894, after a brawl in a saloon.

> The Pinkertons were frustrated at not being able to catch Kid Curry, and attempted to portray him as desperate as Jesse James, another bandit that they had much trouble trying to apprehend. Many writers and historians seemed to have a need to portray at least one Wild Bunch member as a psychopathic killer. Curry cannot be compared to a Harry Tracy or John Wesley Hardin, the latter supposedly shooting a man for snoring. (Mark T. Smokov, interview with author, December 10, 2012)

The scene where Logan tries to take over the Hole-in-the-Wall gang from Cassidy is also an embellishment. Most historians say there never was any official leader, and Smokov said: "It would have been more accurate if the movie had been titled *Kid Curry and the Sundance Kid*" (Mark T. Smokov, interview with author, December 10, 2012).

Sundance and Logan participated in several train robberies from 1897 to 1900, whereas Cassidy's early bank and payroll heists were done with Lay. Logan also started out rustling cattle with other Wild Bunch members, including Currie, O'Day, and Punteney. Logan's "leadership abilities were soon recognized by the Wild Bunch fraternity when he switched to robbing trains after the Belle Fourche bank fiasco," Smokov said. "Contemporary sources often relegate Cassidy to the background by referring to this bunch as 'Kid Curry's gang'" (Mark T. Smokov, interview with author, December 10, 2012).

The back-to-back Union Pacific train heists are loosely based on fact. In the film, Butch, Sundance, and gang members stop the Flyer, but a dedicated express agent named Woodcock (George Furth, 1932–2008) refuses to open the express car, so News Carver uses dynamite to get inside. When the Union Pacific Express was robbed near Wilcox, Wyoming, in 1899, one newspaper reported that mail clerks W. G. Bruce and L. L. Dietrich were locked inside the express car. After the train was stopped, the engineer told the robbers that the clerk's name was Sherman, so they called out the name. "I told them Sherman was not there," Bruce said. "They told me to open the door and come out anyway" (Special to the Herald 1899, 1). The outlaws told him to open the door anyway, but Bruce and Dietrich refused and blew out the light inside the car. Bruce continued:

> The bandits then fired several shots through the mail car, sending bullets crosswise, lengthwise and cornerwise. We still refused to open the door, and the robbers placed some giant powder in the door and exploded it, tearing the door off its hinges. One of the robbers then shoved his pistol through the doorway and fired another shot. They were going to put more dynamite under the car, when we came out. (Special to the Herald 1899, 1)

The Chicago Inter Ocean, however, said the Pacific Express manager's name was Woodcock—as in the movie—and after dynamite blew the doors "to atoms," the robbers dragged the unconscious Woodcock out of the car. "Once more dynamite was used and with terrible effect, the door of the safe being blown off, a hole torn in the top, and the roof and sides of the express car being demolished, and the end of the adjoining mail car being badly damaged. The express matter was blown into small fragments and the contents of the safe suffered also" (Special to the Inter Ocean 1899, 1).

Woodcock was also the express messenger when the outlaws robbed the Union Pacific train near Tipton, Wyoming, on August 29, 1900. Conductor Ed J. Kerrigan said that the robbers ordered Woodcock to open the door, but he refused. "Then when I saw they were going to blow up the car I told him to come out, and he did so," Kerrigan said. The outlaws moved Kerrigan,

Woodcock, the engineer, fireman, and brakeman down the tracks, while making sure none of the passengers got off the train, and then used dynamite in the express car. "They blew the roof, sides and end out of the baggage car and demolished the next car to it," Kerrigan said. "They put three charges on the safe before they could break it open" ("BANDITS TACKLE OVERLAND" 1900, 1).

So the line Redford says to Butch after the express car is blown to smithereens in the movie—"Think you used enough dynamite there, Butch?"—is not farfetched.

In the movie, Joe Lefors leads the "Superposse," which is guided by a Native American out of Oklahoma who is called Lord Baltimore, a fictional character. On the other hand, Lefors was elected captain of a posse that pursued the Hole-in-the-Wall gang, at least in Wyoming. After the Wilcox robbery, the Burlington Railroad asked Lefors to join the posse. Lefors did not need a Lord Baltimore; the respected stock detective had a reputation as a good tracker. For five days, Lefors followed the trail nearly 200 miles before a Lander lawman sent the posse "on a wild goose chase" (Pointer 1977, 153). Lefors suggested that the lawman might have intentionally misled the posse, which wasn't exactly a Superposse.

In the movie, the Superposse kills Carver and Currie after the second train robbery, which is also inaccurate. But when friendly lawman Bledsoe tells Butch and Sundance, "[Y]ou're gonna die bloody, and all you can do is choose where," he spoke accurately about most members of the Wild Bunch.

A posse caught up with Currie while rustling on April 17, 1900, in Utah and killed him near the Green River; Carver was shot to death on April 2, 1901, in Sonora, Texas, in a gunfight with a sheriff and four deputies while Carver and George Kilpatrick, Ben's brother, were buying feed for their horses; Kilpatrick was wounded. A posse trapped Logan near Parachute, Colorado, after he and two other men robbed a train. His accomplices escaped, but rather than be recaptured, Logan killed himself with a gunshot wound to the head. The last of the Wild Bunch's most wanted to die was Kilpatrick. After he was arrested, tried, and convicted in 1901, Kilpatrick was released from prison in 1911. On March 12, 1912, he and another outlaw were killed while attempting to rob a train near Sanderson, Texas. "The gang fell apart—killed or captured—when Butch and Sundance went to South America because they couldn't plan their robberies like Butch could plan them," Hatch said (Thom Hatch, interview with author, May 2, 2019).

Most historians say that Cassidy and Sundance's end was bloody, too, but not quite the way depicted in the movie, which also omits the duo's time in Argentina and Chile. Cassidy and Sundance did serve as payroll guards in Bolivia, only to quit after Sundance got drunk and started talking about previous criminal activities. On November 3, 1908, the two attempted to rob a Bolivian mining enterprise of its payroll. They expected to net 80,000 pesos, but they were a week early for the larger payroll, and they collected only 15,000 pesos. On November 6, they arrived in San Vincente, where Cleto Bellot, the village's chief administrative officer, told them that, although the village had no inn, they could stay in a spare room at Bonifacio Casasola's home. Sundance gave Casasola money to buy sardines and beer for their supper. Bellot then went to another home, where a posse led by Captain Justo P. Concha was being housed. The four-man posse had arrived in town earlier that day, telling Bellot to watch out for two Americans and a mule. Concha was asleep, but the other posse members loaded their rifles and accompanied Bellot to Casasola's house.

It was dark when they entered the patio. As they walked toward the room, Cassidy stepped into the doorway and fired a pistol, hitting soldier Victor Torres in the neck. Torres managed to return fire before retreating to a nearby house, where he soon died. The other posse members shot multiple times with their high-powered rifles before retreating out of the patio with Bellot. Bellot left to find other villagers willing to help watch, and the soldiers opened fire again. Concha arrived to take command while more villagers showed up with weapons. Bellot said he heard "three screams of desperation" from inside the spare room.

Gunfire ceased. The guards waited in the cold and wind until dawn. Then Concha ordered Casasola to check the room, where he found the two Americans dead.

> They found Butch stretched out on the floor, one bullet wound in his temple and another in his arm, and Sundance sitting on a bench behind the door, hugging a large ceramic jar, shot once in the forehead and several times in the arm. According to one report, the bullet removed from Sundance's forehead had come from Butch's Colt. From the positions of the bodies and the locations of the fatal wounds, the witnesses apparently concluded that Butch had put his partner out of his misery, then turned the gun on himself. (Meadows and Buck 1997)

But outlaws can be hard to kill. Just as stories exist that Billy the Kid and Jesse James weren't killed as reported, rumors persisted that Cassidy or Sundance survived and returned to the United States. A Spokane, Washington, resident named William T. Phillips claimed to be Butch Cassidy and wrote an unpublished biography titled *The Bandit Invincible, the Story of Butch Cassidy* in 1934. Most historians dismissed Phillips's account. In 2011, an unabridged version of the Phillips manuscript was discovered, putting Phillips, who died in 1937, and Cassidy in the news again. Buck called the manuscript "Total horse pucky" (Gruver 2011, M-6). In 1983, Edward M. Kirby's book *The Rise & Fall of the Sundance Kid* claimed that Sundance wasn't killed in Bolivia but returned to the United States as Hiram BeBee, also known as George Hanlon, a convicted murderer who died in a Utah prison in 1955. "BeBee was nearly nine inches shorter than Sundance," Donna B. Ernst wrote, "and even osteoporosis doesn't shrink a person that much" (Ernst 2009, 180). Stories continue to resurrect Cassidy and Sundance; a 2011 movie, *Blackthorn*, starred Sam Shepard (1943–2017) as an aging Cassidy living in Bolivia in 1927—19 years after his supposed death. Investigations by Buck and Meadows, however, show "that two North Americans using aliases attributed to Butch and Sundance had died in San Vicente, and very little evidence to support the competing theories about their fate" (Buck and Meadows 2008).

Conspiracy theories, however, have always been practically impossible to silence. "It's easier to believe the Hollywood version, the romantic version," award-winning historian and documentarian Paul Andrew Hutton said in The History Channel's series *Investigating History*'s episode "Butch Cassidy & the Sundance Kid" that first aired in 2004. "It's hard to believe that outlaws that had eluded the Pinkertons, that had eluded the Superposse that chased them across the West would wind up shot down in a pathetic and sad end to a glamorous and romantic career."

CONCLUSION

Butch Cassidy and the Sundance Kid remains an important movie for multiple reasons. Blending history and myth, Goldman's screenplay helped revive a genre that was fading fast. Win Blevins, film critic for the *Los Angeles Herald-Examiner* in 1969, recalled:

> In 1969, the Western movie was breathing its last. The world had turned Hippie. *Midnight Cowboy*, about a male prostitute, got the Best Picture Oscar. Amazingly, from this madness emerged what may be the best two Westerns ever made, and they were hits—Sam Peckinpah's *The Wild Bunch* and George Roy Hill's *Butch Cassidy and the Sundance Kid*. . . . *Butch* dances gracefully and charmingly to a Burt Bacharach tune. Peckinpah's world is a huge, tragic Beethoven symphony. Each holds forth today on the major lists of the best 100 American movies ever made. (Win Blevins, interview with author, May 10, 2019)

Partly because of those two movies, the Western managed to hold on— sometimes by its fingernails—until the financial disaster of *Heaven's Gate* (1980). After that box-office bomb, Westerns became a hard sell in Hollywood, although occasional upswings have helped temporarily resurrect the genre.

Perhaps more importantly, the movie revived an interest in historical Western figures. Butch Cassidy and the Sundance Kid had been depicted in previous movies, but usually superficially. In *Wyoming Renegades* (1954), a former gang member is blamed for one of the gang's robberies, forcing him to rejoin Butch, Sundance, and the boys in order to clear his name and bring the outlaws to justice. *Badman's Country* (1958) sent Pat Garrett, Wyatt Earp, Bat Masterson, and Buffalo Bill Cody against Butch Cassidy, the Sundance Kid, and Wild Bunch members. Obviously, those films, like other Westerns, had nothing to do with history.

After the success of *Butch Cassidy and the Sundance Kid* at the box office, however, the title characters "became household names because it was Robert Redford and Paul Newman in the lead roles. Before that, Butch was the main focus of Old West buffs. Sundance was oh-by-the-way" (Thom Hatch, interview with author, May 2, 2019).

Goldman said he had to find magazine articles to research his screenplay in the 1950s and 1960s because no books were available (a slight exaggeration; books had been published). No screenwriter would face such an obstacle today. Biographies and histories are easily available, and more continue to be published—thanks to *Butch Cassidy and the Sundance Kid*.

FURTHER READING

"BANDITS TACKLE OVERLAND: Five Masked Men Hold Up Union Pacific Flyer in Wyoming. DYNAMITE USED TO GET THE PLUNDER. Robber Climbs Over Tender and Covers Engineer with Revolver—No One Is Injured, but Much Property Is Damaged." 1900. *Omaha Daily Bee*, August 31, 1900, p. 1.

"BANK ROBBED IN DAYLIGHT. Three Masked Men Take All the Cash in a Montpelier, Ida., Bank." 1896. *Beatrice Daily Express*, August 14, 1896, 2.

"Bank Robbers Recognized." 1889. *St. Louis Post-Dispatch*, June 20, 1889, p. 8.

"Bank Robbery." 1889. *El Paso Times*, June 26, 1889, p. 1.

Boardman, Mark. 2017. "Will Carver Checks Out: The Outlaw Buys It during a Visit to the Store." *True West*, November 2, 2007. https:// truewestmagazine.com /will-carver-checks-out

Bronson, Fred. 2003. *The Billboard Book of Number 1 Hits: The Inside Story behind Every Number One Single on Billboard's Hot 100 from 1950 to the Present: Revised and Updated Fifth Edition*. New York: Broadway Books.

Buck, Daniel, and Anne Meadows. 2002. "The Wild Bunch: Wild, but Not Much of a Bunch." *True West*, November 1, 2002. https://truewestmagazine.com/the -wild-bunch

Buck, Daniel, and Anne Meadows. 2008. "Needles and Cats." *True West*, November 1, 2008, https://truewestmagazine.com/needles-and-cats

Callan, Michael Feeney. 2011. *Robert Redford: The Biography*. New York: Alfred A. Knopf.

Canby, Vincent. 1969. "Slapstick and Drama Cross Paths in 'Butch Cassidy.'" *New York Times*, September 25, 1969, p. 54.

Champlin, Charles. 1969. "'Butch Cassidy,' a Tale of 2 Outdated Outlaws." *Los Angeles Times*, October 1, 1969, Part IV, pp. 1, 15.

Clagett, Thomas D. 2018. "Hybrid Western: *Butch Cassidy and the Sundance Kid*." *Roundup Magazine*, December 2017, pp. 14–15.

Ebert, Roger. 1969. "Butch Cassidy and the Sundance Kid." October 13, 1969. https://www.rogerebert.com/reviews/butch-cassidy-and-the-sundance-kid-1969

Ernst, Donna B. 2009. *The Sundance Kid: The Life of Harry Alonzo Longabaugh*. Norman: University of Oklahoma Press.

Gauguin, Lorraine. 1968. "WHAT MAKES PAUL PRODUCE? FOR MONASH, IT'S NOT THE MONEY IN MOVIES." *Independent Press-Telegram Southland Magazine*, November 3, 1968, p. 8.

Goldman, William. 1984. *Adventures in the Screen Trade: A Personal View of Hollywood and Screenwriting*. New York: Warner Books.

Goldman, William. 1997. *Four Screenplays with Essays: Marathon Man—Butch Cassidy and the Sundance Kid—The Princess Bride—Misery*. New York: Applause Books.

Goldman, William. 2001. *Which Lie Did I Tell? More Adventures in the Screen Trade*. New York: Vintage Books.

Gruver, Mead. 2011. "Old Text, New Wrinkles: Did Butch Cassidy Survive?" *Great Falls Tribune*, August 16, 2011, p. M-6.

Hatch, Thom. 2014. *The Last Outlaws: The Lives and Legends of Butch Cassidy and the Sundance Kid*. New York: New American Library.

"The HOLE-IN-THE-WALL." 1899. *Daily Pioneer-Times*, June 15, 1899, p. 4.

Horan, James D. 1949. *Desperate Men: Revelations from the Sealed Pinkerton Files*. New York: Bonanza Books.

Horan, James D. 1970. *The Wild Bunch*. New York: Signet Books.

International News Service. "Rebuild Ghost Town in Order to Make Movie: After 50 Years Town of Grafton, Utah, Reconstructed to Make 'Ramrod.'" *New Castle News*, April 4, 1947, p. 28.

Kelley, Charles. 1996. *The Outlaw Trail: A History of Butch Cassidy & His Wild Bunch*. Lincoln: Bison Books.

"Kid Curry Died Game. Last Raid of the Famous Train Robber and Bandit Thief. Led the Jackson's Hole Gang of Desperadoes in a Siege of Crime and Died at Last by His Own Hand." 1904. *Salisbury Globe*, October 26, 1904, p. 3.

Kirby, Edward M. 1983. *The Rise & Fall of the Sundance Kid*. Iola, WI: Western Publications.

Levy, Shawn. 2009. *Paul Newman: A Life*. New York: Three Rivers Press.

"Local Items." 1887. *Daily Yellowstone Journal*, April 12, 1887, p. 3.

"LONGABAUGH'S STATEMENT." 1887. *Daily Yellowstone Journal*, June 9, 1887.

Meadows, Anne. 1996. *Digging Up Butch & Sundance: Revised Edition*. Lincoln: Bison Books.

Meadows, Anne, and Daniel Buck. 1997. "The Last Days of Butch Cassidy and the Sundance Kid." *Wild West*, February 1997. https://www.historynet.com/butch-cassidy

Metz, Leon Claire. 2003. *The Encyclopedia of Lawmen, Outlaws, and Gunfighters*. New York: Facts on File, Inc.

"MOST DESPERATE PLOT UNEARTHED. Connection of the Montpelier Bank Robbery with the Murders Near Vernal Last Spring. THERE MAY BE A BATTLE. How Cassady and His Gang Proposed to Liberate Their Pals. WARNER, WALL AND COLEMAN. Looted the Bank to Get Defense Money. Prepared to Take Their Friends from Custody by Force of Arms as a Last Resort—The Arrest of the Desperadoes Confidently Expected This Morning—They Are Located Near Ogden at This Time—A Story of Daring and Crime That Recalls the Deeds of Jesse James—Clever Work at the Detectives and Officers in Bringing the Facts to Light—The Indicted Men Now on Trial at Junction City." 1896. *Salt Lake Herald*, September 9, 1896, p. 1.

". . . New Type Western." 1969. *Cincinnati Enquirer*, January 30, 1969, p. 13.

Nix, Elizabeth. 2018. "6 Things You May Not Know about Butch Cassidy: From the Origins of His Famous Name to the Mystery Surrounding His Death, Get the Story on This Legendary American Outlaw." *History*, August 22, 2018. https://www.history.com/news/6-things-you-might-not-know-about-butch-cassidy

"OUTLAWS READY FOR DESPERATE WORK: Story from Rock Springs, Wyo. Relates of Preparations of Hole-in-the-Wall and Robbers' Roost Gang and of Their Intentions—Caring Deeds of 'Butch' Cassidy's Bad Gang." 1902. *Anaconda Standard*, April 30, 1902, p. 4.

Patterson, Richard. 1998. *Butch Cassidy: A Biography*. Lincoln: University of Nebraska Press.

Pocock, Geoffrey A. 2007. *Outrider of Empire: The Life & Adventures of Roger Pocock, 1865–1941*. Edmonton: The University of Alberta Press.

Pointer, Larry. 1977. *In Search of Butch Cassidy*. Norman: University of Oklahoma Press.

Smokov, Mark T. 2012. *He Rode with Butch and Sundance: The Story of Harvey "Kid Curry" Logan*. Denton: University of North Texas Press.

Special to the Herald. 1899. "BANDITS HELD THE TRAIN UP. Bold Robbery of Union Pacific Express in Wyoming. DYNAMITE USED TO BLOW OPEN SAFES. Make Their Escape and Posses are after Them. Daring Work of Six Men, Believed to be Members of Utah's Famous 'Hole-in-the-Wall' Gang—Destroyed a Bridge and Wrecked Cars—Brutal Treatment of Trainmen—The Amount Secured Is Not Unknown." 1899. *Salt Lake Herald*, June 3, 1899, 1.

Special to the Inter Ocean. 1899. "U. P. FLYNER HELD UP: Daring Robbery on Railroad's Main Line Near Laramie, Wyoming. DYNAMITE WAS USED. Six Bandits Signal and Stop Overland Flyer and Destroy a Bridge. BLOW OPEN DOOR OF CAR. Contents of Safe Removed in Sacks and Escape Made to the Medicine Bow Mountains—Posse in Pursuit." *Daily Inter Ocean*, June 3, 1899, 1.

Tribune Special. 1900a. "BANDITS' RICH HAUL. Express Messenger Said the Robbers Got $55,000." *Salt Lake Tribune*, September 1, 1900, p. 1.

Tribune Special. 1900b. "WILCOX TRAIN ROBBERS. Two of Gang Believed to be in Tipton Hold-Up." *Salt Lake Tribune*, September 1, 1900, p. 1.

"Utah Picked for Major Movie Location." *Tooele Bulletin*, July 23, 1968, p. 7.

Chapter 8

Little Big Man (1970)

Based on a popular 1964 novel by Thomas Berger (1924–2014), *Little Big Man* "could not possibly have been filmed at the time it was published" (Herzberg 2008, 246). Although movies like *The Vanishing American* (1925), *They Died with Their Boots On* (1941), *Fort Apache* (1948), *Broken Arrow* (1950), *Devil's Doorway* (1950), and *Tomahawk* (1951) depicted Native Americans in a positive light, the majority of Western films still portrayed them as savages as in *Apache Rifles*, *Bullet for a Badman*, and *Rio Conchos*, all 1964 releases. Another 1964 film, *Cheyenne Autumn*, directed by John Ford (1894–1973), was sympathetic to the plight of Cheyenne Indians but failed to impress critics or moviegoers at a time when Westerns were falling out of favor at the box office. That didn't stop producer-director Arthur Penn (1922–2010) from buying screen rights for Berger's novel in 1965. "There has been so much nonsense about the Indian in Westerns that it's time someone showed how he was wronged by history," Penn said. "Custer's Last Stand offers a good opportunity" (Thomas 1969, 8B). But four years passed before the movie went into production.

By then, the mood of the country was changing. In 1968, President Lyndon B. Johnson (1908–1973) asked Congress for $500 million to provide Native Americans with economic, social and educational opportunities, and signed an executive order creating the National Council on Indian Opportunity, saying that Native Americans deserved "an opportunity to remain in their homelands, if they choose, without surrendering their dignity, an opportunity to move to the towns and cities of American, if they choose, equipped with the skills to live in equality and dignity" (United Press International 1968, 3). Protests by Native Americans led to the founding of the American Indian Movement in 1968, and a peaceful occupation of Alcatraz

Island in San Francisco by Native Americans started in 1969 and lasted 19 months. Protests against the war in Vietnam also continued, while reports of the 1968 massacre of unarmed Vietnamese civilians in My Lai hit the news in 1969. Three Western movies released that year—director Sam Peckinpah's *The Wild Bunch*, Henry Hathaway's *True Grit*, and George Roy Hill's *Butch Cassidy and the Sundance Kid*, the year's top box-office draw—breathed new life into the genre. The time was right for a movie that depicted unjust policies against Native Americans while also condemning actions in Vietnam.

In *Little Big Man*, 121-year-old Jack Crabb (Dustin Hoffman, 1937–) tells a historian (William Hickey, 1927–1997) his life story from the time he and his sister Caroline (Carol Androsky, 1942–) survived an Indian massacre, circa 1852, to just after the Battle of the Little Big Horn in Montana Territory in 1876. After their parents were killed by Pawnee Indians while heading to California, Caroline and Jack are rescued by Cheyenne Indians, but Caroline abandons her 10-year-old brother with the Cheyennes, whose leader, Old Lodge Skins (Chief Dan George, 1899–1981), adopts the young boy and brings him up as a Cheyenne. Crabb saves the life of Younger Bear (Cal Bellini, 1935–2017) during a raid against Pawnee Indians and is given the name Little Big Man. After the army kills Cheyenne women and children in an attack on a village, Old Lodge Skins decides to fight the whites, and Little Big Man is almost killed before he convinces an army soldier that he isn't an Indian.

Returned to "civilization," Crabb is taken into the home of the Reverend Silas Pendrake (Thayer David, 1927–1978) and his promiscuous wife (Faye Dunaway, 1941–). Crabb leaves the Pendrakes and joins a con artist (Martin Balsam, 1919–1996), but the two are tarred and feathered by angry citizens, including Caroline. Back with his family, Crabb learns gunfighting skills from his sister and befriends Wild Bill Hickok (Jeff Corey, 1914–2002). More adventures follow as Crabb marries Olga, a Swedish immigrant (Kelly Jean Peters, 1940–); meets General George Armstrong Custer (Richard Mulligan, 1932–2000); sees his wife kidnapped by Cheyennes; and joins Custer's regiment as a civilian muleskinner to find Olga; when he does find her, she has married Younger Bear. During another cavalry massacre of women and children, Crabb saves a Cheyenne woman, whom he marries. But Custer and his soldiers attack a peaceful camp on the Washita River, killing Little Big Man's Cheyenne wife and newborn son. After rejoining the whites, Crabb becomes a drunk before Hickok straightens him out just before Hickok is gunned down. Living alone in the wilderness, Crabb is about to kill himself when he spots Custer's soldiers. He rejoins Custer, who leads his men to annihilation in a battle against Lakotas and Cheyennes at the Little Big Horn River, but Old Lodge Skins knows that the Cheyennes' days as a free people are numbered. "We won today," he tells Little Big Man. "We won't win tomorrow." After hearing the story, the surprised and saddened historian leaves Crabb alone.

By 1966, Stockbridge Productions, run by Penn and Stuart Millar (1929–2006), and studio Metro-Goldwyn-Mayer (MGM) agreed to terms to make *Little Big Man*. Playwright Jack Richardson (1934–2012), who had written *Lorenzo*, a 1963 play directed by Penn, started on the screenplay. Penn said a screenplay was finished by 1967, but the deal with MGM fell through. In 1969, Cinema Center Films agreed to finance the movie. Penn told Gordon Stulberg (1923–2000), head of CCF: "This is going to be my response to concentration camps—to genocide. And he kept saying, 'But it's got to be funny.' I said, 'It will be funny. And it also will carry that tone.' He was utterly confused by the conversation. I thought he was gonna scotch the deal, but he said, 'Okay. But make sure it's funny'" (Segaloff 2011, 193).

Hoffman agreed to play Crabb, and Calder Willingham (1922–1995), who had cowritten Hoffman's 1967 hit *The Graduate*, replaced Richardson as screenwriter.

Berger's 440-page novel was an episodic adventure that "packed so many characters into his book that you could make half a dozen completely different films from the novel," Penn said (Chaiken and Cronin 2008, 82–83). Characters were cut, added, and the timeline was altered. In one of the biggest changes, Old Lodge Skins dies in Berger's novel, but survives in Penn's film. "We talked long and hard about this and in the first draft of the script he does die," Penn said, "but his death would have introduced an element of sadness into the film and we didn't want this" (Chaiken and Cronin 2008, 84).

Dunaway, who had starred in Penn's *Bonnie and Clyde* (1967), wanted a part in *Little Big Man*, and despite Penn's argument that no role was big enough for her, Dunaway insisted. Willingham came up with the idea of merging the Mrs. Pendrake character with a prostitute involved with Hickok. Dunaway landed that part.

The budget was set at $7 million, but it reportedly grew to an estimated $15 million with filming in California, Montana, and Canada. Those locations including the Crow and Northern Cheyenne Indian reservations in Montana and the Stony Indian reservation in Morley, roughly 40 miles west of Calgary, Alberta. The tribes allowed filming on their lands providing that tribal members were hired as extras at $21 a day. According to Hoffman biographer Jeff Lenburg, "Millar approved of these agreements as a means of strengthening relations with the Indians and warding off protests against the film as 'denigrating to Indians'" (Lenburg 1983, 52). Pie Glenn, a 35-year-old Crow Indian, landed a speaking part, which upped his salary to $125 daily, although it is not clear if Glenn's scene survived the film's final cut. "If it weren't for this movie, a lot of us would be fighting fire, or stacking hay," he said (*New York Times* Service 1969, 15). Much of the Crow Agency location included the Little Big Horn River adjacent to what is now Little Bighorn Battlefield National Monument. The scenes of the final battle took eight days of filming and used between 500 and 600 Native American extras.

The film wasn't without incidents. Actor James Anderson (1921–1969), who played a racist cavalry sergeant, died of a heart attack in Montana after completing his scenes. Trip wires to cause horses to fall angered the American Society for the Prevention of Cruelty to Animals. And Penn said that although Crow Indian extras were given rubber-tipped arrows, the young men "would get so jazzed up that they'd take the tips off the arrows." One stuntman reportedly lost an eye after an arrow struck a tear duct. "We had to go around and be very careful, take after take after take, that they wouldn't touch those tips," Penn said (Segaloff 2011, 195). Penn and Millar also thought filming in Calgary in November would allow them to recreate the snow-covered massacre scene, but the weather did not cooperate. Snow-making machines brought in from ski areas broke down. Plastic snow had to be used. The producers even agreed to pay a Stony medicine man $100—$10 as a down-payment—but when no snow fell by deadline, the production moved to Hollywood for studio work before returning to Morley when there was enough snow. Snow and cold arrived when the film crews returned in January, with temperatures dropping to 44 degrees below zero. "I'd never realized it could be so cold that you lose feeling in your fingers when you have your gloves off for 30 seconds," Hoffman said (Wedman 1970b, 27).

The movie premiered in mid-December. But two other Westerns about Native Americans were released first: *A Man Called Horse*, about an Englishman captured and adopted into a Lakota band in the 1840s, in April; and *Soldier Blue*, about the 1864 Sand Creek massacre, in August. American Indian Movement members picketed *A Man Called Horse* in Minneapolis, although another Native American group said the movie's depiction of the Lakotas was accurate. The *Los Angeles Times* called the graphically violent *Soldier Blue* "revolting," "appallingly and unforgivably vile," and "a shallow entertainment" (Champlin 1970a, IV, 4), but Penn did something different. "I could either make it very physically painful for the audience or do it without showing a single drop of blood. I chose the latter," he said. "In the film nearly all the wars and killings are immaculately clean" (Chaiken and Cronin 2008, 68). Viewers might disagree; a fair amount of blood is shown in the Washita massacre recreation.

Reviewers had mixed feelings about *Little Big Man*. Charles Champlin of the *Los Angeles Times* called it "a densely packed, episodic, daring, uneven but unrepentant gallop through the winning of the West" (Champlin 1970b, IV, 1), while Dan Lewis of the *Record* in Hackensack, New Jersey, said the movie was "a conglomeration of emotions, sometimes blending, at other times discordant" and found "some technically superb movie moments" and "ridiculous moments" (Lewis 1970, B-24). While noting it as "an important movie by one of our most interesting directors," the *New York Times'* Vincent Canby said *Little Big Man* "is not terribly funny" and "sometimes wears its social concerns so blatantly that they look like war paint" (Canby 1970, 53).

The box office, however, was decisive. *Little Big Man* grossed roughly $31.56 million domestically, making it one of the year's biggest hits. "I thought it was pretty good," said Jim Real Bird, a Crow Indian who was as an extra during filming in Montana. "They put a little humor into the story" (Jim Real Bird, interview with author, June 26, 2018). Chief Dan George was nominated for an Academy Award as Best Supporting Actor, and the film's success cemented Hoffman as a major star. "*Little Big Man* was the film that put him [Hoffman] over the top to stay" (Lenburg 1983, 59).

HISTORICAL BACKGROUND

Fur trappers, explorers, missionaries, and other Americans had been exploring the West for decades, but the opportunity of new land brought 70 farmers west from Independence, Missouri, to Oregon Territory in 1841— five years before the United States and England signed a treaty that gave England claim to north of the 49th parallel, plus Vancouver Island, and the United States land south of the line. More settlers headed West in 1842, and roughly 1,000 took the journey on the Great Emigration of 1843. The emigrants followed the Oregon Trail, some 2,000 miles from western Missouri and across present-day Kansas, Nebraska, Wyoming, Idaho, and Oregon. After gold was discovered in northern California in 1848, roughly 300,000 people rushed to California, many of them following the California Trail, which used the Oregon Trail to Fort Hall, Idaho, before turning southwest through present-day Nevada and into California.

At first, Native Americans in the Great Plains and Rocky Mountain West considered the covered wagons and emigrants as curiosities, and they were more prone to steal from the emigrants than kill them.

When migration west began on the California and Oregon trails, "every acre of land between the Kansas River and the Pacific Crest belonged to Indian peoples," historian Will Bagley wrote. "When it ended three decades later, they owned almost none of it" (Bagley 2010, xvi). As the number of white travelers increased, concern among the various tribes grew. White travelers did not help matters in 1849 when a group from Missouri reportedly raped and killed Snake Indian women; the Snakes retaliated by attacking other wagon trains. Two years later, emigrants fired shotguns over the heads of Native Americans while chasing them from a popular campsite on the Snake River.

The westbound travelers also introduced disease to the tribes, killing scores from cholera, measles, smallpox, and other diseases. In 1849, a Cheyenne Indian killed a white emigrant in retaliation for the deaths of the Indian's wife, father, mother, and brother from cholera. The killer blamed whites for bringing the disease to his people and had vowed to kill the next white man he saw. The Cheyennes—not the whites—executed the killer for murder.

For that matter, disease and trail accidents killed plenty of emigrants, too. Of the estimated 10,000 emigrants who died on the trails, Native Americans killed fewer than 400. Yet by the 1850s, the distrust between the two peoples had widened. "Their interactions," wrote historian John D. Unruh Jr., "were slowly becoming less frequent, less friendly and more dangerous" (Unruh 1982, 139).

The run to California was not the only rush for riches in the western United States. After gold was discovered in present-day Colorado, men and women flocked across Kansas to Pike's Peak and the Colorado Rockies between 1859 and 1862, often traveling in covered wagons displaying "Pike's Peak or Bust" signs. Gold discoveries in western Montana in 1862 and 1863 sent adventurers along the Bozeman and Bridger trails. All of these routes crossed lands occupied by Native Americans.

Cheyenne and Lakota Indians raided across the western plains. On August 24, 1864, warriors attacked a party of teamsters on the Platte River near present-day Lexington, Nebraska, and a small wagon train, killing 13 and taking two captives. Hostilities increased between Native American tribes and white settlers. On November 29, a group of volunteer Colorado soldiers under the command of John M. Chivington (1821–1894) attacked a peaceful camp of predominantly Cheyenne Indians at Sand Creek in southeastern Colorado. Chivington's men killed roughly 200 Native Americans. "No Indians were left wounded," historian Gregory F. Michno wrote, "and the soldiers took no prisoners" (Michno 2003, 159).

The resulting friction between whites and Plains Indian tribes led to what became known as Hancock's War. In 1867, General Winfield Scott Hancock (1824–1886), hero of the 1863 Civil War battle at Gettysburg, Pennsylvania, arrived in Kansas to stop the war. Instead of negotiating, though, Hancock sent a show of force to scare the gathered tribes, who—never forgetting Sand Creek—fled. Until the signing of the Medicine Lodge Treaty that October, the Kansas plains turned into a war zone of mostly hit-and-run skirmishes. In early July, Lyman S. Kidder (1842–1867), a second lieutenant in the 7th Cavalry, 10 soldiers, and a Lakota scout were killed by a party of Cheyennes and Lakotas near present-day Goodland, Kansas. Kidder was carrying dispatches to Lieutenant Colonel George Armstrong Custer (1839–1876).

Born in New Rumley, Ohio, Custer was appointed to the U.S. Military Academy at West Point in 1857, where he found himself at the bottom of his class and with a high number of demerits—enough to come close to being expelled—before graduating as "one of the worst cadets in the history of the U.S. Military Academy" (Schultz 2017). Yet in the Civil War (1861–1865), Custer earned a reputation for boldness to the point of recklessness and rose to the brevet (a temporary or battlefield commission usually for meritorious service) rank of major general. General Philip H. Sheridan (1831–1888) thought enough of Custer that he gave Custer the table upon which the terms of surrender signed by Confederate General Robert E. Lee (1807–1870)

CUSTER'S FIGHT SONG

In *Little Big Man*, George Custer's band plays "Garry Owen" during the Washita attack, which is accurate. Custer's own report noted that "The moment the charge was ordered, the band struck up 'Garey [sic] Owen,' and with cheers that strongly reminded me of scenes during the war, ever[y] trooper, led by his officer, rushed towards the village" (Custer 1868, 2).

"Garry Owen" can be heard in many Custer and Western cavalry movies. A popular Irish tune whose origins have been traced to the early 1800s, "Garry Owen" became a favorite song for several military units. Either Custer or Ireland-born Captain Myles Keogh (1840–1876) recommended it for the 7th Cavalry's regimental song.

Custer began humming and whistling the tune at Fort Riley, Kansas, although "[h]owever stirring 'Garry Owen' might be if rendered with bagpipes and all, the lyrics evoke little else than the virginal camaraderie of pipe-smoking undergraduates worshipping the whiffenpoof" (Connell 1984, 293).

Sources

Connell, Evan S. 1984. *Son of the Morning Star: Custer and the Little Bighorn*. San Francisco: North Point Press.

Custer, George A. 1868. "THE INDIAN WAR. BATTLE OF THE WASHITA. Gen. Custar's [sic] Report to Gen. Sheridan." *Topeka Weekly Leader*, December 10, 1868, p. 2.

and Union General Ulysses S. Grant (1822–1885). Sheridan wrote a note to Custer's wife, Elizabeth "Libbie" Bacon Custer (1842–1933), saying, "[T]here is scarcely an individual in our service who has contributed more to bring this about than your very gallant husband" (Monaghan 1971, 246).

After the war, Custer was appointed lieutenant colonel of the 7th Cavalry, headquartered at Fort Riley, Kansas. His frontier service was not without controversy, either. Custer's style of command appeared borderline tyrannical; he alienated many junior officers, and the regiment had a high number of desertions—35 in a 24-hour period—and Custer left his command to rejoin Libbie. That act got him court-martialed: suspended in rank and command, with no pay, for a year. "All things considered," historian James Donovan wrote, "it was a relatively mild sentence, since he could have been dishonorably discharged" (Donovan 2008, 58).

By the summer of 1868, the Medicine Lodge Treaty was deteriorating, and Cheyennes resumed raids. Army attempts to stop the bloodshed failed, so Sheridan requested that Custer's sentence be commuted and Custer reinstated. Sheridan also planned a winter campaign, designed to strike the unsuspecting Native Americans when their horses were weak. Custer rejoined the 7th Cavalry on October 11, 1868, and moved out of Camp Supply in present-day Oklahoma toward the Washita River, where thousands of Cheyennes, Arapahoes, Kiowas, Comanches, and Plains Apaches had set up winter camps. A camp was discovered and surrounded, and on the morning of November 27, the soldiers charged into the camp of Black Kettle, a Cheyenne peace chief who had survived Chivington's attack at Sand Creek four years earlier. Custer said more than 100 Cheyenne warriors were killed, including Black Kettle and his wife, but most historians put the actual number at closer to 30 or 60. Twenty-two U.S. soldiers were killed—most of those following Major Joel Elliott's pursuit of retreating warriors. When a search party could not find Elliott or his men, Custer left them, creating a rift in the regiment. Some officers loved Custer; many others despised him. The bodies of Elliott and his 17 men who rode with him were found two weeks later two miles downstream.

The village was burned, hundreds of Cheyenne horses were slaughtered, and Custer marched away with 53 Cheyenne women and children captives. "Although some branded Custer's attack as a slaughter of innocents," Western historian Paul Andrew Hutton wrote, "the 7th's commander emerged as the most famous Indian fighter on the western frontier" (Crutchfield 2011a, 157).

Ever flamboyant, Custer wore his hair long, often dressed in buckskins, and wrote a series of magazine articles that helped establish his celebrity. In one article he wrote, "If I were an Indian, I often think that I would greatly prefer to cast my lot among those of my people who adhered to the free open plains, rather than submit to the confined limits of a reservation, there to be the recipient of the blessed benefits of civilization, with its vices thrown in without stint or measure" (Custer 2009, 18). In 1874, Custer's articles were published in a book titled *My Life on the Plains: Personal Experiences with Indians.*

Custer also led a 1,200-man expedition into the Black Hills of present-day South Dakota in 1874. Ostensibly a surveying operation, Custer had been ordered to explore the Black Hills in search of a site for a military post that could be established to protect white settlers traveling along the Platte River to the south. The expedition included a geologist, who said he found no traces of gold. But others on the expedition said they had seen plenty of gold, confirming rumors that the Black Hills was a bonanza. A *Chicago Inter-Ocean* correspondent reported: "The gold discoveries have awakened an interest second only to the great California excitement of '49, and parties on the frontier are already thinking of starting out as soon as an expedition can be formed and equipped" ("GOLD!" 1874, 3). News spread across the country, and miners and others swarmed into the Black Hills.

There was a problem. Under the terms of an 1868 treaty, the Black Hills remained part of the Great Sioux Reservation. The 7th Cavalry, now based at Fort Abraham Lincoln near Bismarck in present-day North Dakota, received orders to stop the miners, but the *New York Tribune* reported: "If there is gold in the Black Hills, no army on earth can keep the adventurous men of the west out of them" (Utley 2018, 191). Prospectors continued to sneak into the Black Hills, and when gold was discovered at Deadwood Creek in

1875, the boomtown of Deadwood, founded illegally on Native American land, was born. Thousands of people rushed to Deadwood, including gunfighter/gambler James Butler "Wild Bill" Hickok (1837–1876), who was murdered at a Deadwood saloon while playing poker. The federal government offered to buy the Black Hills, but the Lakotas considered the land sacred and refused. Facing demands to open the newly discovered gold country to settlement, the government issued an edict that any Lakotas who had failed to report to an Indian reservation by January 31, 1876, would be declared hostile. By then, Lakotas, Cheyennes, Arapahoes, and other tribes on the Great Plains were in their winter camps. Even if they had received the orders, they could not have complied. The table was set for another Indian war.

The army developed a three-pronged attack plan. General Alfred H. Terry (1827–1890) led the command, including Custer, out of Fort Abraham Lincoln. Cavalry and infantry under Colonel John Gibbon (1827–1896) moved east from Fort Ellis in Montana; and General George Crook (1828–1890) led troops north from Fort Laramie in Wyoming. After an astonishing defeat by Native Americans at the Rosebud Creek in southern Montana on June 17, Crook's command turned back. On June 25, Custer's troops discovered a large Indian camp on the Little Big Horn River; the Lakotas called the river as Greasy Grass. Custer divided his command and attacked, but warriors stopped the charge led by Major Marcus Reno (1834–1889), who retreated to hilltops and dug in. Custer sent orders to Captain Frederick Benteen (1834–1898): "Come On. Big Village. Be quick. Bring Packs. P.S. Bring packs" (Monaghan 1971, 386). Benteen, who despised Custer, did not hurry and instead stopped to help Reno. There, the soldiers heard gunfire to the north.

The attackers kept Benteen's and Reno's soldiers pinned down on the hills before breaking camp and moving away on the evening of June 26. The following day, Gibbon's command arrived at the battleground. Terry was with them. When Benteen asked where Custer was, Terry said Custer and his command were dead, but Benteen did not believe it, saying, "At the Battle of the Washita he went off and left part of his command, and I think he would do it again" (Donovan 2008, 307). Terry ordered Benteen and his company to the site. When they first saw the bodies, Captain Thomas Weir said, "Oh, how white they look! How white" (Donovan 2008, 310). The 7th Cavalry buried 204 of its soldiers, but "[d]espite their best efforts," some soldiers were left unburied, and their remains "were discovered on or near the battlefield" for the next 50 years (Donovan 2008, 311).

The Lakotas, along with their Cheyenne and Arapaho allies, had won their greatest victory, but the army retaliated. In less than a year, the famed Lakota leader Crazy Horse (ca. 1840–1877) surrendered at Fort Robinson in Nebraska, where he was betrayed by his own people as well as whites, and killed four months later on September 5 after a soldier stabbed him with a bayonet. After what became known as Custer's Last Stand, Sitting Bull (ca. 1831–1890) and perhaps as many as 2,000 Lakotas hurried into Canada, where they lived until returning to reservations in the United States in 1881. In 1890, Sitting Bull was killed in an attempted arrest by tribal policemen on the reservation. On December 29, 1890, the 7th Cavalry killed hundreds of Lakotas—most of them women and children—at Wounded Knee, South Dakota, while attempting to disarm them and return them to the reservation. Several reports said that the soldiers sought revenge for what had happened at the Little Big Horn. "The Seventh," one soldier reportedly said, "has a bloody score to settle with them" (Donovan 2008, 389).

The massacre at Wounded Knee marked the end of the Indian wars.

DEPICTION AND CULTURAL CONTEXT

Jack Crabb begins his story by telling of the massacre of his parents by Pawnees while his family crossed the Great Plains. Although the year is never indicated in the movie, Crabb states in the novel that it was 1852; Crabb is 111 years old in Berger's novel, but the screenplay made him 10 years older, probably because Berger set the contemporary section of the book in the 1950s; the novel was published and the screenplay begun in the mid-1960s.

Crabb's family is apparently traveling alone across the Great Plains in the film, but such an undertaking would have been foolhardy. More than 50,000 people came to California by the overland trail in 1852, but few traveled alone. "People traveling overland by wagon joined together in wagon trains that could be a few wagons, or hundreds," trails historian Candy Moulton said. "They did so to share the work of traveling on the trail. By having at minimum several wagons together there were people to drive wagons, people to scout ahead for campsites, people to hunt. Other duties also were shared such as herding livestock, and guarding the camp and livestock at night" (Candy Moulton, interview with author, May 4, 2019).

Pawnees are responsible for the attack on the Crabb family, and although it's true that Pawnees troubled emigrants more than other tribes, rarely did they kill travelers or burn wagons. Many accounts from emigrants accused Pawnees of stealing, primarily horses, on the journey west. "The Pawnee Indians are the greatest thieves I ever saw—the best way I think to civilize them is with powder & lead, & this is the way we shall do hereafter," one traveler complained (Bagley 2010, 362).

Attacks by Native Americans on wagon trains were rare, especially in the early migration years of 1843–1862, but they did happen. One of the most significant, Moulton said, was the so-called Utter-Van Ornum massacre near the Owyhee River in western Idaho. On the night of September 8, 1860, Native Americans attacked a party of eight wagons and 44 people and stole some livestock. Attacks intensified over the next few days, and several emigrants were killed. While some members of the wagon train escaped and hurried west, others remained pinned down. Of those left behind, Native Americans killed some; others survived, but still others, too weak to continue traveling, starved to death. Which band or bands of Native Americans led the attack was never determined, although most historians believe they were Bannocks and Shoshones.

Warring Indians, flaming arrows, and circled wagons made for exciting cinema, but historically Native Americans often helped the white travelers by providing them with clothing and food in trades—and sometimes even serving as guides. "There are accounts of Lakota tribesmen using their horses to tie onto the handcarts pushed and pulled by Mormon emigrants [1856–1860] to help propel the small carts," Moulton said (Candy Moulton, interview with author, May 4, 2019).

Historically, the attack on the Blinn-Buttles Wagon Train provides the closest resemblance to the attack depicted in *Little Big Man*. On the evening of October 9, 1868, approximately 75 Cheyennes attacked a party of eight wagons near Sand Creek in southern Colorado. One wagon, carrying Clara Blinn, not quite 21 years old, and her young son Willie, moved ahead of the others when "warriors cut off the men with the rear wagons, circled around, and shot flaming arrows, setting several wagons on fire. The defenders dug a breastwork around the wagons and were trapped there for five days, with the number of attacking Indians growing to nearly 200" (Michno 2018, 111).

The Blinns were traveling east—Ohio-born Clara reportedly feared Indians—to relocate from Colorado to Kansas, where Clara's parents had settled. Two men were wounded, none killed, and one man got away and reached Fort Lyon, where a small group of soldiers of the 7th Cavalry rode out to assist the wagon train. The Cheyennes, however, had captured Clara and Willie Blinn. Clara dropped a note about four miles downstream, pleading with her husband to save them.

While the aftermath of this attack resembles the one in *Little Big Man*, the actual attack occurred on the Santa Fe Trail, not the Oregon/California Trail, and in the late 1860s, not the early 1850s. It also happened not far from where Chivington had committed the Sand Creek massacre against Cheyenne Indians almost four years earlier. The attack and abduction of Clara and Willie Blinn would be one of the reasons Custer attacked the Cheyenne camp on the Washita River the following month. That attack caused the death of the two Blinns.

But *Little Big Man*'s depiction of the Washita engagement is closer to the Sand Creek massacre than what happened in 1868. More than 150 years after the attack, the Washita engagement remains controversial. "Washita is the most misunderstood episode of Custer's career," Black Kettle biographer Thom Hatch said. "Black Kettle went to Fort Cobb and was told to make nice with Sheridan in the field or he would be subject to attack. He was not camped on a reservation and had been offered no protection by the military" (Thom Hatch, interview with author, May 2, 2019).

While other historians call the Washita a legitimate military operation, Kent Blansett, assistant professor of history and Native American studies at the University of Nebraska at Omaha, and a Cherokee, Creek, Choctaw, Shawnee, and Potawatomi descendant, disagrees.

Especially in that it's Black Kettle's band that had just survived Sand Creek, was this necessary? A person who absolved for peace within Colorado and continued in that notion by saying we'll even go to Indian Territory now and completely leave the state of Colorado in order to seek protection. Was a military response really dictated in this scenario in regards to Black Kettle, or was this motivation coming from someplace else? The Washita was very much in following with Chivington and a generation that had been completely—I don't want to say sanitized to war—but coming out of the Civil War, that was the solution. Don't stop to compromise. You just go in, guns a-blazing a lot of times. Only then will you have complete subjugation. It's that total war that happens at the end of the Civil War. That idea of total war, of slash and burn, is carried out into the West. The time of complacency and gentility in the field of battle were completely dismissed. (Kent Blansett, interview with author, May 6, 2019)

Added historian Louis Kraft: "It is doubtful that [Custer] would have aborted the attack had he known that it was the village of the one man who had never wavered from his quest of maintaining peace with the white man" (Louis Kraft, interview with author, May 11, 2019).

Custer captured 53 Native Americans, mostly women and children, but he also found evidence of raids against white settlers in the camp. When Custer and Sheridan returned to the village later, they found the bodies of Clara and Willie Blinn. Black Kettle was a Cheyenne peace chief, but he could not, or would not, control all of the Cheyenne warriors, and he had allowed the Indians and their captives into his camp. Most likely, the Cheyennes thought that they could use the two white captives as leverage with future peace negotiations. An Indian trader at Fort Cobb learned that a white woman and child were in Black Kettle's camp, and, through a mixed-blood emissary, asked her for information. Clara Blinn wrote she and her son would be released when the Cheyennes and whites made peace. The trader was authorized to begin negotiations for the Blinns' release, but it was too late. At some point during Custer's attack, the two white hostages were killed. "Assistant surgeon Henry Lippincott said Clara had one bullet hole above the left eyebrow, her head was scalped and the skull extensively fractured. Willie's body showed evidence of violence about the head and face. There was a report that one or both of Clara's breasts were hacked off, and that Willie was killed by holding his feet and swinging his head against a tree" (Michno 2018).

The movie also depicts the slaughter of Cheyenne horses as an act of barbarity on the part of a psychotic Custer. "Yet, there was a military necessity to capture the horses needed for your own force and destroy the rest to prevent their use by the enemy," Gregory F. and Susan J. Michno wrote (Michno 2018, 114–115). After the attack of a Comanche camp in Palo Duro Canyon in the Texas Panhandle on September 28, 1874, Colonel Ranald S. Mackenzie ordered the slaughter of more than 1,000 captured Indian horses. "Custer had shot horses on the Washita in 1868, but that was mere expediency, since his column was in grave danger of annihilation. Mackenzie now did it as a military tactic, to take away the Indians' means of survival" (Gwynne 2010, 282). At the Washita, soldiers captured 875 Indian ponies, and Custer allowed some officers (including himself), women prisoners, and Osage scouts to pick horses for their own use, and then he ordered the destruction of the rest. Four dismounted cavalry companies opened fire for at least 90 minutes.

"Other controversies came out of the battle, but they were just more envy of Custer," Hatch said. "Only someone like Custer would have attacked in freezing cold and a blinding snowstorm. He carried out his orders to the letter" (Thom Hatch, interview with author, May 2, 2019).

The Washita earned Custer credentials as an Indian fighter. Custer biographer and noted Western historian Robert M. Utley said Custer earned that reputation. "The Washita was a classic in Indian warfare. Custer followed the Indian trail in the snow, disposed his troops to surround the village, and launched a surprise attack at dawn. It worked. The village was taken, captives rounded up, and he withdrew in time to avoid more Indians arriving on the field. Yes, it was deserved despite all the controversy that ensued" (Robert M. Utley, interview with author, May 1, 2019).

After the Washita, Kraft said:

> The Cheyennes knew who the white man was and had since the Sand Creek massacre, knew that his word was no good, knew that Black Kettle had stood firmly for peace with the hated *vi'ho'i*—the spider—before those that followed his lead were butchered [at Sand Creek] but still tried to maintain peace. Now he was dead, murdered, all his efforts for peace in vain. They knew that their freedom was no more and that they would do what the white man demanded or be slaughtered. (Louis Kraft, interview with author, May 11, 2019)

And *Little Big Man*'s depiction of Cheyenne culture was not entirely accurate. "Rather, they reflect the fashions of mores of the [1960s'] counterculture, whose practices included a return to the land, experimentation with drugs and alternative lifestyles, communal living, sexual freedom, and a search for peace and harmony," historians Margo Kasdan and Susan Tavernetti wrote (Rollins and O'Connor 1998, 131).

Perhaps *Little Big Man*'s biggest twist in history involves the killing of Wild Bill Hickok. After shooting Hickok in a saloon, the young killer yells, "He killed my daddy. He killed my daddy. He ain't never gonna shoot nobody again. It took me seven years, but I got him." Crabb rushes into the saloon and kneels on the floor beside the dying Hickok, who speaks briefly to his friend before dying.

On August 2, 1876, Hickok was playing poker with three men at Nuttall & Mann's No. 10 Saloon in Deadwood, Dakota Territory. Around 3:00 p.m., John "Jack" McCall, going by the name Bill Sutherland, moved from the bar to behind Hickok, fired a round from a pistol, and shouted, "Damn you, take that!" The bullet passed through Hickok's head and struck one of the other poker players, former riverboat pilot William Rodney Massie, in his left arm just above the wrist. "Wild Bill's head jerked forward, and for some moments his body remained motionless," historian Joseph G. Rosa wrote. "Then it toppled back from the stool to the floor." Killed instantly, Hickok said nothing after he had been shot. His last words came just before McCall's shot: "The old duffer [Massie]—he broke me on the hand" (Rosa 1974, 298).

In a quick trial the following day, Joseph Miller, appointed defense lawyer, advised McCall to testify that he shot Hickok because Hickok had killed his brother—not his father—in Kansas a few years earlier. It worked. The jury acquitted McCall. But that trial "was nothing more than an illegal miner's court. Deadwood City was still located on a Federal Indian Reservation subject to federal law under military rule" (Turner 2001, 152). McCall fled to Wyoming, where he bragged about killing Hickok. That got him arrested by legal authorities, and McCall, who had no brother, wound up being tried for murder under a proper court in Yankton, Dakota Territory. After his conviction, McCall was hanged in Yankton on March 1, 1877.

Little Big Man rearranges the calendar because the movie places Hickok's murder before the Battle of the Little Big Horn when in reality Hickok was killed on August 2—38 days after Custer's immediate command was wiped out at the Little Big Horn.

Regarding the most famous battle between the army and Native Americans, Crabb tells the historian that Custer "figured he needed one more dramatic victory over the Indians to be nominated for President of the United States. That is a historical fact." Historians say otherwise. "Custer had indeed performed notable service for the Democratic Party and had been severely bruised for his effort, but that the party's gratitude extended to the presidency transcends absurdity," Utley wrote. "That Custer fantasized such an absurdity cannot be disproved, of course, but that presidential aspirations governed his tactical decisions demands more weighty evidence" (Utley 2001, 129).

Early Custer movies, from *On the Little Big Horn; or, Custer's Last Stand* (1909) and *Custer's Last Fight* (1912) to the patriotic *They Died with Their Boots On* (1941) depicted Custer as the hero, but he became flawed and far less heroic in later films such as *Tonka* (1958) and *The Great Sioux Massacre* (1965). By 1970, just after a decade of turbulence, civil disobedience, and assassinations, Custer was being portrayed as "the lunatic leader" (Langellier 2000, 72) in *Little Big Man*.

Given that no members of Custer's immediate command survived and that Native Americans were reluctant to tell what happened, the events at Last Stand Hill and those fateful minutes will never be known. But most historians say that Custer did what was expected of a combat veteran in the 1870s.

"He did do almost everything right," said Paul Andrew Hutton, award-winning author and distinguished professor of history at the University of New Mexico. "But nothing he could do would have worked that day. He had to attack, dividing his forces, which was obviously a mistake since he didn't have a clear determination of the size of the village. His actions as an experienced Indian fighter—and at the time, he was the man—made perfect sense. He's worried about the Indians escaping. He's not worried about fighting two or three thousand Indians. Until he gets to the top of the ridge and looks down. And then he knows he's in a world of hurt" (Paul Andrew Hutton, interview with author, May 1, 2019).

Historians debate whether or not Custer could have won. Some blame the loss on Reno's weak charge at the beginning of the battle. Others fault Benteen, who did not obey Custer's orders to rejoin Custer quickly and bring much-needed ammunition. Custer "is burdened with one incompetent officer [Reno] and one officer with a terribly bad attitude [Benteen]," Hutton said. "If [Custer] made a mistake, it was keeping his loyal officers with him. If Benteen had come riding to the rescue like he should have, the Indians would have pulled back. Or Benteen and all of his men would've been killed. It's all what-if stuff" (Paul Andrew Hutton, interview with author, May 1, 2019). Whether Benteen disobeyed a direct order is also debated. "You're always allowed to 'exercise your own judgment,'" said Pulitzer Prize-winning author Thomas Powers, author of *The Killing of Crazy Horse*. "You're never under orders to get yourself and your whole command killed" (Thomas Powers, interview with author, June 26, 2011).

Little Big Man's ending, though, in which Old Lodge Skins laments the future of the Cheyenne Indians, rings true. "Custer's defeat and death became an opportunity to win public support," wrote Lakota historian Joseph M. Marshall III, who grew up on the Rosebud Sioux Indian Reservation. "Now the government *had* to subjugate the Lakota for what happened at the Little Bighorn. That was the rallying point. The 'Indian wars' became something of a holy war because American blood had been spilled in the cause of Manifest Destiny. Uncivilized minions had blasphemed civilization. There was nothing to be done but punish in the name of righteousness" (Marshall III 2007, 227).

A number of historians dislike *Little Big Man* because of its historical distortions, overlooking the fact that Penn wasn't making a movie about Custer and the American West but rather about the United States, Vietnam, and the turbulent period in which the film was released. "It's still the situation in America, as it was then, as it is now," Penn said while making the movie in 1969. "We're talking about 100 years ago and the wars against the Indians. At the same time we're talking about the wars against the blacks—racist divisions that we are all experiencing in all countries—as well as a search for identity. It's the 'what kind of human being am I, and how am I going to live my life?' thing. And that seems to be very much a contemporary scene" (Westgate 1969a, 61).

Little Big Man's depiction of the Washita massacre was an allegory to the My Lai massacre in Vietnam. On March 16, 1968, U.S. Army soldiers massacred unarmed inhabitants of a village province called Son My, with one company killing more than 100 in a hamlet the Vietnamese called Xom Lang that U.S. Army maps identified as My Lai. Although the soldiers received no enemy fire, "they began killing men, women, and children. Some raped and sodomized young girls, mothers, and elderly women, then killed them" (Allison 2012, 38). More than 500 Vietnamese were killed at Son My, with a military criminal investigation determining that 347 were murdered at My Lai. Army pilot Hugh Thompson landed his helicopter between villagers and approaching U.S. soldiers, instructing his crew to open fire on the American troops if they fired at the villagers or Thompson, who was credited with saving the lives of several villagers. Other soldiers refused to participate in the bloodletting. My Lai became a 1960s version of the 1864 Sand Creek massacre.

> The American soldiers and junior officers shot old men, women, boys, girls, and babies. One soldier missed a baby lying on the ground twice with a .45 pistol as his comrades laughed at his marksmanship. He stood over the child and fired a third time. . . . They shot the water buffalos, the pigs, and the chickens. They threw the dead animals into the wells to poison the water. They tossed satchel charges into the bomb shelters under the houses. A lot of the inhabitants had fled into the shelters. Those who leaped out to escape the explosives were gunned down. All of the houses were put to the torch. (Sheehan 1988, 689)

Another helicopter pilot wrote to his wife: "I'll tell you something it sure makes one wonder why we are here" (Allison 2012, 51). Although several Americans were charged in courts-martial, only one, Lieutenant William Calley, was convicted, and although sentenced to life imprisonment, he was only confined for roughly three years before being paroled.

American media did not break the news of the My Lai massacre until September 1969, and the scope of the slaughter was not revealed until the following months, before Penn began to film the Washita massacre scenes for *Little Big Man*. Even film critic Les Wedman of Vancouver, British Columbia's *The Sun* newspaper, said the massacre resembled "current headlines from Vietnam" (Wedman 1970a, 37).

"Westerns often—maybe always—tell us more about the era in which they were made than the one in which they happen to be set," said Kirk Ellis, the Emmy Award–winning producer and screenwriter of *John Adams*

(2008), *Into the West* (2005), and *Anne Frank: The Whole Story* (2001). He continued:

> Berger's intention in the novel is in part deconstruction of the frontier myth, and in their film adaptation, director Arthur Penn and writer Calder Willingham go even further. Their film is easily the best of the Vietnam-era Westerns that used the genre to reflect on the turmoil roiling then-contemporary America. The film's restaging of the Washita Massacre, one of the most breathtaking scenes in any Western from any decade, is deliberately staged to recall images from My Lai, which would still have been fresh in the minds of audiences—an incident Berger, writing in 1964, could not have anticipated, but one which nonetheless finds a tragic mirror in Native American history. (Kirk Ellis, interview with author, April 23, 2019)

CONCLUSION

Little Big Man was woefully historically inaccurate, but that was never the point. Berger's novel tackled the myth of the frontier; Jack Crabb is an unrepentant liar. Penn's film version, while showing the wrongs inflicted on Native Americans in the nineteenth century, also echoed social injustices and an ugly foreign war haunting twentieth-century America.

"The box office shows that [Penn] really had his finger on the pulse of America," Hutton said. "*Little Big Man* is just a perfect representation of the '70s in the same way that *They Died with Their Boots On* is the perfect representation of America in December of 1941 when it's released: valiant soldiers sold out by venal politicians and businessmen dying honorably" (Paul Andrew Hutton, interview with author, May 1, 2019).

Little Big Man also helped ignite a movement among Native American actors for better roles in films and television and for depictions far more accurate than that of the old-school bloodthirsty savage. "I don't think our people were that mean," Chief Dan George said, while Jay Silverheels (1912–1980), best known for playing Tonto on the 1949–1957 *The Lone Ranger* television series and, in 1971, the only Native American on the Screen Actors Guild's board of directors, added, "Throughout the world the image of the Indian is wrong. Movies have always projected the Indians as the aggressor, interested only in acquiring scalps. This is an inaccuracy. Many of the tribes were peaceful people who fought only when their territory was threatened" (Thomas 1971, 9-D).

Little Big Man paved the way not only for similar-themed movies such as *Dances with Wolves* (1990), the Academy Award winner for Best Picture, but also helped recalibrate "the Native presence" in Western films. In 1995, Russell Means (1939–2012), one of the American Indian Movement's founders, said the only films about Native Americans "worth anything" are *Little Big Man*, *The Outlaw Josey Wales* (1976), *Last of the Mohicans*

(1992), and *Thunderheart* (1992) because "[t]hey showed Indian people as human beings with feelings and relationships, four-dimensional and not just two-dimensional" (Kiley 1995, 2).

Blansett points to *The Outlaw Josey Wales* in which an old Cherokee Indian (Chief Dan George) assists gunfighting outlaw Josey Wales (Clint Eastwood) in the years after the Civil War.

After *Little Big Man*, Native Americans began to show up "in unexpected places," Blansett said. "It's changing the narrative—that's essentially flipping the script on Tonto and Lone Ranger in a major way. At least Chief Dan George does that because he's not going to be Jay Silverheels. It's kind of outstanding in the role [George] takes in that, and it's not to the lesser degree of Clint Eastwood, but it's raising Clint Eastwood's standards. It's more or less, how do we come together as a nation despite this very violent past that we share now, and, in essence, how do we move forward as a people overcoming insurmountable odds" (Kent Blansett, interview with author, May 6, 2019).

FURTHER READING

Allison, William Thomas. 2012. *My Lai: An American Atrocity in the Vietnam War.* Baltimore, MD: The Johns Hopkins University Press.

Bagley, Will. 2010. *So Rugged and Mountainous: Blazing the Trails to Oregon and California, 1812–1848.* Norman: University of Oklahoma Press.

Berger, Thomas. 1964. *Little Big Man.* New York: The Dial Press.

Blumberg, Arnold. 2011. "Wounds from the Washita: The Major Elliott Affair." *Wild West*, October 6, 2011. https://www.historynet.com/wounds-from-the-washita -the-major-elliott-affair.htm

Boggs, Johnny D. 2003. *Great Murder Trials of the Old West.* Plano: Republic of Texas Press.

Canby, Vincent. 1970. "Film: Seeking the American Heritage." *New York Times*, December 15, 1970, p. 52.

Chaiken, Michael, and Paul Cronin. 2008. *Arthur Penn: Interviews.* Jackson: University Press of Mississippi.

Champlin, Charles. 1970a. "Blood Flows in 'Soldier Blue.'" *Los Angeles Times*, August 14, 1970, Part IV, p. 1.

Champlin, Charles. 1970b. "Tragedy of Indian in 'Man.'" *Los Angeles Times*, December 22, 1970, Part IV, p. 1, 9.

Clark, Karen. 2017. "How Many Gold Rushes Were There in the 19th Century?" *Sciencing*, April 24, 2017. https://sciencing.com/many-gold-rushes-were-there -19th-century-19423.html

Connell, Evan S. 1984. *Son of the Morning Star: Custer and the Little Bighorn.* San Francisco: North Point Press.

Connery, Allan. 1969. "How to Make a Big-Budget Western Movie out on the Morley Flats: Just Round Up an 80-Man Crew of Technicians, a Few Cowboys and Indians—Then Pray for Snow." *Herald Magazine*, November 7, 1969, pp. 2–3.

Crutchfield, James A., ed. 2011a. *The Settlement of America: Encyclopedia of Westward Expansion from Jamestown to the Closing of the Frontier: Volume 1.* Armonk, NY: Sharpe Reference.

Crutchfield, James A., ed. 2011b. *The Settlement of America: Encyclopedia of Westward Expansion from Jamestown to the Closing of the Frontier: Volume 2.* Armonk, NY: Sharpe Reference.

Custer, Elizabeth B. 1977. *Boots and Saddles, or: Life in Dakota with General Custer.* Williamstown, MA: Corner House Publishers.

Custer, George A. 1868. "THE INDIAN WAR. BATTLE OF THE WASHITA. Gen. Custar's [sic] Report to Gen. Sheridan." *Topeka Weekly Leader*, December 10, 1868, p. 2.

Custer, George A. 2009. *My Life on the Plains.* Carlisle, MA: Applewood Books.

Deutsch, Linda. 1970. "American Indian Seeks Change of Image from Bloodthirsty Savage Movie Villain: Want Cliches Rejected by Industry." *Pensacola News-Journal*, August 16, 1970, p. 15A.

Donovan, James. 2008. *A Terrible Glory: Custer and the Little Bighorn: The Last Great Battle of the American West.* New York: Little, Brown and Company.

Gaver, Jack. 1969. "10 Survive Broadway Hatchet." *Journal-News*, May 17, 1969, p. 10.

GOLD! 1874. "GOLD! THE WONDERFUL RESOURCES OF THE BLACK HILLS. Gold Bearing Quartz in Mountain Piles. GEN. CUSTER WILL RECOMMEND EXTINGUISHMENT OF INDIAN TITLE." *Bismarck Tribune*, September 9, 1874, p. 3.

Greene, Jerome A. 2004. *Washita: The U.S. Army and the Southern Cheyennes, 1867–1869.* Norman: University of Oklahoma Press.

Gwynne, S. C. 2010. *Empire of the Summer Moon: Quanah Parker and the Rise and Fall of the Comanches, the Most Powerful Indian Tribe in American History.* New York: Scribner.

Hardorff, Richard G., editor and compiler. *Washita Memories: Eyewitness Views of Custer's Attack on Black Kettle's Village.* Norman: University of Oklahoma Press.

Hatch, Thom. 2004. *Black Kettle: The Cheyenne Chief Who Sought Peace but Found War.* Hoboken, NJ: John Wiley & Sons, Inc.

Herzberg, Bob. 2008. *Savages and Saints: The Changing Image of American Indians in Westerns.* Jefferson, NC: McFarland & Company, Inc.

Kiley, Mike. 1995. "Dances with Disney: 'Pocahontas' Is More Than a Movie to Russell Means." *Chicago Tribune*, Tempo section, June 14, 1995, pp. 1–2.

King, Gilbert. 2012. "Where the Buffalo No Longer Roamed: The Transcontinental Railroad Connected East and West—And Accelerated the Destruction of What Had Been in the Center of North America." *Smithsonian*, July 17, 2012, https://www .smithsonianmag.com/history/where-the-buffalo-no-longer-roamed-3067904

Kraft, Louis. 2011. *Ned Wynkoop and the Lonely Road from Sand Creek.* Norman: University of Oklahoma Press.

Lamar, Howard R. 1998. *The New Encyclopedia of the American West.* New Haven, CT: Yale University Press.

Langellier, John Philip. 2000. *Custer: The Man, the Myth, the Movies.* Mechanicsburg, PA: Stackpole Books.

Lenburg, Jeff. 1983. *Dustin Hoffman: Hollywood's Antihero.* New York: St. Martin's Press.

Lewis, Dan. 1970. "Film Dulls Image of Gen. Custer." *Record*, December 15, 1970, p. B-24.

Marshall III, Joseph M. 2004. *The Journey of Crazy Horse: A Lakota History*. New York: Penguin Books.

Marshall III, Joseph M. 2007. *The Day the World Ended at Little Bighorn: A Lakota History*. New York: Viking.

Michno, Gregory F. 2003. *Encyclopedia of Indian Wars: Western Battles and Skirmishes, 1850–1890*. Missoula, MT: Mountain Press Publishing Company.

Michno, Gregory F. 2018. "Captive Clara Blinn's Plea: 'If You Love Us, Save Us.'" *Wild West*, October 3, 2018. https://www.historynet.com/captive-clara-blinns-plea-love-us-save-us.htm

Michno, Gregory F., and Susan J. Michno. 2009. *Circle the Wagons! Attacks on Wagon Trains in History and Hollywood Films*. Jefferson, NC: McFarland & Company, Inc.

Monaghan, Jay. 1971. *Custer: The Life of General George Armstrong Custer*. Lincoln: University of Nebraska Press.

New York Times Service. 1969. "Dustin Hoffman Makes Indian Film." *News-Herald*, December 31, 1969, p. 15.

"Presley to Star in More Films." 1966. *Daily Advertiser*, February 3, 1966, p. 22.

Rollins, Peter C., and John E. O'Connor, eds. 1998. *Hollywood's Indian: The Portrayal of Native American in Film*. Lexington: University Press of Kentucky.

"Roosevelt on Cow Boys and Indians." 1886. *River Press*, January 27, 1886, p. 7.

Rosa, Joseph G. 1967. *Alias Jack McCall*. Kansas City, MO: Kansas City Posse of the Westerners.

Rosa, Joseph G. 1974. *They Called Him Wild Bill: The Life and Adventures of James Butler Hickok*. Norman: University of Oklahoma Press.

Schultz, Duane. 2017. "West Point's Worst Cadet: George Armstrong Custer." *America's Civil War Magazine*, July 6, 2017. https://www.historynet.com/west-points-worst-cadet-george-armstrong-custer.htm

Segaloff, Nat. 2011. *Arthur Penn: American Director*. Lexington: University Press of Kentucky.

Sheehan, Neil. 1988. *A Bright, Shining Lie: John Paul Vann and America in Vietnam*. New York: Random House.

Stanley, Donald. 1967. "Donald Stanley on Books: Bizarre Mass Murder." *San Francisco Examiner*, p. 33.

Thomas, Bob. 1969. "'LITTLE BIG MAN': It's a New Look at the Old West." *Ogden Standard-Examiner*, August 14, 1969, p. 8B.

Thomas, Bob. 1971. "Indians Join the Protest for Better Image, Jobs." *Detroit Free Press*, February 25, 1971, p. 9-D.

Turner, Thadd. 2001. *Wild Bill Hickok: Deadwood City—End of Trail*. Deadwood, SD: Old West Alive! Publishing.

United Press International. 1968. "Johnson Asks $500 Million for Aid to U.S. Indians." *Philadelphia Inquirer*, March 7, 1968, p. 3.

Unruh Jr., John D. 1982. *The Plains Across: The Overland Emigrants and the Trans-Mississippi West, 1840–60*. Urbana: University of Illinois Press.

Utley, Robert M. 2001. *Custer: Cavalier in Buckskin*. Norman: University of Oklahoma Press.

Utley, Robert M. 2018. *The Commanders: Civil War Generals Who Shaped the American West*. Norman: University of Oklahoma Press.

Wedman, Les. 1970a. "Debunking Gen. Custer—At 21 Below Zero: Massacre by American War Hero Filmed on the Plains Near Calgary." *Sun*, January 15, 1970, p. 37.

Wedman, Les. 1970b. "'I Made a Bad Film,' Says Dustin." *Sun*, January 16, 1970, p. 27.

Westgate, Barry. 1969a. "THE HOTTEST TANDEM IN FILMS TODAY: Penn, the Bold, Exciting Director; Hoffman, the Inconspicuous Anti-Star." *Edmonton Journal*, November 7, 1969, p. 61.

Westgate, Barry. 1969b. "Where's All the Glamor in Moviemaking?" *Edmonton Journal*, November 7, 1969, p. 61.

Chapter 9

Young Guns (1988)

Dozens of films had covered the outlaw Billy the Kid's life, times, and death, but by the time *Young Guns* came along on August 12, 1988, Hollywood hadn't released a movie about Billy the Kid since 1973, when *Pat Garrett and Billy the Kid* failed at the box office and became the last period Western directed by Sam Peckinpah (1925–1984). In fact, Westerns had become box-office poison, and most reviewers dismissed *Young Guns* as more proof that the Hollywood Western was dead. *Young Guns*, however, defied the critics. Headlined by a cast of young actors popular with moviegoers, the film became a box-office hit; led to a hit sequel, *Young Guns II*, released two years later; and resurrected the genre.

Rather than offering a biopic about Billy the Kid, *Young Guns* confines its story to Billy's role in the Lincoln County War, which historian Robert M. Utley called "a war without heroes" (Utley 1987, ix), a bloody episode in southern New Mexico Territory that propelled Billy the Kid, born William Henry McCarty, to fame.

Played by Emilio Estevez (1962–), the wayward Billy is rescued from certain lynching in the town of Lincoln by rancher-merchant John Henry Tunstall, played by Terence Stamp (1938–). Tunstall, an Englishman, has practically adopted the "flotsam and jetsam of frontier society" as his ranch hands—young runaways and miscreants who happen to be handy with guns. The boys, none older than 21, include foreman Dick Brewer, played by Estevez's brother, Charlie Sheen (1965–); Doc Scurlock, played by Kiefer Sutherland (1966–); part-Indian Chavez Y Chavez (Lou Diamond Phillips, 1962–); Dirty Steve Stephens (Dermot Mulroney, 1963–); and Charley Bowdre (Casey Siemaszko, 1961–). The boys call themselves Regulators.

Lawrence G. Murphy, played by Jack Palance (1919–2006), is a cutthroat Irishman who runs a competing store, controls the sheriff, and is backed by the corrupt Santa Fe Ring, which includes local, territorial, and federal officials. After Murphy's men murder Tunstall, attorney Alexander McSween (Terry O'Quinn, 1952–), Tunstall's friend and partner, persuades a justice of the peace to deputize Tunstall's young riders as constables, and the Regulators are sent to arrest those suspected of murdering Tunstall. Billy is after revenge, not justice, and after a series of violent encounters, the war reaches its inevitable conclusion in a showdown in Lincoln between the Regulators and Murphy and his henchmen.

"Everybody turned [*Young Guns*] down," said Christopher Cain (1943–), the writer-director-producer of mostly low-budget, family-oriented dramas who directed *Young Guns*. "It had to be financed outside the studio system" (Southam News 1988, 21). Morgan Creek Productions, an independent film company owned by Joseph E. "Joe" Roth (1948–) and James G. Robinson (1935–), provided that financing.

Screenwriter John Fusco (1959–), a high school dropout, blues musician, and factory worker who had studied at New York University's Tisch School of the Arts, had one produced screenplay, *Crossroads* (1986), to his credit. But Fusco had an "obsession" with Billy the Kid:

> As my career was heating up, I saw an opportunity to create something bad-ass that would allow me to tell the story while also reaching a young generation. I wanted to turn a new generation onto the Western. My agents almost collapsed when I told them that I was leaving L.A.—I had only been there less than two years—and moving into the mountains in a cabin to write a Western on spec [a publishing term meaning there's no guarantee the finished product will be bought]. "The Western has been dead for two years," they pleaded with me. "It's actually so dead it's a joke in Hollywood." I said, "It's not a joke to me," and I left. (John Fusco, interview with author, July 10, 2018)

Fusco had visited Lincoln, New Mexico, and done plenty of historical research, but he was savvy enough to give his first Western something of a contemporary feel. "I think the opening line said 'Six guys come over the hill on horses. If it was 150 years [later] they'd be on Harleys,'" Fusco said. "I have been told that this made everyone want to read the script—and, for better or for worse, it helped them market it in their heads" (John Fusco, interview with author, July 10, 2018). Fusco sent the script to Cain, "who flipped for it." A South Dakota native living in Malibu, California, Cain had connections with many young actors, and he took the script to Sean Penn, whom Fusco had envisioned playing Billy. But Penn was in jail, sentenced to 60 days for violating probation by hitting a movie extra, and he passed because of his legal problems. Finding a studio was the hard part, said Cain, who heard rejections like, "Oh, it's a great script—it's a western" and "Oh, it's exciting—we don't want to do it" (Chase 1988, 29). 20th Century Fox decided to release the movie with Morgan Creek financing production and advertising costs. Using a nonunion crew, the producers managed to bring in the picture for a little more than $11 million.

With Penn out of consideration, Fusco eyed Sutherland for the lead role, and Sutherland was interested, "but Emilio Estevez made an impassioned pitch and that sold us all on him," Fusco said. "I took him to Lincoln with me; we bonded on that road trip and I gave him everything I had on the Kid" (John Fusco, interview with author, July 10, 2018). It wasn't just young actors. Fusco coaxed Jack Palance, who had earned an Oscar nomination for supporting actor in the Western *Shane* (1953), out of what Palance's agent insisted was retirement. Brian Keith (1921–1997), whose Westerns included *Nevada Smith* (1966) and a short-lived 1960 TV series called *The Westerner*, got the part of Buckshot Roberts. "Those legends added such gravitas and ballast," Fusco said (John Fusco, interview with author, July 10, 2018). Even Patrick Wayne (1939–), son of the late Western icon John Wayne (1907–1979), played Pat Garrett.

"I still have the framed *Variety* front page with the main headline reading 'GUNS HITS BULL'S EYE AT BOX OFFICE,'" Fusco said (John Fusco, interview with author, July 10, 2018). Negative reviews, however, likely outnumbered positive. While saying that it was "less like a real movie than an extended photo opportunity for its trendy young stars," the *New York Times'* Janet Maslin went on to note that *Young Guns* "doesn't make the mistake of taking itself too seriously. It's a good-humored exercise, if also a transparent one, and it sustains its spirit of fun right up to the point of a final shootout, in which the young heroes are badly outnumbered. Even so, the film manages to end on a cheery note" (Maslin 1988, C18).

The *Rocky Mountain News'*s Robert Dennerstein called the film "an ensemble movie that's violent, occasionally funny and as prone to meander as the tumbleweed in a strong wind. . . . 'Young Guns' wants to whip up a few laughs and, ultimately, to turn itself into a touching ode to the days when friendship meant something, like putting a bullet through an enemy's forehead" (quoted in Kinsler 1988, P9). Michael Healy of the *Los Angeles Daily News* called *Young Guns* a "deadly bore of a movie," an "obnoxious exercise in meaningless violence and actors' egotism," and said the "shoot-'em-ups are almost as dull and ineptly filmed as the stupid and everlasting dialogue scenes that separate the bits of action" (Healy 1988, 2H).

Young Guns earned more than $7 million, best for the week, on its opening weekend and went on to gross roughly $45 million. By the summer of 1989, Roth, who had also produced the 1989 hit baseball movie *Major League*, was appointed chairman of 20th Century Fox's filmmaking unit. "He took me to lunch and said, 'Is there a sequel?'" Fusco recalled. "I pitched it before our salad even came and we made the deal that day. To get the opportunity to keep going with it, to punch the critics in the face, and to get back on a horse with my boys—that was the ultimate dream. Very, very hard to top" (John Fusco, interview with author, July 10, 2018).

Young Guns saved the Hollywood Western, for the time being. Western series returned to television, including *Paradise*, retitled *Guns of Paradise* for its last season, on CBS (1988–1991), *The Young Riders* on ABC (1989–1992), and *Dr. Quinn, Medicine Woman* on CBS (1993–1998). *Lonesome Dove*, a four-part miniseries based on Larry McMurtry's Pulitzer Prize-winning novel, premiered on CBS in February 1989 and won seven Emmy Awards. Westerns also returned to the big screen. Fusco's sequel, *Young Guns II*, became another hit when it reached theaters in 1990, a year that also saw the release of *Dances with Wolves*, a mammoth hit that won seven Academy Awards, and *Quigley Down Under*. Soon to follow was another multi-Academy Award–winner, *Unforgiven* (1992), along with *Tombstone* and *Posse* (both 1993), *Wyatt Earp* (1994), *The Quick and the Dead* (1995), and others. There would be peaks and valleys, hits and misfires; and although the Western would never return to its heyday of the 1940s and 1950s, Hollywood had decided that the genre was not ready to be buried on Boot Hill.

HISTORICAL BACKGROUND

Early information about the outlaw who became known worldwide as Billy the Kid remains cloudy. He might have been born in New York City on November 23, 1859. That's what Pat Garrett and ghostwriter Ash Upson used in their 1882 book *The Authentic Life of Billy, the Kid, the Noted Desperado of the Southwest, Whose Deeds of Daring and Blood Have Made His Name a Terror in New Mexico, Arizona and Northern Mexico, by Pat F. Garrett, Sheriff of Lincoln County, N. Mex., by Whom He Was Finally Hunted Down and Captured by Killing Him.* Skeptics say Upson substituted his own birthday for Billy's. Others argue that's how Upson remembered it. As far as Billy being born in New York City, usually in an Irish slum, biographer Michael Wallis points out that "no records that can prove beyond a reasonable doubt that he ever lived there have ever been uncovered" (Wallis 2007, 6).

Other birthplace suggestions include Ireland, Illinois, Indiana, Kansas, New Mexico, Ohio, and Missouri, the latter given to census taker Lorenzo Labadie in mid-June 1880 by one listed as William H. Bonney, Billy's last alias. According to that census, Billy was 25 years old, and his parents were also born in Missouri. "Except for those who are enamored of his legend, there does not seem to have been any credible reason for him to have lied about either his place of birth or his age," Jon Tuska argued (Tuska 1997, 1). On the other hand, Billy lied about his name, possibly to "create a whole new identity to go along with his Bonney alias," Mark Lee Gardner countered (Gardner 2010, 36). It might not have been Billy who gave the information to Labadie. Besides, based on census records, Billy's brother, Joseph, was born in 1854, 1855, 1856 or 1863. Census records aren't always reliable.

What is known is that Billy's mother, Catherine McCarty, was living in Indianapolis, Indiana, in 1868 and reportedly told city directory compilers that she was the widow of Michael McCarty. (Children were not listed in the directory.) Catherine struck up a courtship with a Union Army veteran and Indiana native named William Henry Harrison Antrim, some 12 years Catherine's junior. By the summer of 1870, Catherine, her sons William Henry and Joseph, and Antrim had settled in Wichita, Kansas. At some point, Catherine developed tuberculosis, a lung ailment called consumption and considered a "death sentence" in the nineteenth century. With no known cure for the disease, doctors commonly recommended that sufferers move to drier climates, so the McCarty family and Antrim left Kansas in 1871.

On March 1, 1873, Catherine McCarty married William Antrim at the First Presbyterian Church in Santa Fe, the territorial capital of New Mexico, with her sons serving as witnesses. The family next moved south to the mining town of Georgetown and later to Silver City, where they found a small cabin in town. Antrim worked as a carpenter and butcher but spent more time gambling and prospecting. Catherine sold pies and sweetcakes and took in boarders to help support the family. But as tuberculosis ravaged Catherine's lungs, she was forced to bed, while her husband spent most of his time chasing elusive riches. Catherine's two sons were beside her when she died in their cabin on September 16, 1874, at age 45.

With his mother dead and a stepfather who had no interest in bringing up two young boys, Billy, who had been a popular and good student in school, began hanging out with ne'er-do-wells, including George "Sombrero Jack" Shaffer, a drunk and a thief. About a year after Catherine's death, Shaffer and Billy stole clothing from a Chinese laundry, and Billy hid the plunder. Finding the contraband, county Sheriff Henry Whitehill took Billy to jail "to scare him" but gave him access to the corridor outside the cell. "And right there," Whitehill lamented, "is where we fell down" (Utley 1989, 8). The undersized boy escaped by climbing up the chimney.

Billy eventually turned to horse theft in southern New Mexico and Arizona territories. On the night of August 17, 1877, in Camp Grant, Arizona, he killed his first man. Francis P. "Windy" Cahill was a blacksmith by trade and a bully by choice. Cahill and Billy traded insults in a saloon. Cahill had delighted in tormenting Billy, and on this night, he used his knees to pin down Billy's arms and began slapping the boy. Billy, however, slipped an arm free, grabbed his revolver, and shot Cahill in the stomach. Billy fled back to New Mexico and wound up in the middle of a feud in Lincoln County, the largest county—nearly 30,000 square miles—in the United States.

Over time, the boy born William Henry McCarty assumed a number of aliases—the Kid, Kid Antrim, William H. Bonney, El Chivato—Spanish for "the young goat," or "the kid," it's the nickname Chavez Y Chavez often calls Billy in *Young Guns*—and finally Billy the Kid. He called himself William H. Bonney when he arrived in Lincoln. By late 1877, he was working at the ranch of London-born John Henry Tunstall, who had settled in Lincoln in 1876 with plans to start a cattle ranch and open a mercantile. However, Irish-born Lawrence G. Murphy and his protégé, James J. Dolan, already operated an established store in Lincoln: L. G. Murphy & Co, known as "The House," which Murphy built in 1873. Although Murphy founded The House, he retired on March 14, 1877, and Dolan took over with John Henry Riley, a junior partner. The L. G. Murphy & Co. became the J. J. Dolan & Co.

Partnering with Lincoln attorney Alexander McSween and cattleman John Chisum, Tunstall opened his store in October 1877. It has often been argued that Tunstall did not know what he was getting into, but the store's walls were three feet thick, and the shutters were made of heavy wood sandwiching steel plates. In *Chisum*, a 1970 film depicting the Lincoln County War, a character complains that Tunstall's store "is built like a fort." That's pretty close to the truth, and the store's construction suggests that Tunstall wasn't totally naive. Still, Tunstall opened the store over the objections of McSween's wife, Susan, who said, "I told Tunstall and Mr. McSween that they would be murdered if they went into the store business" (Bell 1996, 44).

Elected sheriff of Lincoln County in 1869 and 1876, William Brady was a native of Ireland; former army soldier; and friend of Dolan, Riley, and Murphy. He was also "bound in allegiance to Murphy and his partners because he was heavily in debt to The House for years" (Wallis 2007, 177). That's what Tunstall and McSween were up against. What they had were loyal riders.

Born in Vermont in 1850, Richard M. "Dick" Brewer lived in Wisconsin when he was 18 but left after a girl spurned him by marrying his cousin. In 1876, Brewer bought a ranch on the Ruidoso River, befriended Tunstall, and served as foreman on the Englishman's ranch. Mississippi-born Charles Bowdre and Alabaman Josiah "Doc" Scurlock arrived in Lincoln in 1875, said to have come from the Gila River in Arizona, where they had operated a cheese factory (and might have employed Billy). Broke when they arrived, they bought a ranch on the Ruidoso River for $1,500 and were given a $3,000 line of credit—the financial assistance coming from, ironically, The House—and married Hispanic women. José Chávez y Chávez settled in Lincoln County in the late 1860s, married in 1871, and served as San Patricio Precinct's constable in 1874 and justice of the peace in 1875. In 1877, he was reappointed San Patricio's constable, but he would not join the Regulators until after Brewer's death in April 1878.

The least known among the Regulators depicted in *Young Guns* is Dirty Steve Stephens (or Stevens), who was among those indicted for Buckshot Roberts's murder and took part in the final battle in Lincoln before fading from the historical record. There were many other participants on both sides of the war.

On February 18, 1878, a subposse led by William "Buck" Morton and including Frank Baker shot and killed Tunstall. Tunstall's riders said the Englishman was murdered in cold blood, but Brady refused to listen. So McSween persuaded "Green" Wilson, the justice of the peace, to appoint Brewer as a special constable to arrest members of the posse that had killed Tunstall. Brewer formed a posse of roughly 15 men, including Billy. They were called the Regulators.

After Morton and Baker were captured by Regulators and then killed, along with Regulator William McCloskey on March 9, Governor Samuel B. Axtell canceled Wilson's legal appointment of the Regulators. On April 1, Billy took part in an ambush on Lincoln's one main street that killed Sheriff Brady and a deputy, George Hindman. Three days later, Brewer died at Blazer's Mill in a gunfight in which Buckshot Roberts, who had ridden in the posse against Tunstall, was also killed and a number of Regulators wounded.

The climax of the Lincoln County War began when McSween and several Regulators returned to Lincoln on the night of July 14. The next day, the men prepared for a siege in McSween's house and other buildings. What became known as the Five-Day Battle ended on the night of July 19. With McSween's house set on fire by Dolan's men, Billy and a handful of others escaped; McSween and others weren't as lucky, and they died in what was called the Big Killing.

That chapter of the Lincoln County War ended, more or less, but the story was far from over. President Rutherford Hayes dispatched Frank Angel to New Mexico, and the investigator's report led to the removal of Axtell, who was replaced as governor by Lew Wallace, at that time busy finishing his novel *Ben-Hur: A Tale of the Christ*. Wallace was sworn in on September 30, declaring overconfidently, "If peace and quiet are not restored in Lincoln County in the next 60 days I will feel ashamed of myself" (Boggs 2013, 9). The widow McSween hired Ira Chapman as her attorney in October, Wallace issued an amnesty proclamation in November, Chapman was murdered in February, and Wallace arrived in Lincoln in March, where he met with Billy and reached an agreement. If Billy testified about what he knew of Chapman's murder, Wallace would "let you go scot free with a pardon in your pockets for all your misdeeds" (Wallis 2007, 227). Billy lived up to his end of the bargain, testifying in April 1879, but the district attorney, William Rynerson, rumored to be part of the Santa Fe Ring, refused to honor the governor's promise of pardon. Eventually, Billy took up rustling livestock and gambling. He even killed a gunman named Joe Grant on January 10, 1880, in a Fort Sumner, New Mexico, saloon.

In November, former buffalo hunter Pat Garrett, backed by Chisum, was elected Lincoln County sheriff on a law-and-order platform, and the lawman went after Billy. Wallace published reward notices—$500 for capture and delivery to any New Mexico sheriff—in territorial newspapers. In December, Billy and several companions rode into Fort Sumner, where Garrett waited. Billy's pal, Tom Folliard (commonly misspelled O'Folliard) was killed, and the following day Billy and others were surrounded at a rock cabin at Stinking Springs. There, Bowdre was shot to death before Billy and those trapped with him surrendered. Eventually, Billy was tried in Mesilla for Brady's murder, convicted, and sentenced to hang in Lincoln. But Billy escaped from the Lincoln courthouse—headquartered in what had once been The House—killing two deputies left to guard him and other prisoners. Instead of fleeing the territory, Billy returned to Fort Sumner, where he had many friends and, reportedly, a lover. There, on the night of July 14, 1881, Billy, after spotting Garrett's small posse, slipped inside Pete Maxwell's bedroom, not realizing that Garrett was in the room questioning Maxwell. Garrett shot Billy in the chest, and Billy the Kid hit the floor dead.

DEPICTION AND CULTURAL CONTEXT

Historian Paul Andrew Hutton called *Young Guns* "the most historically accurate of dozens of Billy the Kid films" (Hutton 2018, 33). That's an accurate assessment, keeping in mind that Hollywood rarely followed history by the book. *Young Guns* embellished some events, created its own, changed some of the chronology, added fictional characters (including a love interest for Sutherland's character), jazzed up gunfights considerably, and did its share of other historical alterations for entertainment purposes. But the basic facts remained the same.

In movies attempting to document Billy the Kid's life and times and/or the Lincoln County War, Tunstall or a Tunstall-like character is portrayed as a fatherly or grandfatherly figure (*Young Guns* is no exception). In reality, the Englishman was just a few years older than Billy. Also, Lawrence G. Murphy is depicted as the villain behind The House, but by the time the Lincoln County War erupted, he had retired, and Dolan ran the business. The number of Regulators remains constant in *Young Guns*, whereas, in reality, riders came and went. At the start of the Five-Day Battle, they numbered roughly 40. But having characters disappear and then reappear can confuse moviegoers, and increasing the number of good guys by 34 significantly impacts a movie's budget. Fusco played it smart.

Still, *Young Guns* also followed history rather closely. Pat Garrett and Billy, often portrayed as bosom buddies in movies, are acquaintances in *Young Guns*, which appears more accurate. Garrett reportedly said of Billy: "He minds his business, and I attend to mine" (Boggs 2013, 226). The Irish faction, the political corruption, the costumes, and the locations felt and looked right, too.

THE LEFT-HANDED GUN?

Young Guns avoids one common misconception about Billy the Kid. In the film, when Billy reads an account of his escapades that says he's left-handed, he responds, "I ain't left-handed." Paul Newman played Billy that way in *The Left Handed Gun* (1958) and right-handed Robert Taylor learned to draw and shoot left-handed for his role in *Billy the Kid* (1941).

The mistake can be attributed to the lone authenticated photograph of Billy, taken in Fort Sumner in late 1879 or early 1880 by an itinerant photographer. The photograph was a tintype, however, and tintypes are reverse images; thus, Billy appeared to be left-handed. That led to Billy the Kid often being a left-hander in film and fiction.

Actually, Billy was likely ambidextrous. "My mother could write equally well with either hand, and so could Billy," said Patience Glennon, the daughter of Billy's Silver City schoolteacher. "He noticed this and he used to say to my mother that he was sure they were related because she was the only other person he had ever seen, besides himself, who could do things equally well with either hand" (Nolan 1998, 29).

In the movie, Murphy has accused Tunstall of "plundering" merchandise bound for The House and is upset that the Englishman plans to bid against him for a government beef contract. When Tunstall refuses to back down, Murphy warns him, "Get ready for hell." After leaving a New Year's Eve party in Lincoln with his Regulators, Tunstall drives a buggy, flanked by his hired hands on horseback. Excited at the opportunity to chase wild pheasants, the boys leave Tunstall, except for Billy, until Tunstall gives him his blessing. "Boys will be boys," Tunstall says, and Billy rides away. Almost immediately, several armed riders come up behind Tunstall. Billy stops his horse and turns around just in time to see Tunstall riddled by bullets and sent flying to the ground. The horse harnessed to the buggy is killed, too. Doc Scurlock stops Billy from opening fire, warning that the Regulators are outnumbered, so the boys flee. The film's depiction of Tunstall's murder is close to history, but the actual details leading up to the killing were much more complicated.

"Scratch behind the surface and you will find one thing as the prime mover in most of the Lincoln County troubles—money," historian Maurice J. Fulton wrote (quoted in Mullin 1968, 95). McSween handled a $10,000 life insurance claim for the heirs of one of The House's partners, Emil Fritz. McSween received the money, but delayed sending it on to the heirs until he was certain he would get his fee. Likely smelling at least a portion of that money for himself, Dolan managed to get one of the heirs to file suit against McSween for embezzlement. After a series of arrests, jailings, and court proceedings, a writ of attachment was issued on February 7, 1878.

The court-ordered writ, a common legal procedure that allows the plaintiff to secure a lien on the defendant's property, gave Sheriff Brady authority to seize assets of up to $8,000. Those assets could include Tunstall's as well, a move that "seemed calculated as much to ruin a competitor as to satisfy the claim of Emil Fritz's heirs and creditors" (Caffey 2014, 67).

With that writ, Brady deputized Jacob B. "Billy" Mathews, one of Dolan's silent partners, to lead a posse to Tunstall's ranch to seize some of Tunstall's livestock. That led to confrontations but no deaths until February 18. On that morning—not New Year's Day—Tunstall and four riders began driving nine horses, six of which Brady had released from the list of attachments a week earlier, toward Lincoln. Meanwhile, Mathews deputized William "Buck" Morton and sent him and a posse of more than a dozen men to catch up with Tunstall and get the horses. "Hurry up boys, my knife is sharp and I feel like scalping someone," Morton said before riding out (Utley 1989, 45).

Around dusk, Morton's posse found Tunstall and his men in rough, wooded country near present-day Glencoe. Tunstall, Brewer, and Robert Widenmann rode in front while John Middleton and Billy pulled up the rear. When Billy spotted the posse closing in, he and Middleton spurred ahead to warn the others. Morton's posse opened fire, and Tunstall's riders loped for a boulder-lined hilltop for protection. Tunstall appeared confused, said Middleton, who urged Tunstall to follow him into the rocks before riding away.

According to posse member George Kitt, Tom Hill called out to Tunstall that he would not be harmed. When Tunstall was near enough, Morton shot him in the breast and Hill shot him in the head. For spite, they also shot and killed Tunstall's prized bay horse. Morton later told Mathews that Tunstall fired on the posse and was killed. Kitt had another version: "Tunstall fired no shots . . . and was killed in cold blood," he said (Nolan 1992, 199). Contrary to the film's portrayal, none of Tunstall's riders witnessed the shooting.

The film also stays close to the truth in depicting the gunfight between the Regulators and Buckshot Roberts. In the movie, the Regulators are eating alone inside an adobe house when Dirty Steve, on guard duty, sees a lone rider coming toward them. Bowdre recognizes the lone man as Buckshot Roberts, who had "killed more men than smallpox." The Regulators step outside, and Brewer announces that he has a warrant for Roberts's arrest. Roberts, armed with two rifles, says he "ain't got no business with that war no more" but is after Billy—Sheriff Brady has posted a $150 reward for the Kid. The others are worth only $110. "Let's dance," Roberts says and opens fire.

Chavez Y Chavez and Scurlock are wounded as the Regulators take cover, while Roberts finds shelter in an outhouse. Brewer dares Billy to "cut the son of a b— in half," and with a grin, Billy attempts but is quickly driven back. The boys send a barrage of bullets through the outhouse's walls, and Brewer slowly walks toward the privy. Roberts shoots Brewer dead, and the Regulators put many bullets through the privy in retaliation. Knowing the place will be "crawling with Murphy men," the Regulators mount up and gallop away, leaving Brewer's body in the dirt.

The incident is wrong chronologically—it happens before Brady's assassination instead of three days later—but it's not a bad interpretation. On April 4, 1878, the Regulators arrived at Blazer's Mill on the Mescalero Apache Reservation to eat a noon meal at an adobe house occupied by Indian Agent Frederick Godfroy, his wife Clara, their two daughters, and a cook. Clara regularly took in boarders and served meals to travelers. While they ate, Bill Williams, also known as Andrew L. "Buckshot" Roberts, rode up. Roberts had ridden with the posse but had not taken part in Tunstall's murder. He wasn't seeking a reward on Billy—there was no reward for the Kid at that time—but wanted to see if a check from someone buying his farm had arrived.

Regulator Frank Coe, who knew Roberts, tried to persuade him to surrender, promising that he would not be harmed. Roberts declined, saying, "The Kid is with you and will kill me on sight" (Nolan 1998, 128). As the conversation dragged on roughly 30 minutes, several Regulators walked outside. Bowdre demanded Roberts to surrender. Roberts refused, guns were drawn, and Roberts put a bullet from his Winchester into Bowdre's belt buckle that ricocheted and struck the gun hand of George Coe, Frank's cousin. Bowdre shot Roberts in the abdomen, but the mortally wounded man shot John Middleton in the chest (Middleton miraculously survived), fired a round that struck Doc Scurlock's pistol and zipped down Scurlock's leg, and creased Billy with another bullet. Roberts then found shelter in Blazer's office, not an outhouse. Demanding that Roberts be captured or killed, Brewer took a position at a footbridge. He fired once. So did Roberts, whose bullet went through Brewer's head. The death of their leader, coupled with the wounding of many men, sent the Regulators into retreat. Roberts died the following day; he and Brewer were buried in the same grave. Billy later told a friend that Roberts "licked our crowd to a finish" (Nolan 1998, 133).

Young Guns turned to pure fiction, however, for the killing of Sheriff Brady. Brady and four armed men are walking down Lincoln's main street when Billy happily walks up behind them. He tosses his hat over Brady's head, which causes Brady to stop. Billy grabs Brady's own pistol and when the surprised sheriff turns around, Billy shoots him and then opens fire at the others. Chavez Y Chavez, on horseback, throws a knife into a deputy's throat. Dirty Steve and Bowdre keep shooting, while Scurlock, on a rooftop, shoots another. Brady is still alive as Billy stands over him and kills him with one more shot.

History reveals the incident as assassination. Brady walked with four deputies, and where they were going has never been verified, but when they reached Tunstall's store and corral, "a withering hail of lead blasted Brady off his feet" (Nolan 1998, 121). Brady and Hindman fell wounded in the street. A stray bullet hit Justice Wilson in the buttocks while hoeing his garden. The other two deputies took cover behind nearby buildings. Brady tried to sit up, but more shots left him mortally wounded. When Hindman begged for water, saloon owner Ike Stockton came out and tried to help him away, but another bullet killed the deputy. "Bullets were flying through town through and around our house; and we labored and prayed for quieter days," Reverend Taylor Ealy recalled, "but they did not come" (Bell 1996, 61).

Billy and Regulator Jim French left the corral for Brady's body, but deputy Billy Mathews's gunfire drove them back. What did Billy and French want? The most popular theories are that Billy went after his Winchester, which Brady had taken from him earlier, or that they were after warrants. In addition to Billy and French, the suspected assassins were Middleton, Widenmann, Fred Waite, and Henry Brown. Billy was the only one tried for Brady's murder.

The film's climactic gunfight is also fiction. Tipped off that Murphy plans to murder McSween, Billy leads the Regulators to Lincoln, but once inside McSween's house, Murphy's men surround the house, and army soldiers arrive, complete with a Gatling gun, to assist. "I love these odds," Billy says with a grin. Eventually, the house is torched, and the Regulators make a dash for freedom. Dirty Steve is killed, as is Bowdre, who guns down manhunter John Kinney before dying. Scurlock, Chavez Y Chavez, and Billy manage to escape, but soldiers riddle McSween's body with bullets from their Gatling gun. Billy then ends the Lincoln County War by putting a bullet through Murphy's forehead. "Now it's over," he says, and then he rides after his comrades. "This is a good piece of story development," Hutton wrote, "but alas, some bad history" (Hutton 2018, 33).

In actuality, Bowdre, Stephens, Kinney, and Murphy were not killed in the Five-Day Battle. Bowdre died two years later at Stinking Spring when Garrett's posse captured Billy; Kinney died in 1919. Stephens faded from history after the Lincoln County War. Practically destitute, Murphy died of cancer on October 20, 1878, not from a bullet to the head fired by Billy.

On the night of July 14, McSween, who had been running and hiding from Dolan's men, entered Lincoln with dozens of Regulators and took up positions at McSween's home, a granary behind Tunstall's store, and other buildings. Dolan, newly appointed Sheriff George W. "Dad" Peppin, and their men quickly found defensive positions. As the siege stretched on, the Regulators blundered when they fired upon soldiers entering town from nearby Fort Stanton. Post commander Nathan Dudley responded by sending troops, armed with a mountain howitzer and a Gatling gun, into Lincoln on July 19. Susan McSween was allowed to vacate her home unharmed—she had a heated exchange with Dudley—while Billy made plans to make a break for freedom that night.

By that time, Dolan's men had set fire to McSween's house. Around 9:00 p.m., Billy led four others outside. Regulator Harvey Morris, a law student, was killed at the gate, but despite a barrage of gunfire, Billy and the others escaped. While this was going on, McSween and others were supposed to make their break, but McSween delayed and did not leave the house until after the shooting stopped. More gunshots drove them back to cover. McSween said he would surrender, changed his mind, and he, or someone else, yelled, "I will never surrender" (Utley 1987, 98). When Deputy Robert Beckwith was shot and killed, Dolan's men opened fire again. McSween, struck by five bullets, died. Two Regulators were killed with him, and another, Yginio Salazar, was wounded, presumed dead, but managed to crawl away—after the Dolan men finished celebrating by drinking whiskey and forcing two McSween servants to play their fiddles near the corpses.

Walter Noble Burns (1866–1932) deserves some credit for *Young Guns* being filmed at all. Charles Greene, who owned the *Santa Fe New Mexican* newspaper, published Garrett's book shortly after Garrett killed Billy, but *The Authentic Life of Billy, the Kid* likely sold no more than a few hundred copies. After that, Billy was briefly mentioned in books by Charlie Siringo and Emerson Hough in the late 1800s, and a four-act melodrama titled *Billy the Kid* opened in 1906 and became a hit, though it had nothing to do with the real outlaw. Billy the Kid faded from memory so much that in 1925, Harvey Fergusson wrote an article for *The American Mercury*, asking, "Who remembers Billy the Kid?" A year later, Burns's *The Saga of Billy the Kid* became a best seller—and put Billy the Kid back into American pop culture.

When *Young Guns* opened, Hollywood—and American moviegoers— had all but buried the Western genre. After all, John Wayne's last movie, *The Shootist*, premiered in 1976, one of roughly 19 Westerns released that year. In 1979, the year Wayne died, only four Westerns made it to the big screen. The next year, the critical and box-office failure of the $40 million epic *Heaven's Gate*, directed by Academy Award–winner Michael Cimino (1939–2016), led to MGM's absorption of *Heaven's Gate* distributor, United Artists. In 1985, two highly anticipated summer releases—*Silverado*, directed by Lawrence Kasdan (1949–), and *Pale Rider*, directed by and starring Clint Eastwood (1930–)—were expected to resurrect the genre but only proved, the *New York Times* noted, "that audiences in the [1980s] prefer their horse operas set on distant planets with the feckless heroes riding spaceships" (Harmetz 1985, 33).

In the 1980s, moviegoers' tastes changed to favor science fiction, adventure, and comedy films. Westerns dramatically fell out of audiences' favor in the 1970s, and audiences of the 1980s, especially young audiences, spurned the genre. The top-grossing movies of the 1980s included the powerhouse *Star Wars* franchise's later installments, *The Empire Strikes Back* (1980) and *Return of the Jedi* (1983); even the decade's biggest comedies blended with science fiction, such as *Back to the Future* (1985) and *Ghostbusters* (1984). Other than Mel Brooks's 1974 Western spoof *Blazing Saddles*, the last Western to top the box office was 1969's *Butch Cassidy and the Sundance Kid*. Bridging the generation gap became crucial for *Young Guns*.

"Seven out of eight studio heads would say it's not going to make money," said Roth, adding that *Young Guns* might appeal to young ticket-buyers because "We have six of the 12 best actors among that age group" (Willistein 1988, D1). Members of Hollywood's "Brat Pack," known for their carousing lifestyles, headlined *Young Guns* cast. The term "Brat Pack" was a play on the fabled Rat Pack (Joey Bishop, 1918–2007; Sammy Davis Jr., 1925–1990; Peter Lawford, 1923–1984; Dean Martin, 1917–1995; Frank Sinatra, 1915–1998) of the 1960s.

David Blum coined "Brat Pack" in a 1985 issue of *New York Magazine*. "It is to the 1980s what the Rat Pack was to the 1960s—a roving band of famous young stars on the prowl for parties, women, and a good time" (Blum 1985). The Brat Packers included stars like Estevez, Penn, Rob Lowe, Tom Cruise, and Judd Nelson—friends who worked together and played together. The moniker "Rat Pack" caught on in the 1960s, when its members of actors, singer-actors, and comics were in their mid-30s to early 40s. In the Go-Go 1980s, the Brat Pack consisted of stars in their 20s. "Their films are often major hits," Blum wrote, "and the bigger the hit, the more money they make, and the more money they make, the more like stars they become" (Blum 1985).

Not that the Regulators of history were anything like the Rat or Brat Packs. Little is known about Stephens; Brewer was considered brave; Scurlock was well read and wrote poetry; there's no documentation that Chávez y Chávez was part Native American; and historian Leon Claire Metz wrote of Bowdre: "Calling Bowdre 'indecisive' would be an understatement" (Metz 2003, 25). For Billy, Estevez played him as a charming psychopath who reads well and shoots better. The real Billy knew how to read, had terrific penmanship, and definitely knew his way around guns. What isn't captured in the movie, though, is how many women adored him and the fact that he was fluent in Spanish, which made him popular among the Hispanics populating New Mexico Territory.

Los Angeles Daily News critic Michael Healy called *Young Guns* "the first teen-age exploitation rock 'n' roll Western" (Healy 1988, 2H). Healy ripped the movie in his review, but his opening statement pretty much nailed the movie—and why it proved to be an enormous hit. One poster depicted the six stars wearing badges and Western duds underneath the headline "SIX REASONS WHY THE WEST WAS WILD." "But none is wearing a cowboy hat," Richard Aquila wrote. "They look more like an eighties boy band than rugged western heroes. Yet, their striking appearance suggests that these six neatly dressed, well-coiffed men may be young and may look different from most cowboys, but they mean business" (Aquila 2015, 302–303).

Young Guns and its sequel, the Fusco-penned, Geoff Murphy-directed *Young Guns II*, were not neo-Westerns. "Although the *Young Guns* westerns feature young heroes, they clearly endorse old myths," Aquila said. "They demonstrate that the mythic West was alive and well in [President Ronald] Reagan's America. . . . [E]ven the supposedly revisionist premise of *Young Guns II*—that Billy the Kid was not killed by Pat Garrett but survived as Brushy Bill Roberts—is just a rehash of an old legend" (Aquila 2015, 306). The sequel, which included Estevez, Sutherland, and Phillips reprising their roles while adding Christian Slater (1969–) and William Petersen (1953–), the latter replacing Patrick Wayne as Pat Garrett, added to the youth factor by including songs by Jon Bon Jovi (1962–), who earned an Academy Award nomination for best original song, "Blaze of Glory."

Youth Westerns suddenly became popular. In May 1989, the cable network TNT premiered *Billy the Kid*, a Western film written by Gore Vidal and starring Val Kilmer (1959–). That fall, a new Western series debuted on ABC. It told the story of a bunch of young Pony Express riders and was titled *The Young Riders*; it lasted three seasons. Westerns, however, weren't just about and for the young. *Old Gringo* hit big screens in 1989, and in 1990, when even *Back to the Future Part III* sent its heroes to the American West of 1885, *Grim Prairie Tales*, *Quigley Down Under*, and *Dances with Wolves* joined *Young Guns II* in theaters.

CONCLUSION

While accurately depicting some events and characters involved in the Lincoln County War, *Young Guns* also added more than its share of embellishment and testosterone-laden nonsense. Too complicated to be boiled down into a 107-minute running time, the story of the Lincoln County War is likely better suited to a miniseries format. The importance of *Young Guns*, however, cannot be overlooked because of what it did for Western filmmaking. "If any movie can revive the western," arts editor Paul Willistein wrote for *The Morning Call* in Allentown, Pennsylvania, "'Young Guns' might" (Willistein 1988, D1).

It did—so much, in fact, that arguments have been made that without the franchise's commercial success, *Dances with Wolves* and *Unforgiven*, the first Westerns to win Oscars for best picture since *Cimarron* (1931), likely would never have been made. "I agree with that," Fusco said. "Something had to break it wide open, and my gut had told me that the young West could do it. Others would go on to do it better and win awards and prestige, but I'm proud that *Young Guns* arguably brought the Western back" (John Fusco, interview with the author, July 10, 2018).

FURTHER READING

Aquila, Richard. 2015. *The Sagebrush Trail: Western Movies and Twentieth-Century America*. Tucson: University of Arizona Press.

Argetsinger, Amy. 2015. "How the Brat Pack Got Its Name—And Spoiled Celebrity Journalism Forever." *Washington Post*, August 10, 2015. https://www .washingtonpost.com/news/arts-and-entertainment/wp/2015/08/10/how-the -brat-pack-got-their-name-and-spoiled-celebrity-journalism-forever

Bell, Bob Boze. 1996. *The Illustrated Life and Times of Billy the Kid: Revised & Expanded Second Edition*. Phoenix, AZ: Tri Star-Boze Productions Inc.

Blum, David. 1985. "Hollywood's Brat Pack: They're Rob, Emilio, Sean, Tom, Judd, and the Rest—The Young Movie Stars You Can't Quite Keep Straight. But They're Already Rich and Famous. They're What Kids Want to See and What Kids Want to Be." *New York Magazine*, June 10, 1985. http://nymag.com /movies/features/49902

Boggs, Johnny D. 2013. *Billy the Kid on Film, 1911–2012*. Jefferson, NC: McFarland & Company, Inc., Publishers.

Caffey, David L. 2014. *Chasing the Santa Fe Ring: Power and Privilege in Territorial New Mexico*. Albuquerque: University of New Mexico Press.

Caulfield, Deborah. 1985. "Kasdan: Hi-yo, 'Silverado'." *Los Angeles Times*, July 7, 1985. https://articles.latimes.com/1985-07-07/entertainment/ca-9339_1 _lawrence-kasdan

Chase, Donald. 1988. "Young Guns Attempts to Revive Spirit of Westerns: Ambitious Film Takes Fresh Look at Billy the Kid." *Winnipeg Free Press*, July 9, 1998, p. 29.

Gardner, Mark Lee. 2010. *To Hell on a Fast Horse: Billy the Kid, Pat Garrett, and the Epic Chase to Justice in the Old West*. New York: William Morrow.

Harmetz, Aljean. 1985. "A Bleak Summer for Movie Makers." *New York Times*, September 2, 1985, p. 33.

Harmetz, Aljean. 1988. "Fox: Lights, Action, More Movies." *Syracuse Herald-Journal*, July 13, 1989, p. C5.

Healy, Michael. 1988. "'Young Guns' Punks Are Shooting Blanks." *Madison State Journal*, August 21, 1988, p. 2H.

Hutton, Paul Andrew. 2018. "A Fool's Errand: Does Such a Thing as a Historically Accurate Western Exist?" *True West*, February 2018.

Kinsler, Robert, compiler. 1988. "Should You See? 'Young Guns.'" *Orange County Register*, August 26, 1988, p. P9.

Loy, R. Philip. 2004. *Westerns in a Changing America, 1955–2000*. Jefferson, NC: McFarland & Company, Inc., Publishers.

Maslin, Janet. 1988. "Hollywood's Young Bloods in 'Young Guns,' Tale of Outlawry." *New York Times*, August 12, 1988, p. C18.

Metz, Leon Claire. 2003. *The Encyclopedia of Lawmen, Outlaws, and Gunfighters*. New York: Facts on File, Inc.

Mullin, Robert N., ed. 1968. *Maurice G. Fulton's History of the Lincoln County War*. Tucson: University of Arizona Press.

Niemietz, Brian. 2018. "The Rat Pack Might Not Have Survived #MeToo, Says Dean Martin's Daughter." *New York Daily News*, June 3, 2018, http://www .nydailynews.com/entertainment/ny-ent-rat-pack-metoo-20180601-story.html

Nolan, Frederick. 1992. *The Lincoln County War: A Documentary History.* Norman: University of Oklahoma Press.

Nolan, Frederick. 1998. *The West of Billy the Kid.* Norman: University of Oklahoma Press.

"Penn Out of Jail Early for Good Behavior." *Desert Sun*, September 17, 1987, p. A11.

Southam News. 1988. "Young Guns Rejected at First." *Medicine Hat News*, September 10, 1988, p. 21.

Tatum, Stephen. 1992. *Inventing Billy the Kid: Visions of the Outlaw in America, 1881–1981.* Albuquerque: University of New Mexico Press.

Tuska, Jon. 1997. *Billy the Kid: His Life and Legend.* Albuquerque: University of New Mexico Press.

Utley, Robert M. 1987. *High Noon in Lincoln: Violence on the Western Frontier.* Albuquerque: University of New Mexico Press.

Utley, Robert M. 1989. *Billy the Kid: A Short and Violent Life.* Lincoln: University of Nebraska Press.

Wallis, Michael. 2007. *Billy the Kid: The Endless Ride.* New York: W. W. Norton & Company.

Willistein, Paul. 1988. "Western Loaded with Young Guns: Hotshots Estevez, Sheen and Sutherland Aim for a Hit." *Morning Call*, August 12, 1988, pp. D1-2.

Chapter 10

Tombstone (1993)

The fact that *Tombstone* even showed in theaters exceeded some insiders' expectations. Turmoil followed the film's production from the development process through its filming, editing, and release, and there were other concerns. *Wyatt Earp*, a movie with a bigger budget ($63 million), star (Kevin Costner, 1955–) and director (Lawrence Kasdan, 1949–) that was covering the same subject—Wyatt Earp and the O.K. Corral gunfight—was in production and already receiving major publicity. Despite the recent success of *Dances with Wolves* (1990) and *Unforgiven* (1992), both commercial hits and Academy Award winners for Best Picture, Westerns were still considered a commercial risk in Hollywood. *Tombstone* producer James Jacks (1947–2014) said: "It was a miracle [*Tombstone*] ever got made" (Blake 2017, 10). Despite minimal publicity and mostly unfavorable reviews, this "miracle," released on Christmas Day 1993 by Hollywood Films, a division of the Walt Disney Studios, became "the surprise hit of the post-holiday season" (Beale 1994, 39), a best seller on the home video market the following summer, and today is regarded as a cult classic.

Tombstone opens with a band of cutthroats known as "the Cowboys," led by Curly Bill Brocious (Powers Boothe, 1948–2017) and Johnny Ringo (Michael Biehn, 1956–), murdering a Hispanic wedding party to avenge the deaths of two of their own. Meanwhile, retired Kansas lawman Wyatt Earp (Kurt Russell, 1951–) arrives in Tucson, Arizona Territory, with his common-law wife, Mattie (Dana Wheeler-Nicholson, 1960–), and joins his brothers Virgil (Sam Elliott, 1944–) and Morgan (Bill Paxton, 1955–2017), and their wives to settle in Tombstone, a booming silver town southeast of Tucson. In Tombstone, Wyatt is reunited with his friend John "Doc" Holliday (Val Kilmer, 1959–), a Georgia-born gambler and killer dying of tuberculosis.

FARO

Faro, as depicted in *Tombstone*, was a popular card game on the American frontier. Known as "bucking the tiger," faro could be played fast and with many players. It used a dealer's box, a faro layout with all card denominations for placing bets, and a regular 52-card deck. The first card turned up was not counted, the second won for the players, and the third won for the dealer. The odds should have been even, but the 1864 *American Hoyle* warned that "*all* regular faro-players are reduced to poverty, while dealers and bankers, who do not play against the game, amass large fortunes" (*The American Hoyle* 1864, 209). That's because "there is no game in which the opportunities of cheating are more numerous or varied" (Maskelyne 1894, 214). Decks could be stacked in favor of the dealer or filled with textured cards that would allow the dealers to stack the deck to their advantage. The faro box could be "gaffed," allowing the dealer to see the card about to be drawn, or to draw two cards after which the dealer's sleight of hand would hide the card that would have lost money for the bank.

Faro's "reputation for being a cheating game finally caught up with the dealers" historian G. R. Williamson wrote (Williamson 2011, 18). Arizona outlawed faro in 1907, and the last Nevada casino offering faro closed in 1985.

Sources

The American Hoyle, or Gentleman's Hand-Book of Games. 1864. New York: Dick & Fitzgerald, Publishers.

Maskelyne, John Nevil. 1894. *Sharps and Flats: A Complete Revelation to The Secrets of Cheating at Games of Chance and Skill.* New York: Longmans, Green, and Co.

Williamson, G. R. 2011. *Frontier Gambling: The Games, the Gamblers & the Great Gambling Halls of the Old West.* Kerrville, TX: Indian Head Publishing.

Tombstone is raucous and highly profitable for the brothers as Wyatt lands a job dealing faro, a popular card game of the era. The Cowboys aren't the only unruly element, but Wyatt rejects attempts by town or territorial leaders to make him a lawman again. He does, however, take action after Brocious shoots town Marshal Fred White (Harry Carey Jr., 1921–2012) dead by arresting Brocious, who is high on opium, but charges are dismissed. With Mattie addicted to laudanum, a painkiller containing opium and alcohol, Wyatt becomes attracted to actress Josephine Marcus (Dana Delany, 1956–). Repulsed by the violence in town, Virgil takes the job of town marshal and deputizes Morgan, irritating Wyatt, and Tombstone bans the carrying of firearms in town. The brothers and Holliday make enemies of Brocious, Ringo, and other Cowboys, including Ike Clanton (Stephen Lang, 1952–); his brother Billy (Thomas Haden Church, 1960–); and the McLaury brothers Frank (Robert John Burke, 1960–) and Tom (John Philbin, 1960–). After threats from the Clantons and McLaurys, the Earps and Holliday try to disarm them for violating the town antigun ordinance. A gunfight follows, leaving Billy Clanton and the McLaury brothers dead and Virgil and Morgan wounded.

The Cowboys get vengeance, though, maiming Virgil with a shotgun blast to his left arm and killing Morgan with a bullet to the back while he's playing pool. After leaving town, Wyatt seeks revenge and justice, killing a would-be assassin at the Tucson train depot and warning Ike Clanton to tell his friends that Wyatt is coming after them. Armed with a commission as a deputy U.S. marshal, Earp and a posse that includes Holliday kill several Cowboys. Brocious and other Cowboys ambush Earp's party, but Wyatt miraculously kills Brocious and several accomplices. Sheriff John Behan (Jon Tenney, 1961–) and his posse, however, have warrants for the arrest of Wyatt, Holliday, and their friends, who take shelter at the ranch owned by Henry Hooker (Charlton Heston, 1923–2008). After Ringo challenges Earp to a gunfight to finish the feud, Holliday gets to the meeting spot first, where he kills Ringo. Wyatt and his friends proceed to kill many of the remaining Cowboys before running Ike Clanton out of the territory. After Holliday dies in a sanatorium in Glenwood Springs, Colorado, Wyatt finds Josephine in Denver, where they dance in the snow before starting their new life together.

Screenwriter Kevin Jarre (1954–2011), who had received a Golden Globe nomination for writing the highly praised Civil War drama *Glory* (1989), became fascinated with the O.K. Corral story after Earp historian Jeff Morey gave the writer a copy of a photograph of Earp. Jarre spent more than a year researching and writing the screenplay, often asking Morey questions. Morey told film historian Michael F. Blake: "He called me up one night out of the clear blue, and said, 'Why do you think Wyatt liked Doc?' I said, 'I think he made him laugh" (Blake 2007, 157). A similar line wound up in the finished film.

Universal agreed to make *Tombstone* until Costner announced that *Wyatt Earp*, originally planned as a six-part miniseries, would be a theatrical film. "Is Tinseltown big enough for two Wyatt Earp movies?" Hollywood columnist Michael McGovern asked (McGovern 1993, 19). Jarre said the announcement was "an attempt to crush my picture," but producer Jim Wilson, Costner's partner, denied any competition between *Wyatt Earp* and *Tombstone* (McGovern 1993, 19). Still, Universal decided against making Jarre's film, citing concerns with the budget, but Blake argued, "The *real* reason was the studio did not want to lose its deal with Costner for *Waterworld*" (Blake 2017, 12), a science-fiction movie starring Costner that the studio released in 1995.

Brad Pitt (1963–) and Johnny Depp (1963–) reportedly agreed to play Wyatt and Holliday but withdrew after Costner's film was announced. Russell, however, found the script and agreed to play Earp. That was enough to get Cinergi, an independent film company, to produce it and Disney's Hollywood Pictures to handle U.S. distribution. Jarre would make his directorial debut on the film that had a $25 million budget and 62-day shooting schedule. Jarre wanted Willem Dafoe (1955–) to play Holliday, but Disney rejected the actor because of his portrayal of Jesus in the controversial film

The Last Temptation of Christ (1988). Kilmer got the part. Older movie stars Heston and Robert Mitchum (1917–1997) signed to play Hooker and Old Man Clanton, Ike's father, but after Mitchum's role was cut, the actor was hired as to narrate the movie's opening and closing.

A stickler for detail, Jarre wanted to make a movie that looked authentic, including costumes. Costume designer Joseph A. Porro, making his first Western, had trouble finding period costumes available for rent. With *Wyatt Earp, Geronimo: An American Legend* (1993), and Turner Network Television's *Geronimo* (1993) also in production, Porro said, "There wasn't even a cowboy hat left anywhere at any of the studios" (Farkis 2019, 48). Porro received help from cowboy reenactors and small, custom clothiers like Penrose, Colorado, hatmaker Tom Hirt. "Working with Kevin was great because he wanted to do a Western that was historically correct in all aspects," Hirt recalled (Tom Hirt, interview with author, November 17, 2001).

With casting set, filming began May 17 in southern Arizona, primarily at Old Tucson, a movie set first built for *Arizona* (1940) and used in several films, and its sister set, first built for *Monte Walsh* (1970), in Mescal, roughly 40 miles southeast of Tucson. The movie quickly fell behind schedule, leading executive producers to suggest cutting scenes. As a director, Jarre irritated actors by telling them how to read their lines, and he ignored suggestions from cinematographer William Fraker (1923–2010), who had been nominated for four Oscars in cinematography and another for visual effects. Elliott complained that Jarre failed to get needed coverage shots. On June 14, Jarre was fired; George P. Cosmatos (1941–2005) replaced him. The production "sort of took another direction at that point in time," Hirt said (Tom Hirt, interview with author, November 17, 2001). Cosmatos cared so little for detail, Kilmer said, "I think I got nine or 10 shots out of my six-gun" (Boggs 1999, 56). Summer monsoons and blistering heat took a toll on cast and crew. "Every day was such a trial," Kilmer said. "It was a unique kind of hell" (Boggs 1999, 57). Cosmatos, profane and belligerent, managed to anger even the hard-to-rile Elliott, but Elliott wasn't alone. Three times Fraker quit, but he returned each time and finished the film. "There always used to be laughter on a movie set," veteran actor Carey said, but on *Tombstone*'s set, "It was like everybody was going to a lynching or something" (Farkis 2019, 166).

Russell said he had been asked to direct after Jarre was fired and Cosmatos came in as a "ghost director . . . I'd go to George's room, give him the shot list for the next day, that was the deal. 'George I don't want any arguments. This is what it is. This is what the job is'" (Beck 2006). Those long days left Russell so exhausted, he said, it affected his acting performance.

On August 10, principal photography ended—18 days over schedule—and the editors went to work, cutting the film and rushing for a Christmas release. "The picture wasn't screened for anyone until days before the opening, which is usually seen as a sign of disaster in a paranoid industry," Lewis Beale wrote in the *New York Daily News* (Beale 1994, 39).

While praising Jarre's script and Kilmer's performance, *San Francisco Examiner* critic Barbara Shulgasser said that "the movie often seems intent on undermining its own momentum" (Shulgasser 1993, D-3). "'Tombstone' is a big, handsome, intermittently engaging barrel of clichés that fails to add any insight or revisionist thinking to an overtold legend," Dan Craft wrote for Bloomington, Illinois's *The Pantagraph* (Craft 1994, B-3). *Tombstone* "wants to be at once traditional and morally ambiguous," Stephen Holden wrote for the *New York Times.* "The two visions don't quite harmonize" (Holden 1993, C6). "Despite some fine photography and [Kilmer's] masterful performance, 'Tombstone' is pretty much dead on arrival," M. Scot Skinner opined in the *Arizona Daily Star* (Skinner 1993, D1).

Audiences, however, were drawn to the movie, which grossed $60 million domestically. More than 600,000 home-video units were sold in *Tombstone*'s inaugural release in July 1994, which came just after the June premiere of Costner's 192-minute *Wyatt Earp*. Unlike *Tombstone*, *Wyatt Earp* was a colossal failure, earning $22 million in four weeks before withdrawing from first-run theaters. "The battle of the dueling Earps was over," John Farkis wrote. "At the end of the day it was *Tombstone* 1, *Wyatt Earp* 0" (Farkis 2019, 2010).

But not everyone was happy. Russell said *Tombstone* "could have been one of the greatest Westerns ever, ever, ever made" (Beck 2006). Jacks told Cosmatos after a preview screening: "George, you had a great script and a great cast and we made a good movie. It's not something we should be doing cartwheels over" (Farkis 2019, 206).

HISTORICAL BACKGROUND

Wyatt Berry Stapp Earp (1848–1929), the fourth of Nicholas Earp's six sons, was born on March 19, 1848, in Monmouth, Illinois. The farming family moved around Illinois and Iowa, and Wyatt's father and older brothers Newton, James, and Virgil served as Union volunteers during the Civil War (1861–1865). Always restless, the Earps moved in 1864 to California, where Wyatt worked as a stagecoach driver and freighter as a teenager. By 1869, the Earps had moved to Missouri, where Wyatt was elected constable of Lamar in 1870 and married Urilla Sutherland, who died along with her child while giving birth. In 1871, Wyatt was indicted and jailed in Arkansas for stealing horses in Indian Territory (present-day Oklahoma), was freed on bail, and fled west. After hunting buffalo in Kansas, Wyatt was hired as a police officer in Wichita, Kansas, a cattle town on the Chisholm Trail, in 1875. The following year, Wyatt joined the police force in Dodge City, another Kansas cattle town, where he also served as a deputy sheriff for Ford County.

In November 1879, Wyatt Earp, likely burned out from serving as a peace officer in Dodge City, arrived in Prescott, territorial capital of Arizona, where his brother Virgil (1843–1905), a local lawman, and Virgil's wife, Allie (1849–1947), had settled in 1877. With Wyatt were his common-law wife Mattie Blaylock (1850–1888); James Earp (1841–1926) and his wife and two children; and John "Doc" Holliday (1951–1887) and his female companion, Mary Katharine Haroney (1850–1940), who went by the name Kate Elder. It's unclear whose idea it was to relocate in Tombstone, more than 275 miles southeast of Prescott, but the Earps had always been clannish. Virgil quit his job, and the Earps moved south. Elder, who never liked Wyatt, and Holliday stayed behind but joined the Earps in Tombstone later.

After the events in Arizona, Wyatt drifted, gambling, running saloons, and speculating in real estate and mining. He and Josephine Marcus became a couple in 1882, and she was with him until his death in California in 1929. Marcus died in 1944.

John Henry "Doc" Holliday was born in Griffin, Georgia, on August 14, 1851, and attended dental school in Pennsylvania, where he graduated in 1872 and opened a practice in Atlanta, Georgia. The following year, Holliday was diagnosed with pulmonary tuberculosis, a lung disease then known as consumption. With no cure, consumptives often went West, where the dry climate was thought to ease their lung troubles. After moving to Dallas, Texas, Holliday struggled with his dental practice and took up gambling. Eventually, he left dentistry behind and gambled full time. He developed a reputation as quick-tempered and quick-triggered, although there is little evidence that he killed anyone before the O.K. Corral, and most of his known arrests were misdemeanors for gambling. Along his travels he befriended Wyatt Earp and became involved with Kate Elder. He came to Arizona to be with Earp, and once he left Arizona, he drifted into Colorado. In 1887, Holliday traveled to Glenwood Springs, Colorado, where the hot springs were believed to help consumptives. On November 8, 1887, Holliday died of tuberculosis and was buried in a town cemetery.

The town of Tombstone was the result of the persistence of Edward "Ed" Schieffelin (1847–1897). Born in Pennsylvania, Schieffelin and his brother and mother left their home in 1856 to join Schieffelin's father, who had joined the 1848–1849 Gold Rush to California. Clinton Schieffelin's luck as a miner never panned out, and he focused on farming and breeding cattle along the Rogue River in Oregon, but he encouraged his sons to prospect. Ed ran away from home at age 12 to join the Salmon River strike before a neighbor brought him home. As an adult, Ed Schieffelin continued hunting for riches across much of the West. He never found riches until he came to Arizona in January 1877. With two mules, $30, and prospecting equipment, Schieffelin roamed across a country occupied by Apaches, who did not like white trespassers. Several times Schieffelin was warned, "All you'll ever find in them hills'll be your tombstone" (Burns 1929, 5), so when Schieffelin filed his first claim in Arizona, he called it "Tombstone." Schieffelin's first haul of silver bullion to Tucson proved that he "indeed had found his El Dorado in the Tombstone Hills" (Craig 2017, 7).

When Schieffelin and his brother, Al, sold their Tombstone mining interests in March 1879, they received more than $1 million each. "I have been told," Schieffelin recalled, "that nearly fifty million dollars' worth of mineral has been taken out of the Tombstone district" (Breakenridge 1928, 98). Schieffelin continued prospecting, as far away as Alaska and Africa. He died in a cabin near Medford, Oregon, of natural causes at age 49 while looking for another fortune. A small bag of quartz that assayed at more than $2,000 a ton was discovered near his body, and he had written his mother: "I have found stuff here in Oregon that will make Tombstone look like salt. This is GOLD" (Craig 2017, 101). No fortune has ever been found in that area.

Tombstone boomed. By December 1879, just after the Earps arrived in town, a *Chicago Tribune* correspondent wrote:

> One year ago to-day there were but sixty voters in the district; but little work done on any of the mines; no works for the reduction of ores; no mail-service, or stage-coaches for the conveyance of comers and goers; and comparatively little said, thought, or known by the outside world of Tombstone's splendid prospects. To-day we can boast of three good-sized towns; the arrival and departure of fifteen stages per week,—giving us daily communication with the end of the Southern Pacific Railroad; more work done on our mines than has been done in any other camp in the Territory; on the San Pedro River three first-class mills are to be found; and throughout the Union the wealth of Tombstone is proverbial. (Stone 1879, 9)

Like many frontier towns, Tombstone went through growing pains and was prone to violence. Elected town marshal on January 6, 1880, Fred White (1849–1880) was shot and killed by Curly Bill Brocious on October 28, 1880, and a devastating fire swept through the town on June 22, 1881, burning two square blocks with losses estimated at $175,000. Rebuilding started immediately, and after two weeks the majority of the saloons were "back up, bigger, better and roaring" (Bell 2000, 48). By 1881, Tombstone's population was estimated at 2,000. Cochise County was created on February 1, 1881, Tombstone became the county seat, and John Behan (1844–1912) was appointed county sheriff. That summer, Virgil Earp, who had received a commission as a deputy U.S. marshal after arriving in Tucson in 1879 on the way to Tombstone, became Tombstone's chief of police. Morgan Earp, who had joined his brothers after quitting his job on the Butte, Montana, police force in early 1880, was appointed a Tombstone police officer on October 17.

On the morning of October 25, 1881, Ike Clanton (1847–1887) and Tom McLaury (1853–1881) arrived in Tombstone to drink and gamble; Billy Clanton (1862–1881) and Frank McLaury (1849–1881) joined them later. After verbal altercations between Doc Holliday and Ike and Tom, Virgil Earp clubbed Ike with a pistol the next day and arrested him for carrying a Winchester, a violation of the town ordinance prohibiting the carrying of weapons in the town limits. Ike paid a fine and was released; moments later Tom McLaury threatened Wyatt. Tension intensified, and shortly after 2:40 p.m., Virgil, Morgan, and Wyatt, joined by Holliday, went to disarm or arrest the Clantons and McLaurys, all reportedly armed. In a vacant lot off Fremont Street behind the O.K. Corral, a gunfight left Billy Clanton and the McLaury brothers dead and Holliday and Virgil and Morgan Earp wounded. Neither of the two principals—Wyatt Earp and Ike Clanton—was injured.

In a preliminary hearing, Justice of the Peace Wells Spicer (1831–1887) began a hearing to determine if the Earps and Holliday should stand trial for murder. On November 29, Spicer cleared the defendants of any wrongdoing. Spicer and Holliday received anonymous threats. Fearing assassination, the Earps moved out of their rented homes and into the Cosmopolitan Hotel.

On December 28, Virgil Earp left the Oriental Saloon around 11:30 p.m. and walked to the hotel. As Virgil crossed Fifth Street, two shotgun blasts maimed his left arm, but he survived. Tombstone resident George W. Parsons wrote in his diary on Tuesday, January 17, 1882:

> Much blood in the air this afternoon. [John Ringo and Doc Holiday came nearly having it with pistols. . . . Bad time expected with the cowboy leader and D. H. I passed both not knowing blood was up. One with hand in breast pocket and the other probably ready. Earps just beyond. Crowded street and looked like another battle. Police vigilant for once and both disarmed. (Parsons 1972, 206)

On March 28, while Morgan and Wyatt played pool at Campbell and Hatch's Saloon, a killer or killers shot through a door window. Morgan was hit in the back, and another bullet struck the wall above Wyatt's head. Morgan died 40 minutes later.

The Earps, Holliday, and Earp partisans left Tombstone for the railroad in Tucson to send Morgan's body, the wounded Virgil, and most of the women to California. Ike Clanton and Frank Stilwell (1856–1882) came to the depot (to ambush the Earp party, according to the Earp faction; to meet a witness for the grand jury, according to Ike Clanton). Wyatt Earp said that he killed Stilwell with a shotgun blast and that Clanton fled. Parsons wrote in his diary: "A quick vengeance and a bad character sent to hell where he will be the chief attraction until a few more accompany him" (Parsons 1972, 221).

What became known as Wyatt Earp's Vendetta Ride began. Behan and a posse, ordered to arrest Earp for Stilwell's murder, pursued Earp's posse. The body of Florentino Cruz, part–Native American believed to have taken part in Morgan Earp's murder, was found on March 23, 1882, shot multiple times the day before. At the coroner's inquest, a witness testified that he had seen Wyatt Earp and his younger brother Warren (1855–1900), accompanied by Holliday and three other men after hearing gunfire at the site where Cruz's body was found ("CORONER'S INQUEST" 1882, 1). "Killing Cruz inarguably put Wyatt Earp beyond the pale of the law," historian Jeff Guinn wrote (Guinn 2011, 281). Earp said he killed Brocious, whose body was never found and identified. The body of John Ringo (1850–1882) was found with a gunshot wound to the head in July. In later years, Wyatt claimed to have killed Ringo, although his Vendetta Ride had ended when his posse left Arizona around that spring.

Attempts by Arizona authorities to extradite Wyatt Earp and Doc Holliday failed. Ike Clanton was killed in June 1887 while rustling cattle, and his brother Phin (1843–1906) was sentenced to ten years in prison after surrendering. John Behan wasn't nominated for reelection in 1882, but he served as Yuma Territorial Prison's warden and as a customs inspector in Texas before his death in 1912. Virgil Earp died of pneumonia in Goldfield, Nevada, in 1905.

Tombstone hit hard times in 1882 with mines flooding and the economy faltering. Silver prices fell, and mines began closing in 1886. By 1900, only 647 people remained in Tombstone, yet "the old town refused to die" (Burns 1929, 378). Tombstone lost the county seat to Bisbee in 1929, the year Tombstone started "Helldorado Days," a festival celebrating the town's Western history. That ended in 1932, but the festival was revived in the late 1940s when tourism and interest in Western history helped resurrect the town. Instead of drawing gamblers, miners, and outlaws, Tombstone today attracts 400,000 tourists a year, helping Tombstone live up to its moniker as "The Town Too Tough to Die."

DEPICTION AND CULTURAL CONTEXT

Moviemakers had favored the Gunfight at the O.K. Corral for decades, covering the event in *Frontier Marshal* (1939), *Tombstone: The Town Too Tough to Die* (1942), *My Darling Clementine* (1946), *Gunfight at the O.K. Corral* (1957), *Hour of the Gun* (1967), and *Doc* (1971). Doc Holliday appeared as a character in other movies, such as *Masterson of Kansas* (1954), while Wyatt Earp was the hero in *Wichita* (1955) and various films that skipped the gunfight. *Law and Order* (1932), *Frontier Marshal* (1934), *Powder River* (1953), *Dawn at Socorro* (1954), and *Warlock* (1959) used themes, characters, and/or gunfights loosely based on the O.K. Corral incident. By the time *Tombstone* hit theaters, Earp, Holliday, and the gunfight had been done to death. Few of those movies came close to recreating actual history, however; director John Ford's *My Darling Clementine*, widely regarded artistically as the best movie about the event, even got the year of the shootout wrong and killed Doc Holliday in the fight. What *Tombstone* had going for it was Jarre's attention to history. Morey, hired as the film's historical consultant, said Jarre's script "had all the period vernacular. I thought it had the potential to be one of the great classic Westerns" (Blake 2007, 160).

Regarding the two main characters, Jarre got close to the real Wyatt Earp and Doc Holliday. "Kurt Russell nailed Wyatt Earp as a genuinely tough man who came to Tombstone with the sole goal of making a fortune" (Jeff Guinn, interview with author, January 5, 2019). Loren D. Estleman, author of *Bloody Season*, a critically acclaimed 1987 novel about the O.K. Corral shootout, agreed, adding this insight into why Earp became a lawman:

> In interviews, [Earp] referred to himself as a businessman. He set out to become a frontier robber baron, traveling to towns where money was to be made, and invested heavily there; but since they were rough places, he had to arm himself in order to protect his interests. The towns had strict gun-control laws, so he became a lawman in order to carry a gun in order to secure his investments. (Loren D. Estleman, interview with author, April 16, 2019)

Russell "accurately portrayed Wyatt's wandering eye and growing estrangement from Mattie" (Jeff Guinn, interview with author, January 5, 2019). The movie also captured Earp's ability as a leader. "More than anything else, he was a man who inspired loyalty," Estleman wrote in an introduction to a reprint of Stuart N. Lake's biography *Wyatt Earp: Frontier Marshal* (Lake 1994, xiii). But Earp was not the famous lawman, bordering on a living legend, when he arrived in Tombstone. The Gunfight at the O.K. Corral gave Earp some notoriety in newspapers, but likely not as much as he received in 1896, when Earp headlined news as a boxing referee. On December 2, 1896, Earp refereed a fight between Ruby Bob Fitzsimmons (1863–1917) and Tom Sharkey (1871–1953) in San Francisco. In the eighth round, Earp ruled that Fitzsimmons struck Sharkey below the belt and called the fight for Sharkey. That wasn't the only controversy. When Earp stepped into the ring and removed his coat, he was carrying a revolver. He surrendered the .45-caliber Colt and was charged with carrying a concealed weapon.

Tombstone has Earp telling his brothers that in all his years as a peace officer in Kansas, he killed only one man—"a good fact to get into the film," Guinn said (Jeff Guinn, interview with author, January 5, 2019). Early on the morning of July 26, 1878, three Texas cowboys fired pistols through the walls of Dodge City's Comique Theater, where Eddie Foy (1856–1928) was reciting the poem "Kalamazoo in Michigan." As Jim Masterson (1855–1895), a brother of then–Ford County Sheriff William Barclay "Bat" Masterson (1853–1921), and Earp ran to investigate, the fleeing cowboys, were said to have shot at the lawmen. Earp and Masterson, and possibly some bystanders, returned fire. One bullet struck George Hoy in the arm and knocked him off his horse. The wound became infected, a surgeon amputated the arm, and Hoy died August 21.

Kilmer also captured much of Doc Holliday, giving the Georgia-born Holliday a Southern accent, something other actors failed to do. "Kirk Douglas [who played Holliday in *Gunfight at the O.K. Corral*] came up to me and said, 'I wanted to play him Southern,'" Kilmer said (Val Kilmer, interview with author, March 23, 1999). Kilmer "captured both Doc's otherworldly aspects and the sense of doom that often propelled him into violence," Guinn said, but the movie also painted Holliday as a deadly gunfighter when "Doc was a god-awful shot and was probably given the Wells Fargo shotgun prior to the gunfight because he was less likely to miss completely with that rather than a handgun" (Jeff Guinn, interview with author, January 5, 2019).

The also film depicted Holliday's friendship with Wyatt and the fact that Wyatt's brothers did not care much for Holliday. This scene during the vendetta ride rings true. Why Earp befriended Holliday puzzled historians for years, but Guinn unearthed notes handwritten by John Flood (1878–1958), who helped Earp write an unpublished memoir. Earp told Flood that a group of cowboys had trained their guns on Earp outside the Long Branch Saloon in Dodge City. Inside the saloon, Holliday, playing a card game called monte, saw what was happening, borrowed the dealer's revolver, and leaped through the doorway armed with two revolvers and yelled. That distracted the cowboys long enough so that Earp drew his gun. The cowboys were disarmed and arrested. Ironically, a similar scene was created in the screenplay by Leon Uris (1924–2003) for *Gunfight at the O.K. Corral*, a movie not known for getting many facts right.

Tombstone also accurately depicted the mining camp's culture and refinement—although the Bird Cage theater, where the Earps and others watch Josephine Marcus's performance, did not open until December 1881. Jarre's original idea was to set the theatrical troupe's performance at Tombstone's Schieffelin Hall, historically correct, but changed the setting because of the Bird Cage's "ambiance" (Blake 2007, 160). The Tombstone in *Tombstone* didn't look like the raw, rough town of facades depicted in most Western films. It resembled the actual Tombstone. "Profitable silver mining fueled Tombstone's wealth and made it a city where residents enjoyed many of the same things that San Francisco and Denver offered," historian Sherry Monahan said. "They dined on trendy French cuisine and oysters in restaurants that were illuminated with gas lighting. Men and women wore fashions from England and France, and many sipped champagne and high-class spirits in ornately decorated saloons and halls. Tombstone may have been in a remote Arizona location, but that didn't stop its citizens from being cosmopolitan" (Sherry Monahan, interview with author, April 13, 2019).

However, Jarre often took historical liberties or ignored facts. Curly Bill Brocious wasn't the leader of the Cowboys, and the gang did not wear red sashes; Jarre added the sashes so the villains would be easily identified by movie audiences. The Earps arrived in Tucson by wagon, not train, and the Earps beat Holliday to Tombstone. James Earp was left out of the movie altogether (one of Wyatt's older brothers, James, was depicted as the kid brother, and killed off, in *My Darling Clementine* and *Gunfight at the O.K. Corral*).

Virgil Earp did not take the marshal's job because of the town's lawlessness. After Fred White was killed in October 1880, Virgil served as acting marshal for two weeks. He ran for the permanent position but lost to Ben Sippy. Virgil wanted the town marshal's job because his "federal marshal appointment continued to provide little real power and less money. The Tombstone city marshal, on the other hand, enjoyed a regular income of a hundred dollars a month, plus a percentage on city taxes, and daily held a position of authority within the community" (Marks 1996, 114). Sippy defeated Virgil in the 1881 election, but Sippy wasn't the kind of lawman Tombstone wanted, and after a few minor scandals, he was granted a leave of absence and left town. When it became clear that he wasn't returning, Virgil was appointed marshal.

The movie also omitted the inquest and hearing after the O.K. Corral incident. Other movies about the O.K. Corral, such as *Frontier Marshal*, *My Darling Clementine*, *Gunfight at the O.K. Corral*, and *Doc*, used the gunfight as the climax. *Tombstone: The Town Too Tough to Die* and *Wyatt Earp* briefly touched upon the hearing, while *Hour of the Gun* opened with the gunfight, depicted Spicer's hearing and the shootings of Virgil and Morgan Earp, and then focused on Earp's Vendetta Ride. Jarre skipped the inquest and hearing to keep the action moving.

Despite quite a few Hollywood exaggerations, most historians say *Tombstone* got the gunfight's details closer to history than any other movie.

"The film depicted Virgil anxious to go and take the Clantons and McLaurys on, when in fact he wanted to let them cool off, then ride off, and only after pressure from town leaders who made clear they'd utilize civilians if [Virgil Earp] didn't do something," Guinn said (Jeff Guinn, interview with author, January 5, 2019).

When Holliday joins the Earp brothers before they walk to the O.K. Corral, Wyatt tells Holliday, "It's not your problem, Doc. You don't have to mix up in this." Holliday's response—"That's a hell of a thing for you to say to me"—makes *Tombstone* the only movie to use that line. (An episode of the ABC series *The Life and Legend of Wyatt Earp* used a modified version of the quote, "hell" being taboo for TV viewers' ears in 1961.) That quote defines the essence of Holliday's loyalty to Wyatt Earp, but there's some question if the exchange actually occurred. Stuart Lake was the first historian to use the quote in 1931, but Lake was more mythmaker than biographer and wrote nonfiction during an era when, Estleman noted, "the publishing industry . . . seldom allowed facts to get in the way of a healthy bottom line" (Lake 1994, xiii). Regarding Holliday's alleged comment, Guinn said, "I've seen no record that [Holliday said that], but the sentiment expressed fits" (Jeff Guinn, interview with author, January 5, 2019).

In the movie, when the Cowboys reach for their pistols, Virgil yells, "Hold it. That's not what I want." After a long pause, Holliday winks at Billy Clanton, and guns are drawn. In Jarre's script, "the screen EXPLODES, everything happening in SPLIT SECONDS" (Jarre 1993). Wyatt shoots Frank McLaury and Billy Clanton in the opening volleys, while Tom McLaury stays behind his skittish horse. Ike screams his brother's name, and Doc fires one round from the double-barreled shotgun to scare Tom McLaury's horse and then guns down Tom McLaury with the second barrel. There is a brief pause as Ike runs toward Wyatt, pleading for the lawmen not to shoot him. Wyatt yells, "The fight's commenced. Get to fightin' or get away!" Ike runs inside the nearby photographer's studio, takes John Behan's gun, and fires wildly through a window before he is driven to flee by gunshots. Virgil is shot in the leg, and Billy shoots Morgan in the shoulder. Billy is then cut down by bullets from Holliday and Wyatt, and badly wounded Frank McLaury tells Doc, "I've got you now, you son of a b—," to which Doc replies, "You're a daisy if you do." Before McLaury can fire his pistol, he is shot and killed by Holliday and Morgan. *Tombstone*'s gunfight lasts more than two minutes after weapons are drawn—much shorter than the seven minutes of screen time in *Gunfight at the O.K. Corral*, but a good deal longer than the actual half-minute gun battle.

Regarding the historical accuracy of the setting, Guinn said the movie accurately placed the gunfight in a vacant lot near the O.K. Corral, whereas the all of the previous films, from *Frontier Marshal* to *Doc*, placed the fight within the corral. Guinn said, "The action was brief and bloody—they got that right. Problem is, the lot was much more confined than portrayed in the movie, but I get that filming in such tight quarters would have been difficult" (Jeff Guinn, interview with author, January 5, 2019). Unlike in the film, there was no dramatic pause with a stare down that's become a Western genre cliché. In reality, the participants opened fire quickly. Further, Guinn noted that Ike Clanton "did not dive into Fly's photo studio, grab a gun, and start shooting out through the windows." Instead, "Ike ran and kept running—at the beginning of the fight, not toward the end as *Tombstone* depicted it" (Jeff Guinn, interview with author, January 5, 2019).

According to Wyatt's testimony, Billy Clanton drew first, and Wyatt, knowing the reputation of Frank McLaury, aimed at Frank. Clanton and Wyatt fired first. "I don't know which was fired first," Earp said. "We fired almost together. The fight then became general" (Bell 2000, 76). McClaury was hit in his abdomen; Billy Clanton's shot missed Earp. Without modern-day ballistics and crime-scene investigation, it's hard to determine who shot who after that. Frank likely wounded Virgil Earp and perhaps Morgan, too. Tom McLaury—witnesses offered conflicting testimony as to whether he was armed—used his horse as a shield, and Ike ran to Wyatt, pleading that he was unarmed, and fled. *Tombstone* correctly captures the exchange between Wyatt and Ike. Wyatt probably wounded Tom McLaury's horse, and Holliday mortally wounded McLaury with a shotgun blast. McLaury staggered away before falling down near Third Street. Virgil and Wyatt probably shot down Billy Clanton. Still game, Frank McLaury aimed at Holliday. Jarre used the verbal exchange between Frank and Holliday, and Holliday's "You're a daisy if you do" became one of the movie's many oft-quoted lines. Frank shot Holliday in the hip—*Tombstone* has Holliday unscathed—before the wounded Morgan killed Frank with a bullet to the head. "Had Frank not been shot on the first exchange, he might have single-handedly killed them all," Bob Boze Bell observed (Bell 2000, 77). Thirty shots had been fired in roughly half a minute. Billy Clanton lay dying, begging for more bullets for his revolver (a scene in Jarre's script that reportedly was filmed, but not used).

Although he was a history buff, Jarre knew he was writing a movie. Historically, Curly Bill Brocious shot Marshal Fred White in Tombstone, but only after the revolver reportedly accidentally discharged. In the movie, Brocious isn't charged because no one witnessed the actual shooting. In reality, White's deathbed statement in which he said the shooting was an accident cleared Brocious. Jarre also puts the assassination attempts on Virgil and Morgan Earp on the same night when Virgil was shot on December 28, 1881, and Morgan was killed three months later. Historian Jim Dunham pointed that out to Jarre, who said, "Jim, we're just making a movie" (Farkis 2019, 16).

Jarre moves up the night of Morgan's assassination, but Morgan's dying words to Wyatt—"I can't see a damn thing"—are based on one report. In an earlier scene, Morgan and Wyatt discuss the afterlife. According to Stuart Lake, Wyatt told him of a conversation about death he had with his brother in which Wyatt and Morgan agreed that, if possible, the dying brother would tell the survivor what he saw. Though not his last words, Morgan told Wyatt: "I guess you were right, Wyatt. I can't see a damn thing" (Lake 1994, 326). Other sources speculated that Morgan whispered to Wyatt to exact revenge for his murder. *The Tombstone Epitaph* reported that regarding Morgan's last words, "all that were heard, except those whispered into the ears of his brother and known only to him, were: 'Don't, I can't stand it. This is the last game of pool I'll ever play.' The first part of the sentence being wrung from him by an effort to place him upon his feet" ("THE DEADLY BULLET" 1882, 3).

Regarding Johnny Ringo's death, *Tombstone* at least got Ringo's dead body right. The corpse was found in mid-July 1882, leaning against a tree in an oak grove in the Chiricahua Mountains with a bullet wound to the head and a revolver in the right hand. "Many people who were intimately acquainted with him in life, have serious doubts that he took his own life," the *Tombstone Epitaph* reported, "while an equally large number say that he frequently threatened to commit suicide, and that event was expected at any time" ("DEATH OF JOHN RINGO" 1882, 4). Although Earp later claimed to have killed Ringo, Earp had left the territory by then, and most historians doubt if he, or Holliday, had any hand in Ringo's death, which, officially ruled a suicide, remains one of the Old West's enduring mysteries.

Holliday's dying words in *Tombstone*—"This is funny"—were alleged to have been his last words, but if he actually said that, it went unrecorded at the time. Kate Elder said she was with him at the time, but no contemporary sources have been unearthed that corroborate her account. Neither was Wyatt Earp near Glenwood Springs, Colorado, when Holliday died on November 8, 1887; their last meeting came at a Denver hotel in May 1885. Holliday didn't die in a sanatorium, but in his room at the Hotel Glenwood ("DOC HOLLIDAY DEAD" 1887, 1). According to one report, when Holliday first arrived, he gave bellboys a dollar to bring him a bottle of whiskey and another dollar for a tip. He did die in bed, as depicted in *Tombstone*, with his boots off. "He always expected to die with his boots on," the *Daily Sentinel* of Garden City, Kansas, reported, "and his demise at Glenwood Springs must have been a matter of considerable surprise to him" ("Colorado" 1887, 2).

In 1882, five years before Holliday's death, Wyatt reunited with Josephine Marcus in San Francisco, beginning what Guinn called "a genuine, if occasionally tumultuous, love story" (Guinn 2011, 304). After settling in California, Earp befriended Hollywood actor William S. Hart, who encouraged Earp to find a writer to help write a book about Earp's life. The first writer, John Flood, finished a book that publishers rejected. Walter Noble Burns, author of the 1926 best seller *The Saga of Billy the Kid*, reached out to Earp, but Earp turned him down, remaining loyal to Flood; instead, Burns wrote another best seller, *Tombstone: An Iliad of the Southwest* (1927). Finally realizing that Flood wasn't much of a writer, Earp let Stuart Lake write *Wyatt Earp: Frontier Marshal* (1931).

Earp brought Josephine to the first meeting with Lake. She wanted "a nice clean story" (Guinn 2011, 312) and objected to much of Lake's book before relenting. Earp didn't live to see Lake's book become a best seller, but Josephine served as a technical adviser on *Frontier Marshal* (1939) "to be sure that the character of Earp is correctly . . . portrayed" (Niemeyer 1939, 3D). "Josephine continued to carp about movies that she believed demeaned Wyatt's memory until she died in December 1944," Guinn wrote, "never knowing that the resurrection of Wyatt Earp had barely begun" (Guinn 2011, 318).

CONCLUSION

Many historians agree that while *Tombstone* came closer than other movies in depicting the events surrounding the Gunfight at the O.K. Corral, it was far from actual history. "I enjoy *Tombstone* for the same reason I enjoy the old John Wayne film about the Alamo [*The Alamo*, 1960]," Guinn said. "It's fun to watch. It's just not factual" (Jeff Guinn, interview with author, January 5, 2019).

With a fan base that is borderline obsessive, the movie's popularity hasn't waned in more than 25 years, either, but *Tombstone*'s overall place in film history has nothing to do with Old West history. Instead, *Tombstone* was the last major Western box-office hit of the twentieth century. A decade passed before another Western, *Open Range* (2003), "really rattled the box office," film historian C. Courtney Joyner said (C. Courtney Joyner, interview with author, April 17, 2019). With a $22 million budget, *Open Range*—starring, directed by, and coproduced by Costner—brought in $68.3 million. *Open Range* outperformed *Tombstone* and possibly gave Costner the satisfaction of avenging *Wyatt Earp*'s loss to *Tombstone*.

FURTHER READING

Agnew, Jeremy. 2012. *The Old West in Fact and Film: History Versus Hollywood*. Jefferson, NC: McFarland & Company, Inc.

Beale, Lewis. 1994. "'Don't Write Westerns' 'Tombstone' Yet: With Ticket Sales Going Great Guns, Cowboys Are Corralling New Audiences." *New York Daily News*, January 11, 1994, p. 39.

Beck, Henry Cabot. 2006. "The Western Godfather: Kurt Russell Spills the Beans on Who Really Directed 1993's Tombstone." *True West*. https://truewestmagazine.com/the-western-godfather

Bell, Bob Boze. 2000. *The Illustrated Life & Times of Wyatt Earp*. Phoenix, AZ: Tri Star—Boze Publications, Inc.

Blake, Michael F. 2007. *Hollywood and the O.K. Corral*. Jefferson, NC: McFarland & Company, Inc.

Blake, Michael F. 2017. "The Miracle behind Tombstone: The Drama behind the Making of the 1993 Western Rivaled Anything on the Screen." *Roundup Magazine*, December 2017.

Boggs, Johnny D. 1999. "Val Kilmer: Playing Cowboy." *Cowboys & Country* (Summer): 55–58.

Brand, Peter. 2018. "10 Earp Vendetta Ride Myths." *True West*, March 20, 2018. https://truewestmagazine.com/10-earp-vendetta-ride-myths

Breakenridge, William M. 1928. *Helldorado: Bringing the Law to the Mesquite*. Cambridge, MA: The Riverside Press.

Burns, Walter Noble. 1929. *Tombstone: An Iliad of the Southwest*. New York: Gross & Dunlap.

"Colorado." 1887. *Daily Sentinel*, November 25, 1887.

"CORONER'S INQUEST." 1882. *Tombstone Epitaph*, March 27, 1882, p. 1.

Craft, Dan. 1994. "'Tombstone' Corrals Clichés." *Pantagraph*, January 7, 1994, p. B-3.

Craig, R. Bruce, ed. 2017. *Portrait of a Prospector: Edward Schieffelin's Own Story*. Norman: University of Oklahoma Press.

"THE DEADLY BULLET. The Assassin at Last Successful in His Devilish Mission. Morgan Earp Shot Down and Killed While Playing Billiards." *Tombstone Epitaph*, March 27, 1882, p. 3.

"DEATH OF JOHN RINGO. His Body Found in Morse's Canyon.—Probably Suicice [sic]." *Tombstone Epitaph*, July 22, 1882, 3.

"DOC HOLLIDAY DEAD." 1887. *The Aspen Daily Times*, November 9, 1887, p. 1.

Farkis, John. 2019. *The Making of Tombstone: Behind the Scenes of the Classic Modern Western*. Jefferson, NC: McFarland & Company, Inc.

George, Homer C. 1939. "An Historic Notch in Georgia's Gun Found in the Old West." *Atlanta Constitution Magazine*, December 10, 1939, pp. 1–2.

Guinn, Jeff. 2011. *The Last Gunfight: The Real Story of the Shootout at the O.K. Corral—And How It Changed the American West*. New York: Simon & Schuster.

Holden, Stephen. 1993. "A Fractious Old West in a Modern Moral Universe," *New York Times*, December 24, 1993, p. C6.

Hornug, Chuck. 2016. *Wyatt Earp's Cow-Boy Campaign: The Bloody Restoration of Law and Order along the Mexican Border, 1882*. Jefferson, NC: McFarland & Company, Inc.

Jarre, Kevin. 1993. TOMBSTONE: An Original Screenplay. Fourth Draft, March 15, 1993. http://www.dailyscript.com/scripts/tombstone.pdf

Johnson, David. 2008. *John Ringo: King of the Cowboys: His Life and Times from the Hoo Doo War to Tombstone, Second Edition*. Denton: University of North Texas Press.

Lake, Stuart N. 1994. *Wyatt Earp: Frontier Marshal*. New York: Pocket Books.

Linder, Shirley Ayn. 2014. *Doc Holliday in Film and Literature*. Jefferson, NC: McFarland & Company, Inc.

Lubet, Steven. 2004. *Murder in Tombstone: The Forgotten Trial of Wyatt Earp*. New Haven, CT: Yale University Press.

Marks, Paula Mitchell. 1996. *And Die in the West: The Story of the O.K. Corral Gunfight*. Norman: University of Oklahoma Press.

Masterson, W. B. (Bat). 2016. *Famous Gunfighters of the Western Frontier*. Mineola, NY: Dover Publications, Inc.

McCormack, Kara L. 2016. *Imagining Tombstone: The Town Too Tough to Die*. Lawrence: University Press of Kansas.

McGovern, Michael. 1993. "Duel of Kevins at O.K. Corral." *New York Daily News*, January 6, 1993, p. 19.

Niemeyer, H. H. 1939. "TOMBSTONE LIVES AGAIN: But Real Location of Arizona Frontier Town Was Passed Up for Synthetic Version in 'Frontier Marshal.'" *St. Louis Post Dispatch*, July 21, 1939, p. 3D.

Parsons, George W. 1972. *The Private Journal of George W. Parsons*. Tombstone, AZ: Tombstone Epitaph.

"Population of Tombstone." 1881. *Arizona Weekly Citizen*, January 1, 1881, p. 3.

Roberts, Gary L. 2006. *Doc Holliday: The Life and Legend*. New York: John Wiley & Sons, Inc.

Shulgasser, Barbara. 1993. "A Western with a College Education: Where Else but in 'Tombstone' Could You Listen to Doc Holliday Arguing in Latin?" *San Francisco Examiner*, December 24, 1993, p. D-3.

Skinner, M. Scot. 1993. "'Lackluster' Fitting Epitaph for New Movie." *Arizona Daily Star*, December 25, 1993, p. D1.

Stone, S. L. 1879. "ARIZONA. A Striking Contrast—The Tombstone District One Year Ago and Now. Condition of the Various Mines—The Tough-Nut Displaying Extraordinary Richness. Information to Laborers, Mechanics, Business-Men, and Speculators, as to Chances at Tombstone." *Chicago Tribune*, December 11, 1879, p. 9.

Tanner, Karen Holliday. 1998. *Doc Holliday: A Family Portrait*. Norman: University of Oklahoma Press.'

Tefertiller, Casey. 1997. *Wyatt Earp: The Life Behind the Legend*. New York: John Wiley & Sons, Inc.

Chapter 11

The Assassination of Jesse James by the Coward Robert Ford (2007)

By the time Warner Bros. released *The Assassination of Jesse James by the Coward Robert Ford* in the fall of 2007, one of America's most famous outlaws had done just about everything on Hollywood celluloid. Since the first known movie about James, *The James Brothers in Missouri* (1908), Jesse James (1847–1882) had battled evil lookalikes (*Jesse James at Bay*), battled Bob Hope (*Alias Jesse James*), battled Dracula's granddaughter (despite the title, *Jesse James Meets Frankenstein's Daughter*), and battled the Three Stooges (*The Outlaws IS Coming!*). He had been a womanizer in Mississippi (*Jesse James' Women*), teamed up with future assassin Robert Ford (1862–1892) to go after a fortune in gold (*The Great Jesse James Raid*), and saved Western icon Randolph Scott (1898–1987) from a lynching (*Fighting Man of the Plains*). Jesse had been killed by Robert Ford, not killed by Robert Ford, fought for justice, fought for the little man, been good and been evil. His ghost had even teamed up with the ghosts of Andrew Jackson and others to save a timid bookkeeper (*The Remarkable Andrew*). Heartthrobs, singing cowboys, B actors, supporting actors, a World War II hero, a future Academy Award winner, and his own son had played him. And Hollywood's Jesse James had ridden through glass windows to escape Northfield, Minnesota, too many times to count.

About the only thing Jesse James hadn't done on the big screen was stay faithful to history. *The Assassination of Jesse James by the Coward Robert Ford*, written and directed by New Zealand-born Andrew Dominik (1967–), changed that.

Only a handful of talkies—not including potboilers and programmers—followed Jesse James's post–Civil War career as bank and train robber to his death in 1882: *Jesse James* (1939), *The Great Missouri Raid* (1951), *The True Story of Jesse James* (1957), *The Long Riders* (1980), and *Frank & Jesse* (1995), the latter originally intended for theatrical release before being sold to cable-movie channel HBO.

"The problem with making a good Jesse James movie is his damn career lasted too long," said Bob Boze Bell, executive editor of *True West*, a Western history magazine based in Cave Creek, Arizona. "In the movie biz, the trick is to distill a story down to the essence of the story. Just the bare bones that pack the most impact. Jesse James has always been a hard nut to crack because his career lasted 16 years and there are too many contradictions and messy details that derail a good story. It's best to concentrate on one aspect of the legendary outlaw's career, such as riding with guerrillas, or the Northfield Raid" (Bob Boze Bell, interview with author, December 24, 2018).

Kansas Raiders (1950) and *Young Jesse James* (1960) focused on Jesse's Civil War career, while *The Great Northfield Minnesota Raid* (1972) dealt with the James-Younger Gang's 1876 botched bank robbery. The made-for-TV *The Last Days of Frank and Jesse James* (1986), which is fairly accurate historically until the last act, covered Jesse's last years and Robert Ford's murder. In *The Assassination of Jesse James by the Coward Robert Ford*, Dominik took a similar approach by following the last few months of Jesse's life and the effect Jesse's death had on his assassin.

The film opens on September 7, 1881, with gang members waiting in the woods to rob a train at Blue Cut, east of Independence, Missouri. A voiceover narrator explains: "The James Gang committed over 25 bank, train and stagecoach robberies from 1867 to 1881. But except for Frank and Jesse James, all the original members were now either dead or in prison," which had forced Frank and Jesse to recruit "a gang of petty thieves and country rubes, culled from the local hillsides."

Played by Casey Affleck (1975–), 19-year-old Robert "Bob" Ford tries to convince Frank James (Sam Shepard, 1943–2017) to take Bob along as a "sidekick," but Bob gives Frank "the willies." Jesse (Brad Pitt, 1963–), however, has no problems letting Bob take part in the train robbery. "I don't care who comes with me," Jesse says. "Never have. That's why they call me gregarious."

After the robbery, Frank leaves the gang, and Jesse takes Bob in for a while. Bob is enraptured with Jesse. He collects newspaper clippings and dime novels and can recite obscure facts about the killer. "I can't figure you out," Jesse says before sending Bob away. "Do you wanna be like me, or do you wanna be me?"

Eventually, Bob and his brother Charley (Sam Rockwell, 1968–) return to Jesse's good graces. But Jesse grows increasingly paranoid and unpredictable, and when Bob kills Wood Hite (Jeremy Renner, 1971–), one of Jesse's favorite cousins, in a gunfight involving gang member Dick Liddil (Paul Schneider, 1976–), Bob makes a deal with Missouri Governor Thomas T. Crittenden (James Carville, 1944–). Fearing for their lives, Bob and Charley agree to capture or kill Jesse. That happens on April 3, 1882, when Bob shoots an unarmed Jesse in the back of his head while Jesse is dusting a picture—in his own home, with his wife, son, and daughter nearby. Instead of being feted as a hero, the Ford brothers are shunned and hated, driving Charley to suicide and Bob to an inglorious end inside a Creede, Colorado, saloon a decade later.

In 1983, Alfred A. Knopf published *The Assassination of Jesse James by the Coward Robert Ford*, a novel by Ron Hansen (1947–). By the 1980s, traditional Western novels, unless written by Louis L'Amour (1908–1988), were shunned by most major publishers, but literary Westerns—Lucia St. Clair Robson's *Ride the Wind* (1982), Ivan Doig's *English Creek* (1984), Larry McMurtry's Pulitzer Prize-winning *Lonesome Dove* (1985), Pete Dexter's *Deadwood* (1986), Glendon Swarthout's *The Homesman* (1988)—were raking up good reviews, sales and awards. *The Assassination of Jesse James by the Coward Robert Ford* was shortlisted for the 1984 PEN/Faulkner Award.

Hansen and director James Foley (1953–) shopped the novel around Hollywood, only to learn that no studio wanted the film rights. Hansen noted, "A guy at Columbia nastily said, 'We don't make movies about horses and dust'" (Ron Hansen, interview with author, December 14, 2018). Other directors showed interest, and Hansen got a few options, but nothing happened until Dominik, who had completed his first major film, *Chopper*, in 2000, found a copy of the novel in a used bookstore in Melbourne, Australia.

"He was at first attracted to it because his young son was named Jesse and because a friend who was with him immediately saw a movie in it after scanning only a few pages," Hansen said (Ron Hansen, interview with author, December 14, 2018).

When Pitt telephoned Dominik and said that he would like to work with him, Dominik mentioned Hansen's novel. Although born in Oklahoma, Pitt, like Jesse James, had grown up in Missouri before moving to California and becoming a major star. Pitt and Angelina Jolie (1975–), his girlfriend and future wife, read the novel.

"Angelina was enthusiastic and convinced Brad he should do it, so things were set in motion at Warner Bros.," Hansen said. "My agent and I presumed it was another option that would fizzle, but then we learned Brad was involved, and he has a great deal of clout, of course, so the game changed" (Ron Hansen, interview with author, December 14, 2018).

Hansen's novel "so captivated" Dominik and Pitt, *Los Angeles Times* film critic Kenneth Turan wrote, "that they seemingly would not rest until they brought it to the screen" (Turan 2007, E4). "It was really Brad Pitt and the Missouri connection that pushed this forward," Hansen said (Bailey 2006, D3).

Dominik sought Hansen's input while interviewing actors to play Bob Ford. When Dominik "told me Casey Affleck was a possibility—he'd nailed the audition as no one else had—I was gratified that someone so talented and who looked so much like Bob would anchor the film," Hansen said (Ron Hansen, interview with author, December 12, 2018). Affleck landed the role.

Filming in Alberta and Winnipeg in 2005, the production was plagued by "several delays, poor test screenings, and reports of infighting between its director, producers and studio" (Canwest News Service 2007, B7). Pitt, producer Ridley Scott, and editor Michael Kahn oversaw cuts or suggested revisions, the *Los Angeles Times* reported. "At one point there were competing versions—one from writer-director Andrew Dominik and another from producer and star Pitt, according to a person familiar with the making of the movie" (Horn 2007, C18).

"I had to throw out things that I loved and keep things in that I didn't like," Dominik said. "For a while, it was viewed as a movie in trouble. And it was in trouble. It hasn't been any easy process for anyone" (Horn 2007, D3). Dominik's first cut clocked in at more than four hours long. Another round of editing left it at three hours before, after two more months of editing, the movie was trimmed to two hours and 40 minutes. There were so many revisions, Pitt said, "I've seen this movie more times than any movie I've ever seen in my life" (Horn 2007, D3).

Two years passed before the $30 million film was released, but it received positive buzz from the Toronto Film Festival in September 2007. When the film went into wide distribution the following month, however, reviews were mixed. Calvin Wilson of the *St. Louis Post-Dispatch* called it "one of the best films of the year" (Wilson 2007, E1), while Carrie Rickey wrote in the *Philadelphia Inquirer* that "its excruciatingly deliberate pace makes you wonder if Andrew Dominik's film, as spare as it is self-important, *intentionally* unfolds in narrative slow-mo" (Rickey 2007, W11).

Some reviewers took a middle-of-the-road view, such as the *Los Angeles Times*' Kenneth Turan, who said, "Dominik likely had something like Robert Altman's 'McCabe and Mrs. Miller' [1971] in mind, but what he has achieved is closer to the unfairly denigrated but still disappointing 'Heaven's Gate' [1980]" (Turan 2007, E4).

While the movie grossed less than $4 million domestically in its initial run and only $15 million worldwide, Affleck (supporting actor) and Roger Deakins (cinematography) were nominated for Academy Awards; Dominik's screenplay won the Spur Award from Western Writers of America; and the Venice Film Festival gave Pitt best actor honors.

Over time, the movie has developed a faithful following, which includes Hansen. "I've now seen the film dozens of times—meaning far more than 12; maybe less than 50—and I'm still captivated by the actors' performances, the beautiful script, Roger Deakins's gorgeous cinematography, the attention to detail in costuming and setting, even the haunting musical score,"

Hansen said. "I find it a masterpiece" (Ron Hansen, interview with author, December 12, 2018).

HISTORICAL BACKGROUND

On September 5, 1847, Jesse Woodson James was born at the family farm outside Centerville, Missouri (later renamed Kearney), roughly 25 miles northeast of Kansas City. His father, Robert James, a Baptist minister, and mother, Zerelda Elizabeth Cole James, were Kentucky natives who settled on a 275-acre farm in Clay County, Missouri, in the early 1840s. Franklin Alexander James was born in 1843; another son lived only a month, and a daughter, Susan Lavenia, was born in 1849. The Jameses owned at least seven slaves.

In 1850, Robert James left Missouri for the California gold fields, where he died of fever four months after arriving in Hangtown (present-day Placerville). Zerelda remarried twice. Her strained second marriage ended when her husband, Benjamin Simms, died in 1854. Zerelda's next marriage, to Dr. Ruben Samuel, produced two daughters and two sons and lasted until Samuel's death in 1908. Zerelda died three years later.

Frank and Jesse grew up in turbulent times. The Kansas-Nebraska Act of 1854 allowed the question of slave state or free state be decided by vote. Slave supporters from Missouri invaded Kansas. Abolitionists from Kansas retaliated. Kansas earned the moniker "Bleeding Kansas," but Missouri was equally bloody—years before Southern sympathizers fired on Fort Sumter in Charleston, South Carolina, to start the Civil War (1861–1865).

Frank James joined the Confederate Missouri State Guard, but was captured and paroled by Union forces at the Battle of Wilson's Creek near Springfield, Missouri, in April 1861. In 1863, he violated his parole by joining Southern guerrillas. He became indoctrinated into leader William Clarke Quantrill's "exercise in brutality" (Stiles 2003, 87). Prisoners were executed. "No quarter" became the law of the land for both Southern sympathizers and Union loyalists. For every Centralia Massacre (where Confederate guerrillas executed 24 unarmed Union soldiers in 1864), there was an Osceola (where Kansans executed nine residents before plundering and burning the Missouri town to the ground in 1861).

On May 23, 1863, pro-Union forces seeking Quantrill arrived at the Samuel farm. Interrogators hoisted Dr. Samuel off the ground with a rope around his neck in an attempt to make him talk, and Jesse, caught while plowing the fields, was whipped with a rope.

If Jesse had not hated Yankees before the beating, he certainly did afterward. By the fall of 1863 or spring of 1864, he rode with Quantrill and later joined "Bloody Bill" Anderson, another notorious guerrilla commander. By most accounts, Jesse did not participate in Quantrill's raid on Lawrence,

---

CALL ME . . . DINGUS?

Jesse James lost the tip of his left hand's middle finger and earned the nickname "Dingus" at the same time. After joining Confederate guerrillas during the Civil War, the teenager was cleaning a revolver when he either accidentally shot off or pinched off the top joint. Instead of swearing, he called the revolver a "dodd-dingus pistol." His companions laughed at the word choice, and the name "Dingus" stuck with Jesse for the rest of his life. The missing digit was used to help identify Jesse's body after his death.

Kansas, in August 1863 (his brother Frank was there), a raid that left much of the city in ashes and at least 150 men and boys dead. Yet the tide was turning against the Confederacy and especially against Southern guerrillas. Anderson was killed on October 26, 1864, and Quantrill was mortally wounded in Kentucky in 1865, dying on June 6. Jesse attempted to surrender in May 1865 but was shot in Lexington, Missouri. His first cousin, Zerelda Mimms, nursed him back to health. They married on April 23, 1874.

After the Civil War, Jesse and Frank James turned to crime. "He was a young man trained to bloodshed at a very early age, traveling with a group that continued to carry out violent crimes after peace came," said T. J. Stiles, author of *Jesse James: Last Rebel of the Civil War.* "Easy money and a taste for violence and excitement drove him. What distinguished Jesse James from other outlaws was his insistence on bringing up politics—i.e., politics wasn't his only motivation, or maybe even his primary motivation, but what's *distinctive* is that it mattered to him so much that he made it a part of his 'career'" (T. J. Stiles, interview with author, April 24, 2012).

The number of bank, train, and stagecoach robberies the James brothers committed is impossible to verify. Gang member Cole Younger, perhaps Frank's best friend, never publicly implicated the Jameses in any crime; Frank was acquitted in two trials; and Jesse never got the chance to defend himself in court. Even historians rarely agree on which robberies the outlaws committed and which crimes copycats or precursors pulled off.

The first robbery attributed to the James brothers occurred on February 13, 1866, when a gang of 10–12 men—"believed . . . to be a gang of old bushwhacking desperadoes who stay mostly in Jackson county" ("Horrid Murder and Heavy Robbery" 1866, 2)—robbed the Clay County Savings Bank in Liberty, Missouri, of about $60,000 in gold, currency, and U.S. bonds and killed a 19-year-old bystander. Historians are divided on whether or not Jesse participated, or if any outlaws later associated with the James-Younger Gang (later the James Gang) were there.

Although the James brothers and Younger brothers (Cole, John, Jim, and Bob) would be linked to other robberies between 1866 and 1869, it wasn't until the Daviess County Savings Association in Gallatin, Missouri, was robbed and president John W. Sheets murdered on December 7, 1869, that Frank and Jesse first became suspects.

Mistaking Sheets for Samuel P. Cox, commander of the Union forces that had killed "Bloody Bill" Anderson, Jesse cold-bloodedly shot Sheets and wounded a lawyer who officed in the building as he fled. Outside, Jesse's foot hung up in a stirrup after his panicking horse threw him and dragged him 30 to 40 feet. Frank rode back, and after freeing himself, Jesse swung up behind Frank, and the two escaped.

The horse, a bay mare called Kate, was identified as belonging to Jesse, and although Jesse offered an alibi and said he had sold the mare to a Topeka, Kansas, man, Gallatin residents offered a reward reported at $1,500 for the arrest of the James brothers. Frank and Jesse became wanted men.

Over the years, charges and rewards piled up after robberies in Missouri, Kentucky, Iowa, Kansas, Texas, Alabama, Mississippi, and West Virginia. The gang committed its first train robbery in Adair County, Iowa, on July 21, 1873, by removing a rail from the tracks. That wrecked the train, killing the engineer and injuring the fireman. Later, the bandits refined their train-robbery methods, such as flagging down the train and/or placing a barricade across the tracks, as at Blue Cut.

One of the most brazen displays came on January 31, 1874, when five men stopped an Iron Mountain train at Gads Hill, Missouri, robbing passengers and the express and leaving their own account of the crime aboard the train to be reprinted in newspapers:

> The most daring robbery on record. The south bound train on the Iron Mountain railroad was robbed here this evening by five heavily armed men, and robbed of—dollars. The robbers arrived at the station a few minutes before the arrival of the train, and arrested the agent, put him under guard, and then threw the train on the switch. The robbers are all large men, none of them under six feet tall. They were all masked, and started in a southerly direction after they had robbed the train, all mounted on fine blooded horses. There is a hell of excitement in this part of the country. ("DARING AND SUCCESSFUL TRAIN ROBBERY" 1874, 1)

Not every crime attributed to the James brothers could have been committed by them, such as a bank robbery in Corinth, Mississippi, on December 7, 1874, and a train robbery in Muncie, Kansas, the next day.

On the night of January 25, 1875, National Pinkerton Detective Agency operatives, assisted by locals, attacked the James farm. Allan Pinkerton had ordered his agents to "destroy the house to the fringe of the ground" (Downes 1993, Section 12, 5). Thinking the James brothers were home, agents threw an incendiary device through the kitchen window. Frank and Jesse weren't home, and the explosion mortally wounded their nine-year-old half-brother, Archie Samuel, and mauled their mother's right arm so badly it required amputation.

On July 7, 1876, the James brothers, Cole and Bob Younger, Clell Miller, Charlie Pitts, Bill Chadwell, and Hobbs Kerry robbed a Missouri Pacific train at Rocky Cut near Otterville, Missouri, of more than $18,000. New gang member Kerry was arrested in St. Louis in late July. Kerry wasn't the first gang member to be arrested. He was the first, however, to name his associates.

With pressure rising, the outlaws traveled to Minnesota, where they gambled, raced horses, watched baseball games, and, on September 7, 1876, robbed the First National Bank of Northfield, Minnesota, where residents resisted. Miller and Chadwell were killed in the streets, bank employee Joseph Heywood was murdered inside the bank, and a Swedish immigrant was mortally wounded outside. The six robbers who made it out of Northfield alive had managed to steal $26.70.

Frank and Jesse made it back to Missouri after separating from the Youngers and Pitts. Surrounded by a posse in southwestern Minnesota, Pitts was killed, and the already wounded Cole and Bob and Jim Younger were wounded more, recovered, pleaded guilty to avoid execution, and were sentenced to life imprisonment. Bob died in 1889; Cole and Jim were paroled in 1901. After Jim committed suicide in 1902, Cole was granted a pardon and returned to Missouri.

The reformed James Gang wasn't the same as the old one. "The demise of the James-Younger gang left Jesse and Frank with few good choices for replacements," said Mark Lee Gardner, author of *Shot All to Hell: Jesse James, the Northfield Raid, and the Wild West's Greatest Escape.* Gardner continued:

> The later gang put together by Jesse was generally made up of young scamps who had not ridden with Quantrill or Bloody Bill; there were no bonds forged in fire. And they sure as hell couldn't be counted on to give their lives in the street while waiting on a man in the bank. Tellingly, there are no attempted bank robberies after the disaster in Northfield, only train robberies and a payroll stickup in rural areas. Jesse and Frank were clearly hesitant to go into the middle of a town again and risk getting into another firefight with irate citizens. Now, if we can believe the Ford brothers, Jesse was planning a bank robbery in Platte City before his assassination, but the outlaw leader believed most of the townspeople would be over at the county courthouse to witness a murder trial. (Mark Lee Gardner, interview with author, January 13, 2019)

The new gang robbed a train near Glendale, Missouri, in 1879; a federal paymaster in Muscle Shoals, Alabama in 1881; and a train near Winston, Missouri in 1881. The gang's last holdup came at Blue Cut.

After Blue Cut, Frank had had enough. He took his wife and son away from Jesse's influence and was living in Lynchburg, Virginia, when he learned of his brother's death. He surrendered a short time later, was acquitted for the Winston and Muscle Shoals crimes, and lived out his days peacefully. He died of a stroke at age 72 in 1915.

With Frank's departure, Jesse's hold on his gang continued to slip. Missouri Governor Thomas Crittenden put a $10,000 reward on each of the James brothers, half to be paid upon capture and the rest upon conviction; and $5,000 rewards were posted for the other robbers of the Glendale and Winston trains. Arrested gang members began confessing, increasing pressure on Jesse, who refused to quit his crime spree after 16 successful years.

Living with his family in St. Joseph, Missouri, Jesse invited gang members Robert (Bob) and Charley Ford to live with them while Jesse planned to rob a bank in Platte City, Missouri. Bob, however, had secretly met with Crittenden in January 1882 and, according to Ford, was promised a pardon and $10,000 apiece for bringing in Jesse and Frank, dead or alive.

On April 3, 1882, Bob Ford shot and killed Jesse in his home. A decade later, while at the bar in his tent saloon in the mining town of Creede, Colorado, Ford was killed with a shotgun by Edward O'Kelley on June 8, 1892. Convicted of murder, O'Kelley was released from prison in 1902. Two years later, he was killed during a fight with an Oklahoma City policeman.

DEPICTION AND CULTURAL CONTEXT

Few Western movies went to such lengths to get history right the way *The Assassination of Jesse James by the Coward Robert Ford* did. Hansen had done much research for his novel, and Dominik's script often lifted words directly from Hansen's novel. The film went to great lengths to accurately depict the language, costumes, and sets. The "House on the Hill," where Jesse was killed, was "painstakingly recreated for the film" Hansen said (Ron Hansen, interview with author, December 14, 2018).

Canadian locations could not always pass for Missouri, but that's often the case in movies. After seeing *The Great Northfield Minnesota Raid*, filmed in Oregon, a Northfield resident quipped: "That's when the James gang rode across Northfield and I learned we had mountains down here" (Boggs 2011, 201). And casting political pundit and media personality James Carville as the Missouri governor stuck out, considering the rest of the cast had at least passing resemblance to the characters they played. But for history, Dominik's movie came closer to reality than other Jesse James movies.

Marley Brant, who has written biographies of Jesse James and the Younger brothers, called the film the most accurate depiction of Jesse to date, possibly due to "the involvement of a Missouri boy—Brad Pitt—as the intent to expose the true nature of Jesse at this time in his life is strong." Brant said that other modern films about James depicted him as "a deep thinker" or "crazy and cruel"; however, she noted, "Jesse was very intelligent, but his thought on committing robberies was solidly based in retaliation, profit, and fame rather than intellectual analysis. *The Assassination of Jesse James* gave us a character that came closer to the personality of the real Jesse James, especially in his end days when he was friendless, paranoid and mentally, emotionally and physically defeated by his long career of outlaw and fugitive" (Marley Brant, interview with author, January 9, 2019).

The film makes a few minor changes regarding the Blue Cut robbery, such as blocking the railroad tracks with timber instead of rocks, and portraying the bandits as menacing. During the robbery, Jesse's "demeanor was more lighthearted than cruel" (Stiles 2003, 368). When Jesse told the brakeman to give him all of his money, the brakeman responded, "I gave you 50 cents— all I had" so Jesse gave him a dollar or $1.50, saying, "This is principal and interest on your money" (Miller 1898, 318).

The movie, however, also takes bigger liberties with the holdup. Hansen's novel has 13 men gathering for the robbery, and Dominik's film has at least that many fleeing into the woods after the heist. It's hard to document who took part in most of the James Gang's crimes, but Blue Cut seems a little easier to name names. While early newspaper reports had 10 or 12 men (one witness put the number at 17) taking part in the crime, the true number appears to be much smaller. In his confession, James Andrew "Dick" Liddil named his accomplices: Frank and Jesse James, Clarence and Wood Hite, and Charley Ford. "There was no one participating in this robbery except we six," Liddil said (Miller 1898, 301). A dying Clarence Hite made a similar confession, naming the same robbers:

> Jesse was our leader here also. The arrangement was as follows: We were to blockade the track with rock and stop the train if possible by waving a lantern with a piece of red flannel around it [a red lantern at night, or a red flag in daylight, was a widely used signal to warn the engineer of danger ahead and to stop the train]. Jesse and myself were to take the north side of the train. We were to keep the people from coming out by firing, etc. Frank and Dick were to take the south side of the train, and Wood and Charlie were to flag the train, take out the engineer, make him break open the express car door, and then they, Charlie and Wood, were to rob it. This arrangement was carried out. (Miller 1898, 315–316)

Ten or more bandits did not fit the James Gang's method of operation. With the exception of the Liberty bank robbery in 1866—if the James brothers were involved—the brothers had generally used fewer associates. For the gang's other train robberies, most newspaper accounts put five to seven bandits at the Adair County, Iowa, job in 1873; five or perhaps six at Gads Hill in 1874; five at Muncie, Kansas, in 1874; and eight at Otterville (Rocky Cut), Missouri, in 1876. Tucker Basham said he and five others were at Glendale, Missouri, in 1879; and five reportedly took part in Winston, Missouri, in 1881.

No matter the number of robbers at Blue Cut, Robert Ford, in all likelihood, was not among them. Jesse's wife said she had overheard that both Ford brothers took part in the Blue Cut robbery, but most historians think Robert was not involved.

During the coroner's inquest after Jesse's death, Robert Ford testified that "for a long time the gang have made our house in Ray County their headquarters, and Jesse and Frank have often been there, and I know them well, as also Dick [Liddil] and Wood Hite" ("JESSE JAMES SLAIN" 1882, 2). Ford went on to say that the Jameses, Liddil, and Wood Hite came to Ford's house after the Winston and Blue Cut robberies.

What Dominik's film gets right, according to Liddil's and Hite's confessions, is when Charley Ford clubs the express agent with a revolver to persuade him to open the safe. But the film has the gang robbing passengers while Jesse and others are in the express car. In reality, the passengers were robbed later. Clarence Hite confessed: "After Charlie and Wood came out of the car they told Jesse they did not have any money. Jesse then said: 'We had bettor [sic] rob the passengers'" (Miller 1898, 317).

Another historical revision is replacing Clarence Hite in the robbery with Ed Miller. Arrested in February 1882 in Kentucky and returned to Missouri, Hite confessed and was sentenced and eventually pardoned by Crittenden. Hite returned to his Adair County, Kentucky, home, where he died of tuberculosis on March 19, 1883. With Hite disappearing from the story, it certainly seemed more dramatic to put Ed Miller in his place—especially as Jesse later killed Miller.

The film paints a close relationship between Jesse and Bob Ford, but Brant said the two were not close and that Jesse turned to Bob as a tool only because Jesse had exhausted his "list of trusted comrades." Brant said the other members of the gang didn't particularly like Bob and noted that Jesse never trusted him. However, Brant noted that the idolization of Jesse that Bob's character displays in the film is closer to the truth: "Bob Ford did idolize Jesse, and when Jesse's character asks him in the film if he doesn't in fact want to *be* Jesse, that is likely the truth. But most of Bob's obsession with Jesse was not played out in front of Jesse or Frank or their friends." Brant went on to say, "The major variance to historical fact in both [film and novel] is the interaction of the characters Dick Liddil, Ed Miller, Wood Hite and the Ford brothers as in fact we don't really know exactly how their plots and schemes were created, developed and delivered" (Marley Brant, interview with author, January 4, 2019). Fewer liberties are taken with the killing of Jesse. Either Liddil, who was fond of the Ford brothers' widowed sister, Martha Bolton, or Ed Miller introduced Charley Ford to Jesse, and Charley talked Jesse into taking Bob in for the next planned robbery. "I told him I thought I could get my brother to help if I could go down and see him," Charley testified ("JESSE, BY JEHOVAH" 1882, 1).

Bob, however, had met with Governor Crittenden and law-enforcement officials to negotiate a deal to bring Jesse in dead or alive, all of which are explained rather faithfully in Dominik's movie.

On the morning of April 3, 1882, Jesse, his family and the Fords ate breakfast in their rented home in St. Joseph, where Jesse was using the alias Thomas Howard. An avid reader of newspapers, Jesse learned that Liddil had surrendered, saying that "Dick was a traitor and ought to be hung," Jesse's wife said (Yeatman 2000, 268). Saying he was warm, Jesse removed his coat, vest, and gun belt. "I guess I'll take off my pistols," he said, "for fear somebody will see them if I walk into the yard" (Stiles 2003, 375). Zerelda was in the kitchen with both children; the film puts Jesse's daughter outside.

No longer armed, Jesse decided to dust picture frames, stood in a chair, and used a brush to clean the pictures on the wall. Some accounts say he was hanging a photo. Movies sometimes have Jesse dusting a religious sampler; Dominik's movie uses a picture of a horse (Jesse was an admirer of good horses and often raced them). With his back to them, the two Ford brothers drew their guns, Bob using a Smith & Wesson that Jesse had given him. "He started to turn his head but didn't say a word," Bob testified ("JESSE, BY JEHOVAH" 1882, 4). Bob fired one round; the bullet hit Jesse in the back of the head, and "he came down tolerably easy" ("JESSE, BY JEHOVAH" 1882, 4).

When Zerelda rushed into the room and saw her husband dead on the floor, Charley said that "a pistol had accidentally gone off," to which Zerelda responded: "Yes. I guess it went off on purpose" (Yeatman 2000, 269).

The brothers made no attempt to force Jesse to surrender. "I knew it was no use; he said he would not surrender to a hundred men, and if three men should step out in front of him and shoot him he could kill them before he fell," Charley said ("JESSE, BY JEHOVAH" 1882, 1).

Filmmakers and historians still struggle over the question of why Jesse would take off his guns. Brad Pitt suggested two theories: Perhaps Jesse "had full knowledge of what Robert Ford or the Ford brothers were capable of and were after and was taunting them and was going to take them out at a later time, and it was a bad gamble and a gamble he lost. The other argument is that he was unhinged, he was weary of this life on the run and that it was actually a puppeteered suicide, unconscious or conscious. It remains ambiguous, and I couldn't pretend to know. I kind of played with both and trusted Andrew to shape it" (Vancheri, 2007, E3).

Brant believes Jesse was suicidal. "That Pitt chose to hint at this possibility was a major breakthrough in the cinema dedicated to Jesse James and his story," she said (Marley Brant, interview with author, January 9, 2019).

The other question is why the Ford brothers would conspire to kill Jesse. Both men likely feared for their own lives, especially as Bob had taken an active part in Wood Hite's death. While the movie has Bob firing that fatal shot, witnesses weren't certain if Bob or Liddil actually killed Hite, and

Ford was acquitted in a trial in October 1882. In 1901, Finis Calvert Farr, Crittenden's private secretary, dismissed reports that the governor had given Ford "dead or alive" orders, saying, "Bob Ford killed Jesse James through terror of being killed himself" (Special 1902, 1). Still, most historians believe that the reward and promise of a pardon motivated the two brothers.

Hansen, who was writing the novel when rock icon John Lennon (1940–1980) was killed by a fan and President Ronald Reagan (1911–2004) was shot by a fanatic trying to get noticed by actress Jodie Foster (1962–), offers another theory:

> It was through reading the Kansas City *Star* that I learned about Charles Guiteau, his assassination of President Garfield, and his trial and execution. It was front-page news in 1882 and had to have had a great deal to do with Bob Ford's motivations and expectations of an outcome. No other author I'd read seems to have seen that linkage. We couldn't treat it in the film because of time limitations. That's the luxury of writing a far more capacious novel. (Ron Hansen, interview with author, December 14, 2018)

Most biopics about Jesse end with his death, but there are exceptions. *I Shot Jesse James* (1949), directed and written by Samuel Fuller (1912–1997), focuses on Robert Ford and has Ford befriending his own assassin, played by Preston Foster (1900–1970). The made-for-TV *The Last Days of Frank and Jesse James* sends Frank James (Johnny Cash, 1932–2003) to Creede, Colorado, where he witnesses the murder of his brother's killer.

Dominik's screenplay, like Hansen's novel, remained more faithful in its depiction of Ford's life after the death of Jesse. The brothers did take to the stage, recreating their assassination in what was billed as "a faithful representation of the killing of Jesse James by the Ford Brothers" ("MURDER AS A FINE ART" 1882, 2). The Fords toured the country, appearing at exploitive "dime museums," such as Bunnell's in New York, and in theatrical plays. While the film has Charley playing Jesse, Henry Belmer took that role in *The Outlaw Brothers*, at least when it appeared in Belmer's Novelty and Dramatic Company production in Buffalo, New York, in 1883. "The thrilling events leading up to the killing of Jesse James were heartily applauded," the *Buffalo Evening News* reported ("The Ford Brothers" 1883, 1).

But reaction to the play was not always pleasant, also accurately depicted in the film. "When Jesse James mounted the chair and prepared to arrange the picture, there was a deathly stillness in the theater, which was not broken until Bob Ford stepped forward and drawing his pistol fired the fatal shot," the *Louisville Courier-Journal* reported. "The report had scarcely died away when two-thirds of the men in the theater rose in their seats and hissed long and loud, crying 'murderers' and 'robbers' at them. The curtain was rung down a moment later, and the drama was at an end" ("The Fords in Louisville" 1883, 1).

"THE BALLAD OF JESSE JAMES"

Nick Cave's rendition of "The Ballad of Jesse James" in *The Assassination of Jesse James by the Coward Robert Ford* might sound too modern, but the lyrics are right out of the nineteenth century. "The Ballad of Jesse James," which is also featured in Samuel Fuller's *I Shot Jesse James* (1949) and used over the end credits in Walter Hill's *The Long Riders* (1980) and opening credits in *The Last Days of Frank and Jesse James* (1986), was "sung by lumberjacks, cowboys, and rogues" after Jesse's death (Slatta 2001, 187). As depicted in the film, the original lyrics incorrectly number Jesse's children at three, instead of two. But who wrote the song?

The opening line of the last verse identifies the author: "This song was made by Billy Gashade." But no one knows who Gashade (sometimes LaShade) was, although historian Homer Croy (1883–1965) said Gashade lived near the Jameses in Clay County's Crackerneck section. The songwriter appears as a character in E. B. Ginty's 1938 play *Missouri Legend* and narrates Loren D. Estleman's 1999 novel *Billy Gashade*.

Immediately after Jesse's death, the press and public demonized the Fords. The *St. Louis Post-Dispatch* headline on April 4, 1882, announcing Jesse's death read in part: "A DASTARD'S DEED. Cold-Blooded Treachery at Last Conquers Jesse James. The Noted Border Bandit Shot Like a Dog from Behind. By a Man Who Was Eating His Bread and Was His Friend. By a Coward Traitor's Hand Missouri Vanquishes Jesse James."

Bob defended himself. "I have been severely criticized in certain quarters for the method I adopted in killing Jesse James," Bob told a reporter in 1883. "Very unjustly, too, I think. The man was a curse to the State of Missouri. . . . It's all [nonsense] to talk about treachery towards a man like Jesse James" ("JESSE JAMES' SLAYER" 1883, 2). But the labels of coward and murderer stuck. The "Coward" in the film and novel's title comes from a popular song of the time that said Jesse had been shot by "that dirty little coward." Even after Ford's own death, many newspapers continued the attack on Ford. "AS HE SLEW SO HE WAS SLAIN" read part of one headline announcing Ford's death ("BOB FORD KILLED" 1892, 2), while a short note about O'Kelley's release from prison described Ford as the man "who betrayed and murdered Jesse James" ("FROM OUR EXCHANGES" 1902, 1).

Another accurate depiction is Charley's suicide. Taking morphine and living in his parents' home, he killed himself with one bullet through his breast on May 6, 1884, leading the *St. Joseph Daily Gazette* to proclaim "THE END OF A MISERABLE MAN" (Special Dispatch to the *Gazette* 1884, 1).

The movie also accurately depicts Ford's death, but the reasons for that slaying aren't clear. Even historians aren't certain how Ford's murderer spelled his last name—Kelly, Kelley, O'Kelley, O'Kelly—although O'Kelley is used most often.

Bob Ford drifted into Colorado, running saloons in Walsenburg, Pueblo, and finally Creede, a mining boomtown, in 1892. "He does not look like a desperado, but has a loutish, apologetic air, which is explained by the fact that he shot Jesse James in the back," a *Harper's Weekly* correspondent described Ford's appearance in Creede (*Harper's Weekly* 1892, 10).

On June 8, 1892, Edward O'Kelley entered Ford's saloon while Ford stood at the bar. Armed with a double-barreled shotgun, "heavily loaded with buckshot," O'Kelley called out, "Bob" ("BOB FORD KILLED" 1892, 1), or "Ah, Bob" (Denver Cor. 1892, 10), or "Hello, Bob" (*Creede Dispatch* 1892, 10), the latter used in the movie (which is also what Billy the Kid reportedly called out to deputy Bob Olinger before killing him during the Kid's 1881 jailbreak in Lincoln, New Mexico).

Newspaper reports at the time said the killing was "over a woman" ("BOB FORD KILLED" 1892, 1), but O'Kelley's brother called that theory "poppycock," according to one historian (Breihan 1979, 294). Another theory, touched upon in Hansen's novel but omitted in the finished film, pointed to a conspiracy led by rival saloon owner Jefferson "Soapy" Smith, who might have suggested or hired O'Kelley to murder Ford. O'Kelley, who was convicted of second-degree murder in Lake City, Colorado, on July 12, 1892, never publicly discussed his reasons.

The movie's narrator says O'Kelley's motive was "[n]othing but a vague longing for glory, and a generalized wish for revenge against Robert Ford." Many historians agree with that theory. "Although O'Kelley might have had other reasons for murdering the unpopular Ford, one possible motive was that while growing up in Missouri, O'Kelley had viewed the notorious Jesse James as a hero," historian Ted P. Yeatman wrote (Yeatman 2006).

CONCLUSION

The Assassination of Jesse James by the Coward Robert Ford failed to attract moviegoers the way *Jesse James* did back in 1939. Viewers and critics were divided as to its entertainment value, but most historians agree that Dominik's film, which often literally followed Hansen's novel, is the most accurate interpretation of the real Jesse James.

"Hollywood history goes wrong because they try to give the public what they imagine the public wants," Hansen said. "But the real history of America, to me, is fascinating enough" (Ron Hansen, interview with author, December 14, 2018).

Brant added: "Praise should be granted to the filmmakers for their attempt at historical accuracy while basing their screenplay on a novel. I sincerely hope that Hollywood does not return to depicting Jesse as a buffoon or an evil, one-dimensional lowlife" (Marley Brant, interview with author, January 9, 2019).

FURTHER READING

Advertisement. 1883. *Buffalo Evening News*, May 18, 1883, p. 10.

"ANOTHER LETTER FROM JESSE W. JAMES." 1870. *Lexington Weekly Caucasian*, July 23, 1870, p. 3.

Bailey, Aaron. 2006. "Jesse James Movie Filmed in St. Joseph; Companion PBS Documentary Also Filmed There." *Salina Journal*, February 24, 2006, p. D3.

Boardman, Mark. 2018. "The Death of the Man Who Killed the Man Who Killed Jesse James: Killer Ed O'Kelley's Short-Lived Fame Ended in a Fatal Gunfight with Police." *True West*. https://truewestmagazine.com/death-man-who-killed-jesse-james

"BOB FORD KILLED. JESSE JAMES SLAYER SHOT DEAD AT CREDE [sic], COL. As He Slew so He Was Slain." 1892. *Ottawa Journal*, June 16, 1892, p. 1.

"BOB FORD KILLED. JESSE JAMES SLAYER SHOT DEAD AT CREEDE, COL. AS HE SLEW SO WAS HE SLAIN. Deputy Sheriff Kelly, without Giving His Victim a Moment's Warning, Comes up behind Him and Blows a Load of Buckshot Full into His Neck—Outgrowth of a Quarrel over a Woman." 1892. *Sedalia Weekly Bazoo*, June 14, 1892, p. 2.

Boggs, Johnny D. 2011. *Jesse James and the Movies*. Jefferson, NC: McFarland & Company, Inc., Publishers.

Brant, Marley. 1992. *The Outlaw Youngers: A Confederate Brotherhood*. Lanham, MD: Madison Books.

Brant, Marley. 1998. *Jesse James: The Man and the Myth*. New York: Berkley Books.

Breihan, Carl W. 1979. *The Man Who Shot Jesse James*. Cranbury, NJ: A.S. Barnes & Company, Inc.

Burroughs, Alexandra. 2007. "Online Buzz Turning Tide for Winnipeg-Shot Pitt Film." *Winnipeg Free Press*, August 4, 2007, p. C9.

Canwest News Service. 2007. "After Lots of Bad Buzz, Brad Pitt Flick Is Finally Ready for Theaters." *Nanaimo Daily News*, August 7, 2007, p. B7.

"CLARENCE HITE'S CONFESSION: HE CORROBORATES DICK LIDDELL'S EVIDENCE AGAINST FRANK JAMES." 1883. *New York Times*, September 12, 1883, p. 5.

"CLARENCE HITE'S DEATH." 1883. *Jewel County Republican*, March 23, 1883, p. 2.

"CLOSE CALL, A." 1882. *The Pleasanton Herald*, April 14, 1882, p. 1.

Cornish, Sam. 1984. "The West Is Brought to Light." *Palm Beach Post*, January 22, 1984, p. F6.

Creed Dispatch to the Denver Sun. 1892. "HOW FORD WAS KILLED. The Story of the Killing of the Slayer of Jesse James." *Times*, June 19, 1892, p. 10.

Croy, Homer. 1949. *Jesse James Was My Neighbor*. Lincoln: University of Nebraska Press.

Cummins, Jim. 1903. *Jim Cummins' Book Written by Himself*. Independence, MO: Two Trails Publishing, 1999.

"DARING AND SUCCESSFUL TRAIN ROBBERY." 1874. *Liberty Tribune*, February 6, 1874, p. 1.

Denver Cor. *New York Sun*. 1892. "BOB FORD. Killing of the Famous Desperado. Did Respected Citizens Hire an Assassin to Do It? It Is Singular That Three

Officers Should Have Been Waiting to Arrest Kelly, Although No Effort Was Made to Prevent the Crime. But, No Matter, It Was as Cowardly an Act as Bob's Shooting of Jesse James." *Cincinnati Enquirer*, June 25, 1892, p. 10.

Downes, Brian. 1993. "The Infamous Attack on the James Home." *Chicago Tribune*, May 30, 1993, Section 12, p. 5.

Dyer, Robert L. 1994. *Jesse James and the Civil War in Missouri*. Columbia: University of Missouri Press.

"The Ford Brothers." 1883. *Buffalo Evening News*, May 16, 1883, p. 1.

"FORD'S FAREWELL SHOT. AFTER A HEARTY BREAKFAST, A SWIFT DEATH. The Last of Charlie Ford." 1884. *Richmond Democrat*, May 8, 1884, p. 2.

"The Fords in Louisville." 1883. *Burlingame Herald*, September 29, 1883, p. 1.

"FROM OUR EXCHANGES." 1902. *Winchester Star*, October 9, 1902, p. 1.

"GALLATIN BANK ROBBERS – THEY ARE SURPRISED IN CLAY COUNTY AND FIRED UPON, THE." 1869. *Holt County Sentinel*, December 24, 1869, p. 1.

Gardner, Mark Lee. 2013. *Shot All to Hell: Jesse James, the Northfield Raid, and the Wild West's Greatest Escape*. New York: William Morrow.

Germain, David. 2007. "Brad Pitt Turns Outlaw in 'Jesse James.'" *Asbury Park Press*, September 20, 2007, p. D8.

Hansen, Ron. 1983. *The Assassination of Jesse James by the Coward Robert Ford*. New York: W. W. Norton and Company, 1990.

Harper's Weekly. 1892. "SOCIAL DIVERSIONS IN CREEDE. A Glimpse of the Young Western Mining Camp's Four Hundred." *Los Angeles Times*, June 26, 1892, p. 10.

Harrigan, Stephen. 1998. "A Killer's Metamorphosis: Frank James—Who Preyed on Banks and Railroads and Robbed and Murdered Innocent Civilians—Walked Freely into a New Life." *American History*. http://www.historynet.com/frank-james

Horn, John. 2007a. "'Jesse James' a Shoot-'Em-Up of the Psychological Kind." *Morning Call*, September 15, 2007, D3.

Horn, John. 2007b. "Studio, filmmakers clash over Jesse James movie." *Winnipeg Free Press*, May 5, 2007, p. C18.

"Horrid Murder and Heavy Robbery." 1866. *Liberty Tribune*, February 16, 1866, p. 2

Huntington, George. 1895. *Robber and Hero: The Story of the Northfield Bank Robbery*. St. Paul: Minnesota Historical Society Press, 1986.

"Indicted Robbers, The." 1881. *Kansas Democrat*, November 4, 1881, p. 1.

"Jesse and Frank James: An Interesting Sketch of Their Careers." 1882. *Madison Weekly Herald*, April 12, 1882, p. 1.

"JESSE, BY JEHOVAH: Jesse James, the Notorious Desperado, Instantly Killed by Robert Ford. His Adventurous Career Brought to an Abrupt Close on the Eve of Another Crime. Ford Gets into His Confidence and Shoots Him from behind While His Back Is Turned. Jesse a Resident of St. Joseph since the Eighth of November Last. An Interview with Mrs. James and the Testimony Developed before a Jury." 1882. *Weekly Gazette*, April 6, 1882, p. 1

"JESSE JAMES SLAIN. The Famous Outlaw Shot Down in Cold Blood by One of His Gang—Detailed Account of the Affair—The Coroner's Inquest." 1882. *Iola Register*, April 14, 1882, p. 2.

"JESSE JAMES' SLAYER." 1883. *The Indiana Weekly Messenger.* May 2, 1883, p. 2.

Kansas City Journal. Sept. 9. 1881. "MISCELLANY. CAPTURED. History of Thursday's Effort to Capture the Perpetrators of Wednesday's Outrage." *Larned Chronoscope*, September 16, 1881, p. 1.

"LATER." 1881. *Representative*, September 16, 1881, p. 2.

"Letter from Kansas City. THE RECENT TRAIN ROBBERY—JESSE JAMES AND HIS IMMUNITY FROM PUNISHMENT—THE POOR PROSECTS OF THE CROPS." 1881. *Evening Star*, September 19, 1881, p. 10.

Miller Jr., George, editor and compiler. 1898. *The Trial of Frank James for Murder with Confessions of Dick Liddil and Clarence Hite and History of the "James Gang."* New York: Jingle Bob/Crown Publishers, Inc., 1977.

"MISSOURI ITEMS." 1870. *Holt County Sentinel*, January 7, 1870, p. 2.

Monaco II, Ralph A. 2017. *The Bandit Rides Again: Jesse James, Whiskeyhead Ryan, and the Glendale Train Robbery.* Kansas City, MO: Monaco Publishing, LLC.

"MURDER AS A FINE ART." 1882. *Hartford Courant*, December 22, 1882, p. 2.

"ONCE MORE. MISSOURI'S BANDITTI DISTINGUISHED THEMSELVES. A Train on the Chicago & Alton Railroad the Victims of the Band, and a Point Near Kansas City the Scene of the Robbery. The Wholesale Robbery of Express, Baggage, Mail and Passengers. The Most Complete Job They Have Yet Undertaken. Full Details of One of the Most Brazen and Daring Robberies on Record. Gov. Crittenden Issues a Proclamation Concerning the Affair." 1881. *Atchison Weekly Patriot*, September 17, 1881, p. 4.

The Potter Kansan. 1904. Untitled Article, January 21, 1904, p. 2.

Rickey, Carrie. 2007. "Characters' Sharpness No Match for That Slow Pace." *Philadelphia Inquirer*, October 5, 2007, p. W11.

"Robberies, The." 2018. http://www.civilwarstlouis.com/History/jamesgangrobberies.htm

Slatta, Richard W. 2001. *The Mythical West: An Encyclopedia of Legend, Lore and Pop Culture.* Santa Barbara, CA: ABC-CLIO.

Special. 1902. "FOR FEAR OF OWN LIFE. Why Bob Ford Killed the Outlaw Jesse James." *The Courier-Journal*, June 30, 1902, p. 1.

Special Correspondence. 1881. "JEFFERSON CITY. News Notes from the Capital— Ryan's Arrival—Political Gossip and Facts." *St. Joseph Weekly Gazette*, October 20, 1881, p. 5.

Special Dispatch to *The Chicago Tribune.* 1881. "THE OUTLAWS. A Chicago & Alton Passenger Train Robbed Last Night. Passengers of Both Sexes and the Express Car Plundered. The Deed Accomplished Only Fourteen Miles from Kansas City. Contents of the Passengers' Pockets Emptied into a Pillow-case. The Outlaws Blatant in Their Declarations of Contempt for the Law. They Intend to Break up Both the Alton and Rock Island Railroads. There Were about a Dozen of Them, Very Poorly Masked. They Claimed to Be the James Gang, but Are Considered New Hands at the 'Business.'" *Chicago Tribune*, September 8, 1881, p. 2.

Special Dispatch to the Gazette. 1881. "Death of a Noted Outlaw at the Hands of Jesse James." *Chicago Tribune*, October 31, 1881, p. 2.

Special Dispatch to the Gazette. 1884. "CHARLEY FORD SUICIDES. THE END OF A MISERABLE MAN. An Assassin to the Last, He Terminates His Ill-Spent

Life by Murdering Himself at His Father's House Near Richmond, Mo." *St. Joseph Daily Gazette*, May 7, 1884, p. 1.

Stiles, T. J. 2003. *Jesse James: Last Rebel of the Civil War*. New York: Vintage Books.

"STORY OF THE GLENDALE TRAIN ROBBERY OF 1879." 1881. *Daily Capital*, October 5, 1881, p. 6.

"THE TRAIN ROBBERY! Again Near Glendale, Fifteen Miles East of Kansas City. Passengers and Express Robbed of $10,000, to $20,000, But Missed $160,000 That Came on the Next Train. They Pretended to be the James Gang. But Believed to be Residents of Kansas City." 1881. *Democratic Standard*, September 13, 1881, p. 1.

Turan, Kenneth. 2007. "A Drawn-Out 'Assassination': Brad Pitt and Casey Affleck Pull Their Weight, but the Long, Ambitious, Indulgent Epic Is Only Occasionally Successful." *Los Angeles Times*, September 21, 2007, p. E4.

Vancheri, Barbara. 2007. "Brad Pitt Understands the Celebrity of Jesse James." *Pittsburgh Post-Gazette*, October 14, 2007, p. E3.

Wilner, Paul. 2007. "True to His Words: New Film on Jesse James Doesn't Deviate Much from Ron Hansen's Book." *Los Angeles Times*, September 25, 2007, p. E3.

Wilson, Calvin. 2007. "Outlaw haunt in film: Brad Pitt, Casey Affleck Deliver Stellar Performances in One of the Best Films of the Year." *St. Louis Post-Dispatch*, October 12, 2007, p. E1.

Yeatman, Ted P. 2000. *Frank and Jesse James: The Story behind the Legend*. Nashville, TN: Cumberland House.

Yeatman, Ted P. December 2006. "Jesse James's Assassination and the Ford Boys." *Wild West*. http://www.historynet.com/jesse-james

Younger, Cole. 1903. *The Story of Cole Younger by Himself*. St. Paul: Minnesota Historical Society Press, 2000.

"YOUNGERS ARE DENIED A PARDON: BOARD UNANIMOUSLY AGAINST IT. BAD NEWS THAT FOR COLE AND JIM. They May Not Take That Journey Which They Planned to the Missouri Bottoms. Lewis Kellehan Escapes His Gallows, His Sentence Commuted to Imprisonment for Life in the State Prison— Rose Is Released—Other Cases." 1897. *Saint Paul Globe*, July 14, 1897, p. 3.

Bibliography

Agnew, Jeremy. 2012. *The Old West in Fact and Film: History Versus Hollywood.* Jefferson, NC: McFarland & Company, Inc.

Aquila, Richard. 2015. *The Sagebrush Trail: Western Movies and Twentieth-Century America.* Tucson: University of Arizona Press.

Bagley, Will. 2010. *So Rugged and Mountainous: Blazing the Trails to Oregon and California, 1812–1848.* Norman: University of Oklahoma Press.

Ball, Larry D. 2014. *Tom Horn: In Life and Legend.* Norman: University of Oklahoma Press.

Bandy, Mary Lea, and Stoehr, Kevin. 2012. *Ride, Boldly Ride: The Evolution of the American Western.* Berkeley: University of California Press.

Blake, Michael. 2006. *Indian Yell: The Heart of an American Insurgence.* Flagstaff, AZ: Northland Publishing.

Blake, Michael F. 2003. *Code of Honor: The Making of Three Great American Westerns: High Noon, Shane, and The Searchers.* Lanham, MD: Taylor Trade Publishing.

Brant, Marley. 1992. *The Outlaw Youngers: A Confederate Brotherhood.* Lanham, MD: Madison Books.

Brown, Dee. 1981. *Bury My Heart at Wounded Knee: An Indian History of the American West.* New York: Pocket Books.

Burton, Art T. 2006. *Black Gun, Silver Star: The Life and Legend of Frontier Marshal Bass Reeves.* Lincoln: University of Nebraska Press.

Chang, Gordon. 2019. *Ghosts of Gold Mountain: The Epic Story of the Chinese Who Built the Transcontinental Railroad.* New York: Houghton Mifflin Harcourt.

Connell, Evan S. 1984. *Son of the Morning Star: Custer and the Little Bighorn.* San Francisco: North Point Press.

Cox, Mike. 1997. *Texas Ranger Tales: Stories That Need Telling.* Plano, TX: Republic of Texas Press.

Cozzens, Peter. 2016. *The Earth Is Weeping: The Epic Story of the Indian Wars for the American West*. New York: Alfred A. Knopf.

Dary, David. 1982. *Cowboy Culture: A Saga of Five Centuries*. New York: Avon Books.

Davis, John L. 2010. *Wyoming Range War: The Infamous Invasion of Johnson County*. Norman: University of Oklahoma Press.

DeArment, Robert K. 1989. *Bat Masterson: The Man and the Legend*. Norman: University of Oklahoma Press.

DeVoto, Bernard. 1998. *Across the Wide Missouri*. New York: Mariner Books.

Dimsdale, Thomas J. 1988. *The Vigilantes of Montana*. Norman: University of Oklahoma Press.

Dobie, J. Frank. 1941. *The Longhorns*. New York: Bramhall Books.

Donovan, James. 2008. *A Terrible Glory: Custer and the Little Bighorn: The Last Great Battle of the American West*. New York: Little, Brown and Company.

Durham, Philip, and Everett L. Jones. 1983. *The Negro Cowboys*. Lincoln: University of Nebraska Press.

Dykstra, Robert R. 1983. *The Cattle Towns*. Lincoln: University of Nebraska Press.

Etulain, Richard W. 2006. *Beyond the Missouri: The Story of the American West*. Albuquerque: University of New Mexico Press.

Fehrenbach, T. R. 1983. *Lone Star: A History of Texas and the Texans*. New York: American Legacy Press.

Frankel, Glenn. 2014. *The Searchers: The Making of an American Legend*. New York: Bloomsbury.

Frankel, Glenn. 2017. *High Noon: The Hollywood Blacklist and the Making of an American Classic*. New York: Bloomsbury.

Gard, Wayne. 1954. *The Chisholm Trail*. Norman: University of Oklahoma Press.

Gardner, Mark Lee. 2010. *To Hell on a Fast Horse: Billy the Kid, Pat Garrett, and the Epic Chase to Justice in the Old West*. New York: William Morrow.

Gardner, Mark Lee. 2013. *Shot All to Hell: Jesse James, the Northfield Raid, and the Wild West's Greatest Escape*. New York: William Morrow.

Greene, Jerome A. 2004. *Washita: The U.S. Army and the Southern Cheyennes, 1867–1869*. Norman: University of Oklahoma Press.

Guinn, Jeff. 2011. *The Last Gunfight: The Real Story of the Shootout at the O.K. Corral—And How It Changed the American West*. New York: Simon & Schuster.

Gwynne, S. C. 2010. *Empire of the Summer Moon: Quanah Parker and the Rise and Fall of the Comanches, the Most Powerful Indian Tribe in American History*. New York: Scribner.

Haley, J. Evetts. 1949. *Charles Goodnight: Cowman and Plainsman*. Norman: University of Oklahoma Press.

Hatch, Thom. 2004. *Black Kettle: The Cheyenne Chief Who Sought Peace but Found War*. Hoboken, NJ: John Wiley & Sons, Inc.

Hatch, Thom. 2014. *The Last Outlaws: The Lives and Legends of Butch Cassidy and The Sundance Kid*. New York: New American Library.

Herzberg, Bob. 2008. *Savages and Saints: The Changing Image of American Indians in Westerns*. Jefferson, NC: McFarland & Company, Inc.

Hoberman, J. 2011. *An Army of Phantoms: American Movies and the Making of the Cold War*. New York: The New Press.

Howard, Joseph Kinsey. 1943. *Montana: High, Wide, and Handsome*. New Haven, CT: Yale University Press.

Hutton, Paul Andrew. 2016. *The Apache Wars: The Hunt for Geronimo, the Apache Kid, and the Captive Boy Who Started the Longest War in American History*. New York: Crown.

Knowlton, Christopher. 2017. *Cattle Kingdom: The Hidden History of the Cowboy West*. New York: Houghton Mifflin Harcourt.

Kraft, Louis. 2011. *Ned Wynkoop and the Lonely Road from Sand Creek*. Norman: University of Oklahoma Press.

Lenihan, John H. 1980. *Showdown: Confronting Modern America in the Western Film*. Urbana: University of Illinois Press.

Loy, R. Philip. 2004. *Westerns in a Changing America, 1955–2000*. Jefferson, NC: McFarland & Company, Inc., Publishers.

Marks, Paula Mitchell. 1996. *And Die in the West: The Story of the O.K. Corral Gunfight*. Norman: University of Oklahoma Press.

Marshall III, Joseph M. 2004. *The Journey of Crazy Horse: A Lakota History*. New York: Penguin Books.

Marshall III, Joseph M. 2007. *The Day the World Ended at Little Bighorn: A Lakota History*. New York: Viking.

McCarthy, Todd. 1997. *Howard Hawks: The Grey Fox of Hollywood*. New York: Grove Press.

Meadows, Anne. 1996. *Digging Up Butch & Sundance: Revised Edition*. Lincoln: Bison Books.

Metz, Leon Claire. 2003. *The Encyclopedia of Lawmen, Outlaws, and Gunfighters*. New York: Facts on File, Inc.

Michno, Gregory F. 2009. *Encyclopedia of Indian Wars: Western Battles and Skirmishes, 1850–1890*. Missoula, MT: Mountain Press Publishing Company.

Morrell, David. 2016. *Stars in My Eyes: My Love Affair with Books, Movies, and Music*. Colorado Springs, CO: Gauntlet Press.

Nelson, Andrew Patrick. 2015. *Still in the Saddle: The Hollywood Western, 1969–1980*. Norman: University of Oklahoma Press.

Nott, Robert. 2000. *Last of the Cowboy Heroes: The Westerns of Randolph Scott, Joel McCrea, and Audie Murphy*. Jefferson, NC: McFarland & Company, Inc.

Patterson, Richard. 1998. *Butch Cassidy: A Biography*. Lincoln: University of Nebraska Press.

Roberts, Gary L. 2006. *Doc Holliday: The Life and Legend*. New York: John Wiley & Sons, Inc.

Rosa, Joseph G. 1974. *They Called Him Wild Bill: The Life and Adventures of James Butler Hickok*. Norman: University of Oklahoma Press.

Russell, Don. 1960. *The Lives and Legends of Buffalo Bill*. Norman: University of Oklahoma Press.

Simmon, Scott. 2003. *The Invention of the Western Film: A Cultural History of the Genre's First Half-Century*. Cambridge, UK: Cambridge University Press.

Slatta, Richard W. 2001. *The Mythical West: An Encyclopedia of Legend, Lore and Pop Culture*. Santa Barbara, CA: ABC-CLIO.

Slotkin, Richard. 1993. *Gunfighter Nation: The Myth of the Frontier in Twentieth-Century America*. New York: Harper Perennial.

Smith, Robert Barr. 1996. *Daltons! The Raid on Coffeyville, Kansas*. Norman: University of Oklahoma Press.

Smokov, Mark T. 2012. *He Rode with Butch and Sundance: The Story of Harvey "Kid Curry" Logan*. Denton: University of North Texas Press.

Stiles, T. J. *Jesse James: Last Rebel of the Civil War*. 2002. New York: Vintage Books, 2003.

Tefertiller, Casey. 1997. *Wyatt Earp: The Life Behind the Legend*. New York: John Wiley & Sons, Inc.

Tuska, Jon. 1976. *The Filming of the West*. Garden City, NY: Doubleday & Company, Inc.

Tuska, Jon. 1988. *The American West in Film: Critical Approaches to the Western*. Lincoln: University of Nebraska Press.

Utley, Robert M. 1987. *High Noon in Lincoln: Violence on the Western Frontier*. Albuquerque: University of New Mexico Press.

Utley, Robert M. 1988. *Cavalier in Buckskin: George Armstrong Custer and the Western Military Frontier*. Norman: University of Oklahoma Press.

Utley, Robert M. 2002. *Lone Star Justice: The First Century of the Texas Rangers*. New York: Oxford University Press.

Wallis, Michael. 2007. *Billy the Kid: The Endless Ride*. New York: W. W. Norton & Company.

Williamson, G.R. 2011. *Frontier Gambling: The Games, the Gamblers & the Great Gambling Halls of the Old West*. Kerrville, TX: Indian Head Publishing.

Wright, Will. 1975. *Sixguns & Society: A Structural Study of the Western*. Berkeley: University of California Press.

Yeatman, Ted P. 2000. *Frank and Jesse James: The Story Behind the Legend*. Nashville, TN: Cumberland House.

Index

About the Author

JOHNNY D. BOGGS, winner of a record eight Spur Awards from Western Writers of America, has been praised by *Booklist* magazine as "among the best western writers at work today." His novels include *Return to Red River*, *Camp Ford*, and *Hard Winter*. He is also a film historian, author of *Jesse James and the Movies* and *Billy the Kid on Film, 1911–2012*, and is working on a book about U.S. newspaper movies.

Boggs also won a Western Heritage Wrangler Award from the National Cowboy and Western Heritage Museum in Oklahoma City for *Spark on the Prairie: The Trial of the Kiowa Chiefs* and an Arkansiana Juvenile Award from the Arkansas Library Association for *Poison Spring*. He was honored as a 2011 Distinguished Alumnus from the University of South Carolina School of Journalism and Mass Communication.

A native of South Carolina, Boggs worked almost 15 years in Texas as a sports journalist at the *Dallas Times Herald* and *Fort Worth Star-Telegram* before moving to New Mexico in 1998 to concentrate full time on his novels, nonfiction books, and freelance magazine articles.

When not writing, Boggs has acted onstage in local theater and is a volunteer umpire, manager, and league official with Little League baseball.

He lives with his wife, son, two dogs, and extensive DVD collection in Santa Fe, New Mexico. His website is www.johnnydboggs.com.